LIVING CONSCIOUSNESS

SUNY SERIES IN TRANSPERSONAL AND HUMANISTIC PSYCHOLOGY
Richard D. Mann, editor

LIVING CONSCIOUSNESS

The Metaphysical Vision of Henri Bergson

G. William Barnard

COVER ART: inner spiral of Nagasaki Prayerwheel by John Lyon Paul (johnlyonpaul.com)

Published by State University of New York Press, Albany

For information, contact State University of New York Press, Albany, NY
www.sunypress.edu

Production by Diane Ganeles
Marketing by Anne M. Valentine

Library of Congress Cataloging-in-Publication Data

Barnard, G. William (George William)
  Living consciousness : the metaphysical vision of Henri Bergson / G.
William Barnard.
      p. cm. — (SUNY series in transpersonal and humanistic
psychology)
  Includes bibliographical references and index.
  ISBN 978-1-4384-3957-0 (hardcover : alk. paper)
  1. Bergson, Henri, 1859–1941. 2. Metaphysics. 3. Consciousness.
4. Philosophy, Modern. I. Title.
  B2430.B43B26 2011
  194—dc22
                                    2011007662

10 9 8 7 6 5 4 3 2 1

Contents

SECTION TWO:
THE MATTER OF CONSCIOUSNESS AND THE
CONSCIOUSNESS OF MATTER

ACKNOWLEDGMENTS

During the many years that it took to nudge this book into its present form, I was assisted, in ways that I cannot begin to adequately acknowledge, by numerous colleagues, friends, family members, loved ones, and fellow travelers on the journey to better understand the nature of consciousness. I am pleased to be given the opportunity to express my gratitude in this context, even if these expressions of thanks inevitably fall short.

To begin with, I would like to thank my parents, and my brother and sisters. They were constantly there for me, offering their unconditional love and support.

I would also like to thank my colleagues in the Department of Religious Studies at Southern Methodist University for creating an extremely collegial environment in which I could flourish. My research on Bergson was especially encouraged over the years by the various chairs of the department: Lonnie Kliever, Rick Cogley, and Mark Chancey. Thanks also to Fred Olness, chair of the Physics Department at Southern Methodist University, who took the time to read my early (and now heavily edited) section on Bergson and quantum mechanics. Without his detailed and helpful comments, as well as those of Henry Stapp, a world-renowned theoretical physicist who was extremely gracious and generous with his time, I would never have felt up to the task of writing about this complex, but important, topic.

The administration of Southern Methodist University was also generous, offering frequent sabbatical leaves as well as funding for research in Paris (where I was fortunate enough to spend time working in Bergson's library). I would also like to thank my students at SMU, both graduate and undergraduate, who served as astute sounding boards for many of the ideas that came together to form this text.

Nancy Ellegate, my editor at State University of New York Press, has been immensely helpful, as has her staff, in guiding me through the intricate and complex process of publishing this text. I am grateful for the numerous prompt and helpful suggestions. A special thanks also to the production editor, Diane Ganeles and to Anne Valentine, the marketing manager. Thanks also to Richard Mann for his willingness to accept this text into the series that he edits, as well as for the perceptive observations given by the anonymous readers of the initial manuscript of this work.

I also want to express my heartfelt appreciation to John Lyon Paul, a gifted artist and longtime friend. I feel blessed that the luminous energy of his artwork can shine forth from the cover of this book.

I also want to express my gratitude to Mike Murphy, not only for his generosity and warmth, but also for inviting me to take part in several week-long seminars sponsored by Esalen's Center for Theory and Research. During these stimulating and soul-reviving conversations, I often felt that I had entered into a type of academic nirvana where I discovered, and bonded with, a cohort of extremely bright and courageous individuals: Harald Atmanspacher, Bernard Carr, Adam Crabtree, Duane Elgin, Deb Frost, Bruce Greyson, David Hufford, Catherine Keller, Emily Kelly, Sean Kelly, Paul Marshall, Robert McDermott, Gary Owens, Frank Poletti, Joseph Prabhu, David Presti, Robert Rosenberg, Greg Shaw, Henry Stapp, Charles Tart, Jim Tucker, Eric Weiss, Gordon Wheeler, Ian Whicher, Sam Yau, and many, many others. It was wonderful to discover that I was not alone in my attempts to articulate a persuasive philosophical alternative to mainstream reductionistic explanations of consciousness.

My participation in Esalen's Center for Theory and Research was jump-started by my longtime friend and confidant, Jeff Kripal. For decades now, I have been the beneficiary of his academic superpowers and am deeply grateful for his ongoing support and inspiration.

Esalen also put me in contact with several brilliant and hardworking scholars who, to my never-ending amazement, dedicated considerable time and energy to reading early versions of this work. My heartfelt thanks go out to Ed Kelly, Phil Clayton, Loriliai Biernacki, Leslie Combs, and Jorge Ferrer for their extremely helpful comments and suggestions, as well as for demonstrating that academic rigor can go hand in hand with deep and abiding friendship.

This book was also considerably improved through the perceptive comments of several other scholars who dedicated enormous amounts of time reading various iterations of this text: Don Browning, a cherished mentor from my time at the University of Chicago, who offered numerous helpful suggestions; Robert Forman, a longtime friend and fellow traveler of the inner worlds, who selflessly carried my rather unwieldy manuscript with him during a trip to

Sweden and went through it, page by page; John Mullarkey, Bergson scholar par excellence, who read and commented on a later version of the work, even though it was sent to him by a complete stranger; and finally, Pete Gunter, one of the preeminent Bergson scholars in the world who (astonishingly) lives less than an hour away, who offered his invaluable help and encouragement in the form of numerous close and careful readings of this text in various stages of its evolution.

I was also blessed to have several non-academic contexts in which I could work out, and play with, many of the ideas that are found in the ruminations of this work. In Aikido of Dallas, I learned, in my own fumbling way, some of the possibilities of fluid and conscious movement from Sensei Bob Mason and other senior students. I would also like to acknowledge Jonathan Goldman, as well as numerous *padrinhos* and *madrinhas* in Brazil, who all helped me to learn how to navigate in unseen, but powerfully felt, worlds of spirit. In addition, Levent Bolukbasi, the director of the IM School of Healing Arts, opened my eyes to what it means to align myself with the evolutionary energy of the élan vital, a process that deepened over the years through my ongoing interactions with the students of his school as well as with the students of the Full Spectrum Center for Spiritual Awakening, directed with consummate skill and love by Sandra Barnard.

I cannot begin to imagine what life would be without my wife Sandra's patience, clarity, and insight. For decades, she has been the glowing center of my world. She not only read, and carefully edited, numerous versions of this book over the years, but more importantly, offered me wellsprings of love, wisdom, and encouragement that continue to amaze me. My gratitude to her is immeasurable.

And finally, I would like to thank, from the bottom of my heart, the élan vital itself, for flowering in such unexpected and wondrous ways during the unfolding of my life on this earth.

ABBREVIATIONS

Throughout this text, all citations of Bergson's works are given within parentheses at the end of the sentence, using a standardized abbreviation for each work. For the sake of simplicity, the page numbers refer to the pagination in the English translations of Bergson's works, with the exception of references to *Mélanges* (which has not been translated into English). Fortunately, this simplification is made possible by the fact that Bergson was himself fluent in English (his mother was British) and personally approved the authorized English translations. However, I do note where in *Mélanges* or *Oeuvres* the French pagination for each work can be found.

CE   Henri Bergson, *Creative Evolution*, trans. Arthur Mitchell (Lanham, Maryland: University Press of America, 1983). *L'Evolution créatrice* (1907), in *Oeuvres*, pp. 487–809.

CM   Henri Bergson, *The Creative Mind*, trans. Mabelle L. Andison (New York: Philosophical Library, 1946). *La Pensée et le mouvant: essais et conférences* (1934), in *Oeuvres*, pp. 1249 –1482.

DS   Henri Bergson, *Duration and Simultaneity, with Reference to Einstein's Theory*, trans. Leon Jacobsen (Indianapolis, Indiana: Bobbs-Merrill, 1965). *Durée et simultanéité: À propos de la théorie d'Einstein* (1923), in *Mélanges*, pp. 57–244.

L   Henri Bergson, *Laughter: An Essay on the Meaning of the Comic*, trans. Cloudesley Brereton and Fred Rothwell (London: Macmillan, 1911). *Le Rire: Essai sur la signification du comique* (1900), in *Oeuvres*, pp. 381–485.

M   Henri Bergson, *Mélanges*. André Robinet, ed. (Paris: Presses Universitaires de France, 1972).

ME   Henri Bergson, *Mind-Energy: Lectures and Essays*, trans. H. Wildon Carr (New York: Henry Holt, 1920). *L'Energie spirituelle: essais et conferences* (1919), in *Oeuvres*, pp. 811–977.

MM   Henri Bergson, *Matter and Memory*, trans. N. M. Paul and W. S. Palmer (New York: Zone Books, 1988). *Matière et mémoire: Essai sur la relation du corps avec l'esprit* (1896), in *Oeuvres*, pp. 159–379.

OE   Henri Bergson, *Oeuvres*. André Robinet, ed. (Paris: Presses Universitaires de France, 1959).

TFW   Henri Bergson, *Time and Free Will: An Essay on the Immediate Data of Consciousness*, trans. F. L. Pogson (Montana: Kessinger Publishing, no date given). *Essai sur les données immédiates de la conscience* (1889), in *Oeuvres*, pp. 1–157.

TS   Henri Bergson, *The Two Sources of Morality and Religion*, trans. R. Ashley Audra and Cloudesley Brereton, with assistance from W. Horsfall Carter (Notre Dame, Indiana: Notre Dame University Press, 1977). *Les Deux Sources de la morale et de la religion* (1932), in *Oeuvres*, pp. 979–1247.

A BRIEF BIO-HISTORICAL PREAMBLE

Although scholars today are almost completely indifferent to the work of Henri Bergson, at one point he was *the* philosopher par excellence in Europe and America. Bergson achieved the peak of his popularity in the decade after the publication of *Creative Evolution* in 1907. He continued to be very influential in the twenties and thirties, but his impact was negligible after World War II (this despite the fact that someone as highly regarded as Emmanuel Levinas, several decades later, described Bergson's first book, *Time and Free Will*, as among the "four or five . . . finest books in the history of philosophy," and ranked Bergson's work alongside that of Plato, Kant, Hegel, and Heidegger).[1] Even though the story of Bergson's life as well as his historical impact deserve a much more substantive treatment than I am able to accomplish here in the preamble, this admittedly terse account will at least provide a glimpse into his life as well as into the historical currents that helped to shape (and were in turn profoundly shaped by) this remarkable thinker.[2]

Henri Bergson was born in Paris on October 18, 1859 (the same year that Darwin's *On the Origin of Species* appeared). His father and his mother were Jewish, both sharing a Hasidic background. However, Bergson considered himself Jewish only in the sense that he was aware of belonging to a persecuted minority his entire life. His father, Varsovie Michael Bergson, was a Polish music teacher, pianist, and composer. His mother, Katherine Levinson Bergson, was English (a family background that offered Bergson a lifelong facility with the English language). When Bergson was twelve the family moved to London, while Bergson stayed behind in France (eventually taking French citizenship), visiting his family in England only during school vacations.

Bergson studied at the Lycée Condorcet, and after completing his studies there in 1878 was admitted to the prestigious École Normale Supérieure, one year behind Emile Durkheim (Lucien Lévy-Bruhl was a third-year student at the

xvi   A BRIEF BIO-HISTORICAL PREAMBLE

École when Bergson arrived). During his time at the École, Bergson initially focused on mathematics. (He later won the prestigious "consours general" prize in 1897 and proposed an elegant solution to a geometrical problem that Pascal had originally posed to Fermat.) However, Bergson eventually decided to concentrate on philosophy. At this time in France, two schools of philosophy were popular: voluntarism and positivism—and both were present in the École. Although Bergson was exposed to the ideas of voluntarism when he studied with Emile Boutroux during his second and third years at the École, he was primarily interested in the work of John Stuart Mill and Herbert Spencer and was considered, at least by his classmates, to be an ardent positivist/materialist.

Bergson graduated from the École Normale Supérieure with honors in 1881. He then taught philosophy for seven years in the provinces at lycées in Angers, Carcassone, and Clermont-Ferrand. One of Bergson's biographers notes that it was during his time at Angers and at Clemont-Ferrand that Bergson turned against materialism and the philosophy of Herbert Spencer—a shift that was later attributed, at least in part, to long contemplative walks that Bergson would frequently take in the countryside.[3]

After a promotion in 1888, Bergson went on to teach at Collège Rollin in Paris and then at the Lycée Henri IV, also in Paris. Bergson's doctoral thesis, *Essai sur les données immédiates de la conscience* (published in English as *Time and Free Will*), and his Latin thesis, *Quid Aristoteles de loco senserit*, were both completed in 1889. His doctorate was granted from the Sorbonne, University of Paris, that same year. Two years later, he married Louise Neuberger. They eventually had one daughter, who was born hearing impaired but went on to excel in painting and sculpture.

The *Essai* brought a degree of recognition to Bergson, and his philosophical reputation improved even further with the publication of *Matière et mémoire* (*Matter and Memory*) in 1896. In 1898 he returned to the École Normale Supérieure as a lecturer, after applying twice (1894 and 1898) for a post at the Sorbonne. (It was rumored that Emile Durkheim worked hard behind the scenes to ensure that Bergson's application was denied.) Then in 1900, Bergson not only published *Le Rire* (*Laughter*), but also was given a chair of philosophy at the Collège de France, where he taught until 1921.

The Collège de France was founded by Francis I, and was considered during Bergson's time to be the highest institute of learning in France. Its structure was rather unusual: while there were numerous professorial chairs in specialized subjects, the Collège had no official students and no examinations; instead, all of the lectures were open to the public. While the courses given by some professors were sparsely attended, Bergson's inspiring lectures quickly became a social event. People from all strata of the community thronged to hear him, many of whom were turned away because of lack of space. Enid Starkie describes how during Bergson's lectures "philosophers, scientists, men of letters, students, priests, clergymen, rabbis, and fashionable women" would all crowd into the hall and listen, mesmerized by his talk, and then after he finished, they would hold "their finger tips together, high up before him, to show that they were clapping silently, since applause at lectures was not the custom."[4]

Several of Bergson's students wrote about their experience of Bergson at the Collège. Marcel Bataillon, for instance, remembered Bergson's "brilliant style" and "the great charm which emanated" from his voice.[5] Gabriel Marcel in turn described how "the inflections of [Bergson's] voice disclosed what seemed to be contained jubilation," and he wrote of the "tender precaution" that Bergson took approaching a topic "as though he were delicately brushing aside vines to bend over a sleeping infant."[6] And finally, Jacques Chevalier described a typical lecture of Bergson's at the Collège. Chevalier said that Bergson would approach quietly from the rear of the amphitheatre, seat "himself beneath the shaded lamp, his hands free of manuscript or notes," with his fingertips joined together.[7] Chevalier commented that Bergson's way of speaking was "unhurried, dignified, and measured like his writing, extraordinarily confident and surprisingly clear . . . its intonations [were] musical and cajoling" and his language was "finished in its perfection."[8]

Bergson quickly became a dominant voice at the Collège de France, even though he was anathema to many of the key figures at the Sorbonne, including Durkheim. The two schools, while physically close to one another, were ideologically miles apart. The professors at the Sorbonne were, on the whole, scornful of religious experience and human freedom; they attempted to replace psychology with physiology; and they asserted that evolution was simply the result of natural selection and the survival of the fittest. Bergson, as a key spokesperson of the Collège de France, strongly challenged this perspective. He argued against the materialism, mechanism, and positivism of the Sorbonne without ignoring the achievements of modern science; he affirmed the validity of human freedom and the priority of consciousness over matter; and while he acknowledged the data of evolution, he reinterpreted evolution in a way that made it a meaningful cosmic process. As Sanford Schwartz notes, "to many who were caught between the opposing claims of religion and evolutionary science, Bergson appeared as a redeeming angel who conclusively resolved the conflict between them. He achieved this feat by simultaneously spiritualizing biology and naturalizing the spiritual."[9]

Bergson's popularity skyrocketed after the publication of *L'évolution créatrice* (*Creative Evolution*) in 1907. William James, after reading this text, wrote to Bergson saying, "you are a magician and your book is a marvel,"[10] noting that *Creative Evolution* "is a true miracle in the history of philosophy [that] marks . . . the beginning of a new era."[11] William James was not the only reader of *Creative*

Evolution who was impressed by its clarity and insights. *Creative Evolution* struck a deep chord even among non-academics of that era in that it affirmed the reality of spiritual forces working in harmony with the unfolding of the physical universe; it emphasized the inherent freedom and dignity of human beings; and its articulation of the doctrine of intuition seemed to imply that divine levels of knowledge were available to all—a doctrine that was particularly appealing to those who felt alienated from orthodox religiosity, but nonetheless still wanted to discover an underlying connection to larger cosmic realities.[12]

Bergson's sudden fame prompted a surge in invitations from several notable academic institutions: in 1911 Bergson delivered an address at the Fourth International Congress of Philosophy at Bologna, and he offered courses in Oxford, London, and Birmingham. He then visited New York in 1913 to deliver a series of lectures and to receive an honorary degree from Columbia University. As Tom Quirk notes, "No philosopher had excited as much enthusiasm or controversy in America as did Bergson when he visited in 1913. Not even William James himself had enjoyed such widespread and fashionable popularity."[13] (Theodore Roosevelt, linking the two philosophers, claimed, "that every truly scientific and truly religious man will turn with relief to the 'lofty' thought of Bergson and James.")[14] Henry May, commenting on Bergson's enormous celebrity during this time, writes that on the day of one of Bergson's lectures at Columbia, "a line of automobiles . . . clogged Broadway, one lady fainted in the crush at the lecture-room door, and regular students were crowded out of their seats by well-dressed auditors."[15]

Between 1909 and 1911, over two hundred articles on Bergson appeared in the British press, a time period during which intellectuals in both America and in Europe frequently compared Bergson's work to that of Plato, Aquinas, Kant, Descartes, or Emerson.[16] A letter written by Joseph Lotte, printed in the *Bulletin des professeurs catholiques de l'Université* on February 20, 1912, exemplifies the tone of many of Bergson's admirers. Mr. Lotte begins by comparing Bergson to Socrates and then notes that "it was the study of [Bergson's] philosophy—a study which I began as a most stubborn materialist—that opened out to me the path of liberty."[17] Reading Bergson's work, Lotte had the sense that "the breath of God inspired the world"; he claimed that he would "never forget [his] rapturous emotion when, in the spring of 1907, [he] read *Evolution créatrice*," and "felt the presence of God in every page."[18]

While Bergson was often effusively endorsed by readers such as Lotte (who were often conservatives who saw him as leading the fight against materialism and secularism), he was also frequently praised by those on the Left who, like Walter Lippmann, saw Bergson's metaphysics as a way to justify and to catalyze social reform. (Bergson himself, in an interview published in *Harper's Weekly*, actively championed one such reform, that is, feminism, saying that he considered "the present feminist movement the greatest event in the history of civilization since the promulgation of the Christian ideal," asserting that "not till women have every right that men have . . . can we hope for a further development of the race." [19]) Bergson's philosophy was also adopted by figures on the far Left, such as Georges Sorel, the principal theoretician of the Syndicalist movement, who drew upon certain aspects of Bergson's philosophical perspective (e.g., his critique of the intellect and his emphasis on spontaneity) in his reflections on the nature of the class struggle in modern society.[20]

However, Bergson's philosophy was also not without its strident critics. While some of his primary supporters in France were moderate conservatives who saw his philosophy as a way to combat the secular ethos and uncompromising naturalism of many prominent French intellectuals, others on the far Right (e.g., representatives of Action Française) waged an intensely hostile and openly anti-Semitic campaign against Bergson, provoked by the possibility that he might be elected to the Académie Française. (Their campaign failed and Bergson was elected into the Académie Française in 1914, an election that was, in the words of R. C. Grogin, "the highest honor which can fall to a Frenchman."[21])

Bergson's philosophy, therefore, drew both effusive praise and equally impassioned attacks, from both conservatives and progressives. As Schwartz notes, "for every conservative who welcomed Bergson's vindication of the spirit there was another who rejected his naturalization of the divine; and for every progressive who applauded his idea of spontaneous development there was another who dismissed the *élan vital* [Bergson's notion of a cosmic life force] as a pseudo-mystical confection."[22]

During the period following the publication of *Evolution créatrice*, Bergson was also strongly attacked by the Catholic Church. In 1914 (the same year that he was elected to the Académie Française) his major works were put on the index of prohibited books by the Holy Office, due in large part to the activity of Jacques Maritain, a prominent neo-Thomist thinker who, ironically, claimed that both he and his wife were "transported into another world" while listening to Bergson's lectures at the Collège de France and who openly admitted that Bergson's work helped to free them both from a life of relativism, skepticism, and despair as well as to pave the way for their conversion to Catholicism.[23])

The hostility of the Catholic Church toward Bergson's work was due, in large part, to the influence his thought appeared to have on Catholic Modernism. This movement was widespread among Catholic intelligentsia in Europe in the early twentieth century. It was led by Éduoard Le Roy (one of Bergson's most ardent spokespersons and his successor in the Collège de France after 1921) as well as by the New Testament scholar Alfred Loisy. In the preface to the second edition of *La Philosophie bergsonienne*, Maritain is explicit about the affinity between Bergson's philosophy and Catholic Modernism. According to Maritain, many priests in the early part of the twentieth century "spoke of nothing but Becoming, Immanence, the evolutionary transformation of the expressions of faith, the refraction of the ineffable through dogmatic formulas that were always provisional and faulty, [and] the ill effects of all abstract knowledge."[24] As Leszek Kolakowski points out, the Modernists (anticipating currently accepted approaches in the academic study of the Bible) believed that the Gospels were "merely expressions of faith of early Christian communities and not infallible and not divinely inspired records, immune to errors."[25] They taught that the enlightenment of the individual consciousness by God is more important than the Bible and that "the dogmas of the Church, rather than being immutable truth, were provisional and changeable forms in which Christians express their faith according to historical circumstances."[26] Finally, the Modernists also "made a distinction between the Christ of faith and Christ the historical figure, and questioned the belief that he was God's son in a literal sense."[27]

Not surprisingly, this movement, built so strongly on Bergsonian principles, was eventually quashed by the Church: two French Modernists were excommunicated, an anti-Modernist oath was eventually imposed on all priests (an oath that was only abolished by the Second Vatican Council in the early 1960s), and in 1907, Pius X wrote the famous encyclical *Pascendi dominici gregis*. In this encyclical, Pius X claimed that Modernism was "the synthesis of all heresies," noting that adherence to this way of thought "means the destruction not only of the Catholic religion alone but of all religion."[28] According to Pius X, the central principle of Modernism, that is, "vital immanence," had the effect of making "consciousness and revelation synonymous" and reduced Church dogma to "'symbols' subject to evolutionary change."[29]

While authorities within the Catholic Church were deeply opposed to Bergson's work, the French government (with the concurrence of Great Britain) appeared to have such great faith in Bergson that they entrusted him with a secret mission in 1917. As P. A. Y. Gunter points out, Bergson was "authorized to promise President Wilson that if he would bring the United States into the First World War on the side of the Allies, after the war Britain and France would back the creation of a League of Nations, dedicated to maintaining world peace."[30] Bergson eventually made two trips to America during the worst periods of the war, that is, from January to May 1917 and then from May to September 1918, and according to Philippe Soulez, Bergson's diplomacy had a decisive impact on Wilson's decision that the United States should enter the war.[31]

In 1919, *L'Énergie spirituelle* (*Mind Energy*), a collection of essays that Bergson wrote between 1900 and 1914, was published. Then, in 1920 Bergson was awarded an honorary doctorate by Cambridge, only to retire suddenly from the Collège de France in 1921 due to his failing health. (Bergson suffered from chronic rheumatoid arthritis. Nonetheless, he stayed on as the president of the Commission for Intellectual Cooperation—a forerunner of UNESCO—in the League of Nations until he was forced to retire in 1925, once again due to the crippling effects of arthritis.)

In 1922, *Durée et simultanéité* (*Duration and Simultaneity*), Bergson's public dispute with Einstein over the nature of time, was published. (He later refused to allow *Durée et simultanéité* to be reprinted, claiming that his mathematical knowledge had not been up to the task.[32]) Then, in 1928, continuing to suffer from poor health, Bergson was awarded the Nobel Prize for Literature. (There is no Nobel Prize for philosophy.) *Les Deux Sources de la morale et de la religion* (*The Two Sources of Morality and Religion*) appeared in 1932 with little fanfare. By this time Bergson's popularity as a philosopher had already dramatically diminished; the *Two Sources* therefore had much less cultural impact than his earlier works. Then, in 1934, *La Pensée et le mouvant* (*The Creative Mind*), a collection of essays from 1903 to 1923, with the addition of two new chapters, was published. By this time, rheumatoid arthritis had made Bergson a virtual invalid.

June of 1940 brought the tragic collapse of France. Soon, Jews were required by the Nazis to register with the authorities. However, the Vichy French government attempted to exempt Bergson from this regulation and conferred on him the title "Honorary Aryan." Bergson refused the title. Standing many hours in line to register as a Jew, he died of pulmonary congestion two days later, on January 7, 1941, at the age of eighty-two.

Ironically, given the hostility toward him from the Catholic Church, Bergson had, according to a letter published by his wife in the September 9, 1941 edition of the *Gazette de Lausanne*, become increasingly sympathetic to Catholicism—a shift that, according to his wife, began during the writing of his last book (*Les Deux Sources de la morale et de la religion*).[33] This revelation of Bergson's near conversion to Catholicism was confirmed in the same issue of the *Gazette de Lausanne*, which printed a copy of Bergson's will, dated February 8, 1937. In this document he declared: "My reflections have brought me closer and closer to Catholicism in which I see the completion of Judaism. I would have been converted had I not seen being prepared for many years the terrible wave of anti-Semitism about to break upon the world. I have preferred to remain with those who tomorrow will be the persecuted." In his will, Bergson also requested that a Catholic priest be permitted by the Archbishop of Paris to preside at his funeral, and if this was not possible, that a rabbi take on that task, "but without hiding from him nor from anyone my moral adherence to Catholicism." Ian Alexander points out that a priest actually did arrive after Bergson's death, and not only "said official prayers" but "made the sign of the cross on the dead man's head."[34]

After Bergson's death, his philosophical perspective became, if possible, even less well known than it was before. It is difficult to discern exactly when, and more importantly, *why* Bergson's thought disappeared so quickly from view. Various scholars of his work have advanced different theories. Some have argued that the dismissal of Bergson's ideas from the academic world was due to the increasing influence of Freudian thought, while others have argued that it was due to the rise in positivism (especially in the English-speaking world). Other scholars have suggested that Bergson's obscuration was linked to the disastrous aftermath of World War I and the consequent distaste for any "optimistic" philosophical perspectives (a distaste that led, not surprisingly, to the rise of Existentialism). Suzanne Guerlac argues that one factor leading to the dismissal of Bergson's thought among philosophers was the sudden upsurge of fascination with Hegel's ideas, which took place in the intellectual world of Paris in the thirties.[35] Elizabeth Grosz, in turn, posits that Bergson's professional demise began sometime after 1922 (the publication date of *Duration and Simultaneity*), when he was perceived by the educated public, correctly or incorrectly, as having lost the debate with Einstein and was hence "subjected to bitter and often unfair criticism from a wide variety of detractors" and "was reviled and ridiculed more or less from this time on, functioning largely as a historical anachronism, a curiosity, more than a dynamic force in contemporary philosophy."[36]

While no one doubts that Bergson's work has been essentially invisible in the philosophical world for several decades (a process of obscuration that was certainly aided by the fact that no viable Bergsonian movement or school arose after his death), nonetheless, the influence of Bergson's thought upon an extremely wide range of thinkers is undeniable. For instance, several scholars have pointed out that Bergson's work impacted, to a greater or lesser degree, a number of literary figures (e.g., Marcel Proust, Nikos Kazantzakis, Virginia Woolf, Thomas Wolfe, Wallace Stevens, James Joyce, William Faulkner, T. S. Eliot, Willa Cather, George Bernard Shaw, D. H. Lawrence, among others).[37] Similarly, in philosophical circles, in addition to the ways in which Bergson inspired William James (and vice versa), Bergson's influence on Whitehead, as Milič Čapek notes, "is beyond doubt" and is "very rarely denied."[38] P. A. Y. Gunter has also explored, in some detail, the importance of Bergson's thought for the development of Existentialism (especially Bergson's link to the work of Sartre),[39] while Richard Lehan and Joseph N. Riddel have underscored the theoretical connections between Bergson's perspective and that of Heidegger.[40] Furthermore, Richard Cohen has written that "the true ally of Bergson is of course . . . Merleau-Ponty," adding that "it is no mere coincidence, then, that Merleau-Ponty succeeded to Bergson's chair of Modern Philosophy at the Collège de France."[41] And finally, the crucial influence of Bergson's thought on Deleuze is unquestionable [42] and Levinas himself frequently alluded to the philosophical debt he owed to Bergson.[43]

During the last decade, there has been a resurgence of interest in Bergson's work (due, in large part, to Deleuze's reintroduction of Bergson's thought within a poststructuralist context).[44] It is not clear whether this renewed concern with Bergson's perspective will gain momentum. Nonetheless, as the present work attempts to demonstrate, Bergson's thought is clearly worthy of sustained, ongoing attention, and is directly relevant to numerous and crucially important areas of contemporary academic exploration.[45]

INTRODUCTION

For well over a decade, I have been deeply engaged with the work of the French philosopher Henri Bergson. Many of my colleagues have been rather puzzled by my decision to commit so much time to Bergson's thought. While there has been a mini-resurgence of interest in his work in the last decade (primarily among scholars who are familiar with the poststructuralist French thinker Gilles Deleuze, who reintroduced Bergson to a postmodern audience), I think that it is safe to say that until quite recently, even among the philosophically inclined, Bergson's ideas have been for the most part relegated to some metaphorical musty bookshelf of the mind, filled with thinkers who are considered (at least tacitly) to be antiquated relics of a bygone era. Much of this book is dedicated to proving that Bergson's thought should not be so easily dismissed. It is my hope that after reading this text you will come to agree that spending time in the company of this relatively forgotten genius is well worth the effort.

Bergson, like most profound thinkers, is someone who can inspire and provoke; he is someone who, if we listen carefully, if we pay attention, can open up new worlds inside of us; he is someone who can prompt us to reexamine many of our most cherished philosophical assumptions. Do not, therefore, take Bergson lightly. This is philosophy with a kick, philosophy that might, little by little, rearrange your comfortable mental world in unexpected ways.

In addition, do not expect that Bergson's ideas will be assimilated easily, or without protest. Texts such as *Time and Free Will* or *Matter and Memory* (Bergson's first two works, and the primary focus of this book) attempt to articulate a radically counterintuitive understanding of our everyday experience. Therefore, do not be surprised if it takes some time to assimilate and to digest certain aspects of Bergson's philosophy. It is to be expected that a philosophy that is so inherently focused on temporality will itself need a little time to do its work.

Because I recognize that it can at times be a rather challenging task to understand Bergson's thought, I have attempted to present his ideas in a way that is as uncluttered as possible. That is, the majority of this text attempts to do what I would argue any good academic examination of Bergson's thought should do, that is, it seeks to provide a clear, thoughtful, and thorough exposition and analysis of the main tenets of his work, in its own terms, free from any extraneous technical jargon; it also attempts to articulate, to a limited extent, some of the central intellectual currents that were prominent during Bergson's historical period (e.g., mechanism, determinism, and so on).

However, I have to confess that, while I have made every attempt to offer a faithful and accurate representation of Bergson's ideas, I am also keenly aware that the Bergson that you are about to discover in this text is not *the* Bergson, as if his work is frozen somewhere in Platonic cold storage, just waiting to be awakened and given new life by my (or *any* scholar's) words. Instead, given my background as a religious studies scholar interested in the comparative study of the philosophy and psychology of mysticism and non-ordinary states of consciousness, what you will discover here is a "spiritual" Bergson—a Bergson that many recent scholars of his work might well not recognize nor endorse. However, I would claim that, like William James (Bergson's closest and most influential philosophical ally in America), Bergson is multifaceted enough that it is possible to articulate a variety of seemingly mutually exclusive understandings of his thought and yet still remain true to his work. My task, therefore, is to highlight certain aspects of Bergson's thought that have been recently overlooked or ignored (i.e., the more "mystical" implications of his work) in order to provide a more nuanced and balanced understanding of his overall philosophical perspective.

Furthermore, this text attempts to demonstrate that Bergson's work is not some outdated remnant of the past, but rather is a provocative, nuanced, complex perspective that continues to have relevance today for a broad range of compelling discussions that are currently taking place in the fields of anthropology, religious studies, psychology, physics, neuroscience, and philosophy. Bergson's work not only provides a set of thoughtful, persuasive answers to numerous, rather daunting philosophical problems that continue to plague scholars today, but does so in a way that is congruent with the central findings of modern science, even while Bergson's perspective also strongly challenges the implicit, typically unexamined, positivism, determinism, and physicalism that underlies how many, if not most, academics and scientists interpret these findings.

In *Living Consciousness*, I attempt to show that Bergson offers numerous stimulating and provocative insights into the nature of consciousness (and reality itself), insights that offer a fresh and helpful approach to several highly diverse realms of inquiry, for example, the philosophy of mind and cognitive neuroscience; quantum mechanics; various models of psychotherapy and spiritual transformation; and anthropological and philosophical approaches within the field of religious studies. For example, I seek to demonstrate that Bergson's thought provides a coherent and intellectually engaging philosophical framework for reinterpreting the nature of the physical universe—a reinterpretation that places consciousness in the heart of matter itself; I attempt to illustrate how Bergson's controversial understanding of the nature of memory is still worthy of consideration, even after more than a century of research into the structure and function of the brain; I attempt to articulate how a Bergsonian perspective on the nature of the subconscious illuminates the transformative process and underlying goals of various modes of psychotherapy and spiritual practice; and finally, as a scholar of religious studies, I offer Bergson's dense and complex metaphysical perspective as an intriguing way to begin to make sense of such non-ordinary states of awareness as trance, possession, mystical experiences, dreams, visionary events, telepathy, and clairvoyance.

In certain respects, the interdisciplinary nature of Bergson's work itself, with its detailed engagement with issues that are now relegated to separate, often isolated, academic specializations, prompted me to engage in these (careful and cautious!) scouting expeditions into realms of thought that are at times admittedly somewhat outside of the boundaries of my own disciplinary background. However, given the multifaceted nature of Bergson's own work, I became convinced of the need to risk going beyond the familiar and comfortable milieu of my own training and to enter into relatively unknown territory. Therefore, although I am willing to claim that these extradisciplinary forays are essentially accurate and are presented with a reasonable amount of clarity (a claim that I am willing to make in large part due to the diligent and careful reading of several experts from those disciplines), it is also important to underscore that I undertook this task with a keen awareness of my own academic limitations and that I make no claims that these chapters of the book are comprehensive. Instead, I see them primarily as suggestive and inevitably schematic maps of territory that has not previously been explored (at least by me)—maps that nonetheless can still help to open up new and unanticipated vistas of connections between Bergson's perspective and these highly diverse fields of academic specialization.

The not-so-simple job of organizing this book was also often rather daunting in that (as will soon become apparent) *Living Consciousness* itself is the end result of a very delicate balancing act. On the one hand, this book is primarily oriented toward academics (either those who are overtly interested in Bergson's work or more broadly those who are interested in how his work applies to current discussions of the nature of consciousness, the mind/body connection, the question of free will, and so on). On the other hand, I have also made a conscious attempt to write this book for a broader audience in that, not only do I attempt to use nontechnical language whenever possible, but I also include certain subsections—that is, "ruminations" (which I describe in greater detail below)—that are explicitly oriented to readers outside of academia.

In many ways, this book was written for people like my father: intelligent, inquisitive, well-educated readers who are not philosophers or scholars of religion and yet are interested in topics such as the nature of consciousness, intuition, mysticism, and so on—readers who have never had the opportunity or perhaps the inclination to read any of Bergson's works. It is my hope, therefore, that *Living Consciousness* can accomplish what might well be an impossible task: to be clear and vivid enough to speak to this broader audience, while simultaneously presenting a rigorously argued analysis of Bergson's work that will appeal to academics.

For those in the latter category, that is, those who pursue the rarified, often arcane discussions that scholars relish, it will be important not to overlook the collection of endnotes. While I (sadly!) had to dramatically pare down the length and quantity of endnotes that I originally wrote, nonetheless, the endnotes that remain are fully of juicy scholarly information. Here is where I overtly address the secondary literature on Bergson; here is where I offer an exploration of (and occasional arguments with) the numerous scholars of Bergson's thought who have preceded me; and here is where I attempt to establish connections to numerous other lines of thought that can help to shed light on whatever topic is being discussed. The endnotes are also (with the exception of the explicit bibliographical references) self-contained. Each substantive endnote begins with a brief recapitulation of the issue that it addresses, a procedure that attempts to prevent unnecessary and tedious flipping back and forth between the endnotes and the main body of the text.

While the endnotes are my gift to the diehard Bergson scholars, the "ruminations" are my gift to those who might, at least at times, find typical academic writing a bit indigestible. Although the main body of the text is primarily descriptive and analytical in style, in the ruminations I shift the tone of my prose. Here I let my guard down (to the extent possible for a trained academic) and simply say what I think, without having to give a complex series of carefully hedged arguments to hammer my point home. These "ruminations" are the result of my prolonged attempts to chew upon—to digest—Bergson's work; they are the partial record of the long, slow work of assimilating his ideas, and over time, of converting his thought into a vision of life that has become, as it were, a part of my own flesh and bones. In these ruminations I take Bergson further than perhaps even he might have anticipated. Here I speak as vividly and concretely as possible; here I tell stories from my own life; here I write about what matters most to me; here I give myself permission to speak about topics that most "respectable" academics avoid (e.g., dreams, telepathy, mystical experiences, and so on).

In these ruminations there are also statements that are at times explicitly normative. In the main subsections of the book I offer a detailed and nuanced examination of Bergson's understanding of the nature of consciousness and the physical world—that is, I focus on "what is." In the ruminations, however, (and occasionally even in the "margins" and "overtones" of the main text itself) I attempt to flesh out the normative implications of Bergson's understandings of the nature of the self and reality—that is, I focus on "what *could or should* be." While *Living Consciousness* is not a book on ethics, it has increasingly become clear to me that different metaphysical assumptions imply different visions of how human beings could or should live in the world and what human beings could or should aspire to become.[1] For instance, if you believe that the world is a cold, predetermined place, in which inert bits of matter interact mechanically to produce the illusion of freedom and consciousness, then you will quite naturally have a distinctly different sense of the possibilities that life has to offer than someone who believes that the universe is an interconnected, living, dynamic whole and that human beings have the capacity to experience a profound intuitive attunement to levels of consciousness that are, quite literally, cosmic in scope (one guess as to which option is more Bergsonian!).

In this way, the ruminations are an opportunity to think out loud about the normative implications that follow if you accept a cluster of basic Bergsonian metaphysical assumptions. They are an opportunity to "ruminate" on what we, as human beings, can (and perhaps should) aspire to and how we might live our lives in ways that are aligned with these ontological presuppositions. Therefore, even though (ironically) I do not explore in any detail the later works of Bergson in which he overtly discusses the ethical implications of intuition and mysticism (to do so would have expanded an already ambitious book beyond any hope of readability), the teleological thrust of *Living Consciousness* moves in this direction and can be most overtly found in the ruminations.

I realize that by including these ruminations I take a risk of alienating some of my scholarly audience. Once again, however, I feel it is imperative to take this step. Not to do so would be (for me) a deep betrayal of the spirit of Bergson's own work. While Bergson had tremendous respect for clear thought and for vigorous argumentation, he nonetheless also stressed the crucial importance of utilizing modes of philosophical inquiry—for example, intuition, metaphorical imagery, and creative synthesis—that are not given much credence in today's academic world. Therefore, while I have made every attempt to present a clear and accurate depiction of Bergson's work in the main body of the text, in these ruminations I have not shied away from a creative appropriation of several of Bergson's key ideas.

I would argue that this willingness to judiciously adapt Bergson's thought is, ironically, perhaps truer to his perspective than any scholarly attempt to locate Bergson's work solely in the past. Because Bergson repeatedly emphasizes that the universe itself can be best understood as a ceaseless dynamic flux characterized by a constant (albeit often unrecognized) emergence of genuine novelty, any philosophical vision that hopes to remain viable will itself also have to remain open to change (an understanding that Bergson himself frequently acknowledges in his reflections on the nature of the philosophical process).[2] Therefore, in the ruminations, I have been willing to use Bergson's work (without apology and indeed with great gusto) for my own highly individual ends and to make conclusions based on his perspective that he might never have anticipated (or even necessarily approved)—all the while remaining, I would argue, aligned with and true to what is most importantly "Bergsonian" in his thought.

For those who are used to the style of conventional academic prose (a style that is burned into a scholar's very marrow through a daunting initiatory process of graduate training and publishing incentives), these ruminations might at times seem a bit jarring. In the end, I can only hope that my attempt to juxtapose several divergent styles of prose is successful and that readers will find them complementary rather than discordant. It is my hope that the more academic subsections are clear enough to be read (and perhaps even enjoyed) by non-academics, and that the ruminations are substantive and thoughtful enough to be read (and perhaps even enjoyed) by academics.

One further task remains in this introduction: to offer a concise and intelligible summation of the three major sections of this book—a task that I approach with some degree of ambivalence, since any summation simply cannot do justice to the hundreds of pages that follow. Such a summation can, however, at least offer a glimpse of the central issues explored in *Living Consciousness*.

Section 1 focuses on the themes covered in Bergson's first major work, *Time and Free Will* (published in 1889 as *Essai sur les données immédiates de la conscience*). This brilliantly insightful book (Bergson's doctoral dissertation) offers a forceful defense of human freedom via a nuanced, introspective examination of the nature of consciousness. According to Bergson, if we focus on the immediacy of what is occurring moment by moment within the depths of our own experience, what we will discover is that our consciousness, unlike the objects in the world surrounding us, is a freely flowing continuity of ceaseless change, a dynamic flux that is ever new and intrinsically creative. Our consciousness is also (again, in contrast to the world of matter) inherently temporal. In fact, Bergson goes further and claims that our consciousness itself *is* time and that time itself *is* consciousness—not time as we typically understand it, that is, not the time that is measured by the beats of a clock, but rather the time that we each subjectively experience.

Bergson's term for consciousness/time is *durée*. Durée is, arguably, the most important theoretical construct in Bergson's work: it is the living heart of Bergson's perspective; it is the thread that is woven in and through Bergson's entire opus. What Bergson attempts to do in *Time and Free Will* is to use his nuanced depictions of durée to shift our attention to what is happening within ourselves, so that we can examine our own experience in order to determine whether his descriptions of the nature of consciousness are accurate or not. He also notes,

however, that it is extremely difficult to cultivate this mode of intuitive knowledge, in which we directly experience durée, due in large part to our deeply
rooted biological need to focus our attention outside of ourselves in order to
master the objective world.

According to Bergson, this external world, at least functionally, is the polar
opposite of durée, in that it appears to be split up into discrete, clearly bounded,
seemingly stable objects that can be measured, counted, and labeled; it behaves
in highly predictable ways; and it is inherently spatial in nature. Our almost hypnotic fascination with the external world, however, leads to a distorted understanding of the nature of consciousness in that we almost inevitably tend to
perceive durée through the distorting lens of our desire to master this spatial
realm, leading us to believe that our inner life is also quasi-spatial in nature; that
is, we come to imagine that our inner world consists of a collection of "states"
(e.g., thoughts, feelings, sensations) that have clear beginnings and endings—
states that behave according to certain fixed natural laws and that can be reduced
to a quantifiable interaction of mindless automatic forces (e.g., hormonal secretions, economic factors, genetic patterns, and so on).

According to Bergson, our urgent, almost obsessive, need to analyze,
weigh, quantify, and control the external world cuts us off, at least partially,
from the freedom and creativity of our deeper self, that is, durée. Consequently,
we live much of our lives basically like automatons, alienated (for the most
part) from the more profound strata of our being.[3] It is no wonder then that we
are often convinced that freedom is an illusion and that we are nothing more
than the sum total of a multitude of sociocultural-economic-biological forces.
However, Bergson asks us to shift our attention away from the insistent mes-
sages bombarding us from the outside as well as from the superficial beliefs that
we have inherited from others in order to attempt the extremely difficult task of
paying careful attention to what is present within us, *as* us, as the ever new,
inherently creative, flux of our own consciousness. Bergson argues that, to the
extent that we succeed in this task we will gain an intuitive certainty that
human freedom is real, a certainty that, if nurtured, has the potential to rein-
fuse our life with increased levels of dynamism and a renewed appreciation for
the gift of human existence.

The liminal section functions as a type of connecting link between section
1, with its focus on the themes of *Time and Free Will*, and the subsequent focus
in section 2 on the ideas explored in Bergson's second book, *Matter and Memory*.
The primary emphasis in the liminal section is on Bergson's understanding of
the nature of the physical world as articulated in *Matter and Memory* (as well as
in later works). Instead of seeing matter and durée as two substances that are
ontologically distinct from each other (as Bergson appears to do in *Time and
Free Will*), by the time of the publication of *Matter and Memory* (1896), Bergson
begins to envision *matter itself* as "durée-like" in nature.[4] That is, he begins to

emphasize that the external world itself, if understood correctly, is (like our own consciousness) not split into atomistic parts, but rather is a dynamic, flowing, interconnected continuum of processes; that is, the material world in reality is not a collection of "things" bumping into each other in utterly predetermined ways in the "container" of empty space, but rather is constituted by ceaseless movement and change and consequently is also inherently temporal in nature.

The liminal section contains several (unfortunately rather cursory) discussions of the ways in which Bergson's non-atomistic, post-Newtonian understanding of matter proved to be remarkably prophetic in that almost all of his claims about the nature of the physical universe were, several decades later, proven to be true in strikingly specific ways by a series of ongoing (and revolutionary) theoretical advances and empirical discoveries made in physics (first by Einstein and then later by numerous quantum physicists): for example, the fusion of space and time theorized by Einstein; the realization that light can be either wave-like or particle-like depending upon how it is measured; the understanding that matter (seemingly so solid and predictable) is, in actuality, a blur of probabilities and wave functions; and the inescapable conclusion that the act of observation fundamentally alters what is being observed. All of these advances in the realm of physics echoed and confirmed Bergson's prior claims about the nature of the physical world—that is, that there is a degree of indetermination even in matter itself; that mental and physical phenomena may not after all be utterly distinct from one another; that consciousness itself is intimately implicated in the processes of material existence; that the physical world, if understood correctly, is less like a complex rearrangement of tiny billiard balls bouncing off each other and more like an intricate and interconnected dance of vibratory, spatiotemporal processes (in other words, that matter is, if understood correctly, an interactive, overlapping, ever-shifting field of different "rhythms" of durée).

The liminal section also underscores how for Bergson the physical world is not some sort of immensely complicated mechanical object, but instead is closer to a melody. As Bergson notes, like our consciousness, the melody of the physical universe is never static; it does not have clear-cut boundaries, but rather it unfolds. Like our consciousness, the tones of this melody overlap: they interpenetrate each other and yet, interestingly, each tone remains distinct. Like our consciousness, the tones of the melody of the universe are inherently plural and yet are simultaneously held together via the cohesive power of memory. Finally, this cosmic melody (again, like our consciousness) is a manifestation of continual change; it is an ever new play of difference—difference that is inherently temporal in its very nature (i.e., melodies take time).

The "both/and" nature of this sonic metaphor, as I point out in ruminations in both section 1 as well as in the liminal section, can be a very helpful lens with which to view reality and to understand ourselves. Here we have a perspective that argues that *both* unity *and* diversity, continuity *and* change, identity *and* difference are intrinsic and deeply intertwined aspects of both the physical world and the deepest levels of our selfhood. Both sides of this spectrum, therefore, can and should be affirmed, instead of proclaiming the philosophical, psychological, moral, or political superiority of one side over the other. I suggest that by approaching life from this point of view, we are encouraged to cherish differences and otherness, while at the same time we are also prompted to value the underlying connection that exists with other human beings and with the world around us. This point of view allows us to appreciate change, creativity, uniqueness, and individuality, while simultaneously respecting the value of tradition, heritage, and communal solidarity.

While section 1 focuses primarily on the nature of consciousness as it is experienced within us and the liminal section attempts to show how the underlying nature of the world of matter, as understood by both Bergson and quantum physics, appears to possess many of the qualities of consciousness itself, section 2 attempts to show how, in *Matter and Memory*, Bergson takes on the exceedingly difficult task of bringing together the apparent dualities of time and space, inside and outside, mind and matter.

What Bergson accomplishes in this revolutionary book is nothing short of astonishing in that he provides a philosophically coherent way to overcome the mind/body divide, thereby solving what is arguably the most challenging problem posed by Western philosophy during the past several centuries. Amazingly, even though Bergson's answer to this problem was never explicitly refuted, *Matter and Memory* has basically been ignored by philosophers and psychologists during most of the past century. The inexplicable absence of Bergson's thought among these thinkers—that is, philosophers of mind, cognitive psychologists, and so on—is quite a loss, especially in light of the fact that during the past few decades the study of consciousness has finally been resurrected after it had almost completely disappeared from view due to the combined onslaught of behaviorism and positivism.

Section 2 attempts to redress this situation by demonstrating the continuing relevance of *Matter and Memory*, especially in light of some of the central issues that have arisen during recent academic discussions of the nature of consciousness and its relationship to the physical body, especially the brain. For example, the so-called "hard problem" (i.e., understanding how it is possible that our subjective, conscious experiences are produced by the physical processes of the brain) not only remains unsolved, but also according to many thinkers is incapable of *being* solved within the current orthodox paradigms. As I note, however, *Matter and Memory* offers a highly sophisticated and creative solution to the "hard problem," a solution that, until recently, has been studiously ignored by most academics interested in the nature of consciousness. Bergson's solution to the hard problem is a uniquely configured version of panpsychism—the view that experience/mind/consciousness (in some shape or form) is basic to the physical universe—or in other words, the philosophical position that matter itself is associated on the most basic level with mind.

In *Matter and Memory*, Bergson argues that the physical universe is an ever-changing, overlapping, interconnected configuration of "images"—vibratory fields that are, in-and-of -themselves, a form of virtual consciousness. These "images" are the underlying substance, the "raw data" of our *perceptions* of the universe. According to Bergson, our "*pure* perceptions" (i.e., perceptions that are devoid of any overlay of memory) are formed when we subconsciously screen out the vast majority of the proto-conscious images of the universe that are ceaselessly flowing in and through us so that we can pay attention to the tiniest fraction of this universal flux, thereby converting the virtual consciousness of these universal images into the bedrock of our conscious perceptions. Our "*concrete* perceptions" (i.e., our actual, lived perceptions of the world around us) are, in turn, formed when these "pure perceptions" are overlaid with various layers of memory.

For Bergson, every moment of lived experience is an inextricable fusion of matter and memory. (Bergson eventually resolves this interactive functional dualism into an ontological nondualism when he argues that both matter and memory are, in the end, nothing but different "rhythms" of durée.) Our pure perceptions are carved out of the material substratum of the universe (i.e., matter not as inert "stuff," but rather matter as the streaming proto-conscious vibratory fluxes of the cosmos) and yet the vast majority of what we *actually* perceive comes from a highly distilled overlay of memory that is seamlessly superimposed upon the "scaffolding" of our pure perceptions, giving them meaning and significance. Our everyday experience, therefore, is grounded in material reality (in that our perceptions are rooted in a direct, albeit highly truncated, contact with the physical universe); however, simultaneously, our experience of the world, others, and ourselves is powerfully shaped under the surface of our conscious awareness by the utterly unique and ceaselessly changing configuration of our personal memories—not only our specific, episodic recollections of past events, but even more importantly, a condensed, ever-shifting fusion of subconsciously held beliefs, cultural assumptions, bodily memory, and affective patterning. Every moment of experience, therefore, is a participatory, co-created event that, on the one hand, connects us to a shared, objective world, while on the other hand, is utterly unique and profoundly molded by our biographical, cultural, and historical background. In this way, for Bergson memory is not some sort of passive and mute register of the past, but instead actively helps us to interpret and make sense of our unique experience of the world.

When Bergson claims that each of us at every moment is profoundly influenced by our entire past, a past that operates within us on subconscious levels of our being in-and-as different "strata" of memory, he is not making the claim that we are utterly and robotically driven by these past experiences. While, as I note in an extended rumination in section 2, there are numerous levels of our memory that, sadly, appear to have become highly defended, contracted, and walled off due to repeated traumatic experiences; while even if it is true that we can all too often act under the influence of these more "knotted" levels of our inner world, in ways that can seem deadened or mechanical, nonetheless because durée is actively present at all moments in the deepest levels of our being, it is always possible (in our freedom) to cultivate and deepen our connection to these depths and, hence, to generate increased levels of spontaneity, consciousness, and creativity in our daily lives. (I argue that we also can see evidence of these qualities of durée/memory every night in the form of the countless complex dream worlds that effortlessly manifest themselves within and as forms of our own consciousness.)

Section 2 also gives extended attention to Bergson's claim that our conscious experiences are not manufactured for us by the activity of the physical brain. In these chapters, I attempt to explain why Bergson would make such a seemingly outrageous claim, noting that his understanding of the nature of the relationship between consciousness and the brain (and especially that crucial subset of consciousness: memory) is not only philosophically sophisticated, but is also completely congruent with the most up-to-date scientific data on the physiological functioning of the brain.

What Bergson argues is that it is not at all clear that the neurochemical activity of the brain *produces* our conscious awareness. All that we know for sure is that there is *some sort of correlation* between brain activity and consciousness. Bergson, for one, argues that it is better to think of the brain as a type of filter that either screens out most of the "images" that flow into it from the material universe or that restricts the equally expansive, multilayered flux of memories that are subconsciously present within us. (Bergson provocatively suggests that the brain also might well serve to limit our contact with *other* consciousnesses as well.)

An alternative Bergsonian understanding of the function of the brain is that it acts as a type of "receiver," somewhat similar to a radio or television set. Drawing upon this second metaphor, Bergson postulates that the neurochemical activity of the brain does not produce consciousness, but rather enables the brain to "tune into" appropriate "frequencies" of preexisting levels of consciousness—that is, the states of consciousness that correspond to waking life, dreaming, deep sleep, trance, as well as, at least potentially, the consciousnesses of other beings. Just as the programs received by a television set are not produced by the electrical activity within the television itself, but rather exist independently of the television set, in the same way, this Bergsonian understanding of the brain/consciousness relationship postulates that consciousness is neither contained within nor produced by the brain.

Bergson also postulates (again, provocatively) that it is *not* the job of the brain to store memories. It might appear that this claim flies in the face of well over a century of scientific findings, but interestingly enough, the search for memory traces within the brain has been, at best, inconclusive. Similarly, while it might appear that damage to the brain destroys the memories that are stored there, the current scientific data available on neurological impairment and memory loss can easily be interpreted, from a Bergsonian perspective, to indicate that injury to the brain primarily damages the brain's ability to either access or to express memory—not that the memories themselves have necessarily been destroyed.

Bergson therefore forcefully argues that consciousness cannot be reduced to the activity of inert material forces (e.g., the neurochemical activity of the brain) no matter how complex this interaction might be. However, while for Bergson there are crucial *functional* differences between matter and consciousness (i.e., between the body and the mind), nonetheless, from an ontological perspective this duality is understood to be simply two ends of a single, albeit highly pluralistic and dynamic, continuum. For this reason, according to Bergson all of the material forms of the universe, and all of our experiences, in differing ways, are nothing but highly interactive and yet uniquely particular forms of durée.

This understanding that all of reality is a highly diverse, yet unified, spectrum of differing "rhythms" or "degrees" of consciousness (an understanding that, as I point out in section 2, is echoed by the work of David Bohm, an intriguing and highly respected physicist famous for his work on "non-locality") provides a framework for making sense of a wide range of phenomena (i.e., intuition, trance, visions, mystical experiences, telepathy, clairvoyance, and so on) that are often either ignored or devalued if examined from the perspective of a more conventional materialistic worldview. Over the course of his career, Bergson himself became increasingly interested in these types of phenomena. He not only wrote extensively on the nature of intuition and, in his final major work, *The Two Sources of Morality and Religion*, discussed the crucial value of mysticism for ethics as well as more broadly the evolution of consciousness itself, but he was also, to a limited degree, involved in testing the claims made about psi phenomena. He was even made the president of the British Society for Psychical Research in 1913. (Bergson's Presidential Address to the SPR offers his most explicit theorizing on the connection between his philosophy and paranormal phenomena.)

If, as Bergson postulates, the entire universe consists of differing levels of overlapping, interpenetrating rhythms of durée; if our brain's task is to "tune into" only a very small range of these levels of consciousness; if we are, under the surface of our awareness, deeply connected not only to other levels of material reality, but other consciousnesses as well; then as I suggest in a lengthy rumination in section 2, perhaps various spiritual disciplines (such as chanting, fasting, meditation, dancing, the ingestion of psychotropic substances, and so on) serve to open up the filters of the brain or to "change its channel" so that we can perceive what has always been there, even if it has previously been hidden from our sight. While Bergson's perspective does not deny that psychological, cultural, and biological factors can crucially influence the particular form that various non-ordinary phenomena take (in fact, he would insist that this is the case), nonetheless, Bergson's work suggests that various transcultural and/or transpersonal factors may also be operative in the genesis of these types of experiences. (Bergson's philosophical framework also provides an ontological basis for understanding a variety of more prosaic modes of consciousness that are also often not highly valued in Western culture, perhaps in part because they appear to be trans-empirical in nature—for example, intuition and empathy. His work also suggests an alternative and fertile way to understand the genesis of crowd contagion, possession states, and certain forms of mental illness.)

The final chapter of section 2 focuses on how Bergson's theories on psi phenomena were closely linked to his speculations on the possible survival of personal consciousness after the death of the physical body. If Bergson is correct and our consciousness, even now, has a degree of independence from material reality; if our brain does not actually store memories, but instead offers those memories an opportunity to help us to interact effectively with material reality; if there is, in fact, reliable data that indicates that it is possible even now for our consciousness to transcend the boundaries of our physical form (e.g., the numerous critically sophisticated and well-documented studies on telepathy, clairvoyance, near-death experiences, and so on), then we have every right to rationally conclude that there is a high probability that our own consciousness does not dissolve when our physical body dies.[5] In the final rumination of section 2, amplifying Bergson's rather sparse discussion of postmortem survival, I draw upon the implications of his broader work on the nature of consciousness and offer a series of suggestions about how we might envision the specific "textures" of the afterlife—positing that Bergson's insights into how we even now create numerous interacting yet highly pluralistic "worlds of experience" to inhabit might well be applicable after the death of the physical body as well.

As has perhaps become apparent, the thrust of section 2 (and in fact of *Living Consciousness* as a whole) in many ways moves in the direction of an examination of a range of topics that are generally avoided (or more seriously, mocked) within the academy—for example, psi phenomena, mysticism, and postmortem survival. However, no serious student of Bergson's work can deny that this is precisely the direction that Bergson's own scholarship took (even if, tellingly, it would be very difficult to discern this telos of Bergson's work in many, if not most, of the recent academic discussions on Bergson's thought).

Bergson's early work can easily be understood and examined on its own terms, divorced from these more controversial topics of discussion and (as noted earlier) can be profitably applied to numerous and important contemporary philosophical and psychological concerns (e.g., the nature of consciousness, the mind/body problem, and so on). As has been made clear, one of the central goals of this book is to illuminate and underscore the contemporary applicability of Bergson's thought—especially the ideas expressed in *Time and Free Will* and *Matter and Memory*. These early texts are the living seed of all of Bergson's later (and at least in his own time period, more well-known works, that is, *Creative Evolution* and *The Two Sources of Morality and Religion*). My hope is that this text, at the very least, offers a clear and helpful elucidation of these two foundational works. Nonetheless, I would also (in my more optimistic moments) like to hope that *Living Consciousness* provides something more: a glimpse into the ways in which Bergson's metaphysics and epistemology can offer us an intriguing, and to my mind exciting, way to philosophically make sense of a variety of phenomena that are all too often not taken seriously in contemporary academic discussions (e.g., intuition, telepathy, clairvoyance, postmortem survival).

I would also (again, in my more optimistic moments) like to imagine that this examination of Bergson's work can underscore the ways in which Western philosophy, in various ways, was perhaps somewhat premature to pronounce that we now live in a postmetaphysical world. As the subtitle of *Living Consciousness* indicates, Bergson's vision of reality was resolutely metaphysical (it was also, I would submit, truly visionary in its depth and breadth). While I remain in basic agreement with the postmodern suspicion of any one dominant, overarching, triumphal metaphysical stance, I am also keenly aware of how this often worthwhile and liberative deconstructive move in philosophy has all too often tended to create room not for more creative and transformative understandings of the universe and our place in it, but (sadly) has frequently engendered either a destructive nihilism (and its perhaps inevitable opposite, for example, various forms of virulent, and often violent, fundamentalisms/literalisms) or an unquestioned and unexamined philosophical materialism. It is my hope that this work can help to articulate a more attractive alternative—a vision of reality that is fully congruent with scientific findings and scientific methodology, and yet which refuses (unlike many current versions of "scientism") to reduce the universe, and our own consciousness, to the mechanistic end results of blind, inert, utterly predictable, material objects; a vision of reality in which consciousness, freedom, and life are fundamental; a vision of reality that is inherently open-ended and pluralistic, even while simultaneously affirming the numerous ways in which, under the surface, we are deeply and continually intertwined with, and interconnected to, the cosmos itself.

There are, sadly, numerous areas of Bergson's thought that this text was not able to address except in passing (e.g., Bergson's intriguing understanding of the dynamics of evolution and intuition that he offers in *Creative Evolution* as well as the timely and insightful presentation of the complex interaction between social ethics, biology, religious traditions, and mysticism that he presents in *The Two Sources of Morality and Religion*). A Bergsonian worldview is intrinsically unfinished and ceaselessly evolving, so it is perhaps appropriate that I cannot claim that this work is in any way definitive. Nonetheless, if I have done my job correctly, then *Living Consciousness* will not only have sparked further interest in Bergson's work, but will have catalyzed numerous, perhaps unanticipated, questions about the implications of his thought—questions that ideally do not lead to the static closure of final answers, but rather to the creative openness of questioning itself.

SECTION ONE

EXPLORATIONS OF CONSCIOUSNESS, AUTHENTICITY, TIME, AND FREEDOM

1

THE NATURE OF CONSCIOUSNESS

QUESTIONING AND EXPERIENCING CONSCIOUSNESS

What can we really say about our consciousness? At first glance, it would seem that we could say a lot. Consciousness is, after all, almost by definition, that which we feel most immediately; it is, to paraphrase one recent scholar of consciousness, "what it's like from the inside."[1] However, the moment when we turn our gaze inward, we are bound to notice that there is something elusive and highly mysterious about consciousness. For instance, in the very attempt to "turn our gaze" toward consciousness, where exactly do we begin to look? And what are we looking at? And who is doing this looking? How do we become conscious of consciousness itself? Exactly what is this strange "stuff" that seems to be, somehow, both something that is known and the knowing itself? Consciousness is that which is most "us," and yet, somehow, in ways that continue to elude comprehension, it also manages to contain within it all that is not us (for example: Just how does that outer world that is so solid, so bulky, so huge, get, in effect, "inside my head"?).

After centuries of scientific discoveries and technological achievements, we *can* say with some confidence that we know quite a lot about matter and how it works. The physical world seems remarkably pliant and obedient, as if it willingly acquiesces to being weighed, measured, tested, probed, and prodded. The same cannot be said about our consciousness. Unlike the external world that seems so strikingly self-evident, consciousness slips from our grasp the moment that we try to capture it with our often less-than-subtle nets of measurement and quantification.

It often appears as if consciousness resists every attempt to pin it down with words. It should not be a surprise, therefore, that exploring the nature of consciousness generates many more questions than it does either reliable or easily

3

understandable answers. For instance: Is consciousness the constantly changing flux of perceptions, feelings, memories, sensations, thoughts within us (i.e., that which is known), or is it the underlying changeless inner subject, the "I," the knower of this inner flux? (Or is it somehow both? Or is it something more than any of this?) Is consciousness a seamless unbroken inner continuity of awareness (i.e., is it "one"), or is it an endless, yet always new, play of sheer difference? (Or is it somehow both? Or something else?) Is consciousness an impersonal, objective "stuff," an "it," or is it a personal, subjective "I"? (Or is "it" somehow both? Or neither?) Is consciousness the most intimate, unique, ever-changing expression of my individuality, or is it a vast, transpersonal, cosmic Awareness that is simultaneously the creative weaver, and created fabric, of this entire universe? (Or is it somehow both? Or beyond even this?)

As you might have guessed, I have been obsessed with these questions for quite some time. My awakening to the importance of consciousness took place when I was around twelve or thirteen and had my first mystical experience. Until this time, I did the things that kids typically do in a college town in north-central Florida: climbing huge oak trees and watching, fascinated, as rabbits and squirrels emerged out of the underbrush; making forts in the swampy woods nearby with my brother and sisters and our friends; running through these woods with my Labrador retriever; playing elaborately staged games of croquet, and so on.

During all of this quasi-automatic immersion in "doing stuff," I was, as might be expected, somewhat less than self-aware. However, while coming back from school on a hot Florida afternoon, I "woke up."[2] For most of that day, for no apparent reason, I had been obsessing about what would happen to my consciousness after I died. I tried and tried to imagine what it would be like not to be aware anymore, what it would be like to have my consciousness just disappear, what it would be like simply to go blank, even while, somehow, the world would remain, would continue without me. I just could not imagine it. It did not seem to make sense, especially when I was feeling so charged, so alive, and the world felt so vivid and real. Every time I pictured myself, cold, dead, and underground in a grave, I could feel my imagination bounce back, as if rebuffed—not so much in fear or revulsion at the thought of death per se, but rather, recoiling at the thought that my "I-ness," my self-awareness, could blink out, disappear, as if it had never existed, as if it had never known this moment in time, walked through this patch of scruffy weeds and smelled the scent of hot asphalt and pine tar and gazed up at the cumulus clouds floating in the bright, blue sky.

And then "it" happened. I find it rather odd, almost surreal, now, almost forty years later, to communicate in words what happened to me, in me, as me, at that juncture in time. There is such a difference between who I am now and who I was then—how I interpret that event, what philosophical overlays I now naturally superimpose over the experience, the density of life experience that I can draw upon to make sense of it. Now the moment exists within me primarily as a rather distant, almost virtual, but strangely magnetic and densely packed, memory—known, understood, explored, but rather removed, far away. For that boy, however, what happened was utterly unexpected and astonishingly vivid— "it" just opened up, suddenly, and then "I" was gone, and yet also, strangely, I was very, very present. My boundaries (which I had not really questioned or thought about before) no longer existed. This "I" was no longer contained, limited to the confines of my physical body. Instead, "I" was literally *ec*-static—*out of* my usual "place," spread out, freely and joyously, existing in-and-as an almost unbearable flux of surging power and delight and transparent open awareness. The normal tick-tock of time dissolved. I do not really, now, have a clue as to how long, in ordinary time, "I" was in that state of consciousness while standing there in the quiet neighborhood road. Perhaps a minute? A couple of minutes? But when I returned, while I was inwardly reeling from the experience, I knew something crucial had just taken place. I knew that I was no longer the same, that somehow, in a way that I could not even begin to describe, I had woken up.

For a variety of reasons, I decided to keep this experience to myself. I could not have articulated in any clear-cut, overt way, why I kept quiet about this experience. In retrospect, I think that it had something to do with wanting to keep this almost miraculous, but still somewhat fragile and raw event untarnished, free from disturbing questions, protected from the rough and insensitive handling of people, even if they might have had the best of intentions. I knew that I had been given an astonishing gift. What the gift was, I could not begin to articulate. All I knew was that the experience had something to do with awareness, joy, expansion, awakening—and that the best way to keep it safe was to keep it secret.

The memory of this inner opening, over the next few years, acted as a kind of touchstone, a catalyst that prompted me to pay close attention to the nature of my consciousness. I was especially intrigued by any experiences that were at all similar to my gradually receding memory of that ecstatic moment on the hot pavement up the street from my home.

For instance, while still in high school, I increasingly began to notice an intriguing sort of inner bifurcation taking place within my own consciousness. One part was able to step back, somewhere deep inside myself, and just observe. This aspect of me simply took note of what was happening both inside and outside of myself, while the other just did (and thought and felt) all of the things that teenagers do (and think and feel). However, my awareness of this inner duality dramatically altered one day when, in full-bore observer mode, I suddenly became aware of just how multilayered and amazingly slippery my everyday consciousness actually was.

It was a clear, comparatively mild day. I was mowing a neighbor's lawn and I began to observe my sensations, feelings, and thoughts. What intrigued me was that so many different experiences were happening within me simultaneously and sequentially. I noticed that I was aware of the bright blue sky, the throbbing sound and vibration of the mower, the shifting of my weight as I moved forward, the smell of the grass and camellias. I was also aware of numerous ever-changing thoughts and feelings. I noticed that somehow these thoughts and feelings took place on another level than the sensations, that they manifested in a way that had a different internal quality, yet were not isolated and separate from the sensations. My feeling of contentment was intermingled, not only with a vague sense of disquiet on the edges of my awareness (emerging, perhaps, from an earlier argument with a friend), but also with the countless sensations that rushed into me, along with another layering of thoughts (again, each with its unique quality and tone): on one level I was, rather abstractly and preconsciously humming a song to myself, while on another level, I was thinking about when I should send the bill to the elderly couple whose lawn I was mowing, while on yet another level I was remembering, in a vague yet tangible way, a previous interaction with this elderly couple in which they had been warm and friendly with me. Amazingly, to me at least, I was also aware of the fact that I was aware of all of this, and aware of my amazement, not only at the densely interwoven contents of my consciousness, but also of the fact that I was aware that I was aware of the fact that I was aware . . . and where did all of these levels of awareness end or begin?

This process was so prolonged, and vivid, and charged, that I added another layer into the mix: an intense desire to remember this experience, to capture in my memory, not only the specifics of this experience, but also how sweetly thrilling and mysterious and intriguing it was (other layers themselves!), even though I was doing something that was so utterly ordinary and prosaic as mowing someone's lawn.

ENDURING DURÉE

This experience of the multilayered nature of consciousness was, to my knowledge, my first conscious encounter with *durée*. Durée is, arguably, the most important philosophical concept of Henri Bergson, the French philosopher of the later nineteenth and early twentieth century whose ideas are the primary catalyst of this present volume. Durée is Bergson's term for the dynamic, ever-changing nature of consciousness, a consciousness expressed and manifested in-and-through-and-as *time*. From Bergson's perspective, durée is an indivisible fusion of manyness and oneness; it is the ongoing, dynamic, temporal flux of awareness; it is a flowing that is ever new and always unpredictable; it is the continual, seamless, interconnected, immeasurable movement of our awareness, manifesting, simultaneously, as both the knower and what is known.

In English texts, *durée* is often translated as "duration," which is a rather problematic translation in that "duration" is often associated with notions of "endurance" and has connotations of grimly and stoically "enduring" something painful or difficult (which is why I prefer to leave the French word *durée* untranslated). Durée is not something that we have to endure, it is not necessarily painful or difficult. Instead, it is the natural manifestation of our inner being; it surges forth, in reality, with complete ease—it is the most natural occurrence in the world. (Bergson also claims that durée actually is very difficult to experience in its purity—but I will say more on this later.)

Durée is accessed through a subtle intuitive introspective awareness, not simply as the contents of our consciousness, but rather as the dynamic essence of who we really are, both the inner knower and what that inner knower knows.[3] As such, durée is not something that exists separate from us; instead, "it" is the temporal flux of our consciousness—it is our own awareness as it persists (while always changing), that is always present (and always moving), that endures, in time, *as* time. (Please bear with my awkward use of quotation marks: they are simply my way of highlighting the limitations of language, because, as noted previously, "it" is not an "it" at all.)

The attempt to understand durée and to express it in philosophically precise and vivid language is at the heart of Bergson's corpus. As he noted in a letter to Harald Höffding, any attempt to portray his work that does not "continually return to . . . the very central point of the doctrine—the intuition of duration [the English translation of durée] . . . [which] is the point whence I set out and to which I constantly return" is, on some level, a distortion.[4]

STRUGGLING WITH IMMEDIACY

Bergson, from very early on in his philosophical career, focused his attention on the problem of understanding durée. His first attempt was his doctoral thesis, written at the age of thirty in 1889, *Essai sur les données immédiates de la conscience* (*An Essay on the Immediate Data of Consciousness*, published in English as *Time and Free Will*).[5] In this text, as well as in most of his other published work, Bergson attempts to base his philosophical conclusions on what is available to all of us in our own immediate experience. For Bergson, it is crucial that philosophical investigations start from what is, arguably, the most intimate, undeniable, vividly felt knowledge that we possess: what is taking place within our own consciousness.

Bergson (in what may strike some as a moment of rhetorical exuberance), even goes so far as to claim that if we focus our attention inward, while letting go of certain deeply entrenched habits (more on these later), it is actually possible to "have absolute knowledge of ourselves" (*TFW* 235). Now, as Maurice Merleau-Ponty, another French philosopher (who was deeply influenced by Bergson) astutely points out, this is a rather "strange absolute knowledge," given the fact that our awareness of ourselves is rarely, if ever, complete or undistorted.[6] However, as Merleau-Ponty then goes on to suggest, the fact that we typically only have a "partial coincidence" with ourselves is not actually a philosophical obstacle, but instead, is an opportunity, because even if we do not possess some sort of "god-like," utterly complete knowledge of ourselves, there is something that is irreplaceable and immediate (and in that sense, "absolute) about our own self-awareness, in that we know ourselves with a knowledge which "could not be conceived of as being any closer or more intimate."[7]

Merleau-Ponty's comments are an evocative attempt to express a self-evident truth: there is something utterly unique and singular and irreplaceable about our self-knowledge. No one else knows what is going on within us besides ourselves; even if that self-knowledge is flawed and limited, it is still a type of knowledge that is incomparable. We may know a lot about objects and events in the external world (e.g., we may have a degree in veterinary medicine and know all about the anatomy and physiology of dogs and cats and cows), but we can only know *about* these objects or events by studying them from the outside—we cannot have the personal, immediate, inner knowledge of them that we have of our own consciousness (*CE* 1).

In *Time and Free Will*, Bergson typically stresses (perhaps even overemphasizes) the difference between these two types of knowledge, and goes to great lengths to point out that it is crucial that we do not treat these two intrinsically different types of knowledge in the same way. In particular, it is a grave error to assume that our own inner states of awareness should be subjected to the same types of observational techniques that we would use to gather accurate information about external objects (e.g., measurement, controlled laboratory experiments, and so on). According to Bergson, instead of studying inner phenomena as we would study external phenomena, using a methodology which is rooted in the tacit assumption that our inner and outer worlds are the same, it is far better to recognize that our inner states of consciousness are uniquely configured and, as such, are best understood "in their developing, and in so far as they make up, by their interpenetration, the continuous evolution of a free person" (*TFW* 229).

It is important to note that Bergson does not have a naïve or simplistic understanding of the immediacy of our conscious experience. While he consistently maintains that our consciousness is a type of philosophical touchstone, he also argues that this touchstone is not easily accessed.[8] Instead, the immediacy of consciousness ironically only emerges for the philosopher after an arduous inner search (and even then only haltingly and with varying degrees of intensity). As

Bergson points out in the letter to Harald Höffding, the intuitive knowledge of durée "demands a great mental effort, the rupture of many restraining limits, something resembling a fresh method of thinking (for the immediate is far from being that which is easiest to notice)" (*M* 1148). The direct knowledge of our own consciousness, for Bergson, is hidden beneath many layers of psychic habits or predispositions that veil its true nature. Nonetheless, according to Bergson, even with all the difficulties and limitations that we might face in our quest to come to know ourselves, even with all of the wrong turns that we might encounter in our introspective endeavors, when we finally make our way into that inner sanctum (or when it presents itself to us as a gift) our intuitive aware-ness of ourselves is undeniable, nonmediated, and directly evident. As Bergson stresses, once a person has reached this level of awareness, "and is acquainted with it in its simple form (which must not be confounded with its conceptual representation)," he or she cannot and will not remain the same; instead, that inner certainty of awareness is so powerful and self-evident that the person who has this knowledge will feel "constrained" to change his or her "point of view about reality" so that it aligns with this inner perception (*M* 1148).

Nonetheless, even if we have, for a limited time and in a limited way, been privileged to grasp (or be grasped by) this inner immediacy; and even if we admit that this intuitive knowledge perhaps challenges many of our previous philosophical presuppositions, another difficulty quickly presents itself: it is almost impossible to describe this "immediate data of consciousness." Bergson, throughout his career, struggles with the difficulty of articulating that which, it seems, language simply cannot handle. While Bergson often insists that language structures and shapes much of our everyday experience, he also recognizes (and attempts to help us to recognize as well) that language, especially in its more abstract, conceptual formulations (although metaphorical language has problems of its own), just does not work very well when it comes to certain types of expe-riences. This linguistic flat-footedness is apparent, not only in attempts to accu-rately and thoroughly describe altered states of consciousness, such as dreams, trance states, or mystical experiences, but even in our attempts to convey in any meaningful way the deeper levels of our day-to-day awareness.

Our difficulty in articulating the nature of consciousness is due, to a certain extent, to the fact that words (especially written words) do not flow. Words remain fixed on the page. Words have a very specific range of meanings (e.g., "apple" = red, fruit, tasty, not "apple" = motorcycle, fish, flying). Words are sequential; they are lined up next to each other and they are built up from parts (at least in those languages that are alphabetical in nature). Durée, however, is very different—it flows, it never remains the same, it is seamlessly intercon-nected, it has distinctions but no parts. Is it any wonder then that words do not work so well when it comes to describing the nature of durée?

There is also another reason why it is difficult for us to gain clear, easy access to the "immediate data of consciousness." Bergson, drawing upon his interest in evolutionary thought, claims that, as a species, we have an inherent and powerful compulsion to focus our attention outward. Human beings, in Bergson's eyes, are immensely practical. In order to survive as a species our attention has primarily, and understandably, been focused on the mastery of the day-to-day details of the external world. For millennia, our time and energy has been primarily given to the urgent necessities of creating shelter, hunting and growing food, and protecting ourselves against enemies; we have been much less concerned with cultivating an awareness of what is going on within us, to say nothing of the development of philosophically sophisticated, introspective observations about the nature of consciousness.

In this respect, things have not changed much during the thousands of years that we have populated the planet. Our focus is still irresistibly riveted on the outer world. It is as if we are mesmerized by the sensory stimulation that drives our culture: we are almost constantly bombarded with throbbing music, with suggestive ads, with honking car horns and bombastic TV shows. In this torrent of sensory overload and psychic pressure, it is not surprising that we rarely find the time, or the desire, to turn our attention within, and really examine what is happening inside of us.

In addition, as Bergson suggests (especially in several of his later works), we *need* to give a lot of attention to the world around us, because it does not come ready-made. Bergson argues that, from the time of our birth, we have had to work hard in order to successfully create a meaningful and manageable world out of the sensory data that cascades in and through us. In order to not be overwhelmed, in order to function, it is crucial that our senses and our brain carve out certain clearly defined zones of stability in the flux of universal becoming. We are forced to create order by screening out vast amounts of the sensory and mental information that pours into us. Through the ongoing process of biological maturation and cultural assimilation, and with the assistance of our social institutions and communal traditions, we are taught how to name and count and assign meanings to this torrent of data. If we are successful, it then becomes possible to live in a world of relatively unchanging (and therefore, useful) objects—for example, cars, computers, blouses, radios, azalea bushes, and squirrels. Helped by our language, which assigns relatively permanent, distinct words to certain clusters of sensory phenomena, and helped by our brain, which filters out any information that is not in some way useful to us, we in essence "create" objects from the flux of sensation, objects that possess clearly defined boundaries, objects that are distinct from other objects, objects that can be lined up next to each other in space and counted, objects that are seen to possess certain (again, relatively stable) abstract qualities (e.g., hot/cold, soft/hard, wet/dry), objects that can be helpfully compared and contrasted with the qualities of other objects.

Bergson suggests that our desire to shape the seeming "chaos" of experience into objects that are discrete, distinct, stable, and that move in quantifiable, ordered, and predictable ways is accentuated in human beings due to our primary reliance upon our sense of sight. He notes that our sense of sight is almost invariably spatial in orientation—it shows us external objects with definite boundaries, positioned near or far from our equally clearly (and spatially) defined, physical body. This visual world is the world that seems most real and important to us, a reality and importance that is underscored by the tangible solidity of our sense of touch.

However, our sense of hearing can reveal a quite different world to us, if we can let go of certain visual habits that we have internalized. If we focus our attention primarily on our sense of hearing, then it is possible that we might begin to "see" (is the frequent linguistic correlation between sight and understanding accidental?) something different, a world of interconnected and ever-changing movement, a world in which movement itself is the central reality. Bergson, as he frequently does, draws upon the example of listening to a melody to make his point:

> Let us listen to a melody, allowing ourselves to be lulled by it: do we not have the clear perception of a movement which is not attached to a mobile [i.e., a moving object], of change without anything changing? This change is enough, it is the thing itself. And even if it takes time, it is still indivisible; if the melody stopped sooner it would no longer be the same sonorous whole, it would be another, equally indivisible. (*CM* 174)

Many of us might tend to think of a melody as simply a "juxtaposition of distinct notes," but this tendency is only because our sense of hearing has taken on the habits of our sense of sight—we, in essence, "listen to the melody through the vision which an orchestra leader would have of it as he watched its score. We picture notes placed next to one another upon an imaginary piece of paper" (*CM* 174). But if we let go of these spatial and visual images, what do we perceive? If we make the effort, if we listen carefully, it is possible to hear a series of overlapping sounds in which each pulsation is qualitatively unique, and yet is also intrinsically connected to the other pulsations of sound, sounds that have no definite and fixed spatial location, sounds that are both outside and inside us, simultaneously, sounds that have no clear-cut boundaries—sounds that are a continuous, interconnected, yet ever changing, whole.

Normally, however, this is not the way we hear music, or more importantly, it is not the way that we "view" the world. Instead, we prefer to "see" the world as filled with relatively stable objects that possess distinct boundaries. And while such a perception may well help us to function effectively, it is deadly to a clear understanding of our inner world. As Bergson points out, as long as our attention is gripped by the outside world, "we have no interest in listening to the uninterrupted humming of life's depths" (*CM* 176). For the vast majority of us, therefore, it is exceedingly difficult to get back to the real experience of our lived consciousness, a consciousness that flows; in order to do so it is "as if the whole normal direction of consciousness [has] to be reversed" (*CM* 111).

An "Object"-tive Understanding of Ourselves

Bergson emphasizes that due to the magnetic pull of the external world, it is almost inevitable that we will have difficulty turning our attention within. He suggests that due to the artificial and linguistically based superimposition of the external world onto our inner experience, we typically (and tacitly) assume that our consciousness (i.e., durée) is structured like the external world, whereas, in reality, it is radically different.[9] Our awareness may seem to be a reflection of the external world, but it is not. It may appear to be composed of a series of separate, self-contained states of awareness that are, in essence, lined up next to each other like solid beads of different colors, seemingly exchanging places with each other in the passing of time (e.g., sadness changing into happiness, a memory of my aunt changing into a memory of my uncle), but it is not.

To use one of Bergson's favorite metaphorical images, we tend to think of our inner experience as if it were captured on a roll of movie film—essentially turning the undivided and unanticipated flux of our consciousness into a linear series of static snapshots, one frozen moment followed by another, each one inevitably leading to the next. In this "cinematographic" perspective on life, each thought, each memory, each feeling, is tacitly understood to exist separately within us, each having its own discrete identity, each taking up just so much "space" within our psyche, each static snapshot lined up and unrolling, implacably, on the underlying homogenous substance of the film of time.[10] As Bergson points out, our tendency to envision the dynamic flow of our consciousness as static and fragmented, to see it as notes upon a musical score, or as beads threaded together on a string, or as snapshots on a roll of film, may well suit the requirements of logic and language, but this "spatialized" mode of understanding deeply distorts the nature of our consciousness. Durée, understood and experienced clearly, is literally like nothing else found in the world, even if we might wish that this were not the case so that we could more easily grasp it.

As was noted earlier, perhaps the closest external analog to durée is a melody. Listening to a melody takes time, and yet it has to be experienced *in* time as an organic unity in order for it to be what it is. If it were split into separate, disconnected parts, it would not be the same melody—it cannot be reduced to individual notes or different vibrations. Listening to a melody, each note blends into others—the previous notes linger in our memory to produce a seamless flow of sound—and yet a melody has to change; in fact, it is made of changes, it is continual novelty and diversity. As such, as Milič Čapek points out, a melody, like durée, is "neither a bare unity nor a sheer multiplicity."[11] Therefore, we would be justified in asking ourselves, with Čapek: "Is the intuitive fact of a melody a single whole or a sum of distinct parts? Is it a unity or a plurality? It is both of them at the same time, or rather neither of them, at least as long as both terms have their usual arithmetical connotations" (more later on the significance of counting).[12]

The problem is that we normally do not hear the manyness/oneness of our consciousness singing its unique song within us. Instead, seeing ourselves through the distorting lens of our internalization of the external world, we lose touch with the "indivisible and indestructible continuity" of the "melody of our experience"; we divide this melody of consciousness into distinct notes that can be set out, side by side, in a two-dimensional, paper-thin existence (CM 83). Whereas our inner world is in actuality a "melody where the past enters into the present and forms with it an undivided whole which remains undivided and even indivisible in spite of what is added at every instant," what we normally tend to experience is an inner life that is tightly controlled, where ideally every feeling has a label and every idea is carefully weighed and considered (CM 83).

LANGUAGE AND DURÉE

As was mentioned earlier, Bergson suggests that, unknown to most of us, language acts as a type of prism in that it fragments our experience, splitting the dynamic flux of our consciousness into unchanging, self-contained parts (i.e., "states" of consciousness, such as "fear" or "pleasure"). Since words are separate, unchanging units ("fear," as a word, always stays the same and is always a different word than "pleasure"), we tend to assume that as time passes within us one "nugget" of consciousness (e.g., "pleasure") is replaced by another "nugget" of consciousness (e.g., "fear"). Furthermore, we are convinced (again, at least partially because of the stability of words) that not only do we experience the same emotion each time we feel, let's say, "anger," but also that other people, because they use the same word "anger," are feeling the same internal state that we are experiencing. However, as Bergson repeatedly stresses, each state of consciousness is utterly unique and is "tinged with the coloring of all the others. Thus each of us has his own way of loving and hating; and this love or this hatred reflects his whole personality. Language, however, denotes these states by the same words in every case: so that it has been able to fix only the objective and impersonal aspect of love, hate, and the thousand emotions which stir the soul" (TFW 164).

Bergson points out that the need to label inner experience, to give it a clear-cut name (e.g., "loneliness" or "anger" or "soft" or "hungry") comes with a heavy cost. He notes that "language requires us to establish between our ideas the same sharp and precise distinctions, the same discontinuity, as between material objects" (*TFW* xix). This similarity in the way that we treat words and things may well be useful in our day-to-day existence, but it can also lead to philosophical difficulties. We see the world through language, through the lens of words that seem so stable and unchanging, that remain fixed in place and lined up next to each other (at least in written form). Language tacitly, yet relentlessly, chops up the interwoven dynamism of our inner world, creating manageable, useful "chunks" of experience, making it difficult for us to see clearly and accurately the true nature of our inner world. As Bergson notes, "the word with well-defined outlines, the rough and ready word, which stores up the stable, common, and consequently impersonal element in the impressions of mankind, overwhelms or at least covers over the delicate and fugitive impressions of our individual consciousness" (*TFW* 132). Even if we somehow could manage to continually create new words to represent each new facet of the ever-changing nature of our sensations and feelings, these words would fail in their task, if nothing else because of the simple fact that they, as words, inherently stay the same, while our consciousness is ceaselessly changing.

While we might well prefer an inner world that is clear-cut and logically consistent, where every belief can be rationally justified and every emotion comes neatly packaged, where there is no murky ambiguity—only black and white, not shades of gray—this attempt to form a stable inner world, seen from a Bergsonian perspective, is nothing more than a desperate attempt to ignore what is really happening within us; it is, at best, a denial of the unpredictable thrust of newness blossoming at each moment in our consciousness in favor of a managed, carefully crafted, and tightly controlled inner world. However, if we can, at least for a while and to the extent that it is possible, let go of our evolutionary predisposition to fragment and spatialize our consciousness, if we release for the moment our desire to corral our feelings and thoughts into culturally convenient compartments, if we can take the risk necessary to open ourselves to the currents of our inner life, it is possible that we might indeed manage to have an intuitive, immediate awareness of durée, even if it only lasts for a short time and is never fully pure.

The Paradox of Durée

Bergson repeatedly insists that durée, our personal consciousness, is not split up into parts. As Čapek notes, it is not "built out of atomic, independent, mutually separable components."[13] It is not a shuffling of "permanent and pre-existing units," such as ideas, thoughts, feelings, memories, and so on, that are each, so to speak, "fragments" of our consciousness.[14] Rather, durée is characterized by a mutual interrelationship of its various states, each of which is utterly unique, and yet each of which is permeated and suffused by all of the other inner states of consciousness.

Because the manyness/oneness of our consciousness is unlike any external object in the world, it is not irrational to use paradox as a way to accurately describe our inner world. In fact, it is irrational *not* to do so. Durée is that which manifests as sheer and utter internal multiplicity and diversity, and yet it is also that which, if examined carefully, has no breaks, no gaps, within itself.[15] Instead, our consciousness is a seamless continuity, an uninterrupted flow in which, in the words of Ian W. Alexander, "each moment is absorbed into the following one, transforming it and being transformed by it, with the consequent transformation of the whole."[16] Consciousness as such is "pure change and heterogeneity," but it is also "the heterogeneity of organic growth."[17] Durée is, as Bergson emphasizes, that which is "ever the same and ever changing" (*TFW* 101). It is always the same in that it is utter continuity, it is always changing because it is a flux of sheer novelty. It is both, and yet actually neither. No descriptive term, or even any clever combination of terms, will ever adequately represent durée.

In order to give more concrete specificity to Bergson's evocative, if somewhat abstract, conceptual understanding of the inevitable fusion of continuity and heterogeneity within our consciousness, let's imagine that I am looking at a chair—an external object that is seemingly immobile. Even if I keep my head completely still and only look at it from the same angle of vision, and even if the light basically stays the same, my perception of this chair is not one continuous *unchanging* experience. Rather, it is a continuous *changing* experience—its continuity actually consists of a multiplicity of changes from the first moment to the next, simply because the later moment of vision is suffused by my memory of the first moment. Therefore, my inner experience, even of something as seemingly static as a chair, is a seamless flow of constant change, swelling within memory as time accumulates, "rolling upon itself, as a snowball on the snow" (*CE* 2).

Bergson repeatedly emphasizes that memory, while providing a multilayered context of ongoing continuity within myself, also subtly alters the sensations of even seemingly stable external objects. Let's say that I am walking for the first time in the Latin Quarter in Paris. Making my way down the street, I am bombarded by countless sensory impressions: the sound of my shoes on cobblestone streets, the smell of escargot cooking in restaurants, the taste of a freshly baked croissant, the sight of Notre Dame peeking above the rooftops. All of these sensations are fused together, mingling with my excitement at finally being able to visit this area of Paris, my disorientation and minor apprehension at being in a strange place, my desire to find a certain bookstore, my memory of getting out of bed that morning, and so on. Let's say that, after a number of days of continuing to prowl around the Latin Quarter, I go on another walk along the same streets. During this walk, I might well see many of the same buildings, smell many of the same foods, eat a croissant baked at the same little shop, and hear my shoes hitting against the same cobblestones. I might, therefore, for convenience's sake, think to myself that my sensations (the sights, the smells, the tastes, the sounds) were also the same. But, if I look closely at my experience, I would notice that the sensations I experience after being in the Latin Quarter for a week are actually strikingly different than they were before. Now I carry within me the memories from all of the previous walks that I took during that week; now, instead of being disoriented, I feel at ease and at home, almost carrying an internalized map of the city within me; now I greet each new moment of experience with a whole new interwoven matrix of memories (which includes everything that I experienced, thought, and felt during that whole week). This tacit overlay of memory, in and of itself, subtly but significantly, alters my experience of these "same" sights, sounds, smells, and tastes.

The ceaseless inner change of conscious experience combined inexplicably but undeniably with inner continuity is also strikingly apparent when we look carefully at our emotions, our desires, and our efforts of will, none of which correspond, like our visual perception of the chair or a walk through the Latin Quarter, to a seemingly unchanging external object or set of objects. To illustrate this claim, let's say that at this moment I am aware of feeling sad (even calling it a "feeling" is simply a linguistic marker that focuses attention on a dominant "note" in the overall "melody" of my consciousness). This sad feeling, if I examine it closely, is not the same as previous feelings of sadness, even if I might use the same word "sad." This feeling is itself suffused with countless memories of previous experiences that all coalesce, in various gradations, to form the utterly unique quality of this current feeling-state. Then, whether or not I am conscious of it, in the very next moment this feeling will have subtly changed (but without any radical breaks) into something else. Perhaps I have shifted the position of my body, or I have absorbed some new sights or sounds, or I have had some new insight. All of these new experiences combine with the memory of the original feeling of sadness that still lingers as a type of "overtone" in my consciousness. All of these new factors come together to produce a different note in the ongoing melody of my consciousness. As time passes, these changes in my consciousness continue to multiply. In fact, for Bergson, the passage of time *is itself* the changing of our consciousness. Ultimately, these changes, reverberating throughout my being, become so evident that I have to acknowledge that I am no longer feeling the way I once was; I am no longer "sad"; now I am, let's say, "content." Therefore, as Bergson points out:

> No two moments are identical in a conscious being. Take for example the simplest feeling, suppose it to be constant, absorb the whole personality in it: the consciousness which will accompany this feeling will

not be able to remain identical with itself for two consecutive moments, since the following moment always contains, over and above the preceding one, the memory the latter has left it. A consciousness which had two identical moments would be a consciousness without memory. It would therefore die and be re-born continually. (*CM* 193)

Bergson goes to great pains to emphasize that in much the same way that we make a mistake when we think that a perception, or a thought, or an emotion, stays the same within us, we also make a mistake when we think that the transition from one state of consciousness to the next is abrupt or discontinuous; in fact, as Bergson notes, "the passing from one state to another resembles, more than we imagine, a single state being prolonged; the transition is continuous" (*CE* 2). We, in essence, ignore the change that is taking place within us until it becomes too great to ignore any longer. We then act as if a completely new state of consciousness has replaced the previous one. In this way, by separate acts of our attention, we change what is a gentle, unbroken slope into a series of discontinuous steps. According to Bergson, however, even the sudden, unforeseen, seemingly disconnected moments in our psychic life (e.g., an unexpected surge of anger) are "the beats of the drum which breaks forth here and there in the symphony" (*CE* 3). We focus on them because they interest us more than the rest of what is occurring within us, but each of these shifts of our consciousness is, in actuality, "borne by the fluid mass of our whole psychical existence. Each is only the best illuminated point of a moving zone which comprises all that we feel or think or will—all, in short, that we are at any given moment. It is this entire zone which in reality makes up our state" (*CE* 3). In truth, as noted earlier, each of the "elements" of our consciousness are not separate from each other—there is nothing static, nothing that is cut off from the rest. Rather, the entire "mass" of our consciousness continues, moment by moment, in an "endless flow" (*CE* 3).

This flow of durée is, in many respects, the flow of memory. And for Bergson, there is nothing more substantial, more durable, than this swelling advance of memory that continually evolves, carrying with it the past that "grows without ceasing" (*CE* 4). He suggests that our personal past is automatically and continually preserved (perhaps in its entirety) in our memory (not, as we will see in section 2, put away in some neural net in the brain), and that it therefore "follows us at every instant; all that we have felt, thought and willed from our earliest infancy is there, leaning over the present which is about to join it" (*CE* 5). What is significant about the persistence of memory and its infusion into the flux of our present awareness is that "consciousness cannot go through the same state twice. The circumstances may be the same, but they will act no longer on the same person, since they find him at a new moment in his history. Our personality, which is being built up each instant with its accumulated experience, [in this way] changes without ceasing" (*CE* 5–6).

2

AUTHENTICITY

═══════════════════════

THE SUPERFICIAL SELF AND THE DEEP SELF

B ergson argues that our tendency to fragment our inner experience, to isolate and stabilize that which before was fluid, alive, and interwoven,
applies not only to our feelings and sensations, but also to our ideas and beliefs.
At first glance, it would seem that our conceptual life, because of its inevitable
linguistic and social underpinning, would be exempt from a Bergsonian introspective revisioning. But Bergson suggests that, if we look carefully, we will
notice that our conceptual life is also not divorced from the rest of our inner
experience. As he notes, each of our ideas is "incorporated in the fluid mass of
our conscious states"; each idea, in this sense "has the same kind of life as a cell
in an organism: everything which affects the general state of the self affects it
also" (*TFW* 135). (Bergson immediately qualifies this statement, stressing that
while a "cell occupies a definite point in the organism, an idea which is truly
ours fills the whole of our self" [*TFW* 135].) Our ideas and beliefs, even if they
might be expressed in the same words that others have used, are truly our own,
at least to the extent that they have become fully incorporated into the depths of
our being and have been significantly altered by that incorporation; they are
truly ours to the extent that they have been "dyed," not only by the "color of all
our other ideas," but also by all the other latent memories and feelings that
ceaselessly swirl within us (*TFW* 135). (Similarly, the ideas that I am writing
right now, while initially expressed by Bergson, have become my own, simply by
virtue of my prolonged attempts to understand and "digest" them.)

Nonetheless, Bergson also insists that some of our ideas are *not* fully ours,
some ideas simply "float on the surface, like dead leaves on the water of a pond"
(*TFW* 135). Whether taking the form of religious dogmas, advertising jingles, or

political slogans, these ideas, most of which "we receive ready-made," are typically beliefs that we have accepted from others without a close examination; therefore, as Bergson puts it, they "remain in us without ever being properly assimilated" (*TFW* 135—136). These ideas, interestingly, are often the ideas which we can easily and clearly articulate, ideas which may be very logical, ideas which can and do tumble off our tongues effortlessly, ideas which we may angrily defend. Nonetheless, these ideas are also, to some degree, lifeless, impersonal, and external to us; they are mechanical platitudes which do not truly express our deepest truths.

Our deepest truths may be less clear-cut and easily expressed than the ideas of others which we are so ready to affirm and to proclaim. Our more profound insights are discovered within ourselves when we dig below the surface of what seems readily apparent, when we, as Bergson says, "penetrate into the depths" of our "organized and living intelligence" in order to "witness the joining together or rather the blending of many ideas, which . . . seem to exclude one another as logically contradictory terms" (*TFW* 136). Here, within "the deeper strata of the self" (*TFW* 136), within the "deep-seated self" which "heats and blazes up" (*TFW* 125), is an inner life that is deeply felt if not readily understood, an inner life where states of consciousness "intermingle in such a way that we cannot tell whether they are one or several" (*TFW* 137), where concepts and feelings interweave to such an extent that they can only be compared with "the strangest dreams, in which two images overlie one another," dreams in which we might, for instance, see two separate individuals who are, at the same time, one person (*TFW* 136).

As Bergson emphasizes, most of us do not give much sustained effort to inner exploration in that, for most of us, "our outer and, so to speak, social life is more practically important to us than our inner and individual existence" (*TFW* 130). Therefore, we prefer to substitute "the symbol for the reality," or more subtly, we are inclined to perceive "reality only through the symbol" (*TFW* 128). In this way, by refracting our self, breaking it into pieces, we create a "conventional ego" (*TFW* 133) that is "much better adapted to the requirements of social life in general and language in particular," even if in doing so we inevitably lose sight of our more "fundamental self" (*TFW* 128).

Many scholars of Bergson have commented on the distinction he draws between the "superficial self" and the "deep self." John Mullarkey points out that, according to Bergson, "modern, social and mechanized existence has cleaved our consciousness in two. The mind exists in two layers, one facing outwards and formed after the external, public realm, the other remaining behind in 'profound' seclusion."[1] Suzanne Guerlac comments further on this internal split in consciousness, pointing out that "in Rousseauistic fashion, Bergson speaks as if social life were radically alienating. He suggests that the pressure of social life requires the doubling of the subject, the engendering of a second self that covers over the first, like a second skin made up of dead leaves, or dead cells."[2] Similarly, according to A. A. Luce, the superficial self is "that side of our nature which we present to the outside world," it is that aspect of our being which attempts to fit in, to blend with the crowd, to put on a pleasing smile, to wear the latest fashions, to react in a habitual, knee-jerk way to what life brings to it; it is as Frederick Burwick and Paul Douglas note with some amusement the "automatistic evil twin" of our deeper nature.[3]

In reality, of course, the superficial self is simply one, very basic and self-evident, aspect of our selfhood. In many ways, we have constructed it by internalizing and reacting to an enormous amount of cultural cues as to how we should behave in various situations, what we should like and dislike, what roles we should play. This surface-level self serves us well enough in our day-to-day lives (in fact, it is "designed" to do this—learning how to objectify ourselves in the same way as we objectify the world permits us, almost literally, to "fit" in). However, as Bergson emphasizes, the more that we identify *solely* with this social, external aspect of ourselves, the more that we will remain cut off from our depths, from the more profound dimensions of our selfhood. This "deep self," as Garrett Barden points out, unlike the superficial self, is "not a construct. It is also, however, not a transcendental ego, it is not a 'metaphysical' self," nor some unchanging substratum of existence. Instead, "it is simply oneself as enduring."[4] This self, while inherently difficult to describe, is not far from us or inherently difficult to access (in fact, it is, in some ways, that which is most evident, once we let go of certain tacit, deeply engrained habits of self-understanding). The deep-seated self is "us" in the truest sense, it is the ceaseless flux of durée, it is us in our freedom and aliveness, it is who we are when we flow with and respond to life, moment to moment.

It is important to recognize that Bergson does not claim that we have a *radically* split personality. As Mullarkey comments, no part of ourselves is irreconcilably divorced from the other. Instead, there are "different parallel processes in the different strata of the self. The deeper ones are (and here it gets subtle) 'not unperceived, but rather unnoticed.'"[5] Bergson suggests that simply by orienting our attention in a different "direction," we can discover that the seemingly distinct, solid, and stable inner states of the superficial self will "melt into one another like the crystals of a snowflake when touched for some time with the finger" (*TFW* 138–139). With a simple shift of awareness and intention, it is possible to discover, beneath the posturing and manipulation and frozen smiles, a dimension of ourselves that has always been present (even though it has never stayed the same).

As we will see further on, this deeper self is us as sheer creative potentiality, this is us as utter freedom and aliveness. However, ironically, we typically prefer to remain safely cut off from this deeper self; we typically prefer living a life that is as predictable and ordered and controlled as possible. We tend to think that we gain a certain inner solidity and stability by depending upon that part of ourselves that has been socialized, as superficial as it may be. We believe that, by acquiescing to and internalizing the rules and regulations imposed on us by authorities (e.g., our parents, our teachers, our pastors), we gain freedom from a life of impulse and capriciousness. But as Bergson points out in an evocative passage from *The Two Sources of Morality and Religion* (his last full-length book):

> In our innermost selves, if we know how to look for it, we may perhaps discover another sort of equilibrium, still more desirable than the one on the surface. Certain aquatic plants as they rise to the surface are ceaselessly jostled by the current: their leaves, meeting above the water, interlace, thus imparting to them stability above. But still more stable are the roots, which, firmly planted in the earth, support them from below. (*TS* 14–15)

Bergson goes on to note that for most of us, "the effort to delve down to the depths of our being" is exceedingly difficult, and often not even attempted (*TS* 15). Most of us prefer to live "on the surface," intertwined with "the close-woven tissue of other exteriorized personalities," remaining comfortable with a world (and a self) that is more or less manageable, scheduled, and seemingly secure, even if, by doing so, we lose touch with the deeper, albeit less-defined and more open-ended dimensions of our selfhood—a process of self-alienation that leads, as suggested later, not only to a distortion in our self-understanding, but also to a loss of emotional, moral, and intellectual fluidity and spontaneity (*TS* 15).

RUMINATION: AUTHENTIC SELFHOOD

Over the years as I have immersed myself in Bergson's thought, I have increasingly begun to ponder the normative overtones of Bergson's notion of the contrast between the superficial self and the deep-seated self. Underneath the surface of Bergson's evocative notions of selfhood and consciousness, emerging out of the descriptions of "what is," there are, it seems to me, numerous tendrils of ideas that are reaching in the direction of "what should be." It is not a stretch, for instance, to suggest that Bergson's understanding of a "superficial" self is not only a vivid analysis of how we inevitably see ourselves in and through the images that we internalize from our social context, but is also a muted, yet carefully crafted, plea for us to go deeper within ourselves, an implicit, yet vivid, nudge in the direction of profundity. Therefore, it makes sense to ask: in light of Bergson's understandings of the contrast between the deep-seated self and the superficial self, what does it mean, to me, right now, to be true to myself, to be real, to be authentic? How do I know when I am being authentic and when I am not? Are these qualities that I would want to nurture within myself? If so, then what stands in my way?

One appealing aspect of Bergson's vision of the deep self (i.e., who we are *in* and *as* durée) is the implication that we have enormous freedom, if we so choose, to create who we are and who we want to become. What is refreshing about this understanding of freedom, especially seen in the light of how certain existentialists conceive of freedom and self-determination, is that the process of self-creation, at least as understood by Bergson, does not have to be filled with angst and dread. Instead, creativity (at least at its deepest level, at the level of durée) is an effortless and ongoing process that takes place of its own accord. It is what is most natural, most true, about who we are. Therefore, embracing our true nature is, from a certain perspective, not difficult at all. It is simply a matter of relaxing into ourselves, paying attention to what is arising, and embracing the newness that is being created at each moment of our existence. Being truly who we are, in a very real sense, does not take any work at all. All that is required is the willingness to tune into the "melody" of the ongoing, ceaselessly creative flux of our consciousness as it proceeds onward, creating newness in the most natural way imaginable.

I would argue, however, that we can also actively nurture and deepen that innate creative thrust with our intent—even through something as simple as noticing the times in which we have, perhaps unknowingly, been satisfied to remain in the superficial levels of our being. However, as Bergson repeatedly points out, even the simple attempt to pay more attention to the natural flow of our consciousness is extremely difficult. Not only can it be psychically tiring to go in the opposite "direction" of the normal current of our human awareness (which is usually, as was noted earlier, strongly oriented toward the external world), but in addition, shifting our attention inward in order to affirm our freedom and creativity can be exceedingly difficult as well. Because we have been shaped so profoundly by our family, our schools, our religious institutions, our ethnic heritage, our immersion in music, TV, movies, and so on, it is, in many ways, much easier to remain comfortably cradled in the womb of who we assume we are than it is to explore and affirm the deeper levels of our being. In this way, the decision on our part to align more closely with our deep-seated self is often an act of great courage.

This courage becomes especially important if-and-when we are willing to acknowledge that we do indeed have the freedom to take our lives into our own hands. It often then quickly becomes apparent that along with that freedom comes the responsibility to decide (albeit, not without difficulty) who and what we wish to become. It can be extremely frightening to simply be ourselves, in large part perhaps because to be ourselves is to not know for sure who we are going to become. To be ourselves, in our depth, is to walk, each moment, into the abyss, not knowing what, if any, support is going to rise up at each moment to help carry us forward. Seen from this perspective, that is, from the perspective of living in-and-as our deep-seated self, we are the most fully ourselves when we are willing to let go at each moment, let go of what we were planning and where we thought we were going in order to fully appreciate the newness of life that is emerging.

What I am attempting to do here is to argue for the value and validity of a certain attitude toward life that is congruent with Bergson's discussion of the deep-seated self. I call this attitude "fluid responsiveness." Fluid responsiveness is not creativity for its own sake; it is not a creativity that is cut off from tradition and lived history; it is not nihilistic anarchy. Instead, it is a creativity of continuity and memory—a creativity that is an expression of the richness of our past infusing the present. As in much of postmodern thought, this creativity is inherently a play of sheer difference. But in the case of Bergson's notion of the deep-seated self, it is difference with a difference. This is difference that is rooted in an ongoing seamless inner connection—a connection to our past, our culture, our social structure, our economic reality, and our bodily existence. Fluid responsiveness is the act of taking the fullness of what we have been given and encouraging it to blossom into the irreplaceable particularity of who we are in-and-through-and-as time. Not who we are as a compressed atom of unyielding sameness (as most Enlightenment thinkers contend). Not who we are as the fragmented shards of that atom exploded out to the horizons (as some postmodern theorists would argue). Rather, fluid responsiveness is a vision of ourselves as the ever-shifting sum total of all that we have experienced, in addition to how we have responded and how we continue to respond to these experiences.

Fluid responsiveness (a mode of life that seeks to embrace durée) is a vision of selfhood and reality that, for a variety of reasons, seems to be difficult to embody. As Bergson notes, the ceaseless creativity and ongoing change of durée can be either a cause for celebration or a catalyst for anxiety. For example, at one point, toward the end of his essay "The Perception of Change," Bergson suggests that, in his attempts to persuade his readers that "reality is mobility itself," he might well not only encounter intellectual resistance from fellow philosophers and scholars, but might also end up provoking a more deeply felt, existential reaction within his readers as they are forced to grapple with the entrenched human need to minimize change.[6]As he notes:

> Before the spectacle of this universal mobility there may be some who will be seized with dizziness. They are accustomed to terra firma; they cannot get used to the rolling and pitching. They must have "fixed" points to which they can attach thought and existence. They think that if everything passes, nothing exists; and that if reality is mobility, it has

already ceased to exist at the moment one thinks it,—it eludes thought. The material world, they say, is going to disintegrate, and the mind will drown in the torrent-like flow of things. (*CM* 177)

Bergson is aware that the philosophical perspective that he is attempting to cultivate in his readers quite likely might catalyze a negative response—ironically, not because of our inability to understand it, but because, on some level, we *have* understood what he is saying and yet are frightened by what such a worldview might imply.[7]

Bergson's claim is persuasive. It *can* be extremely difficult, both intellectually and existentially, to even begin to acknowledge the extent to which our inner (and outer) worlds are undergoing a process of ceaseless change. We often pay lip service to how wonderful it is to be creative, but in actuality, we are deeply frightened of change. We often feel more secure when someone in power tells us what to do, what to say, or what to think. We frequently prefer to remain child-like rather than to take on the frightening responsibility that is implied if we were to really grow up and consciously make the attempt to shape the texture of our lives. As human beings, we often seem to prefer to live in societies and/or subcultures that give clear-cut guidelines and rules instead of taking the risk to honor and cultivate our own freedom to live the life that we choose. It seems that we often prefer to pretend that we know, at all times and in all places, what is right and what is wrong, who is good and who is bad, rather than live in a world in which there are no absolute, rock solid, moral codes, a world in which every human being is a complex, ever-shifting amalgam of good and bad, right and wrong. It is almost as if we prefer to pretend that somehow we can convince the world (and ourselves) to stop changing, as if we want to somehow make ourselves and everyone else stay eternally the same.

But, as Bergson never ceases to point out, it never works this way. Change is both continual and inevitable. So the question becomes: how do we respond to this torrent of newness? Do we attempt to control the behavior of others as well as our own feelings and actions? Do we seek to build higher and thicker and stronger walls around ourselves to hold back the onrushing tsunami of change? Do we attempt to (self-righteously) battle with the threatening forces of otherness and difference? Or, is there perhaps another option? Could we, instead, embrace the change as it comes our way? Could we recognize that change is the very nature of who we are?

Most of us try to muddle through life as best we can, willing to change in certain respects, resisting change in others. It is this resistance to change that is one of the hallmarks of our superficial self. In-and-as our superficial self, it may well, at least for a time, feel comfortable to put on a false smile, or to blindly follow the leader, or to unquestioningly get in line. And yet, in the end, we always pay a price if we continue to live a life that is inwardly dictated by others, if we remain so mesmerized by our fear of the unknown that we no longer have a clue as to what it is that we really want out of life. But I would argue that the pain of awakening to our superficial self is crucial, at least if it helps us to cross some inner threshold so that we can begin to long for something more. That pain is worth it if ultimately some deep part of us finally decides: enough is enough.

Unfortunately, it often seems that, in our attempts to penetrate to the heart of our being, we have to pass through a twisting labyrinth of funhouse mirrors. We perhaps think that we are becoming more spontaneous and free, only to discover that we have just been impulsive and stupid. We perhaps fight against passive acquiescence to social norms, only to discover that we are merely playing out its perverse flip side in the form of our knee-jerk rebellion against authority.

I would like to suggest that genuine and worthwhile inner change does not come from an arbitrary effort of will or from a strained insistence on being different. For myself at least, when I try overly hard to change, when my jaw is clenched with the effort to force myself to be better than I am, I often notice that there is a lot of hidden anxiety and self-judgment underneath all of that effort—deeply engrained psychic patterns that are, themselves, some of the very aspects of myself that I might be attempting to change!

Beyond recommending an intensive introspective effort, Bergson is not very clear about how we could or should access what he calls the "moi fundamental"—the fundamental me, the foundational me, the me of my depths. He claims that this "me" is what is genuinely real, that this "me" is what cannot be denied or doubted. Yet this "me" is also what cannot be pinned down, cannot be analyzed or dissected. Therefore, it is often bewilderingly difficult to figure out who in the world we really are, to say nothing of who we could potentially become. What can be frustrating about attempting to grasp the deep-seated self that Bergson describes is that there is no "it" to find, there is no solid, unchanging essence of "me-ness" anywhere. As soon as I come upon myself, I am already gone. As soon as I turn around to see myself I have disappeared, only to reappear again in a different guise. So how am I to open up to who I truly am, when who I am keeps changing?

Yet fortunately, as Bergson acknowledges, we are also given these cherished, precious moments when we are given a taste of what we are longing for, a quick glimpse into a state of freedom and creativity. These are the times when we sink back and breathe deep. These are the times that act as a beacon in the dark, that nudge us forward, that help to convince us that the search is, indeed, worthwhile.

Every now and then, particularly toward the end of his life, due in part perhaps to his increased interest in the mystics of various traditions, Bergson would write about such moments. For instance, toward the end of "The Perception of Change," he writes about how the "vision of universal becoming" that he describes in this essay, if allowed to "penetrate into our everyday life," can catalyze a type of pleasurable aesthetic transfiguration, in which "all things acquire depth,—more than depth, something like a fourth dimension" in which reality is no longer static and frozen into separate bits, but instead, "affirms itself dynamically" (*CM* 185–186). In moments like these, he says, "what was immobile and frozen in our perception is warmed and set in motion. Everything comes to life around us, everything is revivified in us. A great impulse carries beings and things along. We feel ourselves uplifted, carried away, borne along by it. We are more fully alive" (*CM* 186). For Bergson, these types of moments come about the more that "we accustom ourselves to think and to perceive all things *sub specie durationis*, the more we plunge into real [durée]" (*CM* 186). These moments arise "the more we immerse ourselves in [durée], the more we set ourselves back in the direction of the principle, though it be transcendent, in which we participate and whose eternity is not to be an eternity of immutability, but an eternity of life: how, otherwise, could we live and move in it?" (*CM* 186).

The problem is that, as Bergson admits, it is extremely difficult to cultivate an attitude in which we perceive each and every moment *sub specie durationis*.[8] We may be able to affirm, intellectually, that this is a worthwhile goal, but how, specifically, do we go about getting there? How do we, not just philosophically, but experientially—with our whole being—wake up and remember who we really are? How do we become who we already are?

These are the types of questions that propel many people, for good reasons, into a lifetime of intensive spiritual work. And, understandably, there are no pat or simplistic answers to these questions. However, a good beginning, for me at least, might be to pay attention to how I feel when it seems, at least in retrospect, that I have gone in the *opposite* direction, when I am living my life in a way that is contrary to my desire to remain in my deep-seated self. At such moments, I find that it is helpful to look carefully at what is happening within me, on all levels. For instance, I might ask: what is happening inside of me when I find myself driven by anxiety, when I am obsessed with what others think of me, when I attempt to match myself up with a complex, yet typically unconscious, system of internalized models of social expectations. Just the simple, gentle, nonjudgmental awareness of my changing felt-sense of myself in those moments, in some mysterious way, seems to help, especially when I remember to notice what is going on in my body. For instance, I might ask myself, when I am living in my superficial self, in what ways, if any, do my behaviors become mechanical or my voice flat? Do I perhaps feel fragmented, dispersed, or scattered? Segmented and blocked? Do I perhaps find that my chest is constricted, or my jaw is tense? Is my breath shallow? Jerky? Rapid? Does any of this feel pleasurable?

What often seems to help is simply a shift in orientation—away from the surface and toward the depths; it is simply the willingness to pause, to take some deep breaths and settle down into myself, bit by bit. Something almost magical often happens when I allow myself to let go of fretting and self-judg-ment, when I sink below the obsessive and self-propelled tapes of anxiety or regret or anger that might be playing in my mind, when I simply ground myself in my bodily sensations and open up. At these moments there is a sense of solidity and ease, a feeling that I am rooted in a level of experience that is uniquely "me," as if I am laying back on a gentle wave that is carrying me for-ward, even as I am dropping deeper and deeper into this fluid, densely textured awareness. Here, floating in this stream of durée (that, interestingly, never feels insular or isolated), that is effortlessly natural, it is easy to feel something that had seemed so far away before: in these moments, nothing could be simpler, easier, than just being who I am.

3

TIME

═══

DURÉE AS TIME

In the preceding discussion of durée, a crucial quality of our consciousness has perhaps not been sufficiently emphasized: durée is (and subsequently, *we* are) inherently, inescapably, temporal.[1] Durée is time itself, not, as A. R. Lacey points out, the illusory "second-best form of time" that is created when we superimpose our perception of space over the lived experience of consciousness.[2] Durée is not time as we normally understand it; it is not "clock time." The real time of durée is, as Luce notes, "not so many ticks of a clock or swings of a pendulum."[3] Clock time is based on the measurement of some uniform external process—the rotation of the earth, the rate of radioactive decay—that can be separated into consistent, countable units.[4] Durée, which does not consist of material objects but rather of states of consciousness, is not even in principle countable or measurable. Unlike clock time, the real time of durée is not parceled out; it is not split up into seconds, minutes, or hours. In durée, the efflorescence of ceaseless novelty and inner continuity that is our consciousness is not pulverized into units of sameness, each counted and accounted for. The real time of durée has no preconscious internal clock ticking out the seconds. Durée, as experienced within, does not flow uniformly—instead, it is bound up with, and manifests as, the feeling-tone of our various internal states of consciousness. In this way, it is meaningless to claim that time always moves forward at the same rate; instead, as we all know, experienced time is very fluid; as Joseph Solomon notes, "an hour of joy is infinitely shorter than an hour of expectation."[5]

Durée is, by its very nature, qualitative, not quantitative. Clock time, on the other hand, depends upon counting, and counting (in fact mathematics in general) can only deal with that which is fixed, static, and repetitive. Therefore, the act of counting cannot accurately represent the sheer newness and constant change of durée. For example, if a teacher is counting how many of her students are present, during the process of that counting, she basically ignores their differences. When she is counting "one," "two," "three," "four" to herself, she is not focusing on "Johnny," "Betty," "Jill," and "Jim"; rather, she is focusing on a multiplicity of units that are essentially alike, each replaceable by the other. Her attention, while counting, is on neutral, basically identical objects in space, lined up, at least in her imagination, next to each other. These objects, mathematically, can be represented as a line of points set next to each other, each point separated by an interval of space (space understood in this case as an empty, unbounded, homogeneous medium). Mathematics in this way is rooted in, and is most appropriately used, when dealing with material objects in space, objects that can be, at least in principle, set side by side and counted, objects that are indivisible units, distinguishable from one another, at least in the imagination, only by an interval of space.

Durée becomes clock time when that space which allows things to be counted has been surreptitiously smuggled into the equation (so to speak). In clock time, each state of consciousness is understood as if it were an object in space; that is, as distinguishable, cut off from the rest, following each other sequentially, as if lined up side by side. In clock time, the instants of our consciousness are counted off one by one as the clock ticks off each second. In clock time, each second is an atomized unit; each second, as a measurement of time, is identical to every other second; each second follows the next in succession, like a chain in which the separate parts touch, but do not penetrate each other. This timeline (a common way of attempting to picture time) with its fixed points/instants is the time that is created by our need to measure, by our preconscious urge to import measurable space into the living flux of duration. This line of time, the time that can be counted, fragments the indivisible dynamism of durée, and leads us to think that time is, like the line, already a finished product, that it is complete.[6] However, real time is always in the process of being made, it is always incomplete. Real time is not made of instants that can be added together, instants that, like objects in space, exist separate from each other, instants that can be counted and measured. Durée, lived time, the "time of our lives" (as Keith Ansell Pearson so cleverly puns) cannot be plotted on a line, with each discrete moment a separate static point with the past to the left and the future to the right—each moment clearly mapped out, each moment, in essence, occurring next to each other, and in effect, simultaneously present.

The moments or instants that are added together on the line of time cannot be added together to somehow capture the movement of time because these instants are understood, ironically, to be utterly frozen and immobile. In order to be counted they, in essence, have to stand still, and so become "virtual halts in time" (*CM* 11). As P. A. Y. Gunter comments, "an instant . . . has no breadth—

any more than does a spatial point. Nor does it have the slightest dynamism. It is a mathematical, static knife-edge, cleanly severing the past from the future. A series of such knife-edges, no matter how many, scarcely conveys experienced change."[7] It is this sense of constant change, mobility itself, that characterizes real time—not the artificial and clumsy attempts to picture time as a succession of static instants. As Charles R. Schmidtke insightfully notes:

> *Durée* . . . is *not* a metaphysical link (or point or now) between the past and the future. . . . The past is not stored; it continually flows through the present in a cumulative process. The future is not an object at the end of a string of presents. . . . Past-present-future are not three separate points or areas on a line; rather, for Bergson, the past is really memory flowing through consciousness, the present is continuous perception with its characteristic *durée*, and the future is the creation, newness and unforeseeability of experience.[8]

Real time, the time of consciousness, time *as* consciousness, is also not Newtonian (or Kantian) time; it is not a neutral, blank, empty, homogeneous "container" (like Newtonian or Kantian space), which remains unchanged while events take place within it. There is no inert "receptacle" of time that remains unmoved by the changes that take place within it; there is no absolute "now" that contains all events within it while remaining untouched. Durée, unlike Newtonian time, is not divided into two. There is no distinction between the contents of consciousness and durée itself. As Čapek points out, "psychological events are not *in* time, since they in their ceaseless emergence *constitute time itself*."[9] This last point is crucial. For Bergson, time is not a separate something that we experience; rather, time *is* our experience, or more accurately still, time (at least in certain respects) is *us*. As Merleau-Ponty notes in an astute commentary on Bergson's work, durée "is not something that I see from the outside. From the outside I would have only an outline of it, I would not be in the face of the generating thrust. Time, then, is myself; I am the duration that I grasp; the duration that grasps itself is in me."[10]

RUMINATION: CONSCIOUSNESS AS TIME

What Bergson so wonderfully articulates is how each moment of time, each ripple in the river of durée, is irrevocably unique, is an unrepeatable, irreplaceable event. The implication, therefore, is that there is something intensely problematic about discussing time in general. As a way to meet this challenge head on, perhaps the attempt to focus on one concrete event drawn from my own experience might serve to illustrate some of the less obvious nuances of time—or might at least express how one particular stream of time was experienced by someone who was self-reflexively immersed in a Bergsonian-influenced meditation on time itself.

Late one night, in the midst of working on this section of the book, immersed in thinking about time, I began to feel into the quality of time that I was experiencing in that "moment." (It was not some static, atomistic instant of time, but rather the flux of time manifesting itself in-and-as my own consciousness.) It was after 1:00 a.m., my wife was out of town, and I was upstairs in my office. I had just finished watching a DVD—*Donnie Darko* (itself a dark, disturbing, and surreal meditation on time). I was amazed at just how strongly the story and the music had impacted me. The final, deeply haunting, and melancholy song ("Mad World") was echoing in my mind, and I noticed that my throat was tight and constricted, as if I was clamping down tightly on some feeling that was coiled up in my chest and pressing its way upward. Clearly, this movie about a sad-eyed, troubled, tragic traveler through time had stirred up something in me that wanted to emerge, even if it was having difficulty breaking free to the surface.

Sitting there in my office, I began to think about how time, the stream of time that I was experiencing right then, like *all* time, seemed to have this inexorable forward thrust to it, even though, oddly, it didn't go anywhere in space. I began to wonder, what exactly is the felt sense of being carried forward? I began to think about how time just continues to move on, never ceasing, never pausing, bringing with it layer upon layer of specific, idiosyncratic memories, each of them shaping me moment by moment into new forms of "me-ness." As I sat there, I became intensely aware of the way that this time would never return, that this time (the time that carries me and is me) just keeps flowing, ceaselessly, relentlessly, heading toward the inevitable end: death. Whether I want it to or not, the next "moment" in and of time is always arriving. Who I was, the world that I just previously inhabited, is always left behind. I always emerge just that much older and just that much closer to the abyss that looms ahead in the future.

Sitting there in my office, I was also struck by the realization that only I can ever, and will ever, fully undergo the specific textures and nuances of this exact flux of time. This most deeply personal, intimate level of existence of "me" in-and-as time—this experience of time is mine alone.

The more that I sat there, noticing what was taking place within me, the more I began to feel just how poignant it is that time passes. I became increasingly filled with a sense of loss, with an inchoate but heavy awareness of what I had missed in my life, what did not happen, dreams that did not materialize. Yet, as time passed sitting there in my office, another current began to swirl around and through the original melancholy feeling-tone of my consciousness, tingeing it, ever so slightly and slowly, with faint tendrils of another color of feeling. I began to notice that, underneath and suffusing the melancholy, there was something else, an alternative response to the passing of time. It began as this tiny, but dogged, refusal to give despair the last word; it was something like a willingness to look at time differently than I had been before, to see that each moment brought new-ness—new possibilities, new life.

As I became increasingly aware of this bubble of hope surfacing within, I also began to notice that this particular, nuanced, utterly individual sense of time, once again, was beginning to subtly shift. Something new was emerging, so that now, interfused with the melancholy and the hope and the longing, there was almost an "after-scent" of a different quality of feeling—similar to when a stick of incense has been extinguished, leaving nothing but a sweet, evanescent, and yet insistent smoky after-fragrance. This delicate yet pungent "after-odor" slowly began to coalesce within me. It became a type of knowing—an immediate certainty that was not rooted in anything rational or explicable—the knowledge that, right now, in-and-through the loss, sadness, and isolation that I had been feeling so strongly, even deeper than the glimmering hope that was just beginning to arise, there was something more. This "something" was bedrock; it was foundational; it was this elusive yet powerfully felt quality of radiant presence that was underneath and glowing through everything, if I would but notice. It was as if the shifting, flowing, forward thrust of time remained, but I had somehow sunk deeper into it so that I was now washed with time itself in its effortless continuity and potentiality. This level of time was emerging within me (even as it was also uncovered and discovered within me) as a potent, insistent presence that somehow transfigured the ever-shifting, multifaceted stream of my time, my consciousness, into the certain, powerful, even joyous, knowledge that everything was manifesting just as it should be—manifesting *as* the loss, the regret, the longing, the hope, the radiance. Nothing fancy, no fireworks, no inner explosions—just a simple, easy, almost prosaic shift, a shift into cherishing each moment as it arose and passed, an awareness of how that stream of time is absolutely like nothing that existed before or that will ever exist again.

4

QUANTITY AND QUALITY

In the first section of *Time and Free Will*, Bergson spends considerable time and effort attempting to convince his readers that we are wrong to think that the intensity of a feeling or a sensation can be quantitatively assessed or measured. For instance, we might tell ourselves that we are happier today than yesterday, or that we hurt less when we are pricked by a thorn than when we are stabbed by a knife, or that it takes more effort to bend a paper clip than to bend a bar of steel. What Bergson says in this first section is that we are wrong in this assessment.

Despite how outrageous, how counterintuitive it might at first glance appear, after a closer reading, Bergson's argument becomes increasingly persuasive. What he attempts to accomplish in this lengthy first section is to underscore the uniqueness of consciousness and the ways that we often do not recognize that uniqueness because of how we confuse it with our knowledge of the external world. In particular, this section throws into vivid relief the distinction between *quantity* and *quality*.

The difference between quantity and quality will perhaps become clearer with a careful examination of what goes on within us when we are experiencing what seems to be a dramatic increase in the intensity of a particular emotion. Using an example drawn from everyday life, let's say that you are mildly irritated because a cable TV repairman refuses to give you a specific time in which he is going to come. He tells you that you will simply have to wait for him to arrive sometime between 1:00 and 5:00 p.m. Let's say that after four hours of waiting the repairman never shows up or even calls, and you begin to feel angry. After calling the cable company, let's then say that you are put hold for half an hour, only to be dismissed by an incompetent "assistance" person at the company who does nothing to help. Finally, you slam down the phone receiver, furious, after six hours of futile waiting. It seems quite clear that you are more angry at this point than you were when you first called the cable company.

However, if you had read the first section of *Time and Free Will*, then you might assess your apparent escalating emotional intensity quite differently. For instance, you might ask yourself: is it even possible to ascertain with any certainty the magnitude or degree of your anger at each of these moments during those six hours, starting with the initial irritation, moving to the full-fledged anger, and finally arriving at the flat-out fury? Was the anger that you felt when you were furious *twice* as strong as when you were irritated? *Three* times? *Ten* times? How would you go about measuring the *quantity* of your anger each time in order to give an accurate number? Or is it perhaps possible, if you look back in your memory with care, that you might see that each of these moments of anger (the initial irritation, the full-fledged anger, and the flat-out fury) were *qualitatively*, intrinsically, different experiences?

It might seem, at first glance, that you felt only one emotion (anger) that got stronger and stronger within you as time passed. You might think this way for a number of reasons: first, there were no radical breaks within you, there was no clear-cut moment when one feeling suddenly changed into something else. Second, there seemed to be only one basic external cause for your anger (the cable company). Finally, it is just easier to say that you were "angry," rather than to introspectively note the particular shadings of each uniquely "colored" feeling as it occurred and then to search for an appropriate, distinguishing word to match it. As Bergson archly notes, "our language is ill-suited to render the subtleties of psychological analysis" (*TFW* 13). However, if you look back carefully (especially after internalizing Bergson's ideas), you might just come to realize that you were not actually more angry at the end of those six hours than you were at the beginning. Instead, what you experienced were not variations of one common theme called "anger," but rather, each instance of what you felt was inherently, qualitatively, unique. So unique, in fact, that even using separate terms (i.e., "irritation," "anger," and "fury") does not really do it justice, because even here the static nature of the terms masks the reality—an ongoing flux of ever-shifting, qualitative changes of feeling within as time passes.

As human beings with a practical, this-worldly orientation, it is quite normal that we would resist this Bergsonian interpretation of our emotional states. As Bergson comments, a "wholly dynamic way of looking" at the ongoing shifts in our feeling-life "is repugnant" to most of us, since we prefer "clean cut distinctions, which are easily expressed in words" as well as "things with well-defined outlines, like those which are perceived in space" (*TFW* 9). But this desire for clarity and precision does not work well when it comes to noticing, with any subtlety, what is going on within us. Therefore, we might prefer to imagine, for example, that our desire for a new career has grown, whereas in reality, there is no "volume" of desire that has expanded; this "increased" desire does not now take up increased space inside us. The basic problem is that our desire simply is not a separate, clearly delineated, fixed thing that can be measured. What we experience within us is *not* a change in *quantity*, but rather it is a change in *quality*.[1]

As Mullarkey emphasizes, what Bergson attempts to do in this section of *Time and Free Will* is to "restore the specificity and novelty" that get stripped away when we try to understand our inner life using quantitative terminology.[2] What Bergson wants us to recognize is that our introspective awareness of our own consciousness is, if understood correctly, qualitatively different from what we typically experience in our interactions with the external world. In our day-to-day interactions with the physical world we *compare* and *measure* external objects, objects that have clear-cut boundaries in space, that are separate from each other, that stay relatively the same; but we can only *compare* the different internal phases of our conscious experience—for example, our feelings, our sensations—we cannot measure them because they are not separate, static, countable, units.[3] As Lacey points out, we can say how long a board is (quantity) and compare a pine board to an oak board (quality), but we cannot really say that we are literally twice as happy today as yesterday. We can only *metaphorically* say that we are "more" happy than before.[4] Unlike external objects, our feelings are not "things" that can be added up. We can gather together one hundred apples and mash them all together to create a tub of applesauce, a tub that is measurably larger than the half cup of apple sauce that would be created if we mashed up only one apple. However, as F. C. T. Moore notes, "while we can distinguish, no doubt, between someone experiencing a twinge of jealousy, and someone obsessed by jealous passion . . . it would surely be inappropriate to think that Othello's jealousy is, as it were, simply a great agglomeration of constant and innumerable twinges."[5] A powerful feeling is not a lot of weaker feelings added together.

Why, then, are we so convinced that it is not wrong to use words, such as "more" or "less," "stronger" or "weaker," to compare the intensity of our feeling states? Bergson attempts an answer, by looking closely at what happens when a feeling like joy seems to get stronger and stronger within us. (Again, pay attention to how using only one term to describe the experience of "joy" itself complicates this discussion.) What Bergson claims is that this feeling of joy, as it changes over time, is not an "isolated inner state which at first occupies a corner of the soul and gradually spreads" (*TFW* 10). Instead, there are really several different stages of joy, each of which are qualitatively different from each other, and each of which alters the whole of our experience. For Bergson, each of these feelings that we label as "joy" fills our consciousness and has "altered the shade of a thousand perceptions and memories, and that in this sense . . . pervades them" (*TFW* 9).

Bergson has other explanations of why we are so convinced that our feelings and sensations can be quantitatively assessed. For instance, he points out there is always a physical manifestation of our feeling states—the flushing of anger or shame, the sweating palms of fear, the racing heart of anxiety—and these physical correlates *can* be measured and counted, and therefore, might well have something to do with why we use "more" or "less" language to describe our feelings. As Bergson notes, "there is hardly any passion or desire, any joy or sorrow, which is not accompanied by physical symptoms; and where these symptoms occur, they probably count for something in the estimate of intensities" (*TFW* 20). In the same vein, if we look at our sensations (e.g., the conscious awareness of a loud noise), there does indeed seem to be some sort of intimate relationship between the loudness of that sound and the variety of physical accompaniments/causes of that sensation (e.g., the amount of air that enters the ear).

While Bergson is not willing, at least in *Time and Free Will*, to formulate any in-depth, detailed theory that would account for the interaction between the inner state of consciousness and the outer physical manifestation or external catalyst, he is willing to admit that "there undoubtedly exists some relation between the two terms" (i.e., the sensation and its physical correlate) (*TFW* 20). Therefore, Bergson is willing to admit that perhaps one (good!) reason why we think about our conscious experience in a quantitative fashion is because we, unknowingly, confuse and blur together the outer, physical, quantitative reality with the inner, durational, qualitative reality.

To illustrate this idea, Bergson gives a very concrete example: the feeling that we are exerting increasing amounts of effort when we lift increasing amounts of weight. He notes that a careful introspective analysis reveals that when a person (for the sake of this discussion, let's say a female bodybuilder) lifts a *light* weight with her arm (perhaps doing a curl with a dumbbell), she will undergo a variety of qualitatively unique sensations: perhaps a complex of muscular contractions in her hand, along with a vague awareness of a mild constriction in her forearm, and a very obscure, faint series of peripheral sensations in her upper arm. However, when she lifts a *heavier* dumbbell, with the same arm, at the same speed, if she looks *carefully* enough, she will undergo an entirely new and unique series of sensations—new *qualities* of consciousness, not *quantities*. Perhaps this time, lifting the heavier dumbbell, her attention will not be primarily focused on sensations in her hand, but rather on the sensations in her upper arm, in her back, and perhaps even those that radiate from her legs.

Bergson would claim that the sensations of lifting the light weights are qualitatively different than those of lifting the heavy weights. However, he would also point out that in addition to these qualitative, internal differences, it is also the case that *more* muscles were used with the second series of weights. Therefore, the composite experience of the weightlifter (with both sets of weights) involves both inner, *qualitative* sensations and outer, *quantitative* muscular activity. In this way, the unavoidable and insistent presence of the increased muscular activity becomes, in a sense, fused/confused with the unique flux of inner sensations (*TFW* 25). Therefore, it makes sense that we would think that our internal state of awareness is quantifiable. As Bergson notes, because external, physical objects (like muscles) "are common to us all" and "are more important to us than the subjective states through which each of us passes" we therefore "have everything to gain by objectifying these states" and assuming "to the largest possible extent" that our states of consciousness—our feelings, sensations, efforts, and so on—are simply the inner, quantifiable, mirror image of various external causes (*TFW* 70). (Interestingly, there seems to have been no irony present in Bergson's use of the phrase "to the largest possible extent.")

I would argue that Bergson's perspective needs to be taken seriously. For him, a sensation (e.g., hearing a loud noise) is utterly, qualitatively, intrinsically different than molecules vibrating on our eardrum. There is absolutely nothing in common, *on the level of our conscious experience*, between the physical vibrations of air molecules hitting the eardrum and the sensations of hearing. As Bergson puts it, it is impossible to perceive any direct trace of these molecular movements "in the sensations which translate them" (*TFW* 35). Instead, in a way that remains mysterious in *Time and Free Will* (but which is directly and profoundly addressed in *Matter and Memory*), these complicated external movements (not only in the eardrum, but also in the astonishingly complex network of cerebral neural networks) are translated, somehow, into our internal state of consciousness—into our *experience of* the loud sound.

5

DETERMINISM

═══════════════════════

PHYSICAL DETERMINISM

The scientific goal of understanding our consciousness as nothing more than a series of complex neurochemical interactions (a goal that remains prominent, even taken for granted, today) was (and is) rooted in a prior metaphysical assumption: physical determinism. Physical determinism is the view that everything that happens in the universe is predictable if we only have enough information about the atoms and molecules that make up the universe.

The central assumption of physical determinism is that nothing new ever really takes place. This assumption is made because, allegedly, everything that happens at every instant is simply the sum total of reactions to everything that took place in the previous instant. According to this perspective, it is as if the universe is a giant kaleidoscope, with a finite number of fixed parts that are simply rearranged. Each new arrangement of the pieces seems to produce a "new" pattern; in actuality, according to this perspective, the state of existence at each moment is nothing more than a recycling and reshuffling of a limited amount of permanent, preexisting atoms cascading against and rebounding from each other. Based on the law of the conservation of energy, which claims that not even the smallest quantity of force or movement is created in the universe, physicists argue that, while it is a fact that new molecules are created and new chemical reactions are catalyzed, the atoms themselves remain unchanged and unchangeable, and the quantity of energy available to move these atoms around is simply redistributed from one location to another.

Furthermore, according to classical physics, these atoms do not just move any way they please. There are no self-initiated, spontaneous activities that could create anything genuinely new. Instead, physical determinism claims that every movement of every atom is the utterly predictable end result of how these atoms

38

bumped up against each other in the previous instant. The assumption is that atoms are like billiard balls. How fast these balls career around the table and where they end up is not arbitrary. Instead, the pattern of their movement is the inevitable end result of previous movements of these same balls—a quantitative, calculable, utterly predictable process. The future, in this way, is therefore understood to be completely predetermined—nothing unexpected can or will happen; it is simply the logical and mathematically inevitable result of everything that is taking place in the present. Only the limitations of our knowledge keep us from perceiving this fact.

According to this "billiard ball" perspective, we should be able to predict any and all of the future actions of a person based on the knowledge of his/her past. Because it is understood that who we are is allegedly nothing more than a complex grouping of atoms, all of the movements of our nervous system and brain (and therefore all of our feelings, sensations, ideas, hopes, and creative insights) are, in principle at least, completely predetermined. As Bergson notes, mechanistic determinism assumes that a "mathematician who knew the position of the molecules or atoms of a human organism at a given moment, as well as the position and motion of all the atoms in the universe capable of influencing it, could calculate with unfailing certainty the past, present and future actions of the person to whom this organism belongs, just as one predicts an astronomical phenomenon" (*TFW* 144). A determinist would argue that we might fool ourselves and pretend that we could be anything different than who we are, or that we somehow could have done things differently, that we have free will, but for the determinist, all of these beliefs are nothing more than the inevitable end result of mechanical interactions between the unimaginable number of atoms within us.

Time, from the perspective of determinism, is understood to be of little consequence in that, according to the law of the conservation of energy, the effects of past actions of atoms could even be reversed—every change in material existence could, theoretically, be undone. Understood in this way, past events do not really change anything fundamentally, but merely rearrange energy. Nothing new is created in this mechanistic universe, just different forms of what has always been and always will be. Therefore, the world as seen through the vantage point of physical determinism not only lacks any real growth or novelty, but is also devoid of durée. Time is understood to be present, but only a time which is understood to be, like space, a type of empty container in which inert atoms and molecules move, a time that remains utterly untouched by the various comings and goings of the atoms that dance within it.

However, as Bergson points out, for living, conscious beings, turning back in time is meaningless. In *Time and Free Will*, Bergson is willing, temporarily, to posit that matter may well exist in a perpetual present, a present in which there is no memory of the past, a present in which activity simply happens automatically. But for beings with memory, the present is always growing and swelling with the "thickness" of memory. Our consciousness, on the face of it, does not seem to follow the same rules as matter—it does not, it cannot, stay the same; it does not, it cannot, be divided into preset pieces that bump up against each other.

Bergson was willing, at least in *Time and Free Will*, to claim that events in the physical world of inert matter, a matter without consciousness, may well be for all practical purposes governed by deterministic natural laws. The external world of discrete objects may well be utterly predictable and subject to accurate calculations (otherwise we couldn't build bridges or send rockets to the moon). However, it is not at all clear that our consciousness is bound by the same laws that seem to govern inert matter. In living beings, in beings who have consciousness, most of the evidence seems to be otherwise. We experience ourselves, moment to moment, as having the ability to make genuine choices. We repeatedly appear to make decisions between various options, and we certainly seem to initiate activity (e.g., choosing to not curse at someone who cut us off in traffic) not because we were forced to do so, but because we freely did so. As Guerlac points out, Bergson's primary weapon against determinism is to demonstrate the creative power of time that we experience within. As she notes, because "for living beings, duration in time acts as a cause, then time is a form of energy! . . . Time is a form of energy that does not obey the principle of conservation. Nothing remains the same for us in time."[1]

In *Time and Free Will*, Bergson argues that it makes sense to say that the law of the conservation of energy does indeed appear to apply to physical phenomena and that perhaps one day it will be shown to apply to consciousness. However, to automatically assume that our consciousness is subject to the same laws as matter, as Idella J. Gallagher points out, is "no more than a deduction from observations of physical phenomena; it expresses what happens in a domain wherein no one has ever held that there is caprice, choice or liberty," whereas what "we want to know is whether it can still be verified in the cases in which consciousness . . . feels itself in possession of a free activity."[2]

A HISTORICAL INTERLUDE: PREDETERMINISM

Bergson, from *Time and Free Will* onward, opposed any and all attempts to treat human beings as if we are nothing more than highly complex and interesting machines. He vigorously challenged the philosophical presuppositions underlying the "psychophysical" school of psychology that sought to quantify states of consciousness by correlating them with external stimuli; he proposed a vibrant alternative to the atomistic model of the psyche championed by various associationists who claimed that the mind, like physical reality, is nothing but particles (in this case, of consciousness rather than matter) that rigorously obey natural laws; and he opposed several varieties of philosophical endeavors to reduce the mind to nothing more than a ghostly and impotent epiphenomenon of the brain's neural activity. (More on this in section 2.)

Bergson never denied, however, the validity and value of science per se; in fact, he was a staunch supporter of scientific investigation and repeatedly argued that philosophy, at its best, emerges from and reflects back upon empirical data (although his empiricism, like that of William James, was not limited to sense data). What Bergson *did* oppose was any attempt to reduce human beings to automata devoid of any real creativity or uniqueness, attempts that were rooted in a frequently tacit and unexamined mechanistic metaphysics that undergirded most reductionistic *interpretations of* scientific findings.[3] What Bergson fought against was the notion that human beings were completely determined by invariable natural laws. What he fought against was the claim that the methods of modern science could and should provide a complete and final explanation of both the physical world and of human experience and behavior—a claim that was made by several prestigious French thinkers of that era, such as Auguste Comte (1798–1857), Ernest Renan (1823–1892), and Hippolyte Taine (1828–1893).

While in his youth, Bergson had been attracted to English philosophical perspectives, such as the associationism of John Stuart Mill (1806–1873) and the mechanical evolutionism of Herbert Spencer (1820–1903). But as he matured philosophically, he increasingly began to align himself, not with their French counterparts (e.g., the positivism of Comte, the "religion of science" of Renan, or the determinism of Taine), but with a cluster of thinkers whose perspective became known as French spiritualism or voluntarism. As Sanford Schwartz notes, this major philosophical movement in France in the nineteenth century "originated with the works of Maine de Biran (1766–1824), and was then developed by Félix Ravaisson (1813–1900), and was eventually taken up by several late nineteenth-century philosophers, including two of Bergson's teachers at the École Normal Supérieure, Jules Lachelier (1832–1918) and Emile Boutroux (1845–1921)."[4] While Bergson's perspective was by no means a slavish reduplication of ideas already articulated by these thinkers, in many ways his thought incorporated and elaborated many of the central ideas of French voluntarism (a fact which he freely and openly acknowledged). The correspondences were often striking. For instance, as Schwartz points out, like Bergson, "these philosophers distinguished sharply between mental and physical processes, arguing that the activities of the mind are irreducible to physical explanation. They emphasized the spontaneity of the human will . . . and claimed that natural scientific method ignores the element of spontaneity in nature itself."[5]

Bergson and the French voluntarist movement were not just proposing philosophical alternatives to a newly fledged determinism and mechanism. In fact, their emphasis on the efficacy and freedom of human consciousness had to overcome centuries (if not millennia) of theological, philosophical, and scientific thinking that stressed the deterministic (and mechanistic) nature of the universe. Čapek is especially helpful at pointing out the historical connections between the theological determinism of an omnipotent and omniscient God (manifest in the notion of divine predestination) and the depersonalized, secularized determinism of later thinkers, such as Pierre-Simon Laplace (1749–1827), the French mathematician and astronomer who is famous for his claim that time only exists due to the limitations of our intellect. It was Laplace who claimed in a frequently quoted passage that:

> An intellect which at a given instant knew all the forces with which nature is animated, and the respective situations of the beings that compose nature—supposing the said intellect were vast enough to subject these data to analysis—would embrace in the same formula the motions of the greatest bodies in the universe and those of the slightest atom: nothing would be uncertain for it, and the future, like the past, would be present to its eyes.[6]

However, as Čapek notes, Laplace's determinism (resting on a tacit metaphysical mechanism) was simply an echo of the worldview assumed by numerous distinguished philosophers, mathematicians, and physicists from centuries before Laplace's time. For instance, while Sir Isaac Newton (1642–1727) assumed that the forces of nature that permeated the cosmic void (such as the force of gravity that connects everything) emanated from the mind of God, this theological aspect of Newton's physics was soon forgotten or ignored. When God disappeared from view, what remained was an utterly mechanistic understanding of a universe made up of nothing but inanimate matter and energy, a universe governed completely by eternal, mathematically rigorous laws, a universe in which the future was utterly predetermined, down to the last atom.

Other important thinkers also stressed the deterministic underpinnings of reality. For instance, Baron Gottfried Wilhelm von Leibniz (1646–1716) asserted that, if we had a sufficiently powerful and profound insight into "the inner parts of Being," then we should be able, in the present, to see into the future "as in a mirror."[7] Johann Gottlieb Fichte (1762–1814) also assumed a cosmic determinism. As Čapek points out, Fichte argued for the complete determination and predictability of inner states of consciousness. In the words of Fichte:

> Thus my connection with the whole of nature is what determines everything that I was, what I am and what I shall be, and the same mind could infer from any possible moment of my being what I was

before and what I shall be after. All that I am and that I shall be, I am
and I shall be in a necessary fashion, and it is impossible for me to be
something else.[8]

In this way, as Čapek notes, regardless of their numerous other disagree-
ments, "as far as complete determinism was concerned, there was no disagreement whatever between the idealists and the naturalists . . . both accepted the
idea of a mechanistic predetermined nature"[9] and denied any real contingency in
the cosmos.

The notion of the universe as, in the words of Rupert Sheldrake, a "vast
machine governed by eternal laws" was also given a powerful kick-start by the
French mathematician and philosopher, René Descartes (1596–1650).[10]
Descartes' dualistic perspective claimed that the entire material universe (*res
extensa*) was spread out in space and was governed completely by mathematical
laws. Our human minds (*res cogitans*), however, like the mind of God, were not
material in nature, were not spread out in space, and therefore were not subject
to mathematical calculation. What this philosophical assertion meant, however,
was that no consciousness, or life, or purposes remained in nature—these qualities resided, instead, only in the rational minds of human beings. Therefore, all
plants and animals, as well as our own bodies, became, in essence, inanimate
machines. The modern mechanism that is assumed today (and in Bergson's time)
is, in a manner of speaking, a mutilated Cartesianism, or (seen from another perspective) a secularized version of Newtonian physics. As was pointed out earlier,
Newton assumed that the "world machine" was created by God and ran in
accordance to his eternal and immutable laws. However, by the nineteenth century (as aforementioned), an influential cluster of thinkers (most notably
Laplace, Comte, Renan, Taine) began to argue that the universe was a perfectly
ordered, utterly predictable machine that ran just fine on its own. As Sheldrake
points out in his lucid overview of the development of the idea of "natural laws,"
God, in essence, had become "an unnecessary hypothesis. His universal laws
remained, but no longer as ideas in his eternal mind. . . . Everything, even physicists, became inanimate matter moving in accordance with these blind laws."[11]

However, as Sheldrake goes on to note, at the end of the nineteenth century, the discovery of the laws of thermodynamics meant that the universe
could no longer be seen as a kind of cosmic perpetual motion machine. Instead,
it appeared that the universe was heading, inevitably, toward "a state of thermo-
dynamic equilibrium in which the machinery would stop working, never to
start again."[12] Sadly, even the finely tuned, well-oiled world machine seemed as
if it was going to run out of steam. According to the laws of thermodynamics,
while the matter and energy that make up the universe remain constant,
nonetheless, over time, the heat and light and energy of the universe, what
make it a livable universe, will become more and more dispersed and diffuse,

until finally, inevitably, the cosmos will sputter out altogether, with the "remnants of the exhausted machinery" scattered like cold shards of metal throughout the cosmic void.[13]

The idea of a blind, soulless, mechanistic universe predestined to a cold and dark oblivion was, for many, more than simply a scientific theory. Rather, it was often seen, as Sheldrake notes, as "a dreadful truth that no rational person can deny" no matter what "existential anguish it may cause."[14] Bertrand Russell's comments are illustrative:

> That man is the product of causes which had no prevision of the end they were achieving; that his origin, his growth, his hopes and fears, his loves and beliefs, are but the outcome of accidental collisions of atoms; that no fire, no heroism, no intensity of thought and feeling, can preserve an individual life beyond the grave; that all the labors of the ages, all the devotion, all the inspiration, all the noonday brightness of human genius, are destined to extinction in the vast death of the solar system; and that the whole temple of Man's achievement must inevitably be buried beneath the debris of a universe in ruins—all these things, if not quite beyond dispute, are yet so nearly certain, that no philosophy which rejects them can hope to stand. Only with the scaffolding of these truths, only on the firm foundation of unyielding despair, can the soul's habitation henceforth be built.[15]

PSYCHOLOGICAL DETERMINISM

It could be argued that Bergson's entire philosophical work is, in many ways, a direct and ongoing attempt to articulate a coherent, persuasive alternative to this type of philosophical pessimism, a pessimism that is, in many ways, the end result of assuming the reality of a predetermined, mechanistic universe. But in order to effectively counter this deeply engrained and widespread belief system, it was first necessary to shine light on the extent to which this belief in determinism has infiltrated not only our understanding of the external world, but also our understanding of ourselves. For instance (as was discussed in more detail earlier), given the fact that our attention is riveted on the external world (a world that is understood to be completely predetermined), and given that our consciousness is understood to be simply an inner reflection of that predetermined external world, then it only makes sense that we would think that our inner experience is also predetermined.

It should not be surprising to discover, therefore, that various forms of psychological determinism were extremely common among intellectuals from the eighteenth century onward (if not earlier). For instance, as Čapek notes, even

Immanuel Kant, in his *Critique of Practical Reason*, a quarter of a century before Laplace, claimed that not only the human body, but the human mind as well are predetermined. Kant insists that "It may therefore be admitted that if it were possible to have so profound an insight into a man's mental character . . . as to know all its motives, even the smallest, and likewise all the external occasions that can influence them, we could calculate a man's conduct for the future with as great certainty as a lunar or solar eclipse."[16]

Psychological determinism, although it assumes and emerges out of a belief in physical determinism, is subtly different. Let's look, for example, at how these two perspectives would understand the nature of consciousness. Bergson comments that, from the perspective of physical determinism, consciousness arises as the result of molecular movements in the brain or follows in the wake of these movements "like the phosphorescent line which results from the rubbing of a match" (*TFW* 147). He goes on to note that physical determinism assumes that "the drama enacted in the theatre of consciousness is a literal and even slavish translation of some scenes performed by the molecules and atoms of organized matter" (*TFW* 149). However, from the perspective of psychological determinism, the alleged physical "causes" of particular states of consciousness are put to the side for the moment in order to study the activity and structure of consciousness in its own terms. From this perspective, our current state of consciousness is said to be the inevitable, predictable, end result of the actions of prior "atoms" of consciousness. (For example, my anger is the direct and predetermined result of my prior conviction that my friend insulted me.) From this perspective, free will is nonexistent.

6

ALTERNATIVE UNDERSTANDINGS
OF THE SELF

ASSOCIATIONIST IDEAS OF THE SELF

During Bergson's time, a particular type of psychological determinism frequently dominated the psychological/philosophical discussions of the
nature of consciousness. (At the juncture of the nineteenth and twentieth centuries, the boundaries between psychology and philosophy were extremely
porous.) This loose-knit philosophical/psychological consensus, dating back to at
least the seventeenth century, was called "associationism." Associationists, such as
John Locke, David Hume, Étienne Condillac, John Stuart Mill, Hippolyte
Taine, and Bertrand Russell, for all of their other philosophical differences,
claimed that our psychological reality could be understood in a way that directly
mirrored the current scientific understanding of material reality. These thinkers
agreed that the self, in essence, is nothing more than a collection of mental states
(e.g., sensations, ideas, pleasures, pains, emotions, and memories) that are "associated" with each other by factors such as contiguity, similarity, and so on.
Inspired evidently by the spectacular successes that came when physics began to
interpret physical reality as a complex combination of simple, self-identical
atoms clustering together in physical space, associationists argued that our psychological reality should be understood in a similar fashion, that is, as nothing
more than an aggregate of discrete, static, minute, and clearly distinguishable
mental "atoms" of consciousness.

In a variety of ways, associationists insisted that our belief that we have a
cohesive, unchanging, substantive ego is nothing more than a useful illusion. As
a sort of legal and moral shorthand, it might well make sense to think that we
are the same person over time, but if we look carefully, they claimed, we would

discover that there is no permanent "John" or "Jane" underneath the flux of sensations, perceptions, emotions, and thoughts that make up our conscious experience. What we think of as our "self" is, for associationists, nothing more than a makeshift grouping of these isolated, fragmented, and discontinuous mental "elements." In fact, even the seeming complexity of our mental life was from this perspective also illusory. Associationists claim that, like the physical world, our inner world is nothing more than the rearrangement of an assortment of basic, relatively simple, unchanging mental "elements" that passively combine and recombine, appear and disappear—in essence bumping into each other like internal billiard balls cascading and rebounding within the psychological counterpart of physical space—that is, the homogeneous, empty, inert container of time.

Further (and this is crucial), associationists argued that our belief in our ability to initiate actions, our belief that we are able to make decisions that are genuinely free, is also illusory. They claimed, instead, that just as various physical atoms combine and recombine in ways that are strictly determined and utterly predictable to create the complex physical world that we inhabit, in the same way, the configuration of the mental atoms that make up our present conscious state of awareness are nothing more than the completely predictable and utterly determined end result of prior internal interactions, interactions that are strictly governed by psychological laws (such as contiguity, succession, resemblance) that are just as coercive and implacable as the laws that govern the physical world.

A Substantially Flowing Self

Time and Free Will, in many ways, can be seen as a sustained and multifaceted attack against this associationist understanding of the consciousness and the self, as well as an attempt to articulate a viable philosophical alternative to those (like Kant) who claimed that there was an unchanging transcendental ego underneath the ever-shifting, yet separate and encapsulated, sensations and feelings and thoughts that make up the tumultuous inner world of the associationist self.

Bergson acknowledges that, from a certain point of view, the associationist claims make a type of sense. If we posit that the external world seems to be, for all practical purposes, a collection of separate, self-contained objects which interact with each other in predetermined, mechanical ways, then it is understandable that, by a type of psychic osmosis, we might well come to see our inner world in the same light. He is willing to concede that it may indeed be necessary in day-to-day life to think that our consciousness is broken up into separate beads of clearly labeled thoughts and feelings and sensations. The problem is, however, that we frequently confuse these artificial linguistic constructions for the actual nature of consciousness itself. As Bergson points out, "associationism thus makes the mistake of constantly replacing the concrete phenomenon which takes place in the mind by the artificial reconstruction of it given by philosophy, and of thus confusing the explanation of the fact with the fact itself" (*TFW* 163).

Furthermore, as Bergson argues, once we imagine that durée is nothing more than "beads" of consciousness "bumping" into each other in a lawful, predictable manner, once we have artificially separated the "elements" of our consciousness by acts of our attention, then it is understandable that we might seek to reconnect them by imagining that these psychic "beads" are threaded together on an unchanging, formless ego. In order to make sense of the perceived unity, stability, and continuity of our selfhood in light of the seeming crowded cacophony of various emotions, sensations, and thoughts that seem to jostle and shout and mutter in our inner world, it makes a certain type of sense to think of ourselves as a stable, unchanging ego that is undergoing a series of separate, "distinct psychological states, each one invariable" (*CM* 175).

However, as Bergson goes to great lengths to emphasize, there is another possibility. As Garrett Barden points out, associationists like Hume "correctly failed to discover an underlying subject but incorrectly failed to attend to and understand the enduring subject."[1] The truth, for Bergson, is that there is no unchanging ego which serves as a "rigid, immovable substratum nor distinct states passing over it like actors on a stage. There is simply the continuous melody of our inner life—a melody which is going on and will go on, indivisible, from the beginning to the end of our conscious existence" (*CM* 176). Close inspection reveals that this indivisible melody of our experience is not cut into distinct notes. There really are not completely distinct, isolated thoughts and feelings within us. There is simply the interwoven, ever-shifting flow of our consciousness, "a flux of fleeting shades merging into each other" (*CM* 3)[2] There is no need to imagine some unchanging, foundational, invisible self that holds all of the contents of our conscious life, if our consciousness is already cohesive, if it is already an interconnected whole in which each state of consciousness permeates and interpenetrates all the rest.

What Bergson tries to do is to point out that *the associationists are simply not empirical enough.* If we look closely at our psychological reality, we do not discover any self-identical mental "atoms" within us. It is simply not true that our psychic states can be reduced down to simpler, more general and stable atom-like constituent units that can be added and subtracted from each other. Our feelings and thoughts and memories and desires are not made up of a combination of self-contained, immutable, and impersonal "elements" that remain fixed and unchanging. According to Bergson, "even the simplest psychic elements possess a personality and a life of their own, however superficial they may be; they are in a constant state of becoming, and the same feeling, by the mere fact of being repeated, is a new feeling" (*TFW* 200).

The external physical objects of our sensory experience may well have clearly defined boundaries and a type of relative permanence through time. But not so our psychological state of being, in which we can find no clearly defined contours, no mental states that are utterly discrete and fixed and cut off from each other. Associationists might claim, for instance, that we have a specific sensation that inevitably and invariably catalyzes an equally specific psychological reaction. To use an example drawn from Bergson, associationists would argue that, if we smell a rose, this sensation will automatically stir up certain memories (such as walking in a garden as a child). Arguing against the associationists' position, Bergson offers an alternative depiction of what happens during the act of smelling a rose. He writes: "I smell a rose and immediately confused recollections of childhood come back to my memory. In truth, these recollections have not been called up by the perfume of the rose: I breathe them in with the very scent; it means all that to me. To others it will smell differently" (*TFW* 161). For Bergson, it is not as if there is an objective, impersonal smell of the rose, which different people then associate with their own particular ideas and memories. Instead, the experience within us is a unified (yet complex) whole. Smelling the rose is fused with and/or infused by our own unique childhood memories. Someone whom, let's say, is smelling a rose for the first time would have a very different experience than someone else—for example, someone for whom roses were associated with a death in the family.

Bergson argues that the psychological determinism that is assumed by various associationists is radically undermined, if we have an accurate understanding of the nature of the self. Determinism is rooted in the following logic: given the same cause, the same effect will take place. For instance, in chemistry, adding X to Y will always produce reaction Z. However, as Leszek Kolakowski aptly notes, "the same conditions can never, by definition, obtain in the life of the self, because each, artificially isolated, moment of its duration includes the entire past, which is, consequently, different for each moment . . . the same situation never occurs twice in the being endowed with memory."[3] Therefore, the fundamental assumption that underlies physics, that is, that identical causes will produce identical results, does not apply to our psychological reality, since our consciousness has within it nothing that stays the same, nothing that remains still long enough to be measured, counted, and quantified. As Bergson puts it, "states of consciousness are processes, and not things . . . they are alive and therefore constantly changing; . . . in consequence, it is impossible to cut off a moment from them without making them poorer by the loss of some impression, and thus altering their quality" (*TFW* 196). The so-called mental atoms or even mental "states" of consciousness assumed by associationists simply do not exist—they are nothing but artificial, theoretical constructions, cookie-cutter abstractions imposed upon the fluid dynamism of our inner reality.

Furthermore, according to the associationist understanding of the mind, each "existing state of consciousness is . . . thought of as necessitated by the preceding states" (*TFW* 155). Indeed, there does seem to be a relationship between a particular state of consciousness and the one that follows it. It is often true that one idea reminds us of something else, which reminds us of something else in turn. But is it always true that the first idea *causes* the next idea? For associationists, our feelings and ideas are similar to alien influences that "make" us do something, vectors of various impersonal forces that can be plotted, mapped, and predicted. While there may be some truth to this (to the extent that the feelings and ideas within us are not wholly ours, but instead are surface-level "imports" from outside of ourselves), if these feelings and ideas are rooted deeply enough within us, they are permeated, through and through, with all of our past memories. As such, they are intrinsically connected to the totality of our being. As Bergson notes:

> It is only an inaccurate psychology, misled by language, which will show us the soul determined by sympathy, aversion, or hate, as though by so many forces pressing upon it. These feelings, providing that they go deep enough, each make up the whole soul, since the whole content of the soul is reflected in each of them. To say that the soul is determined under the influence of any one of these feelings is thus to recognize that it is self-determined.[4]

7

FREEDOM

DURÉE: EVER-NEW

Determinism is undercut once it is recognized that durée is, in its very nature, a dynamic, ever-new, ceaselessly changing, flowing, temporal reality whose very essence is freedom and unforeseeable creativity.[1] Time/durée/consciousness is not, as many people imagine, something similar to the images that are captured on film, in which everything is present, everything is given, and each static shot is lined up next to one another in space. However, because many philosophers and scientists picture time in this way, they have grave difficulty conceiving a durée that is radically new and inherently unforeseeable. As Bergson notes, "they seem to have no idea whatever of an act which might be entirely new (at least inwardly) and which in no way would exist . . . prior to its realization. But this is the very nature of a free act. To perceive it thus, as indeed we must do with any creation, novelty or unpredictable occurrence whatsoever, we have to get back into pure duration [durée]" (*CM* 19).

As Čapek points out, one of the primary characteristics of durée is that it is "forever incomplete . . . in other words, it is a *continuous emergence of novelty*."[2] The flow of our consciousness, as time passes (or better, while taking the form of the passage of time), ceaselessly and effortlessly assumes utterly unique forms, continually takes on completely unexpected and novel shapes. Solomon underscores this ongoing novelty of durée when he says that, for Bergson, "the mind is ever changing by a sort of self-creation, or, more precisely, by active adaptation. It is this that constitutes its freedom. It is making; it is never made."[3] This constant, self-generated, internal change, a change that is rooted in and propelled by memory, also assures the irreversibility of durée. As Bergson notes, "we could not live over again a single moment, for we should have to begin by effacing the memory of all that had followed. . . . Thus our personality shoots, grows, and ripens without ceasing. Each of its moments is something new added to what was before" (*CE* 6).

51

Consciousness of its own accord never stays still, never repeats itself. Even when we are at our most robotic, living a life of habitual reactivity to others, almost sleepwalking through existence, even then, our consciousness, under the radar, somehow manages to be genuinely, never-endingly, creative. What is almost miraculous about durée, as Bergson notes, is that it is "a reality which is capable of drawing from itself more than it contains, of enriching itself from within, of creating or recreating itself ceaselessly, and which is essentially resistant to measurement because it is never entirely determined, never fully made but always in the process of becoming."[4]

In addition, as Bergson emphasizes, durée "is not only something new, but something unforeseeable" (*CE* 6). As he points out, any pretense of determinism would immediately vanish, if we could only see ourselves immersed in the immediacy of durée, where "the past becomes identical with the present and continuously creates with it—if only by the fact of being added to it—something absolutely new" (*CM* 185). In light of "the continuous creation of unforeseeable novelty which seems to be going on in the universe," Bergson claims that it is impossible to predict, to any degree of accuracy, the richness and variety of what the future will bring (*CM* 107). As he notes, "no matter how [he tries] to imagine in detail what is going to happen . . . still how inadequate, how abstract and stilted is the thing [he has] imagined in comparison to what actually happens!"(*CM* 107).

Bergson does not deny that our present state of awareness is intimately connected with what happened in the past within us and with what was acting upon us in the past. However, just because our state of awareness at this moment is seamlessly connected with the whole of our prior experience, this in no way implies that our present state of consciousness (or our present actions) are somehow the predictable, automatic outcome of our past. In order to underscore this point, Bergson offers the example of the process of painting a portrait. He comments that, looking at a finished portrait, we might say that its form, color, and texture could be explained by the skill of the artist, by how the model looks, and by the properties and color of the paints on the artist's palette. However, explaining how the portrait came into existence is a dramatically different process than the ability to predict, in advance, exactly how the portrait will look before it is painted. According to Bergson, if you succeeded in accomplishing this task, you would not have simply predicted the form, color, and text of the portrait, you would have actually painted the portrait itself.

As Bergson points out, if the outer world that seems to be, on the whole, so amenable to strict, scientific laws, is itself so difficult to predict or anticipate, then the unrolling of our inner life is even more unpredictable, because every moment of our lives "is a kind of creation" (*CE* 7). According to Bergson, we each have within us "the feeling . . . of being creators of our intentions, of our decisions, of our acts, and by that, of our habits, our characters, ourselves. Artisans of our life . . . we work continually, with the material furnished us by the past and present, by heredity and opportunity, to mold a figure unique, new, original, as unforeseeable as the form given by the sculptor to the clay" (*CM* 110). Just as the painter's talent and ability is modified by each new portrait that is painted, our personality is also continually changed by each of the states of consciousness that we experience. Therefore, as Bergson notes, it is correct "to say that what we do depends upon what we are; but it is necessary to add also that we are, to a certain extent, what we do, and that we are creating ourselves continually" (*CE* 7). As Luce helpfully indicates, the freedom that we have as conscious beings is not capricious, it does not mysteriously emerge in an instant from nowhere. Instead, our inner freedom is a development out of our entire past that carries the "past forward into its present. . . . Inherited disposition, instinctive impulses, temperament, the idea that guides, the feeling that motivates"—all of these come together to form who we are in our ability to freely choose, freely decide, freely act.[5]

From a Bergsonian perspective, it is crucial to underscore the difference between movements that are mechanically caused by an external force and movements that come from within us, movements that are voluntarily initiated by ourselves. Voluntary acts, to the extent that they are not habitual and rote reactions, are directly experienced within us as free and unanticipated activities. As Bergson notes, that inner freedom, concretely felt, "also creates something new inside itself, since the voluntary action reacts on him who wills it, modifies in some degree the character of the person from whom it emanates, and accomplishes, by a kind of miracle, that creation of self by itself which seems to be the very object of human life" (*ME* 39). According to Bergson, this creative power, which "overflows the body on all sides" (since our consciousness is not spatially limited), which "endures through time," which initiates "unforeseeable and free" actions, which "creates by newly-creating itself" is the true nature of the self (*ME* 39). It is this creative power that Bergson is referring to when he uses terms such as "durée," or "the 'I,' the 'soul,' the 'mind'—mind being precisely a force which can draw from itself more than it contains, yield more than it receives, give more than it has" (*ME* 39).[6]

For Bergson, who we are, the flow of our durée, is not the simple end-result of a certain number of past experiences that have been rearranged to produce a fixed and calculable end product. Instead, "real duration [durée] is that in which each form flows out of previous forms, while adding to them something new" (*CE* 362). Our current state of consciousness in its ceaseless emergence is not preordained by mathematically complex but theoretically calculable economic forces; it is not the sum total of our immersion in our particular cultural milieu and institutional structures; it does not arise due to the predetermined mindless interaction of bits of brain and neural matter bumping into each other in predictable patterns.[7] Instead, Bergson argues that durée is endlessly, naturally, almost unbelievably, creative. Each "moment" of durée does not emerge from the past like an automobile coming off an assembly line, constructed by drawing from and rearranging a previous and finite supply of parts. The reservoir from which all of this incessant newness springs forth is not a bounded, finished, complete whole, in which all of our memories and beliefs and fears and passions and so on are neatly stacked, like some giant inner warehouse. Instead, it is a *virtual* reality—an open-ended, living, unbounded, nonspatial, protoconscious potentiality whose very nature is unimaginable creativity. Durée, like an inner cornucopia of consciousness, manages to create, almost magically, genuine newness at each "moment," even while it also remains inextricably connected to the past.

ARGUING FOR FREE WILL

Bergson's provocative descriptions of the nature of durée are not simply meant to provide us with a rich and detailed phenomenology of consciousness. In addition, Bergson sets the foundation for a focused, if somewhat unusual, philosophical defense of free will. What is striking about Bergson's arguments is that they are for the most part "anti-argument" arguments. That is, Bergson is convinced that most philosophical attempts to defend free will are inherently self-defeating because they are based on, and take for granted, many if not most of the same presuppositions that underlie the arguments that determinists use against the reality of free will. Therefore, much of Bergson's philosophical energy in *Time and Free Will* is dedicated to a thoroughgoing deconstruction of the very notion that it is even possible from a certain standpoint to rationally justify the reality of free will. In a very real way, Bergson does not want to be linked with either determinism *or* with those who advocate the necessity of a rational defense of the truth of free will, a philosophical position known as "libertarianism."

One striking aspect of Bergson's "anti-argument" argument is his attempt to unearth the assumptions that undergird either determinism (i.e., the claim that given the sum total of prior experiences/stimuli, only one end-result is possible—the action that is chosen) or libertarianism (i.e., the claim that given the same circumstances, it would have been possible to have chosen another action). Bergson points out that *both* positions assume a conception of voluntary action that goes something like the following: a person, after leaving a point in time (M) and going through a series of experiences, reaches another point in time (O) and discovers that a decision needs to be made. In essence, the person has come to a fork in the road. This individual can then, it is assumed, either go one way (from point O to point X) or go another way (from point O to point Y). This understanding of what happens when we make a decision is rooted, therefore, in a type of tacit geometrical symbolization. Basically, we picture ourselves reaching a certain point in time "O," only to hesitate and mull over possible alternatives, and then finally choose either OX or OY. (Of course, this is the simplest version. There could also be many more possible forks in the road—O to W or O to Z, and so on. But the basic principles that underlie this picture of decision-making do not change.)

It may appear, at first glance, that this scenario would only support the position of the libertarians (in that it pictures a person at O, waffling between various preexistent alternatives and finally choosing one). However, the same geometrical symbolism that underlies the normal conception of free will can also be used by the advocates of determinism. The primary difference is that they look at the process from "further down the road," in that their argument emerges out of a later point in the decision-making process: the time after the decision has been made. From that later point in time, as determinists hasten to note, the person has gone on in only one direction—let's say, from O to Y. Both the libertarians and the determinists agree that a person oscillates at O between various possible courses—let's say, toward Y or toward X. The libertarians, however, focus on the moment of decision, and in essence leave the person oscillating at O *ad infinitum*. The determinists focus on the actual decision itself, noting that the individual chooses only one path (let's say OX), a decision that was based on seemingly good (indeed, unavoidably persuasive) reasons (*TFW* 178–179).

What Bergson goes to great lengths to point out, however, is that this geometrical representation of the decision-making process contains numerous distortions. One of the most crucial distortions is that this "map" of deciding what to do could not have been constructed until after the decision has been made. Therefore, the various alternative routes (e.g., OX, OY, OZ) are simply reified imaginary possibilities that have been spatially represented, and as such, this "map" of various forks in the road, as Bergson notes, "does not show me the deed in the doing but the deed already done" (*TFW* 180). Looking at this internal map, we can pretend to ourselves that all of the various forks already exist and that we could, theoretically, try one, and then perhaps go back and try another. However, as Bergson goes out of his way to emphasize, "time is not a line along which one can pass again" (*TFW* 181). Our attempts to mentally represent, after the fact, our progress through time as a line on a map, as a road with a various forks in it, does not successfully symbolize what really happens to time as it passes, but instead, only succeeds in capturing (with multiple distortions) the time which has already passed.

Because of our ingrained tendency to think about our conscious experience in spatial terms, we believe that it is possible to represent what happens within us when we attempt to make a decision as if we were plotting, in Bergson's words, "the march of an army on a map" (*TFW* 180). But as Bergson indicates, in reality "there is no line MO, no point O, no path OX, no direction OY" (*TFW* 180). Therefore, the libertarian notion that we go through experiences from point M to point O, and then choose to go in direction X (all the while imagining that we could have equally gone down the other preexisting path toward direction Y) is a meaningless mental exercise, as is, of course, the determinist version that, having gone through experiences from M to O, it was inevitable that we would choose to go toward X. The bottom line, for Bergson, is that "all the difficulty arises from the fact that both parties picture the deliberation under the form of an oscillation in space, while it really consists in a dynamic progress in which the self and its motives, like real living beings, are in a constant state of becoming" (*TFW* 183).

Put in another way, the main problem with both arguments is that the (almost inevitable) spatial imagination of the process of choice "represents a *thing* and not a *progress*; it corresponds, in its inertness, to a kind of stereotyped memory of the whole process of deliberation and the final decision arrived at: how could it give us the least idea of the concrete movement, the dynamic progress by which the deliberation issued in the act?" (*TFW* 181).

Another significant distortion that is promoted by this spatial representation of the moment of decision is that we tend to think that we remain the same during the process of vacillating between OX and OY. As Luce notes, Bergson never disputes that choice is a "psychic reality; deliberation, indecision, hesitation are as real as any other states of mind."[8] What Bergson emphasizes, however, is that the very acts of mental hesitation and indecision in-and-of themselves change us and are part of the whole process by which a "final" decision is made. Unlike the determinist understanding of the self, with its atomized thoughts and feelings that change only in a lawful, predictable sequence, Bergson emphasizes that during the process of vacillating from one possibility and its alternates, "the self grows, expands, and changes . . . if not, how would it ever come to a decision?" (*TFW* 175). Who we are is not somehow put on hold during the process of decision. Instead, the hesitations and vacillations themselves impact our selfhood. As Bergson insightfully comments, our consciousness "lives and develops by means of its very hesitations, until the free action drops from it like an over-ripe fruit" (*TFW* 176).

The basic illusion for Bergson is the assumption that time is like space. We imagine that we have come to "a road already marked out across the plain, which we can contemplate from the top of the mountain, even if we have not traversed it and are never to do so" (*TFW* 191). But time cannot be seen, frozen from above, as if it is a road already created, but rather, it has to be lived—we make the road ourselves as we move forward in life. It is only when our experience is in the past that the intellect can operate upon it, can understand it— because now it is unmoving and changeless, now it can be analyzed, broken into bits, and rearranged. The intellect, coming from this kaleidoscopic point of view, will understandably either see our inner life as the mechanical end result of prior actions or as the equally (if less obvious) mechanical oscillation "between two or more ready-made alternatives" (*CE* 47). However, as Bergson hastens to point out, a free act is not something that can be analyzed. He goes on to say, "the self, infallible when it affirms its immediate experiences, feels itself free and says so; but, as soon as it tries to explain its freedom to itself," it can only do so by substituting a spatial chart for the concrete flow of its temporal experience (*TFW* 183).

According to Bergson, our inability to provide any rigorous explanation of our inherent freedom does not, however, imply that a free act is a "capricious, unreasonable action"; instead, the freedom that we have to act and to decide is something which we know immediately from within, something that "involves the whole of our person and is truly ours" (*CE* 47). While it may be true that any decision we make "could not have been foreseen, even though its antecedents explain it when once it has been accomplished," this does not mean that the act of making a decision is somehow groundless (*CE* 47). It is, in fact, just the opposite. It is that which emerges from the depths of our being. It is a "real maturing of an internal state . . . [a] real evolution" that "ripens gradually" within us (*CE* 47). Freedom, for Bergson, is the most natural thing in the world.

FREEDOM: AN IMMEDIATE FACT

It is important to reaffirm that, although it may appear that Bergson is making a series of quite detailed and rational arguments for the existence of free will, in reality he is vividly demonstrating the inadequacy of any intellectual attempts either to validate or to deny the reality of free will. Bergson's primary job seems to be to poke and to prod, from a multitude of angles, the very desire to analyze and define freedom. He repeatedly claims that freedom is so fundamental that every attempt to articulate its inherent nature in any positive, clear way, acts like a highly potent acid that dissolves whatever it touches. As he makes clear, freedom "is indefinable, just because we *are* free. For we can analyze a thing, but not a process"; we can break up objects in the external world, but we cannot fragment durée—and if we persist in the attempt to analyze our freedom, "we unconsciously transform the process into a 'thing'" and "in place of the doing we put the already done" (*TFW* 219). In our very attempts to capture freedom in the net of our words we change spontaneity into inertia and "freedom into necessity," thereby guaranteeing the "victory of determinism" (*TFW* 220).

Bergson was frequently accused by numerous philosophers of advocating irrationality. However, to be fair to Bergson's perspective, he does not deny the value of rational discourse. He simply suggests, and I think correctly, that there are certain crucial dimensions of human experience (such as freedom) that rationality, by its very nature, cannot adequately address. Nonetheless, Bergson's stress on the inability of our intellect to adequately grasp our inner freedom does not mean that he therefore claims that freedom is some mysterious, utterly transcendent quality (*TFW* 233). (He explicitly disagrees with Kant's contention that human freedom is unknowable.) We all continually experience our freedom to choose, to act, to think certain thoughts, and so on, throughout our lives. We all know directly, regardless of the opinions of certain learned scholars, that we are not zombies or robotic automata. Our moral codes and legal systems make sense only if we all agree, at least practically, that a person can make a real choice between right and wrong. The reality of our freedom is about as basic and undeniable a fact as there is.

In order to have a direct experience of our freedom, therefore, we simply have to let go of certain entrenched intellectual habits; we simply have to learn how to discard our stubborn insistence that our consciousness is a psychic replica of the outer world and see it as it is: as ever-new, inherently creative, always changing. Bergson advocates that, if we really want to understand our freedom, we need to set aside all symbolic representations of what happens when we make a decision, "all translations into words," and instead simply "attend to what pure consciousness alone shows us about an action that has come to pass or an action which is still to come" (*TFW* 173). The best way to undermine determinism, therefore, is to see clearly what is continually taking place within us. We need to tenaciously affirm the priority of the facts of our experience. And among the most evident of these facts is our freedom. As Bergson puts it, "among the facts which we observe there is none clearer" (*TFW* 221).

Immediate experience is a type of touchstone for Bergson. He argues that it is crucial to start with the assumed reality of what is immediately evident to our senses or consciousness, whether external or internal, unless proved otherwise. Therefore, because "our immediate impression" is that we initiate voluntary, free actions, the burden of proof is on those (philosophers, psychologists, neurologists, and so on) who think that this impression is illusory (*ME* 44). According to Bergson, the belief that everything, including our consciousness and our freedom, can be reduced to quantifiable bits of mechanistic and predetermined matter is actually not scientific, since it is "neither proved nor even suggested by experience" (*ME* 45). The only way in which mechanists or determinists can justify their belief in the nonexistence of free will is, ironically, by a fiat of the will. In essence, they have to arbitrarily assert that our voluntary actions are, in the final analysis, reducible to the robotic movements of inert matter. And how do they attempt to support this assertion? By drawing upon examples of how, in the physical world, everything acts in a calculable, predetermined manner—examples such as chemical combustion in which everything behaves as planned, examples in which conscious choice or will simply do not even enter into the picture (*ME* 44).

A LITTLE HARD-CORE COMMON SENSE

Bergson's strategy in *Time and Free Will* appears to boil down to the following: 1) Demonstrate the inherent differences between durée and matter; 2) show that it is possible to have an immediate experience of durée as ceaseless creative change; and 3) claim that freedom exists based on our direct awareness of durée. As a preparatory maneuver in the argument against determinism, this strategy has tremendous merit. However, even Bergson seems to have realized that *Time and Free Will* was just a starting point and that any philosophy that sets up a complete separation between consciousness and the physical world cannot, in the end, successfully defend the reality of freedom. We are not simply consciousness; we also have a physical body. Therefore, if the mind and body are understood to be utterly separate, then there is no way to adequately explain, for instance, the fact that I can freely choose in my mind to do something physical (e.g., that I can choose to keep quiet, instead of saying something hurtful to someone). There is also no way to explain the fact that this mental choice will lead to a physical response (that I actually keep my mouth shut). (Those who attempt to reduce the mind to the meaningless movements of insentient matter have a similar problem.)

We will have to wait until section 2 for an in-depth examination of Bergson's mature theory of the mind-body connection that he articulates in his second book, *Matter and Memory*. However, even though Bergson's attempt in *Time and Free Will* to rescue free will from the jaws of determinism is not buttressed by the sophisticated and intriguing understanding of the mind-body connection that he maps out in *Matter and Memory*, it is important to emphasize that his work on free will in *Time and Free Will* is neither a wasted effort, nor is it outdated. Bergson's argument that we all are convinced that we freely initiate actions and certainly behave as if we are free (even if we might, theoretically, believe otherwise) continues to play a role in the work of some contemporary philosophers who attempt to defend the notion of free will against the determinism that is assumed by many (if not most) scientists and philosophers.

One recent philosophical work that fights hard for the reality of freedom is *Unsnarling the World-Knot*, by David Ray Griffin. In this book, Griffin notes that, historically, our commonsense assumptions have often needed to be corrected by science. For instance, "common sense said the world was flat: science showed this to be false. Common sense said the sun and the moon were the same size; science showed this to be false. Common sense said the Earth was the center of the universe; science showed this to be false. Common sense said matter was solid; science has shown this to be false."[9] According to Griffin, the commonsense beliefs that science has corrected (such as the belief in a flat Earth or the belief that the Earth is the center of the universe) can be called "soft-core common sense." What he means by this term is that these beliefs that were corrected by science had, from the beginning, a type of built-in "correctability" to them.

Science, in a very real way, is based on the continual examination and revision of various "soft-core" commonsense beliefs. For instance, we might have the soft-core commonsense belief that a table is solid, but then physics comes along and demonstrates that this belief is an illusion: it is, in reality, primarily empty space filled with a swirling mass of particles and energy fields. (We will see soon that even this belief in the reality of empty space is, itself, open for revision.) Therefore, while "soft-core" commonsense beliefs may be stubbornly held by many people, nonetheless, there is nothing about them that makes them intrinsically impossible to challenge and revise.[10]

The recognition that historically we have had many beliefs that we took for granted, and that science has successfully challenged and overturned these beliefs, has led some philosophers to claim that all of our commonsense beliefs are equally "soft-core"; that is, potentially any commonsense belief we possess may in the end be overturned by new scientific evidence. These philosophers are especially eager to argue that two of our most deeply held beliefs are also up for grabs: first, the belief "that we all really do have subjective conscious mental states"; and second, the belief that we really are free, that is, the belief that we can and do make real choices from genuine alternatives.[11] What makes these two commonsense beliefs especially vulnerable and enticing to those who want to dispute them is the fact that these claims do not agree with certain key understandings of the nature of reality (e.g., materialism and determinism) that are assumed by many, if not most, contemporary scientists.

Griffin, however, along with other philosophers, such as Alfred North Whitehead, C. S. Pierce, and (to a certain extent) John Searle, argues that our "common sense" beliefs about the reality of consciousness and freedom are inherently different than our other "soft-core" commonsense beliefs. Our beliefs about our freedom and our subjective experience are what Griffin calls "hard-core" common sense. "Hard-core" commonsense beliefs, Griffin argues, are in no need of correction by science; in fact, Griffin claims that these types of beliefs are so foundational that they cannot be denied without self-contradiction, so foundational that they can and should challenge the mechanistic and deterministic metaphysical presuppositions that typically undergird many scientific worldviews.[12]

As Griffin points out, many philosophers go to great lengths to deny that we actually are free and conscious. However, as soon as we deny that we are conscious or free we run into a raft of troubles that do not arise when we challenge "soft-core" commonsense beliefs. These sorts of claims (Griffin lists several others) are "hard-core" common sense because they are universally presupposed in practice and cannot be denied without inconsistency. For example, some philosophers (as well as neurobiologists, cognitive psychologists, and so on) argue that our day-to-day belief in the reality of free will is simply another variety of "soft-core" common sense just waiting to be corrected; it is just another "folk belief" that needs to be eliminated with enough "hard-core" science. However, as Griffin wryly comments, these philosophers and scientists often miss the irony of their position: they are choosing to argue that there really is no choice. That is, they may verbally deny the reality of free will, but in their daily lives as philosophers and scientists they cannot avoid acting in ways that assume that free will exists—in fact, no one can. Universally, without exception, our behavior as human beings demonstrates that we believe in the reality of consciousness and free will, even if we go to great lengths to protest otherwise.

What is fascinating is that many of the most important philosophers of today who are considered authorities on the nature of consciousness and freedom, reject the reality of freedom and act as if it is simply a "soft-core" belief. They do so in loyalty to the supposedly "hard-core" scientific understanding that the universe (including ourselves) is ultimately reducible to the movement of insentient particles of matter, movements that are completely determined, an understanding that leaves no room for genuine freedom. But, as Griffin insightfully points out, this deterministic understanding of the nature of matter is actually a very vulnerable "soft-core" commonsense idea: we certainly do not universally presuppose it in the activities of our daily lives, and it can easily be denied without any inconsistency. (In fact, as we will see in the next section of this text, the belief that matter consists of insentient, predetermined particles has already been strongly challenged by many of the recent findings of modern physics itself.) Ironically, the current reigning academic understandings about the nature of matter (typically based, at least implicitly, on a superseded set of understandings drawn from classical physics) is actually much less dependable and solid than our "hard-core" beliefs about consciousness and freedom.

However, as Griffin notes, there are other philosophers, such as Searle and Thomas Nagel, who at least recognize that it is extremely difficult to just flatly reject our belief in freedom when our ordinary lives and actions depend upon this assumption. As Searle points out, "We don't navigate the earth on the assumption of a flat earth, even though the earth looks flat, but we do act on the assumption of freedom. In fact we can't act otherwise than on the assumption of freedom, no matter how much we learn about how the world works as a determined physical system."[13] Nagel's position is similar. He stresses that there is no way to reconcile a belief in freedom with the determinism that is implied by science. But he also is at least willing to admit that there is no way that he can avoid the assumption of freedom in his day-to-day existence, noting: "I can no more help holding myself and others responsible in ordinary life than I can help feeling that my actions originate with me."[14]

Ultimately, while it makes complete sense to wish to base one's philosophical beliefs on the latest and most dependable findings of science, these findings by their very nature are continually open to revision. What is much more dependable, from Bergson's perspective, is the evidence of our immediate experience. We can, in our attempts to be loyal to the determinism and mechanism assumed by most scientists, spin out elaborate and intellectually sophisticated theories that claim that freedom and consciousness are illusory. But what is more real, more self-evident, more undeniable: our direct experience or these theories?

DEGREES OF FREEDOM

In *Time and Free Will*, Bergson, unlike most modern philosophers, argues that our freedom does not need to be explained or justified or even defended, because it is immediately evident and utterly fundamental not only to our social and moral lives, but also to what it means to be human. Instead, what needs explanation is why we do not always act in accordance with that freedom. Why is it that we at times feel ourselves "compelled" to act in ways that seem to go against our better judgment or our moral beliefs? Why do we so often find ourselves behaving in a way that *is* almost robotic? How can we explain that many of our decisions seem to be so irrational and often self-destructive?

To Bergson's credit, he does not ignore questions such as these. While he strenuously argues for the reality of free will, he also realizes that our freedom "is not absolute . . . [rather], it admits of degrees" (*TFW* 166). Bergson acknowledges that a sizable amount of our behavior does seem to have a striking resemblance to the mechanical, nonconscious, repetitive activity of inert matter. In fact, according to Bergson, *most* of our actions are little more than automatic reactions to outer stimuli, reactions which "though conscious and even intelligent, have many points of resemblance with reflex acts" (*TFW* 168). When we act on the instigation of solidified and encrusted habits and ideas that have remained on the surface of our psyches, we often *do* behave in many ways like a type of "conscious automaton" (*TFW* 168). As Bergson puts it, when we identify with our "superficial ego," with its clearly defined social roles, its rigidly held dogmas, its tightly controlled postures, "we live outside ourselves, hardly perceiving anything of ourselves but our own ghost . . . we live for the external world rather than for ourselves; we speak rather than think; we 'are acted' rather than act ourselves" (*TFW* 231).

Nonetheless, according to Bergson, we do have the capacity to act differently. We can push aside the "independent growths" which "form and float" on the surface of our psyche "like dead leaves on the water of a pond"; (*TFW* 166, 135) we can turn within ourselves and melt the "clear-cut crystals" of the "ideas which we receive ready-made, and which remain in us without ever being properly assimilated"(*CM* 192; *TFW* 135–136). If we accomplish this task through an intensive introspective effort, it then becomes possible to discover deep within our psyche that aspect of our being which is "the most uniformly, the most constantly and durably" ourselves, that "continuity of flow comparable to no flowing" that we have ever seen; we can once again "get back into pure [durée]" and thereby "recover possession" of ourselves (*CM* 192; *TFW* 232).[15]

According to Bergson, actions that spring forth from this fluid, continually creative "deep-seated self" are indeed truly free; unfortunately, we rarely act in a way that is connected to our depths. Instead, we prefer to relinquish our freedom, even in moments of crisis, due to "sluggishness or indolence"—we let our habits or the beliefs of others take over, instead of acting from the depths of our being in such a way that our whole personality vibrates (*TFW* 169).[16] Bergson suggests that we may well "believe that we are acting freely," but if we are really honest with ourselves, looking back, we can often "see how much we were mistaken" (*TFW* 169). Instead of taking the risk to examine and question and challenge what we are taught, instead of thinking and acting in accordance to what is most authentic within us, instead of tapping into that subtle, yet insistent guidance that bubbles up quietly from within, we typically choose other courses of action: we listen to what others say we should do, we seek their approval, we consult the rulebooks, we write down lists of pros and cons, we cling to old patterns of behavior that worked in the past, we struggle to stay safely within our comfort zone. Much of the time, sadly, this strategy works. We have learned how to live our lives on automatic pilot. Fortunately, according to Bergson, there are also moments in our lives in which something different takes place—moments where in the struggle to make a decision, just when we think we have made up our minds, something unexpected occurs. As he points out:

> At the very minute when the act is going to be performed, *something* may revolt against it. It is the deep-seated self rushing up to the surface. It is the outer crust bursting, suddenly giving way to an irresistible thrust. Hence in the depths of the self, below this most reasonable pondering over most reasonable pieces of advice, something else was going on—a gradual heating and a sudden boiling over of feelings and ideas, not unperceived, but rather unnoticed. If we turn back to them and carefully scrutinize our memory, we shall see that we had ourselves shaped these ideas, ourselves lived these feelings, but that, through some strange reluctance to exercise our will, we had thrust them back into the darkest depths of our soul whenever they came up to the surface. (*TFW* 169–170)

At times such as these, when a decision rises up, as if out of nowhere, from the deep-seated self, it may appear as if we are acting irrationally. From a certain perspective, this perception is correct.[17] It is often the case that we make decisions that contradict all of our carefully crafted reasons. When this sort of unexpected decision surges up from within us, when we act spontaneously, seemingly without thought (a type of action that is, we will see, very different from impulsive action, which is rooted in habitual emotional/motor reactions), we may not be able to give a precise, easily articulated, and justified explanation for our actions. But according to Bergson, we are actually acting out of the depths of who we are at that moment—the dynamic sum total of our most profound convictions, feelings, and aspirations. [18] Therefore, in cases such as this, we have our reasons, but these reasons are, paradoxically, hidden from us. This sort of decision is, Bergson suggests, based on a type of rationality, in that there are a multitude of reasons that catalyze such a decision, but because these reasons are often hidden from our conscious egos, it is a very odd sort of rationality, a nonconscious variety. This type of decision is not planned, it is not worked out in advance, it may even take us by surprise. However, again paradoxically, such a decision can only be made by *ourselves*, it can only emerge from the most profound dimensions of our being.

Bergson claims that many if not most of us distrust this type of decision-making. We either implicitly or explicitly prefer an algorithm or formula that will automatically give us the answer as to how we should act, especially in moments of difficult decisions. We want life to be predictable; we want it to obey the comforting logic of mathematics. We want to believe that if we start with an initial set of premises, then certain conclusions will inevitably follow—no matter who we are or when we work on the problem. But as Bergson points out, unfortunately (or fortunately!), our personal life does not follow mathematical rules.[19] Because human beings are constantly changing, learning, and growing, "the same reasons may dictate to different persons, or to the same person at different moments, acts profoundly different, although equally reasonable. The truth is that they are not quite the same reasons, since they are not those of the same person, nor of the same moment" (*CE* 7). Since life is constantly in flux, Bergson advises that we learn to know and to trust that aspect of ourselves that is also continually flowing—that is, that we learn how to attune ourselves to what is most deeply and fundamentally real within us: the dynamic, ever-new, yet ever connected, stream of our own consciousness, the depths of durée.

Nonetheless, it would seem that not all decisions made from our depths should be trusted. As Bergson acknowledges (although only in passing and without much theoretical amplification), there are many times in which we do and say and feel things that are very negative, and yet these *impulsive* actions or words or feelings seem to be suspiciously similar to the *spontaneous* actions mentioned previously, in that they seem to emerge very suddenly, without any conscious thought or preparation.[20] We may, for instance, find ourselves, all of a sudden, violently angry at some relatively insignificant comment made by a loved one. This anger may seem to come out of nowhere with great force, arising from the "obscure depths" of our being, from some dimension of ourselves, that is, somehow mysteriously hidden from view (*TFW* 166). All of this—the suddenness, the eruption from hidden depths—may seem to be phenomeno-logically identical to what happens in spontaneous actions. What, therefore, is the difference?

Although Bergson himself does not answer this question in any great detail, it is clear that the difference between spontaneous actions and what I am calling impulsive actions is the "level" or "quality" of selfhood from which these actions emerge. Sudden surges of negative and debilitating emotions and impulsive actions, Bergson posits, originate from a level of selfhood populated by what might be called "psychic cysts" (my term). These "psychic cysts" are self-encased, stagnant, pathological clusters of beliefs that are cut off from integration into the wider, more dynamic, flux of the self. These psychic cysts in certain respects are similar to hypnotic suggestions in that they are hidden, but very potent, clusters of beliefs that seem to come from outside of ourselves, beliefs which have not been incorporated into our conscious personality. These beliefs act as if they are, in the words of Bergson, "endowed with a life of [their] own"; and at moments, seemingly of their own choosing, they spring forth out of hiding and "usurp the whole personality" (*TFW* 166).[21]

Bergson claims that these "independent elements" hidden within us coexist (at perhaps different levels?) with other more complex belief systems—for instance, beliefs that we have memorized at school, beliefs that we have learned but which we have not actually assimilated and made our own, beliefs that we have accepted without any critical evaluation. Therefore, Bergson argues that there is within many (most? all?) people a type of "parasitic self which continu-ally encroaches upon" our more "fundamental self," a layer of subterranean psy-chic existence that, unfortunately, keeps many people trapped in a life in which they never really know their "true freedom" (*TFW* 166).

Bergson's notion of consciousness and freedom in *Time and Free Will* involves an intricate series of unexpected reversals. At first glance, it seems that consciousness/durée should be that which we are most conscious of—what else would we expect from consciousness itself? However, in many ways, just the opposite is true. Ironically, according to Bergson, consciousness/durée is often that which we are *least* conscious of. For instance, durée, even before *Matter and Memory*, is understood by Bergson to be integrally linked with memory—it is at least partially due to the fact that we create a memory of what is occurring right now that our consciousness of the next "moment" remains continually new. Without memory, there is no consciousness (or freedom) for Bergson. However, even in *Time and Free Will*, Bergson also recognizes that the vast majority of our memories is inaccessible and needs to be so in order for us to function. Therefore, durée/consciousness is rooted in and cannot exist without memory, but these memories are for the most part not conscious (at least to our everyday self).

Furthermore, Bergson links durée/consciousness with the deep-seated self. This deep self, however, is *also* said to be for the most part hidden from view and very difficult to access. On the other hand, the superficial self, that aspect of our selfhood that is explicitly non-durée-like in nature, is for most of us a very apparent, easily experienced element of who we are. Therefore, once again, consciousness/durée itself, in this case understood as our true nature, as who we are in our depths, is what is most hidden, whereas who we are at our most superficial, when we are most unreal, is what is most apparent, most conscious.

It gets even more complicated. According to Bergson, it seems that in our depths we do not just find the flowing, connected, ever-changing reality of durée that is the source of our freedom. We also find these "psychic cysts" that are the source of so much of our bondage and suffering. To complicate matters even further, it seems as if some of the beliefs that have come into us from the outside and which have not been integrated into our wholeness do not dwell on the surface level of our consciousness as part of our superficial self. Instead, these undigested belief systems coexist in the subterranean depths of our being with the more primitive, more overtly negative, "psychic cysts," creating a sort of unholy alliance resulting in a "parasitic self" that robs us of our freedom.

One further, and for the moment, final, complication: Bergson eloquently describes how we cheat ourselves of our freedom, both by living a superficial life that panders to social expectations and, more mysteriously, by letting ourselves be swept away by hidden dimensions of our own being that are fragmented, isolated, and nonintegrated into the totality of who we are. (This whole process itself is fraught with puzzling paradoxes: How is it possible to have partial selves that are simultaneously both us and not us? Who is swept away by whom?) However, it is not as simple as "we once were free, and now we are not." As Bergson comments (in a lengthy and insightful footnote in *Time and Free Will*), "the process of our free activity goes on, as it were, unknown to ourselves, in the obscure depths of our consciousness at every moment of duration" (*TFW* 237–238). That is, underneath it all, in-and-through our visceral and undeniable awareness of our blocks, our limitations, our superficiality, we are, nonetheless, always free. The very real fragmentation and atomization of our consciousness does not, somehow, amazingly, touch durée; we are still one self, one consciousness. The parts still flow, the fragments still connect.[22]

I want to be clear here. I am not critiquing Bergson for inconsistency or internal contradictions. In fact I think that he could be even more willing to assert the paradoxical nature of the layerings and complications that occur within the very heart of our consciousness. I do, however, think that Bergson's work in *Time and Free Will* is a worthwhile and extremely interesting place to begin to ponder the stunning complexity of what it means to be a human being.

Bergson's discussion of the understanding of the nature of consciousness and its relationship to genuine freedom in *Time and Free Will* is, I believe, extremely persuasive and helpful. However, *Time and Free Will* is primarily a philosophical analysis (albeit an extremely insightful one). It does not really offer much in the way of concrete suggestions as to how we might live a life that is more authentic, more free, more creative. Bergson presents an intriguing vision of the deep-seated self and the superficial self, but there are very few specific suggestions as to how we might cultivate our depths and diminish our tendency to cling to externals.[23] He is clear that genuinely free actions that are attuned to the depths of our being are possible as the result of rigorous introspective work, but he does not really give us any clues as to what factors might block access to the depths of our being, how we might overcome these inner barriers, or (at least in any detail or depth) how these mental and/or emotional obstacles might distort our decision-making process. Nonetheless, by revisioning who we are in our depths as inherently creative, dynamic, fluid, and free, Bergson in *Time and Free Will* sets the stage for his future work, in which he investigates the interplay between matter and spirit, explores the nature of the relationship between our deeper self and reality as a whole, and begins the process of articulating how it might be possible to be attuned to levels of inspiration and guidance that transcend the boundaries of our personality.

LIMINAL SECTION

THE DYNAMISM OF MATTER

8

THE WORLD "OUT THERE"

PLAYING WITH THE SPACE IN-BETWEEN

Section 1 focuses on *Time and Free Will*, Bergson's first book, a text which offers a relatively straightforward, more-or-less accessible account of the contrast between durée and space, inner versus outer, freedom versus determinism, and so on. In section 2, however, we will quite quickly leave behind the basically dualistic mindset of *Time and Free Will* and enter, almost abruptly, into a very different world—the dense, multilayered, highly abstract, almost visionary landscape of Bergson's second major work, *Matter and Memory*. In *Matter and Memory*, without any warning or acknowledgment, Bergson lets go of what Milič Čapek calls the "untenable dualism of the temporal mind and timeless matter" and, instead, articulates a worldview in which durée is seen as the ever-changing substance of not only our psychological experience, but also of the external material world.[1] In *Matter and Memory*, therefore, Bergson essentially affirms a type of nondualism, albeit one that is highly unusual and difficult to grasp—a temporal, dynamic nondualism that ironically strongly affirms the reality of a functional dualism.

However, before we plunge into the oceanic (and highly daunting) waters of *Matter and Memory*, I offer this liminal interlude as a way to start to imagine a world in which durée is, in Deleuze's words, "the variable essence of things," a world in which the fluidity, mutability, interpenetrability, and creativity of durée is found in the world of material objects as well.[2] In this bridge between sections 1 and 2, I explore how things shift when we start to see the outer world through the lens of durée—when we start to see it less as a collection of static, discrete objects exchanging places in an immutable empty space and more as functional islands of semi-stability arising out of a highly mutable flux of becoming.[3]

71

SPLITTING UP THE WORLD

From Bergson's post–*Time and Free Will* perspective, the external world, if understood correctly, is not split up into parts. Rather, in a way that is similar to our consciousness, the material universe is an interconnected, flowing, ever-changing, dynamic process. In both our inner and outer worlds, nothing is static, nothing is immutable. Instead, as Bergson succinctly states, "movement is reality itself" (*CM* 169).

Bergson recognizes that, on a practical level, we need to think that we are stable subjects interacting with a world of equally stable objects and that we will therefore tend to minimize and overlook the constant change that surrounds us. However, even if we intellectually recognize that everything is constantly changing, nonetheless, on a deeper level, as human beings with certain deeply engrained tendencies, we prefer to overlook or ignore the extent and depth of the change that takes place in our lives. At best, while we might grudgingly acknowledge that change occurs, we still *act* as if it only affects the surface of things—that is, we are unconsciously wired with the conviction that, underneath it all, both we and the world are stable and dependably nonchanging. From the perspective of our day-to-day experience, it seems almost impossible to give anything more than a token nod to Bergson's claim that "there do not exist *things* made, but only things in the making, not *states* that remain fixed, but only states in the process of change" (*CM* 222). We can be as Bergsonian (or for that matter as Taoist or Buddhist) as we like philosophically, but in our day-to-day experience we certainly do not act as if "things" do not exist.

In order for us to survive, Bergson argues that we (both as a species and individually) have learned how to convert the ceaseless onrush of universal change into separate, relatively stable objects that "we" (as separate, relatively stable subjects) attempt to manipulate to our advantage. As Bergson puts it, our various needs and desires (e.g., to eat, to procreate, to relate to others) act as "so many searchlights" which shine upon the continuity of our sense experience and "single out in it distinct bodies. They cannot satisfy themselves except upon the condition that they carve out, within this continuity, a body which is to be their own and then delimit other bodies" which they can then interact with in practical ways (*MM* 198).

Bergson argues, therefore, that the external world is *not* innately structured as a collection of separate "pieces" of matter. Instead, *we create* this perception of the physical world due to a series of biological imperatives (to mate, to gather food, and so forth). This set of innate and insistent urges that function outside of our conscious awareness effectively fractures the fluid continuity of life in order to engender the seemingly necessary illusion of a stable "us" that interacts with a series of equally stable objects. Our ordinary lived experience, therefore, while practically useful, is nonetheless philosophically deceptive.

9

MOVEMENT

═══════════

MOTION AS A WHOLE

From a Bergsonian perspective, "reality is mobility itself" (*CM* 177). Bergson is careful with his phrasing here. He does not say that reality is that which moves or that reality is in constant motion—a phrasing that would imply that reality is a "thing" that has motion added to it. Instead, for Bergson, reality is, in-and-of-itself, motion. He continually attempts to disabuse us of the idea that motion is an accidental quality that is added to a preexisting, permanent, self-enclosed, otherwise stable and steady "thing" (regardless of whether that "thing" is as small as an electron or as large as the entire universe). He argues that our "irresistible tendency" to see ourselves as part of a discontinuous material universe that is "composed of bodies that have clearly defined outlines and change their place [in] relation with each other," needs to be examined and forcefully challenged (*MM* 197). As he points out, this way of understanding the universe is not found in immediate intuition, and it is also (as we will soon see) not supported by post-Newtonian scientific understandings.

Bergson asks, therefore, that we change how we think about change. Instead of seeing change as something which happens to permanent, substantive, individual bodies/things in a homogeneous, unchanging space, he asks us to "purely and simply realize that the whole has changed, as with the turning of a kaleidoscope"; he asks us to embrace the notion that the entire "continuity [of material extensity] changes from moment to moment" (*MM* 197). From this perspective, there is no need for us to insist that some unchanging substratum is underneath the change, there is no need for an artificial bond to link together isolated, separate objects. Instead, Bergson argues, if we see "things" correctly, we will recognize that *there are changes, but there are underneath the change no things which change: change has no need of a support. There are movements, but there is no inert*

73

or invariable object which moves" (*CM* 173; Bergson's emphasis). Understood correctly, change is itself "the very substance of things" (*CM* 184).[1]

As we have seen, Bergson's claim that change is the most basic stuff of the universe relies heavily on his subtle and insightful analysis of movement. What Bergson attempts to do is to argue that motion is not something that occurs when unchanging "atom-like" particles move about in space. Instead, according to Bergson, movement itself is what is primary.

However, as we saw in section 1, human beings resist recognizing the primacy of change and motion, even within our own consciousness. Instead, we prefer to take a "cinematographic" view of durée in which we "freeze frame" the ceaseless flux of our consciousness into a successive series of immobile pictures. What Bergson does, after *Time and Free Will*, is to take this "cinematographic" understanding of consciousness as a paradigm for understanding how we perceive *all* of reality. In this way, he is able to claim that we continually "take snapshots, as it were, of the passing reality" and then string these "snapshots" together to form the "film" of our day-to-day experience (*CE* 306).

Another metaphorical way to understand our inherent and deeply human attempt to "freeze" reality is to imagine a gushing fountain of water. Let's say that we are constantly attempting to reach out and grab at this water so that we can contain it and measure it, but it keeps slipping through our fingers. Therefore, in order to get a "handle" on all of this ceaseless change, we turn the water into pellets of ice by blasting the streaming water with a jet of super-cooled air. The problem, however, is that by "pelletizing" the water we lose the very essence of what water is—we lose its flowing nature—especially when we attempt to line these pellets next to each other to count, weigh, and measure them. Furthermore, because we have created separate units where there was once fluid wholeness, we are forced to artificially "recompose" the fragments that we have created in order to patch together a meaningful pattern and purpose to it all. Similarly, Bergson claims that, in our attempts to piece together some coherence from the frozen fragments of life, we overlook the ever-changing organic order and interconnectedness of what was always there: the underlying, fundamental reality of movement itself (*CE* 306).

To further illustrate Bergson's "cinematographic" view of reality, this time using an example that is explicitly Bergson's, let's examine a common understanding of what happens if a person's hand moves from one point in space to another. (Notice how language itself continually reinforces the notions that Bergson is disputing—the notion of fixed points and an empty, container-like space.) Bergson claims that instead of limiting our perception to the actual movement of the hand, what commonly occurs is that we tacitly superimpose a type of mathematical abstraction upon our immediate perception. We do this by imagining that the hand's movement is taking place in a line that could, theoretically, be plotted from, let's say, point A to point B.

However, there is a problem with our superimposition of this imaginary line: a line is mathematically understood to consist of a series of static, motionless points. How can motion possibly come from something that is, by definition, frozen? What happens, therefore, is that in our attempts to analyze the movement of the person's hand, we miss the point; we have frozen motion itself. We might well be able to divide up the abstract trajectory of the person's hand into a multitude of fixed points on an imaginary line, but the actual movement of his/her hand can never arise out of these static points. As Bergson notes, "multiply the number of them as you will, let the interval between two consecutive [points] be infinitely small: before the intervening movement you will always experience the disappointment of the child who tries by clapping his hands together to crush the smoke. The movement slips through the interval, because every attempt to reconstitute change out of [immobile points] implies the absurd proposition, that movement is made of immobilities" (*CE* 308).

However, in science's attempt to measure movement, it acts as if motion actually is the sum total of the static positions in space occupied by a moving body (e.g., a hand or an atom or a planet), it acts as if a movement actually can be plotted as a collection of unmoving points on a line.[2] Science, in many respects, relies on these static points because, like the ice pellets in our earlier example, points are easily and usefully measured and calculated. However, as Bergson notes, even as early as *Time and Free Will*, what classical physics does not do and in fact cannot do is to measure motion itself. All that it can do is to measure various static points, for instance, when an object/particle begins to move, when it stops, and the space it traverses. The problem, however, is that movement, by its very nature, is never *at* a stationary point. It would only be *at* a point if it stopped, but if it stopped, then it would no longer be movement. As Bergson puts it, a "moving body occupies, one after the other, points on a line," but "motion itself has nothing to do with a line" (*TFW* 120). The stopping points on the line of our imagination are simply useful constructs. Mathematics, astronomy, engineering, and technology can do marvels with these mathematical points, but ultimately, these points, as such, are not real.

What *is* real is motion, what *is* real is movement itself. According to Bergson, the only way to come to know what movement is, in-and-of-itself, is to place ourselves within it. It is only in the immediacy of our own perceptions that we can come to know that movement cannot be divided into parts; that is, the reality of movement only truly reveals itself when we plunge into durée. When we are immersed in the immediacy of durée, what we see is a reality that extends beyond the boundary of our personal consciousness; what we see is a reality that is sheer movement, a reality that, in the words of Marie Cariou, "is characterized by the absence of instants and . . . far from being reconstituted by the sum of its parts, excludes the very idea of parts. It is a whole which cannot be broken down without being destroyed in the same gesture."[3]

CATCHING UP WITH ZENO

Bergson's discussion of the indivisibility and continuity of movement emerges out of his novel response to a series of paradoxes that were constructed approximately twenty-six centuries ago by the Greek thinker, Zeno of Elea. Zeno's terse paradoxes are famous for their brilliant attempt to rationally demonstrate something that everyone knows is not true: that motion does not exist. Bergson frequently comments on Zeno's paradoxes—his observations on these logical dilemmas are peppered throughout his work. Yet, perhaps because these paradoxes were so well known to intellectuals in the late nineteenth and early twentieth centuries, Bergson never bothers to actually describe them clearly and concisely. Therefore, in the interest of thoroughness, I present three stripped-down versions of these paradoxes.

1) *The Dichotomy*: A runner, starting a race at a certain point, attempts to reach the goal. However, he cannot reach it except by traversing successive "halves" of the total distance. Thus, if he runs half of the distance to the goal, he must then run half of the remaining distance to the goal, and then he must yet again run half of this distance, and so forth. Keep in mind that, to reach the goal, the runner must traverse *all* of the various half-intervals. However, the problem is there are an *infinite* number of these half intervals. Therefore, because it is impossible to complete an infinite sequence of half-intervals in a finite time, the runner will not and cannot ever reach the goal.

2) *The Race between Achilles and the Tortoise*: In this race the tortoise takes a step. Then Achilles, starting one moment later than the tortoise, takes a step, arriving on the spot where the tortoise had just been, prior to its first step. However, while Achilles is taking his step, the tortoise again has moved on, taking yet another step. So each time, as Achilles takes another step forward, he only reaches the spot where the tortoise had just been, since by this time the tortoise has moved on again. Therefore, Achilles will never be able to pass the tortoise.

3) *The Arrow*: An arrow in flight appears to move, but it does not. Anytime that the arrow actually *is* at any point on the line of its flight, that point is a duration-less, static point. Therefore, anytime that the arrow is actually at a specific point on the line of its flight, it cannot also be moving. Hence, the arrow is always motionless.[4]

What each of these paradoxes have in common is the understanding that in order to get from one stationary point (A) to another stationary point (B), an object or a person has to traverse a line AB, and this line, in accordance with Euclidean geometry, consists of an infinite series of juxtaposed, immobile, successive points.[5] Therefore, as Keith Ansell Pearson notes, because the "interval between two points is infinitely divisible, and if motion is said to consist of parts like those of the interval itself, then the interval can never be crossed."[6]

What Zeno's paradoxes effectively demonstrate is that motion is not and *cannot* be composed of immobile points—a claim that Bergson strongly endorses. Where Bergson differs from Zeno (or at least a common interpretation of Zeno), is that Zeno concludes therefore that motion is not real (a conclusion that is historically linked to subsequent Greek philosophical attempts to ground reality in a realm untouched by time and movement).[7] Bergson, on the other hand, argues that motion (or change) is *all* that is real. The paradoxes of Zeno create a dilemma: either motion and time are illusory or the logical/mathematical structure that underscores classical physics is flawed. For Bergson, the choice is clear: our immediate experience shows us that the runner does reach the goal, Achilles easily passes the tortoise, and the arrow really does fly. Movement as a continuous, temporal flux is a felt, lived experience that each of us can verify. Therefore, instead of giving priority to a certain type of logical argumentation, we should trust what we know directly. As Vladimir Jankélévitch comments, Bergson is in essence saying, "Do not listen to what Zeno of Elea says, look at what Achilles does."[8]

10

AN ATOMISTIC
UNDERSTANDING OF REALITY

UNCHANGING ATOMS OR UNIVERSAL FLUX?

Bergson's claims that motion (or, more generally, change) is all that is real and that this motion is not divisible into parts flies in the face of millennia of philosophical, mathematical, and scientific theorizing in the West. Both the Pythagoreans and the Platonists, in different ways, argued that change was illusory. Similarly, the Greek atomists Leucippus and Democritus, like the Pythagoreans and the Platonists, sought to discover an unchanging Absolute reality underneath the change that we all experience in our day-to-day reality. For these fifth-century BCE atomists, the Absolute was not to be found in the changeless mathematical laws of Pythagoras or the changeless Platonic world of the Forms or even in the changeless, undifferentiated sphere of Parmenides. Rather, as Rupert Sheldrake notes, for the Greek atomists, the Absolute was to be found in "many tiny, undifferentiated, changeless things—material atoms moving in the void."[1] Atoms were understood by these early Greek thinkers to be permanent and indestructible. (The word "atom" itself refers to that which cannot be split.) Further, change was understood to be nothing more than the "movement and combination and rearrangement of these real but invisible particles."[2] For the Greek atomists, the entire universe was, in essence, one giant Lego puzzle, in that every object (regardless of its shape or size) was understood to be constructed from different arrangements of a few basic atomic building blocks. From this point of view, the external world may appear to be changing, but seen correctly, change only takes place on the surface of things. What we call change is really nothing more than a temporary rearrangement of changeless atoms.

This notion of changeless atoms itself changed little over the centuries. As Fritjof Capra notes, from the time of the early Greek atomists through the formulations of Newton, atoms were thought to be "small, solid, and indestructible objects out of which all matter is made."[3] From a Bergsonian point of view, there are several good reasons for the durability of this "building-block" understanding of reality. This canonical perspective of science has lasted the past several centuries not only because of its theoretical usefulness and practical value, but also because it emerges naturally from our sense experience, which appears to show us a world in which solid, compact bodies move through empty space. The notion of atoms is, therefore, simply an abstract version of what our naïve sense experience tells us is the case, applied to the realm of the very small.

It is not surprising, therefore, that the early theorists of classical physics eventually came to envision atoms and molecules as, in essence, minute billiard balls bouncing off each other in a variety of complex configurations with mathematical, lawful, and predictable precision. As Bergson notes, because this image of physical reality springs from our naïve sense experience, it is extremely difficult to let go of the tacit belief that the universe consists of unchanging particles moving in an empty void—a void itself seen as, in the words of Čapek, a "passive, all-embracing, homogeneous container."[4] The tenacity by which we cling to this understanding of reality also seems to be exacerbated by certain deeply rooted biological tendencies. As Jean Piaget's work clearly demonstrates, very early on in their developmental process, children spontaneously tend toward an atomistic understanding of the world.[5] Further complicating matters is the fact that this way of viewing the world, especially when it is combined with the notion of unchanging mathematical laws (a synthesis created by Newton), has had enormous practical utility. In many ways it would not be inaccurate to argue that technological achievements of the industrial age are a direct result of this "corpuscular-kinetic" view of material reality.

MINI-RUMINATION: POROUS BODIES

If our sense experience and our practical life tell us that an atomistic view of the universe is accurate, then why should we not simply accept this way of understanding the world? The problem is that, while our senses, practically speaking, are correct, nonetheless, from a deeper perspective (both philosophically and scientifically), the information that we receive from our senses is, while not entirely false, at least radically oversimplified and incomplete. If we look closely, for example, at our own bodies, it is not too difficult to discern that they are not the impervious, tightly sealed, self-contained objects that we imagine them to be when we see them through the lens of an atomistic point of view. We might like to imagine that our bodies are solid, cohesive wholes that are completely separate from other similarly configured objects. But a closer examination reveals something entirely different.

For instance, as I breathe in and out, it is not exactly clear where my body begins and the external world ends (and vice versa). As I breathe in air, the oxygen and water vapor it contains is taken into my body and becomes an integral component of my physical functioning. That much is clear. However, what is *not* so apparent is exactly when the oxygen and water vapor that begins as an "outside" or a "not-me" becomes, somehow, almost miraculously, an "inside," an integral aspect of "me."

The process of digestion raises similar questions. For instance, the broccoli that I ate for lunch today was, before I ate it, clearly external to my body. And as I bit into it and chewed it in my mouth, it was also external (I could easily spit it out). But when I swallowed it, the question of its "me-ness" becomes a bit murkier. (For instance, what if I was bulimic and decided that I needed to throw up my lunch in order to stay thin? Is the masticated broccoli that emerges part of me?) As with the air I breathe—at what exact point does this external/"not-me" something become internal/"me"? When does the food I eat change from being an external object inserted into my body to being an intrinsic part of my physical body?[6]

As we saw with the example of the bulimic, the act of something exiting the body raises just as many pertinent questions about the boundaries of "me"/"not-me" as something entering the body. As Mary Douglas' work so helpfully points out, it is perhaps not accidental that we treat the substances that exit our body with, at best, suspicion and concern, and at worst, with disgust and revulsion.[7] It is perhaps also not accidental that in numerous cultures, these "liminal" substances (including cut hair or nail clippings) are often hedged about with numerous taboos, and that they are frequently used as the basis for magical rituals. There is an enormous emotional charge that surrounds feces, urine, sweat, spit, phlegm, breast milk, menses, and tears. Could at least part of this emotional intensity have to do with the anxiety that we feel in the face of the fact that these substances powerfully challenge the boundaries that we seek to erect between us and the outer world?

Finally, there are numerous "vibratory" realities (such as gravitational fields and electromagnetic fields)—fields of force that extend to and from the "limits" of the universe—that every moment penetrate and affect my physical body. These energetic fields operate, for the most part, beneath my conscious awareness, but this spectrum of universal influence also provides the physical substratum for many of my most basic visceral experiences. (For example, I can see the world around me only because I am connected to it through the electromagnetic field in which the particular vibratory energy of light travels.)[8] I could not exist, physically, as who I am unless I was constantly interpenetrated by these various energetic waves. But are they, therefore, somehow part of "me" in the same way as oxygen and food? If not, why?

It is clear that our physical bodies as well as all other physical objects are nowhere near as bounded, unchanging, and separate from each other as we might tacitly imagine. Instead, the belief that we, in our physicality, are nugget-like, self-contained, essentially stable objects interacting with other distinct, nugget-like objects is, at best, a simplification brought on by the practical necessities of life. At worst, it is a gross distortion that prompts us to forget our underlying connection to, and dependence upon, the rest of the universe.

11

GOING BEYOND CLASSICAL PHYSICS

BEYOND MECHANISM

In the late nineteenth century it was widely assumed that classical physics had a basically complete knowledge of the external universe. It was taken for granted that the universe was, in essence, a giant, utterly implacable, machine that runs on its own, fueled only by rigorous mathematical laws and (since the time of Darwin) sheer blind chance. This is the vision of the universe that was endorsed by Bertrand Russell in 1903, when he claimed that all of the basic aspects of this mechanistic understanding of the universe (such as atomism, determinism, motionless space, and so on) were "if not quite beyond dispute, are yet so nearly certain, that no philosophy which rejects them can hope to stand."[1] Other influential thinkers of the time shared Russell's perspective. For instance, Ernst Haeckel claimed that all of "the riddles of the universe" had been solved, while Marcellin Berthelot declared that "the world is now without mysteries."[2]

Not surprisingly, however, these assertions were quickly shown to be simply more evidence of human hubris. Beginning in the first decade of the twentieth century and rapidly gaining momentum after that, physicists began to make a series of impressive discoveries (from relativity theories dealing with the macro-universe to quantum theory dealing with the micro-universe). These discoveries were so revolutionary that their philosophical implications have still not made much headway. However, at least within the close-knit circle of physics, it has been acknowledged that the previous atomistic and mechanistic model of the universe that had been assumed by classical physicists as well as by many, if not most, early twentieth-century intellectuals is no longer an adequate account of nature—at least in the realms of the very small (i.e., on the subatomic level) and the very large (i.e., on the level of stars and galaxies).[3]

CONTRA ATOMISM

From the perspective of contemporary physics, a stone may appear to be a thick, heavy, passive, and unmoving object, but in its depths, on a subatomic level, all that exists is a blur of activity, a throb of energy. The inside of atoms resemble not small inert chunks of matter, but an intricate dance of vibrating motion, a dynamic structure of rhythmic patterns. It is at best only partially correct to conceive of subatomic particles as tiny objects that move around with enormous velocity. More accurately, subatomic particles are, themselves, nothing but process. This is a world of "happenings" (and potentialities), not a world of "stuff," a world of verbs, not nouns, a world that, in the words of Fritjof Capra, can best be conceived as "an inseparable network of interactions involving a ceaseless flow of energy manifesting itself as the exchange of particles," not a world of isolated, stable, and solid entities.[4] In this world, what are often (still) referred to as particles are not tiny, unchanging, "objects," but rather, are intrinsically dynamic, fluid processes, involving, on the one hand, a spatial dimension (the material, cloud-like "particle" form), and on the other hand, an equally prominent temporal dimension (the energetic pattern, the wave-like flux).

The wave-like aspect of subatomic reality as envisioned by quantum theory underscores the inherent temporality of matter. Whereas classical physics claims that a particle (or "corpuscle") with its eternally fixed spatial dimensions does not need time to be what it is, a wave cannot be a wave unless it unfolds in time. A wave that is frozen at a certain instant of time, a wave that no longer undulates, a wave that does not develop *in* time (or better, *as* a form of time) is no longer a wave.[5] A wave that has been frozen and chopped up into a series of static Zenoian instants is not a wave any longer. Instead, in order to be a wave, a wave has to occupy a certain quantity of duration (because vibrations take time!).

In a way that is strikingly similar to Bergson's claim that there are no "things" that change, but rather only change itself, quantum physics prompts us to understand physical reality as a "universe which is an inseparable whole and where all forms are fluid and ever-changing."[6] On a subatomic level, physical objects have no real independent existence. Instead, from the perspective of quantum physics, objects exist only as interwoven threads of a vast, all-encompassing, ever-changing pattern, in which each thread is intrinsically interlaced with every other thread. Or to change metaphors, instead of dancers changing positions on the cosmic stage of empty space, there seems to be only the dance of wholeness itself, constantly whirling and spinning, ceaselessly creating new rhythms and movements. In the words of David Bohm (a prominent physicist whose philosophical perspectives put him in opposition to the more pragmatic, "agnostic" Copenhagen interpretation of quantum theory):

> One is led to a new notion of unbroken wholeness, which denies the
> classical idea of analyzability of the world into separately and independ-
> ently existing parts. . . . We have reversed the usual classical notion that
> the independent "elementary parts" of the world are the fundamental
> reality, and that the various systems are merely particular contingent
> forms and arrangements of these parts. Rather, we say that inseparable
> quantum interconnectedness of the whole universe is the fundamental
> reality, and that relatively independently behaving parts are merely par-
> ticular and contingent forms within this whole.[7]

What quantum physics underscores again and again is the fact that the classical notion of atomism is not only misleading, but fundamentally flawed. *All* of
the characteristics previously ascribed to particles from the early Greek atomists
through Newton are wrong—particles are not indestructible or uncreated; they
are not immutable, and they are not clearly localized in space. As Čapek succinctly puts it, "*they are not particles at all.*"[8]

It is very difficult for us, as human beings, to give up the idea that particles
are tiny, self-sufficient balls of matter whizzing through empty space, but as
Bergson argued, decades before physics came around to his way of thinking, this
commonsense understanding is simply not the truth. It is meaningless to think
of "billiard ball-like" particles cascading and rebounding in the void. There is no
void, there are no billiard ball particles. Instead, what we find is a universe filled
to the brim with ceaseless dynamism, a universe permeated with complex, interpenetrating, and overlapping fields, a universe that is *itself* nothing but motion
and change.

From the perspective of quantum physics, the understanding of the universe
as a type of giant Clock has been smashed, not into tiny bits, but rather into a
vortex of interconnecting vibrations and fields. Atoms which were, at one point,
thought to be indestructible and unchanging chunks of matter are now viewed as
complex interactions of dynamic fields of energy. Empty space is now considered
to be a vibrant ocean of potentiality, a matrix from which countless numbers of
particles emerge and disappear. And the rigid determinism assumed by classical
physics has softened into a complex science of tendencies and probabilities.[9]

BERGSON SAID IT FIRST

Astonishingly, the non-atomistic vision of material reality that is articulated by
quantum physics is strikingly similar to what Bergson had anticipated in 1896
(when *Matter and Memory* was published). At this time, the revolutions that
were about to overtake physics were just barely on the horizon. Nonetheless,
even then, Bergson was convinced that we would never be able to explain the

nature of material reality if we continue to think that it is composed of discrete particles, of stable objects that move about from place to place in an unchanging space. In *Matter and Memory*, Bergson argued that matter cannot be reduced to atoms moving in the void, if only because of the fact that something else exists as well: energy or force. Even at the end of the nineteenth century, it was recognized that various types of forces seem to operate *between* atoms (e.g., the forces of attraction and repulsion that bind or separate molecules or the force of gravity). But Bergson was not convinced that there was an ontological difference between these forces and atoms. He hypothesized that the only reason why we distinguish between the seemingly solid matter of atoms and the more amorphous reality of various forces is that, from the standpoint of our survival needs, we urgently attempt to "distinguish, in our daily experience, between passive *things* and *actions* effected by these things in space" (*MM* 200).

In effect, Bergson was suggesting that our tendency to think that atoms are solid objects is based more on our deeply ingrained need to carve up the world into dense unchanging things than from any innate structure that atoms might possess. He was convinced that it was likely that, in the future, as science progressed, we would "see force more and more materialized, the atom more and more idealized, the two terms converging toward a common limit and the universe thus recovering its continuity" (*MM* 200). He predicted that with this convergence of matter and energy (a convergence that was realized with Einstein's famous equation, $E = mc^2$), scientists would continue to speak in terms of individual atoms (if for no other reason than from their habitual and human need to have a distinct "picture" of what they are studying), but theoretically, they would increasingly realize that the seeming "solidity and the inertia of the atom" is not real (*MM* 200). Instead, what is real, what is fundamental, is either a variety of "movements" or "lines of force" (cosmic in scope) that overlap and interpenetrate each other to such an extent that the focus would inevitably shift from extremely tiny, highly localized interactions to a more basic "universal continuity" (*MM* 200).

Therefore, decades before the revolutionary findings of quantum physics, Bergson was sure that science would eventually discover that even atoms themselves are not unchanging. As he put it in the introduction to *Creative Mind* (an introduction that he wrote several years after *Matter and Memory*):

> When I began to write [*Matter and Memory*], physics had not yet made the decisive advances which were to bring a change in its ideas on the structure of matter. But convinced, even then, that immobility and invariability were only views taken of moving and changing reality, I could not believe that matter, whose solid image had been obtained through the immobilization of changes . . . was composed of solid elements. (*CM* 84)

By the time that Bergson wrote the essay "The Perception of Change" (several decades after *Matter and Memory*), he was beginning to feel that his predictions were becoming reality. By that time, his radical claims about the nature of matter were step by step gaining support from the findings of physics. Increasingly, scientists spoke of matter less in terms of elementary bits of solidity and more in terms of motion or vibrations. Year by year, the seemingly solid support of matter increasingly evaporated: molecules were resolved into atoms, which in turn were broken down into subatomic particles, until, finally, it was recognized that these particles were better understood as "a simple concession on the part of the scholar to the habits of our visual imagination" (*CM* 175). The more that scientists began to carefully investigate the properties of matter, the less that the incredibly minute particles studied by quantum physics began to look and act like discrete, self-contained bits of matter, and the more they began to look like vibrating, indeterminate patterns of energy. (This was also, as noted previously, the meaning of Einstein's famous equation $E = mc^2$, which fused together what were previously thought of as two fundamental physical realities—mass and energy.)[10]

It is difficult for us, from our twenty-first-century perspective, to realize just how daring Bergson's vision of matter was. As Čapek points out, when *Matter and Memory* was published in 1896, "hardly anyone could then guess even remotely the extent of the coming scientific revolution."[11] Čapek goes on to note that when Bergson's understandings of the nature of matter first appeared in *Matter and Memory* in 1896, "they appeared, in contrast to the prevailing classical picture of the physical world, so grotesquely improbable, that they were largely ignored."[12] Even after Bergson's ideas on time, evolution, and intuition became well known with the publication of *Creative Evolution*, his previous extremely complex analysis of matter in *Matter and Memory* was essentially ignored. However, seen from the vantage point of our current understandings of the nature of the physical world, it can now be acknowledged that Bergson's theoretical perspective on matter, far from being dated and passé, is actually a remarkably sophisticated philosophical position, one that anticipated and mirrors many, if not most, of the findings of modern physics.

In a commentary on the correspondence between the findings of quantum physics and Bergson's thought, Louis de Broglie (a noted quantum physicist) points out that in the decades before the experimental findings of quantum physics, Bergson essentially came to many, if not most, of the same conclusions.[13] De Broglie points out that several of Bergson's most important insights antedate "by forty years the ideas of [the well-known quantum physicists] Niels Bohr and Werner Heisenberg."[14] Gunter agrees with de Broglie's assessment and goes on to assert that Bergson's understandings of the physical world were "remarkably prophetic," since many of Bergson's philosophical contributions were in fact "both *precise* and *specific* anticipations of the course of twentieth-century physics"—for example, Bergson's insight that motion does not need "a static *thing* which moves"; his notion that matter is composed of interpenetrating and continuous "pulses of energy each having a finite breadth of duration"; and his "recommendation . . . that physicists look for measurable indeterminism in the behavior of very small 'units' of matter."[15]

Therefore, in a way that is remarkably congruent with (but not identical to) the discoveries of contemporary physics, Bergson's vision of matter challenges almost all of the classical Newtonian conceptions of the physical universe: Newton's internally unchanging particles with specific locations in space make way for Bergson's notion of wave-like phenomena that undulate, in a fluid continuity, from one end of the cosmos to the other; Newton's conception of an absolute time created by stringing together a series of duration-less instants is replaced by a pulsational universe in which different textures of durée create the ever-changing "stuff" of reality; and the determinism and reversibility of Newton's linear equations is exchanged for a world in which nothing is ever repeated and genuine newness and creativity have a place.

12

MELODIES OF THE SELF AND THE WORLD

MATTER AS MELODY

If it no longer makes sense to conceive of the universe as consisting of various tiny Lego-like building blocks arranged in different rigidly determined configurations, is there, nonetheless, some sort of workable metaphor that can help us to begin to make sense of the subatomic underpinnings of our sense experience? We have already seen how various contemporary physicists have drawn upon the metaphors of webs and weaving and dance in an attempt to correct our tendency to imagine the cosmos as consisting of a collection of disconnected chunks of matter. Bergson, however, offers us another, less visual, analog drawn from our daily experience: a musical melody.

As we have already seen in section 1, Bergson frequently uses the metaphor of melody to help illustrate some of the qualities that can be found in the temporal onrush of our consciousness. So it is not surprising to find that Bergson would also be drawn to "hearing" the *physical* world as a complex interwoven symphony of sound in his post–*Time and Free Will* writings, especially in light of his decision to extend durée from the confines of our inner world into the external world as well.[1]

There are several reasons why the metaphors of music and melody are a natural way for Bergson to express his understanding of the nature of reality (besides the interesting fact, as we saw in the bio-historical preamble, that his father was himself a musician and composer). To begin with, by shifting the focus of our attention from sight to sound, Bergson attempts to catalyze a radical, if difficult to attain, alteration in how we orient ourselves to the world around us.

As a species whose sense experience is primarily visual in nature, we are predisposed to make sense of the world through the medium and metaphors of sight. Our dependence upon sight means that we intrinsically focus our attention on, and tend to "see," a world made up of an assortment of various permanent objects that stay basically the same, whether they are moving or at rest. For instance (drawing upon a helpful illustration by A. R. Lacey), let's say that we pick up a football and throw it. During the time that the ball flies through the air, our sense of sight tells us that it stays the same shape as it is thrown through the air. What we see is a solid, unchanging object that just happens to be moving. Our sense of sight convinces us, therefore, that the movement of the football is something that is incidental, something that has been added to it.[2]

However, as Lacey goes on to point out, our sense of hearing reveals a very different world to us. For instance, if we listen intently to a young woman singing a song, what will we hear? If we listen attentively enough, we will hear a constant flux of sound manifesting as various changes in pitch, volume, and rhythm. We may, especially if we are musically trained, preconsciously chop up the music into a set of musical notes and hear those specific notes overlaid with our previous experience with musical scores. But if we resolutely return to the "raw material" of what our ears reveal to us and put to one side our visual prejudices and training, what we will hear is not a set of stable, utterly separate notes. Instead, we will hear a variety of constantly changing vibratory qualities that mingle and co-sound. In a way that is very different from our experience with sight, there are no constant, stable "things" that change in all of this sonic dynamism. Rather than hearing notes change, "noting" is happening, "toning" is happening. Substantive nouns do not work all that well in a sonic world of ceaseless flux.[3]

Understanding the world through the metaphor of music underscores the fact that reality is intrinsically temporal. A melody (like an energy wave) cannot, by its very nature, exist without time. A melody cannot just manifest itself in an instant, utterly complete and whole. Instead, it unfolds and appears over time, note by note, phrase by phrase. We might like to think that a melody can in fact exist, timelessly, in the form of a static collection of notes written on the paper of a score (in much the same way that we might prefer to believe that the physical universe is reducible, in theory, to a predetermined, highly complex series of mathematical formula). But as Bergson points out, notes on a sheet of music are not the melody itself, any more than scribbled mathematical equations on a page are the thickness and density of real experience. Both are simply highly abstract symbolic attempts to freeze a dynamic temporal reality into a static collection of manageable, replicable formulations; both are simply expressions of our inherent human tendency to see reality as a collection of separate and unchanging objects.

The similarities between music/melody and the nature of physical reality (at least as revealed by quantum physics) are striking. For instance, melody and physical reality (at least in its pulsational, vibratory, subatomic dimension) are both ever-changing, complexly organized, and inherently temporal. Both manifest themselves as an onrush of overlapping, interpenetrating, and resonant vibratory fields. In neither melody nor physical reality (at least, physical reality as it is understood from the perspective of both quantum physics and Bergson) do we find stable, unchanging objects (whether particles or notes) that have a specific, concrete location in space. (Asking "where" the notes of a melody actually *are* can be an illuminating exercise in futility; unlike visually perceived objects in space, sonic realities seem to be nowhere and everywhere. During their time of sounding, are the tones that we hear "in" the body of the instruments or the singer's voice? Are they "in" the air? Are they "in" our ears? Are they all of the aforementioned?)

Imagining the universe as a vast, ongoing musical creation can also help to free us from the tyranny of an Aristotelian "either/or" logic that, either implicitly or explicitly, pressures us to think that oneness cannot coexist with manyness, that change cannot coexist with continuity. "Hearing" the world through the metaphor of music and melody, it becomes easier to grasp how the world might well be such that individuality (whether in persons, things, or events) can and does coexist with some sort of underlying, even if hidden, connection and continuity. For instance, while it is tempting to think of a melody as an aggregate of separate, clearly delineated tones, if we look (or rather, listen) more carefully, what we discover is that each individual tone, while it maintains its uniqueness and distinctness, is not abruptly cut off from the other tones. Instead, each tone, during the time while it physically sounds, infuses and overlaps with the other tones that are concurrently sounding. What is more, even after each tone has physically faded, it continues to linger in memory, it continues to persist in the mind—in fact, it is this very persistence in the memory that creates a melodic phrase.[4] Melody, in order to be melody, needs both—the individuality and distinctiveness of particular notes and the ongoing continuity and connectedness of many notes brought together in the memory. In much the same way as the quantum reality is understood to be both particulate and field-like in nature, and in much the same way as our consciousness is a dynamic continuity of utter diversity, melody is an inseparable fusion of individual tones and the organic, ongoing gestalt created by memory.

As Čapek points out, the melodic metaphor becomes even more fruitful if we cease to think of melody as simply a single melodic phrase and, instead, begin to envision a multileveled polyphonic (and/or polyrhythmic) musical piece in which several relatively independent melodic movements unfold both successively and alongside each other. (Significantly, it does not matter whether the interaction between the movements create harmony or dissonance.)[5] For example, let's imagine a piece of music in which a saxophone has one melodic movement, a bass has another, and a guitar the third (we can even add the drums as the fourth melodic/rhythmic movement). Even if these various instruments are playing simultaneously, each melodic/rhythmic movement is relatively independent, in that each proceeds "parallel" to the other melodic/rhythmic movements (e.g., the guitar, the sax, the bass, and the drum each have their own parts, even while they are playing together). If we are trained listeners, it is possible to hear each movement separately and distinctly. Yet, at the same time, it is also possible to hear the more inclusive overall musical creation. In this level of hearing, each movement is enriched and gains a greater significance through its interaction with the other melodic/rhythmic movements. Together, they create a more complex, interesting, dynamic whole, a whole that is composed of relatively independent melodic/rhythmic movements that are organically interconnected and held together in memory. In this world of "co-becoming" or "co-fluidity," ceaseless change and seamless continuity coexist, and sheer diversity lives happily with stable ongoing presence.

In much the same way, perhaps we can imagine a world in which each being or entity (e.g., rabbits, clouds, rivers, spiders, wheat) has its own unique, ever-changing melody (or vibratory expression) through time, while simultaneously we could also recognize that each is not utterly separate, utterly cut off from the other beings or entities. Instead, perhaps we could train ourselves to realize the numerous ways in which each of these various "songs of being" overlaps, interpenetrates, and affects each of the other "songs," creating an almost unimaginably complex, dynamic intermingling of beings/entities within the matrix of a more expansive wholeness.

One potential argument against using the melody/music metaphor is that there is a strong tendency on our part to want to treat music as an imperfect translation of an almost Platonic, abstract, mathematically perfect musical score, rather than experience it as a living, visceral, ongoing movement of unique and spontaneously improvised tones. If we think of music in the former way, then we implicitly open the door to a type of musical determinism (in much the same way that, from the perspective of physical determinism, matter can be understood as adhering to, or to be the manifestation of, a complex set of preexistent, mathematically perfect Laws of Nature).

However, if we think of music as more "jazz-like" or improvisational in nature, then the musical metaphor has the potential to overcome the latent Platonism and implicit determinism discussed earlier. Doing so permits the metaphor to become not only more explicitly Bergsonian, but also a closer reflection of the nature of reality itself. A group of polished jazz musicians who have been playing together for a long time will, rarely, if ever, faithfully reproduce, note for note, a predetermined musical score. Instead, they can create, spontaneously, a new musical experience each time they play. Their music is not utter chaos, nor is it formulaic. Instead, it is the unplanned, unpredictable, result of listening and responding to each other, as well as listening and responding to their own intuitive musical sense. At its best, jazz improvisation is a type of "eco-logical" adaptivity. As such, while there are regularities and patterned behavior in jazz, it is also something that is genuinely new, something that emerges organi-cally from the complex, interconnected interactions of a group of skilled per-formers, each playing off the others and yet each also taking the risk to venture into uncharted territory in the service of melodic/rhythmic visions of where the music needs to go.

In a similar way, instead of envisioning the universe as the rigorously formu-laic manifestation of some Pythagorean regularity, as the terrestrial echo of the "music of the spheres" in which matter obeys the preset "score" given by the Laws of Nature, why not think of physical reality as a complex jazz performance, in which old standards are frequently performed (making them the "habits" rather than the "laws" of nature), even if, periodically and regularly, something unexpected also occurs, something genuinely new takes place as the adaptive result of different individuals and groups responding to and interacting with each other.[6]

This jazz-inspired metaphor works best if (and here is where the metaphor, like all metaphors, stretches and perhaps breaks) we can imagine that the music is not the end result of a stable group of performers, but rather, plays itself—as if the various clusters of melodic movements were each conscious of themselves and the other musical patterns. This type of metaphorical imagination helps to underscore the Bergsonian insistence that movement and change itself are what is primary, not stable things or objects that change. It allows us to return to a musical worldview in which each note, while having its own integrity, also res-onates outward, overlapping with and affecting/being affected by all of the other notes that are simultaneously resonating. In such a world, some patterns might repeat themselves, again and again, with almost utter regularity, but other clus-ters of musical movements would be much more "alive" and would appear to emerge and develop in-and-of-themselves—creating/composing new and unpre-dictable musical modes of existence.

A FLOWING IDENTITY

Thinking of reality as a vast, partially improvised musical performance also offers a potentially helpful new way to envision the nature of personal identity. As numerous philosophers and psychologists have repeatedly emphasized, it is not at all clear how a person constructs and maintains a stable sense of identity. Given the countless changes that each of us goes through, it is almost mystifying why we should come to feel any solid sense of inner sameness and psychic solid-ity.[7] On a physical level, our blood constantly flows, our cells never stop metab-olizing, and our breath continually comes in and goes out. On a molecular and subatomic level, we are a blur of dynamic movement. Mentally and emotionally, numerous thoughts and feelings ceaselessly arise and subside. The question therefore is: where are "we" in all of this activity?

Numerous attempts have been made to solve the dilemma of our personal identity, attempts that are, as Eric Matthews points out, typically variations on two themes: 1) essentialism (the conviction that, underneath it all, there is some unchanged essence or core of individual personhood) or 2) conventionalism (the understanding that there really is no inherent personhood to be found and that what we call personal identity is simply a conventional, practical fiction created out of cultural and psychological necessity). However, as Matthews goes on to note, "Bergson's view of a person as unified, not by a continuing essence, but by a developing life-*history* seems . . . to offer the possibility" of a viable third alternative, "a view of personal identity which could accommodate the changeability . . . while retaining the idea, so important to us morally and emotionally, that a person remains the same throughout his or her life."[8]

It seems that Matthews is correct. From a Bergsonian perspective, our experience (of both our "inner" and "outer" world) is characterized by *both* ceaseless change *and* inner continuity. Both aspects of reality need to be acknowledged. The flowing or the passage of life contains within itself both sheer diversity and seamless unity. Our own unique flowings or passages are, in this way, as Bergson stresses, "sufficient in themselves, the flowing not implying a thing which flows and the passage not presupposing any states by which one passes: the *thing* and the *state* are simply snapshots artificially taken of the transition; and this transition, alone experienced naturally, is durée itself" (*M* 98).[9] What is real is the continual, ongoing flux of durée; what is not is our desperate attempt to separate ourselves out from the ceaseless temporal dynamism of life in a futile attempt to create an unchanging ego (us) interacting with other separate and equally unchanging egos (them).

Bergson stresses that our attempts to separate out discrete stages in our life history is rooted in a similar type of confusion. For instance, if we look carefully at the process of how a child grows up to become an adult, there is never a clear-cut moment when that child becomes an "adult." There really is no static, unchanging essence of "childhood" or "adulthood." But we often act as if there are clear signs by which we can discern the difference between different stages of our personal development, whereas in reality all that exists is a ceaseless transition, a continual becoming—an inner dynamism that is often hidden from us because, as Bergson points out, we are typically so focused on static states of being that the more elusive transition process itself typically slips "between our fingers" (*CE* 313).

According to Bergson, if we understood correctly what takes place during the process of growing up, we would not say that a child became an adult. Instead, what we would (or should) say is that "there is becoming from the child to the [adult]" (*CE* 313). Expressed in this way, the emphasis is not on one static subject (the child) turning almost miraculously into another static subject (the adult). Instead, the emphasis is where it belongs: on the highly individualized process of becoming. With this way of understanding the developmental process, the flux of our life history is what is emphasized. With this shift in emphasis, our prior focus on "childhood" and "adulthood" can then be seen as simply "possible stops" along the way, as merely "views of the mind" created by our stubborn and insistent need to overlook and minimize change (*CE* 313).

From a Bergsonian perspective, if we cease thinking of ourselves as some sort of unchanging "nugget-like" essence that undergoes change only on the surface, while underneath remaining the same, if we focus instead on the reality of ceaseless change, then we are not necessarily forced to deny any and all individuality. We can, instead, realize that just as a melody is a combination of both continual change and uninterrupted continuity over time, in the same way, our individuality is, to a certain extent, the ever-changing end result of all of the countless life experiences we have had, held together and unified into a single continuum of experience.

This way of understanding ourselves allows us to acknowledge the very real fact that who we are is constantly changing, while also underscoring the equally real fact that there is an inner continuity and unified identity to our selfhood. With this mode of self-understanding, we can affirm that we are indeed ceaselessly shaped, moment by moment, by each experience we have. The song of our being is continually changing, moment to moment, as it is (at least partially) formed by our life experiences. Nonetheless, this vision of selfhood also permits us to maintain that the melodic stream of our identity is not reducible to, or the inevitable and predictable result of, all of our life experiences. Instead, the song of our being (and again, this is where the metaphor stretches to the breaking point) is itself conscious, and as such, responds to and interacts with these experiences in unique and idiosyncratic ways. It chooses which experiences to highlight and which to mute and it overlays and infuses each experience with various interpretative frameworks that are themselves continually reforming themselves in creative, unexpected ways in the hidden recesses of our memory. (As we will see in section 2, our memory is neither a passive receptacle, nor an utterly neutral mechanical "video camera" that simply records what happens. Instead, our memory possesses an intrinsic and genuine freedom, a freedom that allows us to take our lives in unanticipated directions in response to the promptings it is constantly receiving from the other melodic movements that surround it.)

What is crucial to emphasize is that our identity, understood in this way, is not only constantly in flux, but it is also intrinsically interactive. Who we are can be found, if anywhere, in the in-between-ness of the ongoing relations that take place between us and the various, equally constantly changing "melodies" of experience that surround and interpenetrate us. This in-between-ness means that what is outer and what is inner, where "we" begin (and end) and where the "world" begins (and ends) is extremely difficult, if not impossible, to discern.

And yet, amazingly, we typically act as if we (and everyone else) are solid, bounded, essentially unchanging beings, even while inhabiting a world that is characterized by perpetual flux.

Bergson offers a vivid analogy that can help make sense of how, in all of this constant dynamism, we could ever think that we (and those around us) remain comfortably stable, solid, and clearly delimited. (Bergson's analogy is, by the way, strikingly reminiscent of examples offered by Einstein to help explain certain aspects of relativity theory.) Bergson asks us to imagine two trains moving "at the same speed, in the same direction, on parallel tracks" (*CM* 169). Seated in each of these two trains, it might well appear, from the perspective of the travelers, that the trains themselves are not moving. In fact, if they wished, travelers on the trains could "hold out their hands to one another through the door and talk to one another" with ease, even if the trains were moving at a high rate of speed (*CM* 169). Similarly, while all of life may well be in a constant state of motion, nonetheless, when "my" stream of experience matches the vibratory quality of other streams of experience, when "my" movement or "my" pattern of energy is in harmony with other, similarly vibrating fields, then it may well appear, for all practical purposes, that a stable "subject" is interacting with other equally stable "subjects" or "objects," even if the truth is that, underneath it all, there is nothing but continually shifting patterns of change. As Bergson points out, it may well be that "in order that the uninterrupted change which each of us calls 'me' may act upon the uninterrupted change that we call a 'thing,' these two changes must find themselves, with regard to one another, in a situation like that of the two trains referred to above" (*CM* 172).

Nonetheless, while we seem to need to "freeze frame" the living flux of reality in order to exist, by doing so we typically tend to forget that the world is not, in reality, chopped up into a multitude of separate, clear-cut objects. We forget that, underneath it all, fixed immutable boundaries do not exist, and that even if our selfhood does possess a type of genuine cohesiveness and integrity, it also at each moment emerges organically out of its interaction with other resonating modes of existence—modes of existence that themselves are simply complex patterns of ceaseless change, are themselves simply overlapping and interpenetrating melodies of a single cosmic Song.

RUMINATION: THE "BOTH/AND" PERSPECTIVE OF BERGSON

The more that I immerse myself in Bergson's musical metaphor of the universe, the more I am impressed with its potential to address a host of philosophical as well as psychological and sociological problems. Later on in this text, I will go into more detail about what a Bergsonian perspective might have to offer in the way of potential solutions to these problems, but for now, I simply want to touch upon a few of the issues that I have returned to again and again during the time that I have been immersed in Bergson's understanding of the physical world.

To begin with, it is crucial to underscore the fact that Bergson's philosophical perspective not only anticipated, but remains congruent with, some of the most significant findings of modern physics in the twentieth and twenty-first centuries. Bergson's radical vision of matter as a vibrating sea of interpenetrating, ever-changing fields of energy may have been quickly dismissed and overlooked at the end of the nineteenth century. This vision may even seem far-fetched more than one hundred years later. But it remains one of the few philosophical worldviews that corresponds closely with some of the most recent and revolutionary discoveries of modern physics, discoveries that have been experimentally verified countless times, discoveries that most people, to this day, have yet even to hear about, let alone fully comprehend.

Ironically, even many (most?) highly educated intellectuals of today still act as if the world of matter that is described by science is resolutely Newtonian in its makeup, as if the Cosmic Clock is still up and running at this very moment in physics laboratories around the globe. In many ways, this attachment to Newtonian physics is understandable. Bergson himself says a lot about why this vision of matter as tiny, eternal, solid particles whizzing about in empty space is so tenaciously held by human beings. Practically speaking, for the most part, Newton's understanding mirrors our day-to-day experience of the external world—it seems to work. Furthermore, we can easily "see" it in our mind's eye—the Styrofoam ball "atoms" connected with pipe cleaners that we made in grade school seem to want to keep whirling around inside of our mind, even if we might have heard in passing that, in reality, "things" are much more complex than this in the subatomic world. In fact, it has frequently been pointed out that even those who should know better, the physicists of today, often still catch themselves thinking about the universe in Newtonian ways, even though they know that such a way of thinking profoundly oversimplifies and distorts the true nature of physical reality. However, just because it is difficult, if not impossible, for us to visualize the way that the physical universe actually functions, this does not absolve us of the responsibility of attempting to articulate more accurate and persuasive models of the true nature of reality—models such as Bergson's melodic understanding of durée.

What is valuable about Bergson's work is that while, at first glance, it may seem to be highly abstract and counterintuitive, the more that we study it, the more we come to realize how profoundly empirical and grounded in reality it actually is. Bergson was often criticized in his time for being antiscientific, however, this criticism came from individuals who, unknowingly (and like many/most intellectuals today), still thought that "scientific" equaled "Newtonian." Bergson's relationship with science was complex, but while he did believe that science at times needed a certain prodding and correction from philosophy, he was also deeply respectful of its value and integrity.[10] For Bergson, both philosophy and science should always be in mutual dialogue with each other, and while science at times might well benefit from a philosophical critique, any philosophy that is not grounded in, and responsive to, the ongoing findings of science is at best incomplete, and at worst is the product of idle speculation.

What is astonishing about Bergson's empiricism is that it is not limited to laboratory findings (as important as these may be), nor is it guided by naïve sense experience (a sense experience that shows us a world of discrete objects in space). Instead, it is an empiricism that is profoundly experiential—it is an empiricism that dives beneath the surface of the way things *seem* to be in order to reveal a deeper truth, the way that reality actually moves. This is a philosophical perspective that can, if we give it time, be extremely persuasive, that can, if we are willing to chew on it for a bit, reveal an inner and outer world that looks and acts very differently than what we might have previously assumed.

What Bergson does is to examine, with great care and rigor, what actually takes place in the workings of consciousness. (This is the crucial contribution of *Time and Free Will*.) In this way, his philosophy is grounded in something undeniable: one's own conscious experience. Then, in *Matter and Memory*, he takes a courageous next step. While continuing to respect the unique configuration of consciousness and its intrinsic difference from material reality, with equal care and rigor, Bergson extends his findings about the nature of consciousness to physical existence itself—thereby not only grounding his philosophy in the material world as well, but also (importantly) creating a uniquely configured bridge that crosses the (arguably) previously uncrossable Cartesian divide between mind and matter. By envisioning the durée of our consciousness and the durée that manifests itself in the physical world as interactive aspects of a single dynamic spectrum of becoming, Bergson manages to articulate a philosophical perspective that is not only extremely complex and sophisticated, but that also, crucially, both illuminates and refers back to the two most basic foci of our ongoing experience: our consciousness and our interaction with the material world.

As I mentioned earlier, seeing our inner and outer worlds through the lens of durée has, in many ways, given me an intellectual framework that is subtle and fluid enough to shed new light on a series of philosophical, psychological, and sociological problems.

To begin with, the "both/and" perspective of Bergson's philosophy provides a potentially helpful contribution to many of the thunderous debates on foundationalism/antifoundationalism that continue to rumble in the philosophical stratosphere.

In many ways, it can be quite inspiring to study the postmodern proponents of an antifoundational worldview, a type of self-consciously ironic *anti-worldview* worldview in which the ultimate nature of reality is understood to be so profoundly beyond our grasp that we might as well not bother to discuss it. (In fact, proponents of this perspective often argue that any attempt to do so is not only useless, but is also at times the covert manifestation of an imperialistic urge to impose our will upon others.) What we can, and should do, however (according to this perspective), is to spend a lot of time discussing how we as human beings construct and shape our understandings of ourselves and the world around us—politically, economically, institutionally, religiously, and philosophically. What we can and should do is to continually attempt to expose and root out the distortions and injustices created by any lingering tendencies to deny differences and otherness (or the Other) with our attempts to create an overarching, static vision of Oneness and Unity. What we can and should do is to critique any and all claims that there is a philosophical perspective that is ultimately true due to the fact that it is grounded in some undeniable, secure, trustworthy, ahistorical foundation. What we can and should do is to stress the boundless creativity of the human imagination, the value of diversity, and the ceaseless play of differences.

At the same time, many of the arguments that are put forth by certain thinkers in the opposite camp are also persuasive. This variety of foundationalism (which is sometimes known as "critical realism") typically does not deny that it is important to be alert to the numerous sociological, economic, political, and psychological reasons why we often dogmatically claim an unshakable certainty for our own positions and attack the truth or value of the belief of others (especially those who are marginalized). They frequently will agree that any attempts to establish our claims to truth in some unshakeable foundation is fraught with peril due to the ever-present potential for distortion. Nonetheless, they will also often argue that this awareness of our human limitations and frailty does not mean that we should therefore abandon the quest for a more accurate, more reliable, more trustworthy worldview, or that this quest is somehow doomed from the beginning.

According to this type of foundationalist perspective, some truth claims *are* more accurate, more factual than others, simply because these claims more accurately, more factually, represent the way that reality is actually structured. For these foundationalists, it simply makes sense to base our philosophical claims on something that is broader than or deeper than the various and complex webs of human linguistic creativity (whether that "something" is God, or the material universe, or the nature of our conscious experience). For these thinkers, the sheer relativism and the "anything goes" quality of antifoundationalism is highly suspect (not only because the antifoundationalists have to assert, at least implicitly, that their perspective is truer than the foundationalist perspectives that they are arguing against). For these foundationalists, truth and goodness and justice really do exist, even if we can only partially approximate them with our flawed and limited human capabilities.

Bergson's position can be extremely helpful in adjudicating this philosophical debate. A Bergsonian understanding is, in many ways, aligned with critical realism, especially in its insistence that our knowledge needs to be rooted in the real. (Hence Bergson's concerted and ongoing attempt to base his philosophical claims on a profound examination of the nature of human consciousness, as well as on an insightful and detailed understanding of the hidden structure of material reality.) Nonetheless, Bergson's work is a very odd sort of foundationalism in that it is a foundationalism of ceaseless change. This is not a foundationalism that affirms static Oneness (whether divine or not), rock-solid particles, changeless laws of nature, or any substantive Ego. Bergsonism is, in certain respects, an *antifoundational* foundationalism, a philosophy that affirms that what is true is that truth itself is always changing, a philosophy that affirms continual multiplicity and diversity, a philosophy that celebrates human freedom and creativity, both in ourselves and in others.[11]

Bergson's foundationalism is in many ways so deeply antifoundational that it no longer makes sense to call it foundationalism. For Bergson, the *Same* is never present, neither in our own consciousness nor in the world around us; he posits that every moment is a manifestation of the ceaseless play of difference. In addition, Bergson argues that philosophy itself must not only be continually on the alert for systemic distortions in the perspectives of others, but must also attempt to notice how its *own* outlook needs continual, self-reflexive reexamination and revision.

Nonetheless, Bergsonism is not an affirmation of anarchy and chaos. As human beings, the flux of difference within our conscious experience takes place within an equally evident continuity; that is, the multiplicity and manyness within us emerges within the ongoing unity of memory. In a similar way, the spontaneity of our creative freedom emerges not only out of the deeply embedded patterns of culture that remain active in the hidden layers of our unconscious memory (more on this in section 2), but also out of the equally insistent patterning found in the natural structures of our physicality (a physicality that, itself, emerges organically out of the interpenetrating fields that make up the physical matrix of the cosmos).

Furthermore, Bergson's insistence that reality is not split up into static, disconnected parts, but rather is a resonant, pulsating, overlapping, ever-new "song" gives us good reasons to cherish difference and otherness in the world around us; but at the same time, it also shows us why it makes sense to value the underlying empathetic connection we feel with these other human beings. Bergson's melodic metaphor can also provide a coherent worldview that supports the notion that perhaps our lives would be more rewarding and joyful if we could only learn how to "tune in" to and harmonize with the continually shifting fields or "notes" that are "sounding" in and through and from the variety of beings/entities that make up the world around us.

In addition to the ways in which Bergson's perspective can help us find some middle ground in the ongoing philosophical debate between the foundationalist/antifoundationalist perspectives, Bergson's discussion of our human tendency to fear and resist change and our natural inclination to split the world up into fractured, isolated parts that we attempt to manage and control can also give us some much-needed insight into some of the central, albeit hidden, causes of our most troubling social and psychological problems. For instance (to give only some of the more egregious examples), various forms of religious fanaticism and our troubling historical attraction to totalitarian modes of government clearly have a strong connection to our desire to keep our world the same, to our need to have problematically black and white answers to moral dilemmas, to our intolerance for murky ambiguities, to our yearning for a world in which everything has its systematic, rigidly ordered proper place. Similarly, on a more prosaic level, surely it is not accidental that so many of us work in hermetically sealed offices filled with tidy cubicles, that we design schools with desks bolted to the floor in straight rows, and that we build subdivisions of cookie-cutter houses, carefully separated and isolated from each other by high hedges and manicured lawns. Arguably, all of this behavior (among many more possible examples) is at least in part a sociological/psychological reflection of a visceral, almost instinctual desire either to deny or to suppress the ceaseless change that, according to Bergson, characterizes all of life, and/or a reflection of our seemingly insatiable drive to split a flowing, interconnected world into a manageable set of stable, ordered objects.

Obviously, not all habitual behavior is undesirable. Not all need for order is neurotic and destructive. Not all certainty is unwanted. Some momentary places of stability in the flux are not only helpful, but also seem to be congruent with or reflective of the dynamic interplay between fluidity and structure that appears to make up the nature of our consciousness and physical reality. Repetition and routine appear to be needed, at least to a certain extent, as long as they do not become too engrained. The desire for clear-cut answers seems to have an important purpose, as long as it does not calcify into a rigid oppositional world of right versus wrong, saved versus damned, us versus them.

Seen from a Bergsonian perspective, it makes perfect sense that, as human beings, we are continually struggling with ways to find some sort of workable middle ground between dogmatic, narrow-minded, self-righteous certainty and a paralyzing, indecisive openness to all perspectives; between atomistic, walled-off, fearful isolation from others and a porous, boundary-less dependence upon and merger with others. It makes sense that, as human beings, we need to find some way to simultaneously cultivate creativity, uniqueness, and individuality while also nurturing tradition, heritage, and communal solidarity. From a Bergsonian perspective, it is completely understandable that we would simultaneously be attracted to and disturbed by moments in which we lose our normal sense of ego boundaries (e.g., moments of sexual ecstasy or religious fervor) or that we would work hard to keep our world and our loved ones comfortably regular and secure, becoming anxious (or angry) if they change too quickly or intensely, even while we might also feel trapped or bored if they (and we) remain predictably the same. What is so attractive about a Bergsonian perspective is that it acknowledges and affirms what we already know, but often refuse to acknowledge, that life is rarely black and white, rarely either/or, but instead is a bewildering, frightening, exhilarating, confusing, ever-changing conflux of difference and sameness, oneness and manyness, structure and fluidity. Bergson's philosophy does not offer us any easy answers, but it does offer us at least the hope that we do indeed live in a world that, underneath it all and in a way that we might never fully grasp, makes sense.

Section Two

The Matter of Consciousness and the Consciousness of Matter

13

CONTEMPORARY UNDERSTANDINGS
OF CONSCIOUSNESS

═══════════════

REMEMBERING *MATTER AND MEMORY*

Although it was published in 1896, *Matter and Memory* remains a revolutionary work. In it, Bergson articulates a creative and persuasive solution to what has to be one of the most stubborn and tenacious problems in Western philosophy: the mind-body problem.[1] Sadly, however, at the beginning of the twenty-first century, most Western philosophers and psychologists act as if *Matter and Memory* was never written. What makes this omission in the collective memory of the academy particularly troubling is that during the last several decades, after a prolonged positivist/behaviorist period in which conversations about the nature of consciousness were in essence relegated to the philosophical and psychological garbage heap, there has been a resurgence in interest in the relationship between the mind/consciousness and the body/brain. Numerous highly respected thinkers have taken up the mind-body problem with renewed zeal, each writing texts that approach this difficult issue from her or his particular vantage point. However, in this torrent of philosophical and psychological speculation, it is rare to find even a brief mention of the work of Bergson.

This philosophical lacuna would be understandable if, after serious and careful consideration, there had been a consensus that Bergson's arguments in *Matter and Memory* were fatally flawed and it was therefore only worthy of notice as a historical relic superseded by far more sophisticated perspectives. But this negative assessment never happened. *Matter and Memory*, even in Bergson's own time, was never (with certain exceptions) adequately examined or properly understood by the majority of the philosophers and psychologists of that period.

Instead, it was simply ignored and then forgotten (for reasons that I attempted to describe in the bio-historical preamble). Therefore, far from being outmoded, *Matter and Memory* has yet to be fully understood, let alone appreciated. It is my contention that a detailed critical examination of Bergson's perspective on the mind-body issue, especially as it is presented in *Matter and Memory*, is urgently needed in today's philosophical and psychological climate. If taken seriously it has the potential to open up several potentially fruitful new avenues of inquiry.

However, before I dive into the difficult-to-navigate waters of *Matter and Memory*, it would be helpful first to offer a relatively terse, inevitably oversimplified, overview of some of the central issues that have arisen in the discussions on the nature of consciousness during the last several decades. This overview will make it easier to see exactly how *Matter and Memory* fits into the current conversation and will also help to clarify how its powerful, dense, idiosyncratic, and seemingly counterintuitive perspective might actually have the capacity to untangle the tightly cinched knot of the mind-body problem.[2]

BECOMING CONSCIOUS OF CONSCIOUSNESS

When discussing the nature of consciousness and its relationship to the physical world, it can be helpful to begin with an often-overlooked insight, that is, that there are two seemingly irreconcilable ways to know the world. First, we can know something from the outside. For example, the small wooden statue of St. Francis on my desk can be weighed, measured, probed, and examined by a wide variety of people, all of whom (given a modicum of intelligence, mental health, and educational background) would probably come to a rough consensus about the basic facts of what it is made of, who made it, what wood it was carved from, and so on. The statue is, undeniably, a physical object in a physical world and can be publicly known by others as such. But at the same time, as I look at the statue, or as I hold it, I am having a unique, utterly private, nonsharable, intimate, inner experience *of* that statue. No one else will have, or can have, exactly this quality of experience—an experience that is inherently subjective and intrinsically ineffable.[3] We might be able to imagine what someone else's experience of the statue would be, but our own experience itself, from the inside, is ours alone. A scientist might tell us that our inner experience of the textures and shapes and colors and smells of the statue is nothing more than a complex neurochemical interaction taking place within our brain, but as far as we are concerned, our experience has nothing to do with neurochemical cerebral activity. In-and-of-itself, our experience simply is what it is—it has its own unique quality, or better yet our experience *consists* of this quality. (Philosophers often use the technical term *qualia* to indicate the private, subjective, phenomenological quality of consciousness—what an experience is like, on its own terms, instead of what physical properties, allegedly, are its cause.)

The problem is how our inner, private, subjective experiences (our qualia) are related to the physical world that seems so external, public, and objective. This conundrum is, not surprisingly, virtually identical to the Cartesian impasse: how is it possible that the *mind* (which, according to Descartes, is "unextended," i.e., nonspatial and inner) is related to *matter* (which, according to Descartes, is "extended," i.e., spatial and outer). When I perceive something in my mind (let's say, a television), how is my immaterial consciousness of the television related to the heavy, bulky material object sitting across from me? That television has a specific location (let's say, six feet from the sofa), but where is my *consciousness* of the television? My consciousness of the television does not seem to be anywhere in particular. (It is certainly not six feet from my consciousness of the sofa.)[4] Similarly, the television can be weighed and measured, but what about my consciousness of the television? Consciousness, as such, appears to be inherently nonspatial, that is, "unextended," whereas matter seems to be inherently spatial, that is, "extended." The big question, therefore, is this: how are these two very different "stuffs" related?

A modern variation of this Cartesian conundrum is what David Chalmers calls the "hard problem"; that is, exactly how do "physical processes in the brain give rise to subjective experience"?[5] The "hard problem" forces us to confront and explain how it is possible that each of us at every moment manages, in Susan Blackmore's words, to cross the "fathomless abyss" or "chasm" that exists "between the objective material brain and the subjective world of experience."[6] As Ed Kelly points out, "the fundamental question before us now reduces starkly to this: Can everything we know about the mind be explained in terms of brain processes?"[7] In other words, how is it possible that an "extended" object (like our brain and nervous system), which is physical, external, measurable, wet, and pulpy, can create the wide variety of "unextended" qualia that make up our conscious experience? For example, how do the electromagnetic waves of light entering my eyes become my consciousness of the tree outside my office window? How does this physical, measurable, vibratory reality become transformed into a nonphysical, nonlocatable, immeasurable conscious experience? We can talk as much as we want to about molecular movements in the rods and cones in the retina and neural activity in the visual centers in the brain, but how do these physical and seemingly nonconscious processes miraculously transform themselves into my conscious visual experiences? As A. A. Luce archly notes, "the eye forms images. So does a camera; yet we do not credit the camera with the power of seeing the images it has made."[8]

THEORIES OF CONSCIOUSNESS: DUALISM

Although there are numerous complex philosophical theories that attempt to bridge the chasm between matter and the mind, or between the brain and consciousness, for simplicity's sake, I am going to focus on the three major theories of the mind-body relation that were prominent during Bergson's time: dualism, materialism, and epiphenomenalism. Contemporary philosophers of mind have tweaked these three perspectives, adding several subtly different variations, but these three theoretical positions will serve as a useful starting point.

Descartes' theory of the mind-body relationship is basically a form of dualism, technically known as "substance dualism." Dualism acknowledges that both the mind and the body exist, but it also asserts that they are completely different and separate substances, one (the body) extended and the other (the mind) unextended. The basic assumption of dualism is that the mind (or soul or consciousness) somehow (rather mysteriously) interacts with the body in and through the brain.

The primary advantage of dualism (or "interactionism," as it is sometimes called), is that it affirms what introspection tells us, very clearly: consciousness exists (although, as we will see soon, some philosophical theories deny the value and validity of our introspective awareness of our own consciousness) and consciousness both affects, and is affected by, the external world around it (e.g., my consciousness tells my fingers to begin typing and they do; I drink a few beers and my consciousness becomes altered). The major problem with substance dualism however is that it is not at all clear how physical occurrences in a physical world and a physical brain could possibly create or influence our nonphysical conscious experiences *of* that world, or how our nonphysical conscious experiences (e.g., willing ourselves to press the keys on a computer keyboard) could possibly have any effect on our clearly physical brains and equally physical external world. The perspectives of some ardent supporters of dualism remain active in contemporary philosophical debates (e.g., the philosopher of science Sir Karl Popper; quantum physicists, such as Werner Heisenberg and Wolfgang Pauli; and neurophysiologists, such as Wilder Penfield, John Eccles, and Roger Sperry). However, it is safe to say that dualism is rarely given much credence in current mainstream philosophical and scientific circles.

THEORIES OF CONSCIOUSNESS: EPIPHENOMENALISM

During Bergson's time there was another widely held theory of the relationship between the mind and the body. This theory, *epiphenomenalism*, like dualism, acknowledged the intrinsic difference between our conscious experience and the external physical world. But unlike dualism, epiphenomenalism asserted that consciousness is simply a superfluous by-product of material processes. Many late nineteenth-century epiphenomenalists (including Thomas Huxley, who is credited with coining the term) argued that although it does seem to be true that certain animal species (including human beings) possess conscious awareness, nonetheless, consciousness as such is utterly powerless to affect physical reality. As Milič Čapek puts it, according to these thinkers, "the consciousness of higher living beings merely accompanies certain neural processes without influencing them; it supposedly has as little effect on them as a steam whistle on the motion of a locomotive."[9]

While epiphenomenalism was very influential in Bergson's time, there are few serious advocates for this position today. One of the most serious difficulties of epiphenomenalism, which William James pointed out in 1880, is that if the physiological processes of the brain and nervous system take place regardless of whether consciousness is present or not, if consciousness has absolutely no power to alter our cerebral functioning in any way, then it is almost impossible to understand how consciousness could have emerged during the process of evolution. Čapek echoes this concern when he notes, "the mechanism of natural selection preserves only those features which represent some survival value"; therefore, if consciousness actually is as utterly powerless as the epiphenomenalists claim, it becomes difficult to see how something with so little survival value would ever have been preserved.[10]

Epiphenomenalism has one further theoretical difficulty, a difficulty that (as we will soon see) it shares with materialism. The difficulty is this: our everyday actions and experiences repeatedly and powerfully affirm that our consciousness can and does affect our physical body. While driving a car, we decide to turn left and our body turns the steering wheel in the proper direction. Epiphenomenalists such as Huxley, however, claimed that this introspective awareness of the power of our intentions to influence the actions of our body is simply mistaken. According to Huxley, whether we know it or not, we are "conscious automata"; that is, we are simply robotic physical beings who, mysteriously, are also conscious. While this assertion was (and is) implicitly affirmed by generations of psychologists and philosophers, a handful of contemporary theorists have rebelled against this claim that our conscious intentions have no effect on our physical actions. For instance, Ted Honderich notes that the argument made by epiphenomenalists that consciousness has no effect on the body is immediately self-refuting: the very act of speaking or writing about epiphenomenalism could not have occurred without having been catalyzed by the supposedly powerless conscious beliefs held by the epiphenomenalists themselves.[11]

THEORIES OF CONSCIOUSNESS: MATERIALISM

A similar argument can be made against reductive materialism (or physicalism), currently the most influential theoretical understanding of the relationship between the mind and the body. For materialists, there is only one "stuff" in the universe: physical matter in various forms. If there is only one "stuff" out of which everything is made, then there can be no interaction between the mind and the body, because what we call "the mind" is in actuality simply an alternative way of describing the neurochemical activities of the brain. Therefore, to talk about consciousness as if it were something separate from matter is, according to materialism, a category mistake, since everything that we think, feel, say, and do is reducible to physical activities in the brain/body. For materialists, "minds are simply what brains do,"[12] or mind is nothing more than "the personalization of the physical brain."[13]

Materialists tend to argue that our commonsense dualist understanding that our consciousness is an active agent that can and does initiate physical changes in our body is nothing more than a superstitious relic of earlier, more ignorant, time periods. Therefore, they are happy to follow the advice of British philosopher Gilbert Ryle, who in 1949 urged scientists and philosophers to ignore the "ghost in the machine" (i.e., consciousness in the body). Exorcising this ghost means that we acknowledge that our normal understandings of consciousness are completely mistaken. For instance, according to certain materialists (i.e., "eliminative" materialists), consciousness as we normally think about it does not really exist: our consciousness does not influence our body in any way. Our consciousness is not even caused by, nor does it interact with, the neurochemical processes of our body. Instead, our conscious experience is nothing more than, or is reducible to, the highly complex neurochemical activity in our bodies.

This understanding of the nature of consciousness is voiced by Francis Crick (who, along with James D. Watson, uncovered the structure of DNA), when he claims that we are mistaken when we imagine that our conscious experiences are something more than, or distinct from, our physicality. Instead, our sorrows, memories, ambitions, our sense of personal identity and free will are "in fact no more than the behavior of a vast assembly of nerve cells and their associated molecules."[14] Eliminative materialists, astonishingly, assert that we are mistaken when we think that our conscious experiences, or qualia, even exist. As Blackmore points out, "you may think that it is unquestionable that qualia exist. . . . Most theorists would agree with you, but some think you would be wrong."[15] For instance, one of Daniel Dennett's primary tasks as an eliminative materialist is "to convince people that there are no such properties as qualia."[16]

Dennett's perspective dovetails with the understanding of Paul Churchland, another well-known "eliminative materialist," who insists that we need to let go of our antiquated notion that what we experience introspectively actually exists. As such, we "need to eliminate our old language of the mind" in favor of the purified language of neuroscience in which " 'A-delta fibers and/or C-fibers' will replace our notions of pain; 'iodopsins,' our color after images; and 'vestibular maculae,' our feelings of acceleration and falling."[17] For eliminative materialists such as Churchland, our internal experience of consciousness is irrelevant and it is a waste of time to give it any theoretical attention. What we should focus on, instead, is how to better understand the neurochemical activity of the brain and nervous system.

During Bergson's time, variations on "eliminative" materialism existed, but they generally were discredited in European philosophical circles. After the work of Descartes and Kant, it was commonly asserted that it was difficult to deny, with any credibility, the stark evidence of introspection that clearly shows us that consciousness exists. Several more recent thinkers argue that this basic insight continues to have merit. As Čapek points out, eliminative materialism is that position "whose basic contradiction could be expressed in the absurd statement: 'I am aware that no awareness exists.'"[18] Similarly, Galen Strawson notes that while some materialists claim that "although it *seems* to one that there is experience—for this cannot be denied—there really isn't any experience," this assertion itself "is an immediate reductio ad absurdum. For this seeming is already experience . . . illusion presupposes—it is a form of—experience."[19] Strawson goes on to make the following perceptive comment:

> I find the suggestion that common sense makes any error about the qualitative or lived nature of [conscious experiences such as] pain inexplicable except as an extreme case of theory-driven Procrusteanism. If there is any sense in which these philosophers are rejecting the ordinary view of the nature of things like pain . . . their view seems to be one of the most amazing manifestations of human irrationality on record. It is much less irrational to postulate the existence of a divine being whom we cannot perceive than to deny the truth of the commonsense view of experience.[20]

Some of the most important problems of materialism as a philosophical perspective are discussed in the following, but the inadequacy of *eliminative* materialism is painfully obvious: it simply decides that we can and should ignore perhaps the most important fact of all, that is, consciousness itself.

A PROBLEM FOR MATERIALISM: THE UNITY OF CONSCIOUSNESS

At the present time the vast majority of theorists who write about the mind-body problem are not eliminative materialists, but most do accept some form of materialism. Besides the painfully obvious difficulty of having to explain how nonconscious physical processes can generate conscious experience, many philosophers are also dissatisfied with the ability of materialism to adequately account for the unity of our conscious experience. As these philosophers point out, in our day-to-day experience, we seem to have only one consciousness, a single mind that experiences a unified world. For example, at this moment in time I may simultaneously hear a dog bark, feel the wind blow, see a squirrel run up a tree, and taste a crisp green apple, but these various experiences that are happening within me do not feel as if they are isolated from each other. In addition, my experience does not feel as if it is happening to a multitude of separate observers. Instead, my consciousness during this interval of time feels as if one individual ("me") is experiencing a single cohesive world.

However, while this flood of sensory data is taking place within me (along with the equally complex overlays of thoughts, feelings, memories, and so on—none of which disturbs the sense of an integral "wholeness" within my consciousness), the over one hundred billion neurons that make up my brain are interacting in a stunningly complex fashion. As Blackmore points out, "At any given time, countless different processes are all going on at once [within the brain], and in different areas. . . . All these diverse processes are linked up through multiple routes and connections, but . . . there is no single place in the brain where everything is brought together. All the parts just keep doing their different things all at once."[21] If a single mind does not exist "over and above" the brain, then it is extremely difficult to account for the sense of unity that we all experience within ourselves, both over time (i.e., none of us feel, within ourselves, that we are a collection of different selves from moment to moment) and during a single moment in time (i.e., in this moment, each of us feels that we are a single self experiencing an integral world). As Searle tersely points out, "we have little understanding of how the brain achieves this unity."[22] (One of the philosophical strengths of *dualism* is that it *can* more easily make sense of our experience of unity, because it can attribute that experience to the unity of the mind. As Eccles notes, "a key component of the [dualist] hypothesis is that the unity of conscious experience is provided by the self-conscious mind, not by the neural machinery" of the brain.)[23]

Some materialists, such as Dennett, argue that materialism has no difficulty accounting for our perceived unity of experience because this alleged unity is actually an illusion. Dennett claims that while it may *seem* to us that we are a single self experiencing an integral world, in reality, under the surface, our selfhood consists of a multitude of separate "sub-selves" or "homunculi" with various tasks, desires, and beliefs. These homunculi can themselves, he claims, be further subdivided into smaller and "less clever" homunculi, until at some point we reach a level that is purely mechanistic, in which all that exists are "adders and subtractors."[24]

Dennett's theory admittedly possesses a certain visual appeal (it would make a wonderful shot in a Charlie Kaufman film: I picture lots of little robotic human-like figures in sci-fi outfits running around in each of our skulls). However, the homunculus theory is extremely problematic if looked at carefully. To begin with, if our conscious experience is created by billions of mindless "mini-me's" with no "Big Boss," then it is utterly mysterious why we have even the *appearance* of conscious unity within us. Dennett's homunculus theory is also unpersuasive in a second crucially important respect: Dennett's homunculi are utterly mindless robotic figures, and as John Mullarkey astutely observes, "it is one thing to see how an activity normally performed by a single agent of certain intelligence could be effected by lesser beings with their talents pooled together; it is quite another thing to believe it possible that beings with no intelligence whatsoever could muster anything beyond this level, irrespective of how many of them are collected together."[25]

AN EVOLUTIONARY PROBLEM: WHEN DID CONSCIOUSNESS ARISE?

Dennett's homunculus theory fails because it is blind to an important category mistake: it simply does not make sense to argue that mindless external objects that only have "outsides," no matter how many of them exist and no matter how they are organized, can miraculously come together to form "inner" subjective experiences, experiences of an utterly different quality, that is, consciousness. This same category mistake appears again, in a slightly altered form, when both materialists and dualists discuss the issue of how (and when) consciousness emerged in the evolutionary development of various life forms on the planet (remember: there are almost no epiphenomenalists active today, so their perspective typically is not entertained).

Most of the major figures in the current discussion on the nature of consciousness and its relationship to the physical world, for all of their numerous differences, would probably agree that several billion years ago consciousness did not exist on our planet and that at some point in the process of evolution consciousness appeared. (As we will see further on, there is one notable exception to this understanding: those theorists who support panpsychism, a philosophical position which claims that consciousness, or more broadly, experience, has always existed and is present in various forms in everything. For panpsychists, consciousness/experience did not emerge from insentient matter because it was there already, albeit in a rudimentary, or hidden, or latent form.[26] Although panpsychism is not a popular position today, it has a rather prestigious background: not only Bergson, but Leibniz, William James, A. N. Whitehead, Charles Hartshorne, and others were all, in various forms, panpsychists.)[27]

When we look carefully at the almost taken-for-granted notion that consciousness "emerged" at some point in the process of evolution, several problems appear. As David Ray Griffin points out, one problem is "exactly *where to draw the line* between experiencing and non-experiencing things."[28] Given the continuity that is suggested by evolutionary theory, any place that is chosen for this line is bound to look arbitrary. With his usual acerbic wit, Griffin notes that because both dualists and materialists "know" that the discontinuity between nonconscious matter and consciousness "*must* have happened somewhere in the evolutionary process, they are content to indicate only vaguely where that might have been."[29] For instance, Searle is confident that amoebas have no experience, but perhaps "fleas, grasshoppers, crabs and snails do."[30] Owen Flanagan, on the other hand, while acknowledging that scallops and paramecia have an interactive relationship with their environment, appears to be strangely certain that they feel and experience nothing.[31] All in all, the decision as to where to draw the line between sheer physicality and conscious existence appears to be rather arbitrary and based on rather sketchy evidence. (As Griffin goes on to note, an article in *Science* that appeared in 1974 suggests that even bacteria appear to possess the ability to make primitive types of decisions, based on rudimentary forms of memory—activities that seem to imply the presence of some form of rudimentary consciousness.)[32]

However, the question of *when* consciousness emerged during the process of evolution is nowhere near as pressing as the question of *how* consciousness (or experience, or subjectivity) could have arisen out of inert matter in the first place—and this is a problem for both materialists and dualists alike. For instance, a prominent materialist, J. J. C. Smart, attempting to deflate the dualist position asks, "How could a non-physical property or entity suddenly arise in the course of animal evolution? . . . [W]hat sort of chemical process could lead to the springing into existence of something non-physical? No enzyme can catalyze the production of a spook!"[33] However, as Griffin rightly points out, "although Smart directs this comment against dualism, it can be directed back at his own materialism. One can equally well ask, How can an enzyme catalyze the production of even the *appearance* of a spook?"[34] Thomas Nagel is, if anything, even more emphatic. He asserts that the "gap" between nonconscious matter and consciousness "is logically unbridgeable. If a bodiless god wanted to create a conscious being, he could not expect to do it by combining together in organic form a lot of particles with none but physical properties."[35]

Some philosophers of mind have tried to bridge the huge gulf between insentience and sentience by breaking the gap down into lots of tiny intermediary steps. Nicholas Humphrey, for example, assumes that experience simply did not exist on our planet thousands of millions of years ago. However, because he recognizes that sentient behavior is clearly a reality at our current moment in history, he proposes that, "present-day sensory activities could have developed step-by-step from primitive beginnings, starting with a local 'wriggle of acceptance or rejection' in response to stimulation at the body surface."[36] According to Humphrey, this slight degree of sensitivity in rudimentary organisms is then "selected for" by natural selection and becomes, eventually, an inner life of sorts.

Commenting on the preceding passage, Griffin correctly observes that Humphrey has, perhaps unknowingly, combined "externalist language ['wriggle'] and internalist language ['acceptance or rejection']."[37] This fusion (confusion?) of objective and subjective language obscures the fact that Humphrey has not, in any way, "wriggled" out of the dilemma of how consciousness could have emerged from matter. As Griffin dryly notes, "no matter how tiny, far back, and innocuous one tries to make it, [the emergence of experience/subjectivity] is still a miracle."[38]

Humphrey, however, maintains that we *can* understand how utterly inert physical processes managed to generate consciousness during the course of evolution if we recognize that consciousness, like many other phenomena in nature, is an "emergent property." As Blackmore points out, emergent properties "are properties of a combination of things, but not of those things alone. So, for example, the wetness of water is not a property of either hydrogen or oxygen but emerges when the two form molecules of H_2O."[39] Eccles, although coming from a dualist standpoint, makes much the same argument when he says, "just as in biology there are new emergent properties of matter, so at the extreme level of organized complexity of the cerebral cortex, there arises still further emergence, namely the property of being associated with conscious experience."[40] Here, again, consciousness/experience is said to be simply another example of "emergence."

While these examples of emergence may appear at first glance to be compelling, if we look closer, their argumentative force begins to dissolve. As Griffin points out, the most common examples of emergence that are given are examples drawn from physical things that are described from the outside, that are objective, that are understood to have no subjectivity. However, the alleged "emergence" of consciousness/experience/subjectivity is not simply an issue of one type of objectivity arising out of a previous type of objectivity. Instead, it is "the alleged emergence of an 'inside' from things that have only outsides."[41] The notion of "emergent properties" as applied to consciousness is, once again, an example of a category mistake. In this case, the category of something which has only physical characteristics, which has nothing more than an "outside" (i.e., which has "no features beyond those that are perceivable in principle by others") is conflated with something that exists in-and-for-itself, something that has subjectivity and is capable of experience (i.e., that has an "inside" that cannot be perceived by others).[42]

Thankfully, at least some contemporary theorists recognize that the emergence of subjectivity out of inert physical processes is a major philosophical problem. As Colin McGinn, for example, forthrightly states:

> We do not know how consciousness might have arisen by natural processes from antecedently existing material things. Somehow or other sentience sprang from pulpy matter, giving matter an inner aspect, but we have no idea how this leap was propelled. . . . One is tempted, however reluctantly, to turn to divine assistance: for only a kind of miracle

could produce *this* from *that*. It would take a supernatural magician to extract consciousness from matter, even living matter. Consciousness appears to introduce a sharp break in the natural order—a point at which scientific naturalism runs out of steam.[43]

However, unfortunately, McGinn's "solution" to the mind-body problem is to simply assert that somehow, in some mysterious fashion, consciousness *does* emerge from purely natural causes. According to McGinn, although it may *appear* that the creation of consciousness is miraculous, in fact this is not the case and "we can rest secure in the knowledge that some (unknowable) property of the brain makes everything fall into place."[44] Not surprisingly, Griffin is somewhat less than satisfied with McGinn's hopeful stance, noting that "all [this proposal] does . . . is declare that no miracle occurred while giving not a hint as to how the feat was accomplished without one."[45]As Griffin correctly points out, "blind faith is blind faith whether it be of the supernaturalistic or the naturalistic variety, and blind faith does not provide a secure resting place for most intellectuals."[46]

CONTEMPORARY THEORISTS — VARIOUS "CAMPS"

One way to divide up the current most influential perspectives on the mind-body problem is to ask whether or not a particular theorist believes that the "hard problem" can, or even should, be solved (the "hard problem," once again, is explaining how it is possible that physical processes in the brain can produce subjective states of consciousness). Some thinkers contend that the "hard problem" should simply be ignored. As Blackmore points out, these theorists think that it makes more sense to address the "easy problems" first (e.g., how attention, memory, learning, perception, and so on, function within us).[47] According to this perspective, once we gain solutions to these "easy problems," then our understanding of the "hard problem" will inevitably change; therefore, any attempts to solve the "hard problem" at this point in time are premature.

Another group of theorists who are interested in the mind-body problem (a group which includes both dualists and materialists) have rather recently begun to assert that it is quite likely the "hard problem" will never be solved, or more radically, that it is in principle insolvable. These philosophers are convinced that conscious experience simply cannot be explained using exclusively physical categories (even if they might very much wish that it could!). For instance, the dualist Karl Popper in his 1977 book *The Self and Its Brain*, co-written with John Eccles, concludes that a complete understanding of how the nonphysical mind interacts with the physical brain "is unlikely to be achieved."[48] Similarly, as Blackmore notes, Nagel recently argued that "the problem of subjectivity is intractable or hopeless. Not only do we have no solution—we do not even have a conception of what a physical explanation of a mental phenomenon would be."[49] In addition, as Griffin points out, Collin McGinn "argues that our present perplexity is terminal, that we will *never* be able to resolve the mystery of how consciousness could emerge from the brain."[50] (McGinn argues that just as a dog is "cognitively closed" to reading a newspaper, no matter how hard it tries, we are also "cognitively closed" to understanding the nature of consciousness.) Similarly, William Seager says that "it remains true, and may forever remain true, that we have no idea whatsoever of *how* the physical states of a brain can constitute consciousness."[51] And finally, according to Galen Strawson, the "mysteriousness, for us, of the relation between the experiential and the physical-as-discerned-by-physics is . . . a sign of how much is at present, and perhaps forever, beyond us."[52]

Griffin, for one, is convinced that it is significant that important thinkers from all sides of the consciousness debate are finally and forcefully acknowledging not only that are there major unresolved problems with both dualism and materialism, but even more importantly, that these problems may never be resolved. Griffin believes, and I think that he is correct, that faced with such a situation, it only makes sense that we "think outside of the box" if we are ever to solve the mystery of the mind-body connection. Griffin joins a rather small group of thinkers who claim that the hard problem *is* solvable even if, in order to do so, we need to take seriously Nagel's observation that "the world is a strange place and nothing but radical speculation gives us the hope of coming up with any candidates for truth."[53]

ONE SOLUTION TO THE "HARD PROBLEM": PANPSYCHISM

It would appear then that, if there is going to be a solution to the "hard problem," we might do well to look in atypical philosophical directions. Strawson, for one, seems to agree. As Griffin notes, Strawson argues that "taking alternative views such as idealism and panpsychism seriously . . . is part of 'a proper response' to the fact that, given standard assumptions about the physical and the mental, the mind-body problem has proved to be intractable."[54]

According to Blackmore, panpsychism is "the view that mind is fundamental in the universe, and that all matter has associated mental aspects or properties, however primitive."[55] Griffin, who prefers the term "panexperientialism" (a term that he apparently coined), adds that this philosophical perspective involves "attributing the two basic features that we associate with mind—experience and spontaneity—to all units of nature."[56] Most versions of panpsychism hold that all forms of matter in some way or another possess something that resembles consciousness. However, many versions of panpsychism argue that this underlying consciousness can manifest itself in a wide variety of ways, some of which, paradoxically, are subconscious in nature. (Bergson's own version of panpsychism, for example, is rooted in a very sophisticated notion of the subconscious/unconscious.)

As was noted earlier, Griffin points out that, while panpsychism is basically ignored today, it has a prestigious past. Many renowned thinkers, such as "Leibniz, Fechner, Lotze, James, Bergson, Peirce, Montague, Whitehead, Hartshorne, Wright, Waddington, Rensch, and Bohm," articulated some version of panpsychism.[57] Therefore, while this philosophical alternative is currently neglected, there appears to be no a priori reason why it should not be reconsidered, especially given the impasse that currently exists in resolving the mind-body problem.

What panpsychism allows us to do, in Griffin's words, is to "try a new strategy: Begin with experience, which we *know* exists, and see if we can understand the various phenomena we call 'physical' in terms of various degrees, organizations, and external perceptions of *it*."[58] If everything, including physical existence, is understood inherently to possess experience (albeit, often in very rudimentary, latent, or even unconscious forms), then experience itself ceases to be something which needs to be reduced to something else (i.e., physical processes); it ceases to be something anomalous that needs to be explained away. Instead, our experiential life itself, the one aspect of our existence which is undeniable, that which is most immediately given, that which we know directly from within, becomes our philosophical foundation, becomes in Griffin's words, "the starting point of our analysis of what actual things are really like."[59]

WHY IS PANPSYCHISM SO OFTEN DISMISSED OR IGNORED?

Given the philosophical promise of panpsychism, it is puzzling that most current theorists act as if dualism and materialism were the only two worthwhile options and almost completely ignore panpsychism.[60] As Griffin notes, it is often the case that "if panpsychism is even mentioned, it is usually dismissed in a paragraph, if not a sentence."[61] For instance, Humphrey, during a discussion of how consciousness allegedly emerged on the planet ages ago out of the mindless interaction of atoms, adds this comment: "The alternative idea, that consciousness has always been inherent in every particle of matter, sometimes called 'panpsychism,' is one of those superficially attractive ideas that crumbles to nothing as soon as it is asked to do any sort of explanatory work."[62] A reader, coming across this passage, might assume that Humphrey will provide clear-cut, persuasive reasons for this off-hand dismissal of panpsychism, but this is not the case.[63]

McGinn's approach to panpsychism appears to be similarly nonchalant. He comments that "attributing specks of proto-consciousness to the constituents of matter is not supernatural in the way postulating immaterial substances or divine interventions is; it is merely extravagant."[64] However, as Griffin rightly points out, McGinn's comment is rather perplexing, in that on the same page McGinn claims that "something pretty remarkable is needed if the mind-body relation is to be made sense of."[65] Therefore, as Griffin archly notes, "McGinn has given us a difficult assignment: Our solution must be 'remarkable' and yet not 'extravagant.'"[66]

The almost unanimous rejection of panpsychism as a viable solution to the mind-body problem in today's philosophical circles is telling. Rather than seeing panpsychism as an opportunity to finally make some sense of a problem that has plagued Western philosophy for centuries, most philosophers either ignore panpsychism completely, or dismiss it with a few off-hand comments, preferring instead to cling to materialism.

It seems clear that there are nonrational factors at work in the tenacious defense of materialism, in spite of the fact that it is philosophically so problematic. As Searle notes:

> One of the unstated assumptions behind the current batch of views is that they represent the only scientifically acceptable alternatives to the antiscientism that went with traditional dualism, the belief in the immortality of the soul, spiritualism, and so on. Acceptance of the current views is motivated not so much by an independent conviction of their truth as by a terror of what are apparently the only alternatives.[67]

This fear-based attachment to materialism is, in some respects, understandable. As Thomas Kuhn's work has so helpfully demonstrated, if we are locked into a particular paradigm, we often become blind to phenomena or ideas that do not fit into that paradigm or we reject these alternate possibilities without giving them a careful and thoughtful examination. For a variety of historical and social reasons, detailed so well by Emily Kelly in chapter 2 of *Irreducible Mind*, beginning in the late nineteenth century and continuing up until the present, materialism has been the taken-for-granted assumption of the vast majority of philosophers and psychologists. Given this fact, it is exceedingly difficult to even propose, let alone seriously develop, any alternate hypothesis. As Griffin points out, "we are usually socialized into a paradigm through our schooling, and the paradigm is more or less subtly enforced by hiring, promotion, and tenure committees, by grant-authorizing committees, by journal editors and referees, by book reviewers, and so on."[68]

It is also important to note that advocates of *both* materialism and dualism, for all of their other differences, appear to assume without question a Cartesian/Newtonian understanding of *matter*, in which matter is understood to be atomistic and mechanistically determined and also, significantly, devoid of any experience. However, as we have seen, quantum physics has already challenged the classic understanding of matter as tiny bits of stuff compelled to behave with mathematical certainty. If this is the case (and there is good evidence that it is), then we need to ask whether the other prominent materialist assumption, that is, that matter lacks any dimension of awareness/experience, might also be incorrect. In other words, there seem to be several good reasons why we should take panpsychism seriously.

The majority of this section is dedicated to an examination of the sophisticated version of panpsychism that Bergson articulated in *Matter and Memory*, but before we begin this examination, it might be helpful to summarize briefly the present situation in philosophical and psychological approaches to the dilemma of consciousness:

1) Both materialism and dualism have serious, perhaps insolvable, problems.

2) Many thinkers are convinced that neither materialism nor dualism will ever be able to solve the "hard problem" of how consciousness emerges from material processes.

3) A small group of thinkers is convinced that, if there is a solution to the "hard problem," that we should look in the direction of panpsychism.

4) Panpsychism, as a philosophical position, is typically not taken seriously as a philosophical position, not because it has been refuted by careful, rational argumentation, but rather (in part at least) as the result of a wide variety of non-rational factors and unexamined assumptions.

Given these four observations, it seems clear that panpsychism deserves our thoughtful and sustained philosophical attention. And if in order to proceed further in the study of the nature of consciousness, we need to take panpsychism seriously, then we would do well to look carefully at what is arguably one of the most creative and complex formulations of panpsychism available today: *Matter and Memory*.

14

IMAGES OF THE UNIVERSE

MAKING CONSCIOUSNESS MATTER

In *Matter and Memory*, Bergson builds on the insights that he established in *Time and Free Will*, while also (in ways that he rarely acknowledges) making some subtle (and not so subtle) changes in his understandings of the nature of human consciousness and physical reality. As we saw earlier, in *Time and Free Will* Bergson offered a forceful defense of the freedom and creativity of human consciousness, arguing against those thinkers who claim that our actions are in the end simply the predetermined result of a complicated yet predictable dance of electrochemical interactions. However, in his attempts to underscore the reality of free will, Bergson ended up creating a yawning chasm between matter and consciousness.

According to *Time and Free Will*, matter is a collection of discrete, relatively stable objects, each of which can be measured and counted, objects that interact with each other automatically in ways that are utterly predictable (a type of interaction that causes chemistry experiments to produce the same results every time they are performed). However, according to Bergson's analysis in *Time and Free Will*, consciousness is a dynamic flux of interconnected and interpenetrating states of awareness that never repeat themselves; our consciousness is always new, always creative. The problem is, given this radical distinction between matter and consciousness, how could they possibly interact? Yet this interaction appears to be a basic and ongoing fact of experience. For instance, I make a decision (e.g., to sit down on a chair) and my body responds by sitting down. How is this decision communicated if my mind is utterly different from my physical body? *Matter and Memory* attempts to resolve this dilemma.[1]

In *Matter and Memory*, Bergson argues that we are continually juggling two basic levels of experience. On the one hand, we seem to live in a stable, objective world, a world that is shared by everyone, a world in which objects interact with each other in determined, invariable ways, according to fixed natural laws—a world that does not seem to depend upon anyone's conscious perceptions (e.g., the furniture in my study exists, regardless of whether anyone is present in the room to perceive it). On the other hand, another world of experience also demands our attention. Equally present, equally real, is the world of our conscious perceptions, a level of experience in which the outer world does seem to vary moment to moment, depending upon the subjective perspective of the individual (e.g., if I shut my eyes, the furniture in the room disappears; if I spin around, it seems to move, and so on). In *Matter and Memory*, Bergson attempts to reconcile these two seemingly estranged realities.

Our commonsense understanding of how we come to know the objective world around us is that physical stimuli from this external world impacts our sense organs and these organs then send signals to our brain via the nervous system. Our brain, receiving these signals, promptly translates them into our conscious perceptions. This understanding of the process of perception leads us to assume that we are, in a sense, taking photographs of the universe, using our sense organs as the camera, and developing a picture of the external world by an elaborate electrochemical process in the brain.

The problem with this commonsense understanding, however, is that there still remains a big chasm between the world of matter and consciousness itself. Our consciousness is nothing like a photograph; it is not an inert physical piece of paper coated with chemicals. Consciousness is, on the face of it, inherently nonspatial, inner, subjective, and private, whereas the material brain is inherently spatial, outer, objective, and publicly accessible. We are therefore, as noted earlier, presented with an urgent philosophical question: How are these two very different "stuffs" related? How is it possible that the inert, squishy, neurochemical activity of the brain somehow manages, almost magically, to change into our conscious perceptual experience? Bergson's solution in *Matter and Memory* is ingenious, if perhaps difficult at first to grasp.

MATERIAL IMAGES

Bergson begins by positing a universe that is, below the level of appearances, made up of something he calls "images." (Bergson's use of the technical term "image" is somewhat misleading, in that it is a visual metaphor, and for Bergson, images are much more than simply visual. A cumbersome, yet more accurate phrase, might be "fields of experience.")[2] These images possess qualities that are similar to how both matter and consciousness are often understood.

Bergson's notion of "images" as simultaneously "matter-like" (i.e., as that which comes together to form an external universe that exists independently of us) and "consciousness-like" (i.e., as that which comes together to form our perceptions) may well seem to be some sort of esoteric, highly abstract, philosophical attempt to overcome the Cartesian chasm between our subjective experiences and the objective world described by science—and, to a certain extent, it is. However, in important ways his notion of "images" also emerges out of his attempt to honor the evidence of our common human experience.

Bergson is in certain respects a realist in that he is adamant that perception cannot take place without some sort of contact with the "external" universe. He does not believe (as did certain philosophers active during his time) that perception can and does happen independently of the external world. These philosophers pointed out that, if we look at, for example, a cat curled up in our lap and then shut our eyes, the cat that we just saw can still be "seen" within us by using our imagination—therefore making it appear that the external object (the cat) is not crucial to the process of perception. These philosophers also underscored the fact that dreams and hallucinations "resemble external perception in all their details," but again without any contact with the external world (*MM* 43).

At first glance, these cases would seem to indicate that it is the brain alone that creates our perception of various images (such as the sight of the cat curled in our lap or our dream image of, for instance, an old, beat-up VW van). Bergson notes, however, that in cases such as these what is actually most important is *memory*—and as he will argue vehemently later in *Matter and Memory*, memory is quite different from perception (although they can and do interact). It is memory that, for instance, allows a person who has become blind later in life to recall (or dream, or hallucinate) various visual images from before she or he became blind. However, as Bergson goes on to note, if that same individual had been *born* blind, then he or she would never be able to experience a single visual image. As this case makes clear, perception per se (i.e., perception that is unalloyed with memory) is always dependent upon some sort of interaction with the external world.

A CONSCIOUS UNIVERSE

Before we go any further, it is crucial to note that Bergson's understanding of the external world is radically different from how it is normally understood either by common sense or by classical physics. As we saw earlier, for Bergson the world of separate objects that we normally perceive is not the true nature of matter. Instead, according to him, the physical universe, like our consciousness, is an interconnected, dynamic continuum of becoming in which "numberless vibrations, all linked together in uninterrupted continuity" travel "in every direction like shivers through an immense body" (*MM* 208). This vast, pulsating, interconnected universe consists entirely of dynamic patterns of energy, vortices of

vibrations that radiate outward, contacting and affecting other complexly patterned vortices of energy. Therefore, the external world is *not* made up of
"objects."[3] Instead, it consists of innumerable fields of energy, and these fields of
energy are what Bergson calls "images."

As was underscored in the liminal section, most theoretical physicists today
would almost certainly take for granted Bergson's claim that the physical universe does not consist of tiny unchanging "nuggets" of "hard stuff" whizzing
around in the void, but instead is a highly complex, ever-changing network of
energy. However, Bergson's next step would likely be much more controversial,
in that he postulates that the overlapping fields of energy that make up the universe are neither inert nor non-aware, but instead are a type of "virtual" or
"latent" consciousness. It is quite likely that most scientists (as well as the average
person on the street) would part company with Bergson at this juncture.[4] It is all
well and good to challenge our preconscious Newtonian belief in separate,
clearly bounded, atomistic objects. But to go on to claim, as Bergson does, that
"the material universe itself, defined as the totality of images, is a kind of consciousness," to assert that consciousness, in a latent form, is already present in
this universe of images—that assertion would almost certainly be dismissed out
of hand by many if not most scientists in that it forcibly calls into question one
of the Western world's most central (and unexamined) metaphysical assumptions
about matter, that is, that matter is dead, inert, non-aware (*MM* 235).

Bergson's radical philosophical revisioning of the nature of matter strongly
contests one of the most taken-for-granted presuppositions of modern science.
However, by doing so it offers us a potential gift: the possibility that we might
finally be able to make sense of the mind-body dilemma.

In Bergson's vision of the universe, consciousness is not a mystery to be
solved. Instead, consciousness is always present in the very heart of "things." As
Frédéric Worms astutely notes, "It is not the world which is a content of consciousness, but consciousness which is a property of the world."[5] Consciousness
is not somehow inexplicably and almost magically produced by the interactions
of inert matter. Consciousness is not secretly added into the mix at just the right
moment. Instead, it is already there under the surface as a latent aspect of the
very tangible and material "stuff" of the universe—Bergson's "images." This
dynamic flux of images is itself what allows anything to be perceived—it is as if,
for Bergson, matter is perceiving itself at every moment. Or in Merleau-Ponty's
memorable phrasing, "it is as if my vision took place in them [the images] rather
than in myself."[6]

Bergson postulates that the streaming, interpenetrating, protoconscious
images that make up the universe are a ceaseless whirl of activity in which a constant transmission of energy information is moment to moment passed on from
one image to the next. As such, each image of the universe acts as merely "a road
by which pass, in every direction, the modifications propagated throughout the

immensity of the universe" (*MM* 36). Each image, therefore, is influenced by, and influences, to a greater or lesser degree all the other images of the universe and all of these influences flow through all of the images of the universe basically unimpeded (*MM* 38). Every image, both individually and collectively, reacts to the universal influx of information/energy. However, for the most part (i.e., when these images are acting as the physical universe typically does) they do so without hesitation, automatically, fully, and seemingly out of necessity—transmitting that reaction in turn to all the other "points" of matter in the universe. Therefore, from one moment to the next, each "point" of the material universe (and remember: these "points" are not localized, atomistic entities) receives and transmits a "snapshot" of the entire universe, a type of flash or pulse of universal information through all the lines of force or influence that interconnect all of the images. It is this measurable, predictable, lawful interaction between various images that Bergson claims is the basis for the stable, objective world of matter, a world rooted in the dependable, repeatable patterns of cause and effect studied by the natural sciences.

THE CREATION OF PERCEPTIONS

However, a crucial question immediately presents itself: How is the set of images that constitute the external world related to the set of images that make up our individual perceptions of the universe? These two sets of images certainly appear at least at first glance to be quite different from one another. For instance, at this moment I am certainly not aware of any universal flux of information passing unimpeded through me. My perceptions seem to be quite limited and localized and they seem to center around my body as the primary point of reference. My perceptions also alter with each movement of my physical body. As Bergson observes, when the "privileged image" that constitutes my body shifts in any way, then everything around me changes as well, "as though by a turn of a kaleidoscope" (*MM* 25). It is not at all clear, therefore, how the images that make up the quasi-automatic, orderly, regulated, predictable, objective universe are related to that other set of images (i.e., our personal perceptions) which seem to be so unstable, shifting, contingent, and subjective.

Matter and Memory offers a straightforward (albeit rather abstract) solution. Bergson hypothesizes that the universe of virtually conscious images are for the most part "indifferent to each other"—meaning that they simply act and react to all of the other images of matter automatically out of necessity (*MM* 37). However, this robotic interaction (i.e., the physical world as studied by Newtonian science) is interrupted when the influences radiating out from these images encounter the images that constitute an embodied living being. An embodied living being acts and responds, not out of necessity, but instead with various degrees of spontaneity and freedom, depending upon its level of evolution. (A more evolved organism will react less reflexively or habitually and thus will have a greater range of choices.) This living organism, in F. C. T. Moore's words, is "selectively sensitive" to its environment and responds only to those properties or qualities of the environment that are important to it, ignoring the rest.[7] By doing so, the embodied organism limits and diminishes the universal flux of information. However, this limitation, this choosing to pay attention to only a small segment of what exists, is what actualizes the consciousness that was previously latent in the cosmic dynamism. As Bergson points out, "consciousness—in regard to external perception—lies in just this choice. But there is, in this necessary poverty of our conscious perceptions, something that is positive, that foretells spirit: it is . . . discernment" (*MM* 38).

In *Matter and Memory*, therefore, Bergson postulates that perception (i.e., our personal, subjective set of images) occurs when we select out and actualize only a tiny percentage of the infinitely complex, interpenetrating, multilayered, vibratory field of virtual consciousness that surrounds us. The material universe, according to Bergson, is a kind of "neutralized" or "latent consciousness" in which the potential gleams of full-fledged consciousness "annul each other precisely at the moment when they might appear" in the flux of matter (*MM* 248). Our individual perceptions take place when we remove the obstacle to the emergence of consciousness, when we extract "from the whole that is real a part that is virtual," when we choose and finally disengage from the whole that part of the material world which interests us (*MM* 248).[8]

RUMINATION: OPENING OURSELVES TO THE WHOLE

As someone who has spent much time immersed in various meditative or contemplative traditions, I will admit that it was rather disconcerting when I first read Bergson's discussion of the relationship between perception and matter. Many meditative and contemplative techniques are explicitly intended to help us to open up our awareness, to remove the blocks that separate us from the wider cosmos, to dismantle the subconscious filters that so effortlessly create a world of discrete objects within our perceptions and that so effectively convince us that we are a small, relatively insignificant speck of dust in an uncaring universe. From the point of view of these meditative and contemplative traditions, in order to move toward a more expanded awareness and to cultivate a greater connection with the universe at large, it is crucial to learn how to quiet the mind and to dissolve our egoic sense of separation and limitation in order to perceive directly and as fully as possible our oneness with all of existence. From the perspective of many, if not most mystical traditions, this movement toward what might be called a type of spiritual "super-consciousness" is, or at least should be, the telos of every human being.

At least in *Matter and Memory*, Bergson seems to disagree. For Bergson, moving toward an increased openness to the totality of the universe is actually a movement toward materiality and unconsciousness, not a movement toward increased spiritual awareness. He claims that, understood from a certain point of view, an "unconscious material point" has (paradoxically) a type of awareness that is "infinitely greater and more complete than ours, since this point gathers and transmits the influences of all the points of the material universe" (*MM* 38). Nonetheless, according to Bergson, possessing this type of cosmic awareness is not exactly something to be highly prized, since as he puts it, "to perceive all the influences from all the points of all bodies would be to descend to the condition of a material object" (*MM* 49).

According to Bergson, rather than attempting to open ourselves to the vastness of our innate, but typically unperceived, connection to the universal material flux, we should instead cherish the limitations and exclusions that come hand in hand with the creation of our personal consciousness. While ironically our conscious awareness is much more restricted and partial than that of an "unconscious material point," nonetheless, that limitation is itself a hidden gift: the gift that unlocks and actualizes the virtual consciousness that is always present within the heart of materiality itself. Therefore, in *Matter and Memory* consciousness only becomes actualized when, because of increased limitations (i.e., increased options, increased choices, increased hesitation, increased freedom), a small part of the flux of the whole is reflected back to its source, leaving the rest of the dynamic, pulsing, interpenetrating (and yet deeply habituated) fields of potential consciousness (i.e., images) that are coursing through that organism unnoticed. In *Matter and Memory*, the direction toward increased consciousness is *away* from immediacy, *away* from complete transparency, *away* from full connection to the totality of the material universe.

At first blush therefore it would appear that Bergson would not be supportive of those meditative and contemplative techniques that seek to open us up to an increased awareness of our connection to the universe. However, while this might be a reasonable inference from Bergson's work in *Matter and Memory*, in the later phases of his career, Bergson offers an increasingly affirmative assessment of the value of contemplative and meditative techniques. For instance, in his third major work, *Creative Evolution*, Bergson begins to move strongly toward a positive evaluation of the task of cultivating and nurturing an immediate intuitive awareness of one's connection to the cosmic flux of life. And by the time of *The Two Sources of Morality and Religion*, Bergson asserts in no uncertain terms that those individuals who have developed this intuitive capacity to its fullest extent (i.e., advanced contemplatives or mystics) are able to become extremely effective catalysts of cultural transformation in large part due to their direct, immediate sense of their ongoing connection to the oneness/manyness of Life itself.[9]

It is therefore really only after *Matter and Memory* that Bergson proposes a form of awareness that, in some ways, can be seen as of the capacity to comprehend the depths of the universe and one's own being: *intuition.*

Throughout his career, Bergson offered several different ways to understand intuition. On the most basic level, intuition is that learned (and extremely arduous) capacity to come to know, from the inside, one's own personal durée. As Bergson emphasized, especially beginning with *Introduction to Metaphysics*, this capacity itself has the potential, if developed, to become a type of philosophical method, a way of accessing information on the nature of consciousness, time, and life that the intellect is incapable of accessing (due to its biological imperative to focus on solid, countable material "things" and clear-cut, logical ideas).

Over time, Bergson began to argue that this intuitive immediacy, this alternative way of knowledge, could also be extended to other modes of durée as well. Understood from this point of view, intuition can be seen as "the *sympathy* by which one is transported into the interior of an object in order to coincide with what there is unique and consequently inexpressible in it" (*CM* 190). By the time of *Creative Evolution*, Bergson began to envision the entire universe itself, and all the forms of consciousness within it, as a single, complexly interwoven, dynamic continuum of differing "rhythms" of durée—a continuum that is itself the ever-changing, highly pluralistic manifestation of the élan vital—that cosmic evolutionary life force that propels the universe forward, that universal super-consciousness that manifests in-and-as each level of individual consciousness, that unfolds in each flower petal, and that vibrates in each quantum pulsation. Understood from this perspective (and all perspectives on intuition, according to Bergson, are inescapably partial), intuition began to be seen as not only as a type of higher octave overtone or alternative to both instinct and intellect, but also as the human capacity, cultivated to differing degrees, to align ourselves with, and to have immediate access to the élan vital, that is, to creativity, energy, consciousness, movement, and change itself on a cosmic scale—that is, the capacity to attune ourselves to that which underlies *both* matter and the different levels of consciousness that are found, not only in all living creatures, but also in all material forms.

Therefore, to the degree that we can cultivate an intuitive attunement with the élan vital we are able to discover within ourselves a corresponding sense of cosmic oneness and universal connectedness (i.e., the qualities of materiality), but without the robotic quasi-determinism that is so characteristic of matter. Simultaneously, to the degree that we can cultivate this intuitive attunement with the élan vital, we are also able to find the freedom and spontaneity that is characteristic of human consciousness, but without those "parts" of ourselves that are most matter-like, that is, without the habitual, driven, repetitive, formulaic, predictable aspects of ourselves that are so characteristic of our day-to-day awareness.

The question then becomes: How can we deepen our connection to the élan vital? Bergson does not give a lot of focused attention to this question, but I would argue that he, at least implicitly, suggests that we are able to deepen this connection the more that we can tune into the depths of our own consciousness, the more that we can sense, and feel, and move with that life that is present at all times (*as* time) both within us and around us, the more that we become truly conscious of our own consciousness.

One place in Bergson's work where he explicitly discusses the value of opening ourselves up to the depths of our conscious experience happens toward the end of an essay in *The Creative Mind* ("Philosophical Intuition"). Bergson, in this lyrical section, describes what takes place within us when we "become accustomed to see all things *sub specie durationis*"—that is, when we become conscious of and aligned with the depths of our consciousness as it expresses itself in and through the particularities of each moment (*CM* 152). As he points out, when we become increasingly aware of durée within us, and in all things, "immediately in our galvanized perception what is taut becomes relaxed, what is dormant awakens, what is dead comes to life again" (*CM* 152). As a result of this new way of seeing and experiencing life, "all of us, at all times" are offered a quality of insight which not only revives and revitalizes us, but also breathes "life once again into the phantoms which surround us" (*CM* 152). Because of our immersion in this intuitive level of perception, we become as it were artists of our own lives; that is, we begin to experience the joy that comes from tapping into and expressing the sheer exuberant creativity of life itself.

According to Bergson's later work, this capacity to deepen our intuitive ability culminates in the mystics from various cultures, that is, in those individuals who typically through the ongoing practice of various meditative and contemplative techniques have cultivated within themselves the most profound connection to the élan vital that is possible for human beings. Therefore, while in *Matter and Memory* Bergson endorses the value of *cutting ourselves off* from the whole in favor of the *finitude and limitations* of personal consciousness, by the time of Bergson's discussion of intuition in *Creative Evolution* and his investigation of mysticism in *The Two Sources of Morality and Religion* he articulates a worldview that affirms the value of *reconnecting* to the whole and *expanding* our consciousness—a process that at least for many mystics is often assisted by spiritual techniques such as meditation and contemplation.

15

NONLOCALITY AND BERGSON'S UNIVERSE OF IMAGES

BELL'S THEOREM AND NONLOCALITY

Some might argue that Bergson's hypothesis that the physical universe is not a collection of discrete, localized, individual parts mechanically interacting with each other, but instead is an interconnected, dynamic, unimaginably complex, protoconscious "symphony" in which every "note" of the universe is effected by, and effects, every other "note" is itself closer to a mystical vision than to a viable articulation of the nature of physical reality. However, relatively recently physicists working in quantum mechanics have proposed several theories (confirmed by experimental findings) that appear to support Bergson's vision of the universe: a universe in which each apparently separate "thing" seems to be unceasingly (and instantaneously) communicating with, or intrinsically linked to, every other "thing."

It is impossible, within the limitations of this work, to give a full or detailed account of the theoretical formulations and experimental findings that underlie this vision of universal interconnectedness—an interconnectedness that is so profound that even the notion of separate "things" begins to seem more like a useful fiction than an ontological reality. Nonetheless, a good beginning of this account might be in 1964, when J. S. Bell, a physicist working at the European Organization for Nuclear Research in Switzerland, published a mathematical theorem (later known as Bell's theorem) that, according to some physicists, may well be "the most important single work, perhaps, in the history of physics."[1] The revolutionary implications of Bell's theorem will hopefully become clear further on, but in order to set the stage, let's look first at an experiment that is closely related to the central insights of Bell's theorem, an experiment designed

130

to highlight the uncanny and perplexing connectedness between certain quantum phenomena.

While working as a physicist at the University of London, David Bohm devised an experiment designed to investigate a "two-particle system of zero spin."[2] In this two particle system, the spin of one particle is opposite to the spin of the other in that, if one of the particles has an "up" spin, then the other particle will have a "down" spin (or if one of the particles has a "left" spin, then the other particle will have a "right" spin, and so forth)—that is, the spins of the paired particles in the system are always equal to and yet the opposite of each other. Let's imagine, for instance, that one of the particles of this pair is sent in direction A and that it goes through a magnetic device that registers that it has an "up" spin. The other particle, meanwhile, is sent in direction B. Inevitably and *instantaneously* it is determined that the particle sent in direction B has shifted as well and has taken on a corresponding and equal "down" spin. Somehow, inexplicably, it appears that the particle sent in direction B "knows" that its twin in area A, after going through the magnetic device, has been found to be in a spin "up" state (instead of, let's say, "right") and the particle in area B *instantaneously* acquires a spin "down" state (instead of "left").

This strange phenomenon is known as the Einstein-Podolsky-Rosen (EPR) effect after the paper published in 1935 by Albert Einstein, Boris Podolsky, and Nathan Rosen that described a similar thought experiment.[3] The crucial question raised by these experiments is this: How is it possible for the two particles in this pair to communicate so quickly? Information carried from one place to another typically does so via a signal of some sort. For instance, when we speak to one another, our words are carried by sound waves, which travel around 700 miles per hour. Similarly, if we see something, that information travels to our eyes via light waves, which move at approximately 186,000 miles per second. However, according to the EPR effect, regardless of how far the two particles are, when the particle in area A is affected by the choice of the experimenter to, let's say, give the particle in that area an "up" spin, the particle in area B will *instantaneously* have a "down" spin—even if the two particles were so far apart that there would not be enough time for a signal of light to cover the distance. What makes the EPR effect so fascinating is that it seems that the two particles are (as it were) communicating with each other faster than the speed of light, which defies one of the central assumptions of physics that posits it is not possible for anything in the universe to travel faster than the speed of light.

Because Einstein was convinced that a signal could not travel faster than the speed of light, by proposing this thought experiment, he was attempting to demonstrate that quantum theory was seriously flawed, since quantum theory insists that the results of the experiment should be exactly as was described previously. As Einstein put it in his autobiographical notes, the only way in which it would be possible to make sense of the results of this thought experiment (i.e., the only way that quantum physics would not have a flaw) would be to assume either "that the measurement of [particle A] (telepathically) changes the real situation of [particle B]" or to simply deny that "things are spatially separated from each other. Both alternatives appear to me entirely unacceptable."[4]

Many quantum physicists, however, disagreed with Einstein. And what made Bell's theorem so significant is that it appeared to give mathematical support to those quantum physicists who opposed Einstein's conclusions (Bell's theorem is based upon the correlations that exist between paired entangled particles that act in ways that are similar to the particles described in the EPR effect thought experiment—and in Bohm's experiment as well).

Crucially, in 1982, Alain Aspect, Jean Dalibard, and Gérard Roger, physicists at the Institute of Optics at the University of Paris, provided experimental validation of the predictions of quantum mechanics upon which Bell's theorem is based. Albert Einstein had earlier disparaged this type of "spooky action at a distance," in which subatomic particles seem to know, instantaneously, what has occurred to another particle, even if those changes theoretically took place as far away as another galaxy. However, this "action at a distance," spooky or not, is exactly what appears to have been decisively confirmed by Aspect and his team. Aspect's laboratory findings demonstrated, as Michael Talbot points out, "that either Einstein's ban against faster-than-light communication was being violated, or the two photons were nonlocally connected."[5] Because most physicists still maintain the impossibility of faster-than-light communication, Aspect's findings are "generally viewed as virtual proof that the connection between the two photons is nonlocal."[6]

In order to understand the concept of "nonlocality" we first have to let go of our commonsense understandings of what an object is, and especially our understandings of a specific type of object: a subatomic particle. A particle as it is normally understood is "local"; that is, it is an object that has clear-cut boundaries in space. It is said to be "here," which means that it cannot also be "there." A particle located "here" could, in various ways, communicate to another particle over "there," but this communication should always take time, even if this time is measured in microseconds. And if the two particles are located in different galaxies, because of the limitations imposed by the speed of light, this communication should take centuries.[7] However, in the experimental confirmation of Bell's theorem, the two particles change *instantaneously*—regardless of their distance from each other. What this implies is that, in order for a particle to know instantaneously what is going on "over there," it must also somehow actually exist over there; that is to say, the connection between the two particles is "nonlocal."[8] But if it is somehow possible for a particle to be "both places at once, then it is no longer a particle. . . . This means that 'particles' may not be particles at all."[9]

As has been shown earlier, Bergson theorizes that matter is not intrinsically divided up into particles that have a precise, measurable location; for Bergson, matter is better understood as wave-like, spreading in all directions and penetrating the furthest reaches of the universe. According to this vision of matter each wave would both affect and be affected by all of the other waves that they contact. Nonetheless, as Čapek points out (critiquing Bergson), because of the finite velocity of light this "spreading influence" of matter cannot (or should not) be instantaneous, and therefore local or regional disturbances of the spatiotemporal matrix should not *immediately* affect *every aspect* of the whole. A universal interactiveness may indeed take place, but as Čapek emphasizes, this process necessarily *"takes time."*[10]

However, again, Aspect and his team proved that a quantum entity such as a photon is able somehow to influence another quantum entity *instantaneously* over *any* distance, without any exchange of force or energy.[11] Furthermore, as Paul Davis (a physicist at the University of Newcastle) observed, because subatomic particles are constantly interacting with each other, it would appear that "the nonlocal aspects of quantum systems [are] therefore a general property of nature."[12] If this is the case (and the experimental results appear to be conclusive), then the world, under the surface, behaves in a way that is radically different from how it is typically understood, both by common sense and by classical physics.

NONLOCALITY AND THE WORK OF DAVID BOHM

So how is it possible to explain these extremely counterintuitive experimental results? Several mutually exclusive possibilities have been proposed. Most physicists, at least implicitly, align themselves with the Copenhagen Interpretation of Quantum Mechanics. The Copenhagen Interpretation argues that quantum physicists should, in essence, ignore the philosophical issues raised by these types of experiments. From this perspective, it is simply not possible to articulate any ultimately verifiable model of reality as it is, independent of our experience.

For those few physicists who are not satisfied with the Copenhagen Interpretation and who remain interested in the deeper philosophical implications of Bell's theorem, other options remain on the table, (e.g., superdeterminism and the Many Worlds theory).[13] However, there is yet another option: accepting the notion of nonlocality. This interpretation of the findings of Bell's theorem (and its experimental verification) postulates, in a way that is similar to Bergson's understanding of matter, that there really are no such things as "things" in the universe, even if classical physics (and our common sense) tells us otherwise. From this perspective, instead of seeing the twin particles as separate, independent "things," it makes more sense to understand them as two aspects of an indivisible (albeit highly dynamic) whole.

David Bohm is perhaps the most influential and well-known advocate of this way of making sense of Bell's theorem. In Bohm's complex system, the unbroken, dynamic wholeness of life that underlies and connects all of the apparent atomistic fragmentation that we perceive in our day-to-day existence is referred to as the "implicate order." Bohm postulates that this fundamental matrix of reality underlies and continually gives birth to the "explicate order"— that is, the everyday, tangible world of ordinary reality, a world of separate objects that have distinct boundaries and that interact with each other in space and time according to natural laws. According to Bohm, every form in the explicate order is virtually present or "enfolded" within the implicate order. From this perspective, for instance, an electron is not in actuality an isolated particle, but rather is enfolded throughout the implicate order. When an instrument appears to detect the activity of a single electron, what that instrument is registering is simply one aspect of the electron that has unfolded "from" the implicate order "into" the space/time of the explicate order. As Michael Talbot eloquently puts it, seen from this perspective, "electrons and all other particles are no more substantive or permanent than the form a geyser of water takes as it gushes out of a fountain. They are sustained by a constant influx from the implicate order, and when a particle appears to be destroyed, it is not lost. It has merely enfolded back into the deeper order from which it sprang."[14] Understood in this way, the continual change of forms that takes place on a subatomic level, in which one particle appears to shape-shift into another, is nothing more than the process by which, for instance, one particle, say an electron, enfolds back into the implicate order, while another particle, say a photon, unfolds in its place. Similarly, the mysterious way in which a quantum can manifest as either a particle or as a wave can be understood as simply different manifestations of potentials that are always virtually present in the implicate order, but which are unfolded into the explicate order due to the choices made by the observer in the experimental setting.[15]

According to Bohm, the entire universe is a "holomovement"; that is, it is a dynamic unified field of reality in which every "part" enfolds the whole (and the whole is enfolded in every "part")—so much so that it becomes meaningless to speak of separate "parts." To a certain extent, dividing the "holomovement" of the universe into separate, nameable "things" is an arbitrary process, based as much upon convention as upon the independent properties of the "things" themselves. However, importantly, as Talbot points out, Bohm's emphasis on the underlying wholeness of reality "does not mean the universe is a giant undifferentiated mass."[16] In the same way that ripples and eddies and whirlpools are distinctive and relatively stable patterns of movement within a larger stream, objects in the universe can and do have their own unique characteristics, while simultaneously remaining connected to a larger unified whole. Bohm's point is simply that the process of dividing the "holomovement" of reality into fixed, stable, atomistic "things" is always, to a certain extent, an abstraction from a much more complex, ever-changing, multileveled, and interconnected universe.

In the dynamic "holomovement" of reality, matter and the mind are also simply two aspects of a single interconnected whole. According to Bohm, "the mental and the material are two sides of one overall process. . . . There is one energy that is the basis of all reality."[17] Bohm suggests that "mind" (or some aspect of mind) is always present in every material form and that it is quite possible that "a rudimentary consciousness is present even at the level of particle physics."[18] Moreover, Bohm goes on to propose that something else may also exist underneath this infinite multiplicity of different levels of consciousness, that is, "an indefinitely greater kind of consciousness that is universal and that pervades the entire process [of the universe]."[19]

Bohm's perspective, like that of Bergson's, can perhaps best be described, in the words of David Skrbina, as "a form of participatory panpsychism."[20] Both Bohm and Bergson agree that the process by which "things" interact with each other is not a mechanical collision of atomistic units. Instead, as Bohm puts it, perhaps "the whole system is undergoing a coordinated movement more like a ballet dance than like a crowd of unorganized people"; seen in this way, the "quantum wholeness of activity is closer to the organized unity of the functioning of the parts of a living being than it is to the kind of unity that is obtained by putting together the parts of a machine."[21] In this type of participatory panpsychism, we are engaged moment to moment in a mutually transformative "dance" with the rest of the universe. In this dance, our own choices and decisions become in effect microcosmic exemplars and instantiations of the macrocosm. This is the case because, as Bohm points out, "the whole of the universe is in some way enfolded in everything and . . . each thing is enfolded in the whole."[22]

It is crucial to remember that, while Bohm's philosophical speculations represent a minority opinion within the world of quantum mechanics, he is, nonetheless, highly respected as a theorist by many within the physics community. While it is safe to say that most physicists prefer to focus primarily upon the nuts and bolts of mathematical formulations and experimental work, within the small cluster of physicists who are willing to give focused time to exploring the metaphysical implications of the experimental verification of Bell's theorem, Bohm's work is taken very seriously.

Given the striking correspondence between Bohm's perspective and Bergson's metaphysical vision (especially as it is articulated in *Matter and Memory* and *Creative Evolution*), it seems clear that Bergson's work should be taken very seriously as well. Admittedly, there are several differences in the outlook of these two thinkers—for example, Bergson does not discuss nonlocality or the possibility of the macrocosm existing within the microcosm and Bohm's writings, as a physicist, do not possess Bergson's nuanced understandings of the nature of memory and consciousness. Nonetheless, both thinkers articulate pluralistic or participatory versions of panpsychism: that is, both stress the interconnectedness of existence; both deconstruct the notion of "thing-ness"; both emphasize the dynamism of reality; both argue that consciousness exists in a wide variety of manifestations within every material form; and both postulate the existence of a universal, all pervasive form of consciousness. Therefore, Bergson's work, far from being an antiquated historical relic, can and should be seen, instead, as an extremely relevant and philosophically sophisticated perspective that is mirrored in and echoed by some of the most provocative and intriguing theoretical formulations within the contemporary world of quantum physics.

16

PERCEPTIONS AND THE BRAIN

PURE PERCEPTIONS

It is important to recognize that, up until this point, in the discussion of the genesis of perception, the focus has *not* been on our everyday, concrete perceptions. (These concrete perceptions, according to Bergson, are a fusion of what he calls "pure perceptions" and memory.) Instead, we have been examining the "raw data" of perception—that is, "pure perception": perception as it would appear if we could somehow, impossibly, isolate the process of perception from the ever-present, but typically unnoticed, activity of memory; perception that is as close as possible to the immediacy and seeming nontemporality of matter.

What Bergson calls "pure perception" is, therefore, an analytical construct; it is an intellectual artifact that is never actually experienced directly by anyone, at any time. However, the notion of "pure perception" is a very useful analytical tool, because it enables us to recognize that there is a "that-ness," a stubbornly objective "external" matter-like aspect to our everyday perceptions, a core of our perceptual experience that, while it may be partial, is nevertheless also not relative, not simply our own subjective creation.

According to Bergson, these pure perceptions are a type of filtrate from the totality of the universal flux of potential consciousness in which we find ourselves. Our pure perceptions are, therefore, the result of a radical truncation, a culling process by which we ignore most of what we might potentially know. As such, pure perceptions are not something that is added onto matter; they do not occur when our brains somehow miraculously convert inert, nonconscious images into our conscious perceptual experience. Instead, for Bergson, our pure perceptions are themselves an aspect of the material (albeit implicitly conscious) universe. No mysterious something is added to pure perceptions to make them conscious. Instead, our pure perceptions are what occur when living, conscious beings (themselves made of images) focus their attention on a very small subset of the universal flux of images that interest them, when they select out of that flux only those images that have practical importance for their own existence. The data from which our pure perceptions emerge has always been present, but as far as we are concerned, that data has only a virtual existence. In order for a pure perception to become actual, as living beings, we have to "obscure" or "diminish" some of its qualities; that is, we have to "suppress" those aspects of the image field that do not interest us (*MM* 36). As a result of this radical truncation, we perceive only the "external crust" or the "superficial shell" of what actually surrounds us (*MM* 36).

However, while our pure perceptions, in relation to the universe of images, are simply a small part of the greater whole, Bergson claims that they are neither relative nor illusory. Pure perceptions are rooted in reality, unlike Kantian relativism, "because the relation between the 'phenomenon' and the 'thing' is not that of appearance to reality, but merely that of the part to the whole" (*MM* 230). While our pure perceptions may not reveal to us all that there is to know in the world around us, nonetheless, they are not subjective since they are "in things rather than in me" (*MM* 230). Our pure perceptions are, as Pete Gunter puts it, "in-the-world: that is, [they are] ec-static."[1] They are not "in our heads"; they are not created by our brains. Instead, according to Bergson, our pure perceptions are "matter-like" and extended—they do not take place "in here," but rather "out there," exactly where they seem to be. (In other words, most people do not think that the tree that they perceive is inside of them, but rather that it exists in an external world.) The job of the sense organs, nervous system, and the brain (which are themselves images) is not to *create* our conscious perceptions. Instead, the "raw data" of our perceptions is part and parcel of the world around us.

Bergson does not shy away from the implications of this unique epistemology. As he puts it, "we are really present in everything we perceive" (*TS* 259).[2] In reality, therefore, our body is not limited to the small physical organism with which we typically identify (although that body always remains the vital center of our world). We also possess a massive body made up of the totality of our conscious perceptions, a body that, in a very real sense, "reaches to the stars" (*TS* 258).

PERCEPTIONS AND THE PHYSICAL BODY

However, while we might, unknown to us, possess this huge, quasi-universal body, our smaller body, our "inner and central body," remains vitally important to us in the moment-to-moment process of perception (*TS* 258). Our physical body (especially our senses, nervous system, and brain) acts as a type of dynamic filter that continually screens out the vast majority of the information we receive from the mass of potential consciousness that surrounds us in order that we might act effectively and flourish as a physical organism. Our senses acknowledge only a small percentage of the streaming dynamic fields of virtual consciousness (i.e., images) in the world that surrounds us; these images influence the sense organs, which modify the nerves—and this "data" is then transmitted to the brain. (It is important to remember that, for Bergson, the sense organs, the nerves, and the brain are also all images themselves.)

According to Bergson, our body (in particular, our sense organs, brain, and nervous system) is at every moment influenced by the onrush of images that make up the external universe—images that are constantly transmitting vibratory "movements" to our sense organs, nerves, and brain. Our body, in turn, after screening out those "movements" that do not concern it, influences the external universe as well, transmitting its own variety of movements out into the surrounding cosmos. In this way, our body acts almost identically to the other images that make up the material universe, with one crucial difference: it chooses, with various degrees of freedom, what actions to take. The body of a living organism is unique among other images in that its actions are freely chosen, at least to the extent that is possible, given the evolutionary development of the organism. The actions of a living organism are not automatic, unlike the images of the inanimate physical universe that act in ways that can be measured and predicted.

This way of explaining the genesis of perception is very different from our typical, taken-for-granted understanding of the dynamics of perception, in which we imagine (as was noted before) that perception is similar to taking photographs of the universe with a camera. According to this commonsense metaphorical understanding of perception (which typically focuses on *visual* perception, since our eyes are the sense organ that is most developed in our species), our eyes can be understood to be the lens of the camera and our optic nerve and brain can be seen as mysterious, hidden mechanisms that convert the light into a photograph via an elaborate imaging process. The trouble with this notion of the genesis of perception, however, is that it is exceedingly difficult to conceive of how our brain magically manages to change the inert material vibrations of light and the inert, squishy, pulpy, neurochemical activity of the brain into our conscious perceptual experience.

The benefit of Bergson's model of perception is that the genesis of our conscious perceptions does not have to be explained, since everything in the material world, as the totality of images, is at all times *already* a type of latent or virtual consciousness. For Bergson, the photograph of our perceptual experience of the world, if it is being taken, is being taken (and developed) at every moment "in the very heart of things and at all the points of space" (*MM* 38).

According to this model, the brain does not *produce* consciousness; instead, it receives and responds to those preexisting fields of consciousness that serve its own practical needs. Therefore, as Bergson notes, *"what you have to explain, then, is not how perception arises, but how it is limited, since it should be the image of the whole, and is in fact reduced to the image of that which interests you"* (*MM* 40, his emphasis).

Relationships between the Brain and Consciousness

According to Bergson, it is important to remember that the creation of pure perceptions is intimately linked to the physical activities taking place within our body (especially within our brain and nervous system). He argues, however, that the relationship between the activity of the brain/nervous system and perception is not the simple, one-way, causal relationship that is often assumed by most philosophers, psychologists, and scientists. These theorists often act as if it is self-evident that the neurochemical activity of the brain/nervous system *causes* our perceptions of the world around us; however, as Bergson notes, strictly speaking, "all that observation, experience, and consequently science, allows us to affirm is the existence of a certain *relation* between brain and mind" (*ME* 46). He goes on to emphasize that "the relation of the mental to the cerebral is not a constant, any more than it is a simple, relation" (*MM* 14).

Susan Blackmore makes a similar point. She emphasizes that when we examine the relationship between neurology and consciousness, all that we can legitimately describe are the "neural correlates of consciousness."[3] As she correctly points out, it is important to remember that "a correlation is not the same as a cause."[4] It is crucial to acknowledge, therefore, that while it might indeed be true that specific neurochemical activities cause corresponding shifts in our consciousness, it is equally possible that the changes in the neurochemical activity in the brain may themselves be caused by shifts in consciousness, or in turn that "some other event or process" might have caused *both* to change. (Blackmore also gives a nod to "eliminative materialism" by noting that neurochemical shifts in the brain and shifts in consciousness "might actually be the same thing even though they do not appear to be"; to her credit, for the sake of philosophical completeness, she even notes that "perhaps we have so misconstrued one or [the] other that none of them is true.")[5]

Compelling evidence that the relationship between the brain and consciousness is perhaps more complicated than is often acknowledged is provided by the British neurologist John Lorber (evidence that was popularized by Roger Lewin in 1980, in an article in *Science*: "Is Your Brain Really Necessary?"). Lorber did extensive studies of people who suffer hydrocephalus, more commonly known as "water on the brain" (an ailment that results from an abnormal build-up of cerebrospinal fluid). While many of the individuals suffering from this ailment are severely mentally impaired, Lorber also discovered to his surprise that some of these individuals have IQs greater than 100 and live utterly normal lives, even though in several cases *they have virtually no brain*.[6]

Lorber initially became aware of this phenomenon when a colleague at Sheffield University noticed a young man on campus with a larger than normal head. This young man was referred to Lorber even though his skull size had not caused him any difficulty. (He had an IQ of 126 and was an honors student in mathematics.) CAT scans revealed that his skull was lined with only a paper-thin layer of brain cells, approximately a millimeter in thickness, while the rest of his skull was filled with cerebrospinal fluid. Lorber estimated that his brain weighed only between 50 to 150 grams, instead of the normal 1.5 kilograms.

Lorber subsequently went on to do a systematic study of over six hundred individuals with this ailment. The group with the most severe levels of the disease (i.e., those whose cranial cavity was 95 percent filled with cerebrospinal fluid) composed less than 10 percent of the total sample. Half of these individuals were profoundly mentally handicapped. The other half, however, all had IQs over 100.

When confronted with the evidence that it is possible to possess an above-average intelligence and the ability to function effectively in social settings, while having essentially no brain (or at least only a tiny fraction of the tissue that a normal brain possesses), some neurologists have claimed that this amazing phenomenon is simply a tribute to the brain's redundancy and its ability to reassign functions. However, others have admitted that they remain perplexed and state openly that they have no way to account for this phenomenon within the parameters of conventional understandings of how the brain operates.[7]

UNDERSTANDING THE RELATIONSHIP BETWEEN THE BRAIN AND CONSCIOUSNESS

In light of this startling phenomenon, it is clear that a profound revisioning of the relationship between the brain and consciousness is needed.[8] According to Bergson, the brain plays an important role, but that role is not the one that most theorists assume. The brain's primary function is not productive; it does not produce states of consciousness from the interactions of supposedly inert brain matter. Instead, it is adaptive; it is what allows us to keep our attention on the world around us; it is what "keeps us in touch with realities"; it is what keeps our awareness "tensely strained on life"; it is what prompts us to interact with the world in an effective way (*ME* 59). As Bergson puts it, "the brain is the organ of attention to life" (*ME* 59). It is "the sharp edge by which consciousness cuts into the compact tissue of events"; but, just as a knife is not limited to its edge, our experiential life is not identical to the activity of the brain (*CE* 263). Our brain/nervous system, therefore, is understood by Bergson to be a center of action, rather than as something that creates mental images (*MM* 19).

THE BRAIN'S ROLE IN PURE PERCEPTION

To reemphasize: it is crucial to remember that Bergson agrees with many, if not most, of the basic scientific understandings of the process of perception. Bergson does not question the fact that an incoming flux of external stimulation impacts the afferent nerves of our body—those nerves whose task is to transmit stimuli from the external world to the spinal cord or the brain. (The *afferent* nerves differ from *efferent* nerves in that the efferent nerves transmit stimuli from the spinal cord and brain in order to prompt bodily movements.) Bergson agrees with contemporary science when it asserts that the afferent nerves receive external stimuli, react in complicated ways to these stimuli, and transmit their reactions to the central nervous system.

Nonetheless, Bergson argues (provocatively) that there is only a difference in degree, not in kind, between the brain's role in perception and the reflex actions of the spinal cord. As he points out, the spinal cord receives stimulation from the external world and transforms it automatically into bodily movements. The brain, however, takes the nerve impulses and processes them in complicated ways, so that instead of the automatic reflex actions of the body that are prompted by the spinal cord, we have the partially voluntary actions of the body that are initiated by the brain. Therefore, Bergson argues that in this way the brain is best understood as "an organ of choice" (*ME* 13) in that the brain is that which opens up enormously the possibilities of different choices in response to external stimulation.

The brain, for Bergson, is somewhat similar to "a kind of central telephonic exchange" (the latest technological metaphor available to him) whose task is either "to allow communication or to delay it" (*MM* 30). (Bergson is here envisioning the brain like an old-fashioned "switchboard," similar to the one used by Lily Tomlin's character on *Laugh-In*, in which there is a console that contains a number of pins connected to cables. When a call comes in, the operator pulls the requisite pin/cable out of the console and plugs it into one of the sockets located on the wall perpendicular to the console. In this analogy, the brain is the wall of sockets, with the afferent nerves serving as the pin/cable combination.)[9]

If we understand the brain/nervous system as a type of "central telephonic exchange," then the brain's task is not to create consciousness, whether in the form of thoughts, feelings, memories, or images, just as it is not the task of the pins, wires, and sockets to create the conversations that are pouring through them. As was pointed out previously, the job of the brain/nervous system is not to create conscious "pictures" of the universe within us. Instead, the brain/ nervous system, responding (as will be described in more detail further on) to the prompting of our various levels of memory—promptings which function analogously to the metaphorical human operator—is that which helps us, as an organism, to *act* most effectively. In other words, the brain/nervous system is what enables us to respond, with varying degrees of freedom and effectiveness, to the surrounding world via a complicated system of communication pathways. These pathways, understood very simplistically, channel the flux of perceptions from the surrounding environment to the brain. Then, after varying periods of hesitation (almost instantaneous in some cases or with a consciously experienced time lag in others), the brain relays instructions to the body via the efferent nerves as to what actions it should take (instructions that are given to it from the subconscious dynamism of memory).

Bergson supports his provocative comparison of the brain and the spinal cord by noting that in simple organisms, like protozoa, perceptions of external stimuli are followed, seemingly automatically, by immediate reactions—that is, protozoa act in a way that is almost identical to the activity of the spinal cord. However, in more developed organisms—that is, in organisms with complex nervous systems and brains—we can see a much greater ability to postpone action, to respond with an ever-increasing range of choices to external stimuli. For Bergson, in this way, the degree of complexity of the structure of the brain and the nervous system is a "material symbol" of the degree of free choice of an organism; it is an indication of the amount of independence that the living being has in regard to matter; it is a "symbol of the inner energy which allows the being to free itself from the seemingly determined rhythm of the flow of things and to retain in an ever higher degree the past in order to influence ever more deeply the future" (*MM* 222). As such, the brain and the nervous system are "the symbol . . . of its memory" (*MM* 222).

Bergson argues, quite strongly, that the intimate, seeming one-to-one correspondence between the brain and perception need not be taken as evidence that the brain is that which produces perceptions. And while many, if not most, academics and scientists would almost certainly scoff at Bergson's argument, there have been some who have taken his perspective quite seriously. For instance, as George Wald, a Nobel Prize–winning physiologist from Harvard points out:

> There is no way of knowing whether the brain contains consciousness in
> the sense that it is producing it or whether it is simply a reception and
> transmission mechanism which, as Bergson has argued, has the function
> of selection and realization of conscious images and not the production
> of such images. As a neuroscientist, one can only intervene in the brain
> and record whether the intervention in particular parts of the brain
> results in the evocation or abolishment of conscious experience.[10]

According to Bergson, the fact that there is a correspondence between brain activity and states of consciousness does not indicate that those states were produced by the brain or somehow localized within it. Suppose, for example, that we compare the brain to a television set. There is, apparently, a one-to-one relationship between the electrical and mechanical activity of the television set and the programs that are appearing on the screen. But no one ever claims that the program that is appearing on the screen has been *produced* by the television. Instead, a television set receives, limits, directs, and shapes preexisting electromagnetic signals of various frequencies into the programs that we watch on the screen. Similarly, as Wald notes, if we "pull a transistor out of your T.V. set and it no longer works," we would not (or at least should not) "conclude that the transistor is the source of the program" (or, one might add, the TV set as a whole) anymore than we are forced to conclude that the brain is what produces consciousness simply because of the fact that when a person's brain has been damaged by a severe organic illness or trauma, her or his cognitive abilities are severely impaired.[11]

Bergson suggests that one of the most basic functions of our brain is to carve out manageable islands of stability in the onrush of universal becoming by choosing to focus only on that level of experience that best serves our needs. He points out that it is crucial for our physical body (especially the brain) to alter our perceptions in response to the practical needs of our existence. If we were to perceive and attempt to act upon the physical world as it exists at its most fundamental, subatomic vibratory level, we would become incapacitated; if, for example, we no longer saw an oak table as a solid structure of wood, but instead consciously perceived and responded to the flux of almost infinite energetic patterns that underlie the table, we would become lost in the "moving immensity" of what previously had been a motionless, rectangular solid object (*CM* 69). We are therefore continually, on subconscious levels, carving out manageable islands of stability in the onrush of universal becoming by choosing to focus only on that level of experience that best serves our needs.

In essence, according to Bergson, within certain parameters (determined by the physical regularities that we encounter in the universe) we help to create our experience of the world moment by moment through the power of our choices. Bergson argues that even if these choices happen so rapidly that it may appear that they take place automatically, they are nonetheless still choices, albeit choices that emerge from a subconscious dimension of our being, a dimension that while awash with an ever-changing flux of psychological, cultural, and even biological patterning, still maintains a literally unimaginable level of freedom and creativity. This subconscious level of our selfhood will be discussed in much greater detail in later chapters.

17

THE INTERACTION OF PERCEPTION AND MEMORY

PURE PERCEPTIONS AND "PRIMAL" MEMORY

I n *Matter and Memory*, Bergson insists that "pure perception," as an analytical construct, should be understood as perception in-and-of-itself, that is, as perception minus any and all memory. As was pointed out earlier, a pure perception occurs when, out of a universe of potentially conscious images, only a fraction—those that interest us—are selected. What never becomes clear, however, in Bergson's discussion of this process is exactly what it is that does all of this selecting in the first place. What I would like to suggest is that a highly condensed, multi-layered, fluid, and subconscious form of *memory* plays this all-important role.

Bergson himself never explicitly makes this claim; however, he repeatedly underscores that memory is that which permits an organism to select from a range of possible actions; it is memory that inserts freedom into the almost fully automatic, seemingly lawful and calculable interactions that constitute the physical universe. Therefore, from a Bergsonian perspective, what else but memory could possibly generate and maintain the ongoing culling process by which we select from the universal flux of images only those images that are practically important to us; what else but memory, in its most basic form, could possibly be "choosing" and "selecting"; in other words, what else but memory could possibly act as the catalyst for the very process which creates pure perceptions in the first place?

I would argue that it is memory (in its most fundamental, subliminal form—a form that I term *primal memory*) that is the source of these choices and

145

hence of our freedom. The creation of pure perceptions may well take place con-tinuously and quasi-automatically (in that for the most part there is no *conscious* choice involved); nonetheless, this process simply cannot take place without the discriminating, filtering, and meaning-giving activity of memory. It is this form of memory—subconscious, deeply buried, quasi-automatic and seemingly impersonal—that shapes our perception of the world at its most basic level. Ironically, therefore, even when Bergson attempts, for analytical (and tactical) purposes, to separate memory from perception, he simply cannot ultimately suc-ceed: this foundational, primordial activity of memory (which is, as we will see, another form of durée) is always present, actively inserting itself into the very heart of the perceptual process.

This "primal memory" not only helps to create pure perceptions via this process of preconscious selection, but it is also integrally interwoven with our pure perceptions in another equally important way. For Bergson, memory in its most basic form is simply the continuity of our consciousness; it is the auto-matic and ongoing connection of our past to the present. It is this mode of memory that, according to Bergson, threads together "an uninterrupted series of instantaneous visions," visions or images that, without this form of memory, "would be a part of things rather than of ourselves" (*MM* 65). It is this primal memory which combines the enormous quantity and range of the vibrations of matter into a seamless felt unity; it is this primal memory that takes these countless pulsations of matter and condenses them into the perceived moments of our consciousness.[1]

For example, drawing upon information from the science of his time, Berg-son explains that if we perceive a pulse of red light for a single second, during that time our consciousness has condensed four hundred billion vibrations of that wavelength of light. These vibrations are not, according to Bergson, flashes of inert, predetermined energy taking place in a discrete, ceaselessly repeated present. Instead, even at the most basic atomic and molecular level, these vibra-tions are bound together by a substratum of memory, that is, by a type of proto-consciousness. This memory is not an entirely different "stuff" than matter. Instead, matter itself possesses this primal memory; matter itself is simply a dif-ferent degree or "frequency" or "tension" of duration—the durée of matter.

PURE PERCEPTIONS AND TWO BASIC FORMS OF MEMORY

Bergson's discussion of the role of memory is, however, by no means limited to his investigation of what I am calling "primal memory." He recognizes that the task of memory is not just to bind one moment of experience to the next by connecting the past to the present or to condense the potentially conscious vibrations of matter into our everyday conscious perceptions. Memory is also operative within us either in the form of specific recollections of past events (e.g., remembering one's first time riding a bicycle) or more frequently in the form of impersonal, bodily based distillations of past events (e.g., the set of internalized motor skills it takes to ride a bicycle well). According to Bergson, these two more personal forms of memory (i.e., what I am going to call "*recollection memory*" and "*habit memory*") help to create the fullness of our concrete, lived experience by interweaving themselves into each "pure perception" so seamlessly that "we are no longer able to discern what is perception and what is memory" (*MM* 103).[2]

As Bergson notes, in our day-to-day concrete perceptions, the "immediate and present data of the senses" (i.e., pure perception) is mingled "with a thousand details out of our past experience," details that are so extensive that for the most part they supplant our actual perceptions (*MM* 33). A pure perception by itself is rather thin—it is simply a type of schematic outline which in order to be most effective needs to be filled in with a wide range of memories. These memories are typically not specific memory-images of past events. Instead, they are preconscious, highly distilled internalizations of cultural and psychological patterns of belief that merge with the raw perceptual data, and by doing so, shape these perceptions, giving them order, structure, and meaning. According to Bergson, this interpretive overlay from memory is so extensive that we end up "constantly creating or reconstructing" our present experience based on the sum total of our past (*MM* 103). Therefore, for the most part, what we refer to as our "perceptions" are in actuality, in Bergson's words, primarily a "cloak" of memory covering a "core of immediate perception" (*MM* 34). In the final analysis, perception for Bergson is simply "an occasion for remembering" (*MM* 66).

To illustrate this fusion of memory and perception, let's imagine that we are in a room with someone speaking a language that we do not know (e.g., Italian). Our ears hear the same sounds as the native speakers from Italy who are also in the room. Nonetheless, our experience is quite different from the experience of the Italians. This is so because their past experiences of learning Italian have been condensed within their consciousness, have been compressed into a fluid and useful distillation of memory that can superimpose itself upon the sounds of the language being spoken, thereby enabling them to hear meaningful words and sentences, while we hear nothing but a confused mass of noise.

Similarly, when we look at a purple pansy in a window box, we may think that we are perceiving in a simple and straightforward way a pansy that is "out there"; we may think that anyone who chose to look at this pansy would invariably perceive exactly what we are seeing. However, according to Bergson, only a small "percentage" of our concrete perception of the pansy is rooted in the impersonal, objective, raw data of our pure perceptions. Most of what we actually see is the end result of a preconscious "overlay" or "extract" of memories that is superimposed upon the "sketch" of our pure perceptions of the pansy. Therefore, the pansy that we actually perceive concretely is in many ways co-created by us and is to that extent our own unique experience, an experience that is not shared by others.[3] Indeed, as Bergson notes, it is only because memory is added to perception that the objective, externalized moments of pure perception (which actually take place "outside of us," among the objects themselves) are converted into experiences that seem to be subjective and internal; that is, it is memory that makes it appear that our experience takes place "inside our heads."

RUMINATION: CAPPADOCIA, TURKEY, 2004

I was traveling on a pilgrimage with forty students, all graduates of the Full Spectrum School of Healing and Self Transformation. We had just gotten off our bus late that afternoon in Cappadocia, Turkey, and had walked together up to a barren bluff overlooking a stark, surreal landscape. My wife, Sandra, the director of the school, asked us all to find a place where we could each sit quietly by ourselves. She instructed us simply to observe—carefully, attentively, and mindfully—the expansive vista before us, without analyzing it and with a minimum of internal commentary.

I walked over to a patch of dry ground and sat down between a few scruffy plants on the edge of a rocky slope that sharply angled down in front of me into a vast gorge. It took me a while to get settled, but fairly quickly I began to feel at ease in my own skin, began to become increasingly poised and balanced as I sat there, observing the immensity that surrounded me.

Little by little, I began to sink into the slow, easy rise and fall of my breath, and my mind began to get very still, with very little effort on my part. With each inhalation and exhalation, it was almost as if I could feel layer after layer of memories, meanings, and associations slowly drain away. Increasingly, I felt myself becoming almost transparent, porous, and diaphanous. Increasingly, I felt absorbed in the glowing vividness that stretched out in front of me: the simple, visceral reality of various planes, forms, and patterns of color. More and more, it was as if I left the confines of my physicality, pulled out of my material boundaries by the beauty that called to me. It was as if I became simply an "eye" of awareness, traveling in and through my vision to wherever I wanted to go. I swooped and soared across the chasm of the gorge to a cluster of weathered stone pillars that thrust themselves up into the crystalline blue sky and then traveled past several more complexly configured, strikingly colored rock formations. Wherever I "went," I would feel a surge of joy, as I catapulted from one scene of beauty to the next.

Increasingly, even the sense of "rocks" or "watching" or "Turkey" began to disappear, and I was left with simply this complex, utterly beautiful, layering of geometric patterns, like a cubist painting in stone. Whether diving into dark crevices or flying over the horizontal ridge in the distance where deep browns cut like a blade into the brilliant blue of the sky, it felt as if I was letting my vision itself merge with the rock faces, watching as they subtly began to lose their solidity, noticing that in-and-as my experience, they began to melt and flow and pulse, even though oddly they simultaneously maintained their shape and structure.

This process continued for perhaps twenty minutes, until I heard Sandra's voice asking us all to come together to speak about our experiences. In the sharing that followed, I was struck by how dramatically different everyone's observations were. One young woman began by talking about how caught up she was in the way the landscape revealed to her the balanced interplay of male and female energies, how struck she was by the contrast between the peaks and the valleys, the soft curves and the jagged rock faces. A middle-aged man spoke about how he saw a million years of time embodied in the stone. After him, another woman shared how moved she was by the tenderness she felt in the relationship between herself and what she was viewing. Each person's perceptions were utterly unique.

After listening to all those who wanted to share their experience, Sandra then asked, "Okay. Now tell me: whose perception was the correct one?" While some were perhaps momentarily caught off guard by her question, I think that almost everyone quickly realized that she was asking us this question as a way to underscore the fact that no one's experience was better or worse, more or less true, than the experience of anyone else. What she wanted us to "get" (if anything) was not only the diversity and range of each of our experiences of the "same" landscape, but also how the quality of our experience can and will shift when we approach it with care and respectful attention.

I, for one, was also struck by the congruence of my experience with Bergson's thought. (Yes, I actually made this association. What can I say? I was very much immersed in Bergson's work at the time.) To me, this exercise had been a clear-cut illustration of the interweaving of memory and pure perception. It was clear to me, for instance, that my tacit memories of reading Bergson's work had themselves helped to shape my experience. For instance, it was evident to me (even as it was happening) that, as I sat there on the ground by the edge of the gorge, I had inched a bit closer toward a glimpse of pure perception. Of course, a penumbra of memories remained that infused and helped to shape my experience—memories of "rockness," memories of what that slash of blue above signified ("sky"), memories of different colors and forms (e.g., "yellow"; "angular"). Nonetheless, the memory overlay that I typically superimpose upon experience was less "dense" or "thick" than at other times and so there was, consequently, more transparency, more immediacy. There was also less of a sense of being confined to my body—more of an awareness of being "spread out" and connected to the world around me.

And yet, unlike certain meditative traditions, I would suggest that it was not as if either end of the spectrum (between pure experience and memory) was somehow "better" or "worse" than the other. I had indeed experienced enormous beauty and joy in-and-through the perceptual merger that I had felt with the landscape. However, as Ian Alexander points out, there is also something precious that can be gained through the overlay of memory onto our perceptual experience, because through this process "the mind and world come together; the world becomes constituted 'for me,' 'my world.' It becomes a world of significant perceptions, meaningful acts and artistic creations, in short a transcendent world."[4] It was the totality of my memories that made that experience uniquely "mine," just as the personal memories of all of the students who shared that afternoon helped to shape their experience at the edge of that gorge into something irreplaceable and deeply individual.

Listening to each of the people who shared, it became clear to me the extent to which each one of us at every moment lives in a world that is inevitably, and inextricably, infused with difference. I was reminded, once again, how each of the worlds that we inhabit is tinged with a multitude of deeply personal memories, associations, expectations, and linguistic overlays of meaning. I was struck by how we are each allowed to share in the creation of a universe of experience, we are each invited to contribute to the ever-changing, unexpected, creative uniqueness and multiplicity of the universe. Nonetheless, in-and-through all of that difference, it is evident that we still share a common universe. None of us are in this universe alone; none of us are trapped in solipsistic isolation. Instead, we all perceive, and are rooted in, and emerge out of, and respond to, and help to create, a shared world together.

18

MOVING FROM PERCEPTION TO MEMORY

THE DIFFERENCES BETWEEN MEMORY AND PERCEPTION

At first glance, it might appear that Bergson would claim that memories and perceptions are simply two different forms of the same "stuff" (since they blend together so seamlessly in each moment of concrete perception). In reality, however, until the very end of *Matter and Memory*, Bergson fights hard to separate (at least analytically) perception and memory.

Bergson stresses the radical difference between memory and perception at least in part because he wants to emphasize that perception is not a subjective "internal state," but rather is an activity that contacts an objective reality, an activity "whereby we place ourselves in the very heart of things" (*MM* 67). For Bergson, pure perception "plunges roots deep into the real; and . . . once perception is seen to be radically distinct from recollection, the reality of things is no more constructed or reconstructed, but touched, penetrated, lived" (*MM* 69). Bergson also argues that memory and perception are radically different realities in order to underscore the distinctive "spiritual" qualities of memory, a distinctiveness that allows him to argue that memory, per se, is independent of physical processes (e.g., the neurochemical activity of the brain and nervous system).

While Bergson's emphasis on the radical distinction between memory and perception is understandable and convincing (up to a point), I would argue that in the end the difference between memory and perception is not quite as radical as Bergson, at least initially, seems to want to claim. For instance, if perception and memory are indeed utterly and completely different substances, then it would be very difficult to explain how they so easily and completely fuse with each other in every moment of concrete perception. Furthermore, Bergson himself seems to acknowledge the link between perception and memory when he

151

claims that memory is "the survival of past images" (i.e., that memory is the survival of the very stuff of perception: images) (*MM* 66). There may be, indeed, crucial and significant differences between perception and memory, but I would suggest that it is difficult to argue in the end that this difference is utterly radical.

I would suggest that Bergson's attempt to claim that perception and memory are different in kind from one another is one of many examples of a rhetorical process in Bergson's work in which he begins by analytically separating out two "components" of reality that have previously been (to his mind) illegitimately confused, only in the end to reunite them in a manner that is radically different from the previous, and pernicious, conflation.

In this case, for instance, Bergson needs to advocate a fairly severe form of dualism between perception and memory (or between matter and spirit, respectively) in order to refute materialism, which claims that everything, even our conscious experience, can be in the end reduced to the calculable, predetermined interactions of inert bits of matter. In order to combat this physicalistic monism, it is understandable that Bergson argues strenuously and at length for the independence of perception and memory in *Matter and Memory*. However, this rather strident dualism (I would argue) is primarily rhetorical and strategic in nature. While it is crucial for us, for example, to become disabused of the idea that our consciousness is the slavish product of material objects mindlessly bumping up against each other, nonetheless, if Bergson stopped merely there, we would be left with all of the dilemmas and problems inherent in a Cartesian dualism. Therefore, it is important to remember that the most strongly dualistic statements in *Matter and Memory* (e.g., Bergson's claim that perception and memory differ in kind, not in degree) are ultimately reconciled. While *Matter and Memory* emphasizes the functional and practical differences between mind and matter, in the final analysis, Bergson asks us to conceive that both mind and matter are simply differing manifestations of a unified (albeit continually changing and intrinsically pluralistic) reality: durée—the dynamic flow of consciousness writ large, or expressed in different terms, the ongoing flux of time. In this temporal nondualism, both matter and mind, in the final analysis, are two ends of a single interactive spectrum of temporal becoming and the "stuff" of existence is the creative unfolding, on all levels, of the oneness/manyness of durée.

TWO TYPES OF MEMORIES

We have seen how Bergson analytically separates our experience into two distinct, yet interactive, components: perception and memory. He also (as was briefly mentioned earlier) separates memory itself into two very different forms: "*habit memory*" and "*recollection memory*."[1] (Not surprisingly, Bergson goes on to emphasize how these two forms of memory are "mixed" together in our actual experience.) In the following discussion, for the moment, I will not be giving a

lot of attention to the form of memory that I have termed *"primal memory"*—
that is, that form of memory that binds one moment of experience to another,
that serves as the durée of matter itself. I will also not focus on another form of
memory that Bergson only obliquely acknowledges, a form of memory that John
Mullarkey calls *"virtual"* or *"pure memory"*—that is, memory as the imageless,
utterly open, creative fountainhead of durée. For the moment, this discussion
will primarily focus on memory as we ordinarily understood the term—that is,
memory as that which helps us to learn something (what we mean when we say,
for instance, that we "memorized" a poem) and memory as that which brings to
our mind specific images or representations of past events (what we mean when
we say, for instance, that we have a memory of when we walked in the park with
a friend last week).

Bergson illustrates the difference between these two forms of memory with
the example of learning a lesson by heart (e.g., learning the Gettysburg Address
in the fourth grade). *Habit memory* takes place when we repeat the lesson aloud,
and then gradually, after several repetitions, the words that we are attempting to
memorize begin to connect with one another, until finally all of the words can
be recited as a single, connected unit. As Bergson notes, "when that moment
comes, it is said that I know my lesson by heart, that it is imprinted on my
memory" (*MM* 79).

Recollection memory, however, is completely different. This type of memory,
for example, occurs when I think back on the process whereby I learned the
lesson. If my memory is good, I can see in my mind's eye the various times in
which I repeated the lesson aloud (e.g., perhaps I first repeated it in my study,
then the second time I repeated it in my yard) and "each reading stands out in
my mind as a definite event in my history" (*MM* 79). This type of memory (i.e.,
recollection memory) in essence creates "pictures" of the past within us, and as
such is relatively detached from the immediate needs of the present. Habit
memory, by contrast, is visceral; it is enacted in the present.

It is important to recognize that habit memory does not only take place
when we consciously, with effort, "memorize" something. As Bergson comments,
the example of learning a lesson by heart is actually fairly artificial because "the
memories which we acquire voluntarily by repetition are rare and exceptional"
(*MM* 83). What is much more common is that we learn how to do something
simply via "accidental repetition of the same situations"; that is, most of our
habit memories are generated by frequently repeating similar actions, in similar
contexts, until our body finally "switches into gear" anytime a similar situation
presents itself (*MM* 231).

In fact, according to Bergson, our body moves, either potentially or actually,
every time that we perceive an object or event (e.g., we hear a loud sound and
unconsciously envision ourselves reaching to the nearby remote to turn the
sound down—an imaginary response that catalyzes a corresponding and complex set of reactions in our glands, nerves, and muscles). Given this sort of

moment-by-moment bodily reactivity to the ongoing flux of perception, it makes sense that, if enough similar situations take place, then certain stereotyped sets of bodily movements will begin to happen quasi-automatically creating in essence a type of bodily habit, an enfleshed form of memory, a "record of the past in the form of motor habits" (*MM* 84).

In order to put more "flesh" on these analytical "bones," let's imagine two hypothetical (and admittedly, rather one-dimensional) examples. In the first example, a young girl, at a very young age, reacts to her mother's presence with a smile. The mother, uplifted by her daughter's smile, responds in kind with abundant hugs and laughter. If that scenario repeats itself frequently enough, the child will learn that smiling is a way to provoke positive responses from significant others. Consequently, that particular "bodily attitude" may be carried forward in a variety of ways into the present as she adapts this fundamental "posture" toward the world to fit a wide range of circumstances (for example, learning to be "upbeat" in the face of difficulties).

As a second example, however, another young girl smiles as well; however, her smiles are ignored. She learns, instead, over time, that the only way to get at least some attention is to scream and cry. She may then carry this learning, this "stance" toward life, into her present situation in a variety of ways. (For example, she learns that she can get the "negative attention" that she craves by sulking or glowering.)

In both of these examples, a cluster of distinct bodily reactions to external events eventually becomes embedded in the motor areas of the child's brain, and eventually in her muscles and nerves; it becomes a habituated series of bodily movements that are ready and waiting to be catalyzed by different events that are taking place in the present. As such, these habit memories become a quasi-automatic way of enacting the past in the present; they are one way in which these children can prolong and consolidate an interrelated cluster of past events into present-day reactions to various similar events

Bergson argues that it is crucial that we realize that there is a "profound difference, a difference in kind" between the habit memory that was just discussed and recollection memory (*MM* 81). Habit memories, such as walking, or writing, or knowing how to speak a language or how to play the piano, are part of our present; they are lived and enacted. Recollection memory, however, is quite different. Recollection memory is not concerned with practical utility. Its task is simply to record "in the form of memory-images, all the events of our daily life as they occur in time," neglecting no detail (*MM* 82). All of the memory-images that are a part of recollection memory are unique; they are records of specific moments in the past that cannot and will not ever be repeated. As such, the memory-images of recollection memory are in dramatic contrast to habit memories, which are an impersonal condensation and repetition of past activities that arise, almost effortlessly, in response to the needs of the present moment.

19

THE INTERWEAVING OF RECOLLECTION MEMORY AND HABIT MEMORY

THE CONE OF MEMORY AND THE PLANE OF PERCEPTION

As was pointed out previously, Bergson emphasizes that recollection memory and habit memory are always combined to one degree or another in our daily lives. Each time we have an instant of recognition, each time in which we attempt to recall an event from the past, each time in which we seek to learn a new skill, each time in which we try to understand a passage that we have just read, these "two memories run side by side and lend to each other a mutual support" (*MM* 86). In fact, at every moment of our lives, to the extent that we are both physical and mental beings, habit memory and recollection memory are "so completely mingled we can never say where one begins and the other ends" (*ME* 190).

For instance, I am able to understand the Spanish language (to the extent that I do) only because I possess both of these forms of memory working together within me. While I have numerous highly specific memories of times in which I went to Spanish class and did pronunciation drills, most of my (rather modest) Spanish-language skills are not rooted in my concrete recollections of times spent learning this or that Spanish phrase. Instead, when I hear certain words or sentences in that language, I simply and automatically comprehend them, almost in my flesh and bones. Each language drill session instilled learned patterns of behavior that are almost effortlessly expressed in and through my bodily tone, stance, breathing, and so on, whenever I am speaking Spanish. This type of memory—a highly embodied, quasi-automatic, habitual reaction to the promptings of the present moment—is very different from my mental recollections of specific moments of my past. Nonetheless, and this is crucial, if I did not understand the various words and phrases that were drilled into me in these various sessions, if I did not possess the meanings and associations that I still carry within me in the form of different "distillations" of recollection memory, I would have no comprehension of what it was that I was saying. I could perhaps mouth various words and phrases, but these utterances would be utterly unintelligible to me.

In order to give a better sense of the complex interaction of these two forms of memory in our everyday lives, Bergson provides a geometric diagram. The diagram pictures a cone with its point directed downward and intersecting with a horizontal plane. For those unfamiliar with mathematics, imagine a rounded, upside down pyramid, with its tip balanced on an utterly smooth and flat (and enormous!) sheet of paper. The rounded upside-down pyramid (the inverted cone) represents the total accumulation of our memories. The enormous sheet of paper (the plane) represents all of the images that together make up the physical universe. And crucially (given the inherent dynamism of Bergson's vision of the universe) neither the cone nor the plane is understood to be static. Instead, the plane is said to be in constant motion, while the tip of the cone is pictured as ceaselessly moving forward in time and space (*MM* 152).

In Bergson's cone/plane image, our body is located at the intersection of the plane and the cone, in that at every moment it is receiving and responding to the influences of the images of the physical universe that are flowing, in essence, "up" from the plane, while it is also at all times receiving and responding to the influences that are flowing "downward" from the cone of memory. Our body is that "special image" that "constitutes at every moment . . . a section of universal becoming"; it is "the place of passage," "a connecting link," "a hyphen" between the cone of memory and the plane of physical images (*MM* 151).

Habit memory, as embodied, enacted memory, is also located at the intersection of the cone of memory and the plane of material images. Located in the present and concerned with action, habit memory is, as was noted earlier, primarily sensorimotor and as such needs the recollections from the past, the "lessons from experience," in order to function effectively (*MM* 152–153). However, habit memory in turn also assists recollection memory in that it offers these unconscious, hidden, and ineffective recollections from the past a way to materialize themselves; it gives them an opportunity to "matter" by becoming conscious and enacted in the tangible, present universe of becoming (*MM* 153).

PLANES OF CONSCIOUSNESS

What Bergson suggests is that within the cone of memory, within the everincreasing totality of our recollections, there are an infinite number of possible states of memory or "planes of consciousness." Bergson claims that "between the plane of action—the plane in which our body has condensed its past into motor habits—and the plane of pure memory [the base of the cone] where our mind retains in all its details the picture of our past life . . . we can discover thousands of different planes of consciousness, a thousand integral and yet diverse repetitions of the whole of experience through which we have lived" (*MM* 241). At one extreme, at the upper base of the cone, there is the plane of "pure memory" in which, utterly disconnected from the needs of ordinary existence, every detail of our past life is *virtually* available. (The virtuality of this *pure memory*—that is, this open, creative source of memory—means that pure memory as such does not even possess the concreteness and actuality of images; *that* degree of "embodiment" only happens in planes of consciousness a bit further "down" the cone, with the creation of "memory-images"—the individual specific recollections of past events.)

Bergson argues that at certain moments in our life, moments when we are not gripped with the practical necessities of functioning effectively in the world, moments when we can retreat from the demands of daily life, moments when we can, for instance, dream or slip into periods of reverie, then specific recollections of the past (i.e., "memory-images") can and do often come surging into our awareness. For the most part, however, specific recollections of past events typically do not enter into our conscious awareness. As was pointed out previously, most of this vast reservoir of memory-images is kept out of our conscious awareness by the structure of our brain and nervous system, which acts as a type of filter or reducing valve admitting into consciousness (again, for the most part) only those memory images which "can cast light on the present situation or further the action now being prepared" (*CE* 5). (Bergson rather optimistically overlooks those moments in life when individuals can become overwhelmed with debilitating, emotionally charged memories, and claims that "at the most, a few superfluous recollections may succeed in smuggling themselves through the half-open door. These memories, messengers from the unconscious, remind us of what we are dragging behind us unawares" [*CE* 5].)

Bergson goes on to stress that in order for us to function effectively in the world, what we need are not the highly particular, individualized memory-images of specific events of the past that are located closer to the base/top of the cone of memory. Instead, what we need are the generalities, the "condensations" of memory that are located further down the cone, closer to the tip. For example, my specific memory-image of "that giant cottonwood near White Rock Lake that I lay underneath on the afternoon of April 12, 2002" is typically much less useful to me than my tacit, preconscious, enormously complex and multilayered understanding of "tree"—"tree" with all of its virtual associations, implications, connotations; "tree" as that quintessence of memory that can, most easily and effectively, superimpose itself unto my present perceptions and help me make my way through the world with a minimum of disruption.

Nonetheless, that enormously complex, multifaceted condensation of "tree-ness" does not stand alone within my memory. Bergson repeatedly stresses that memories should not be understood as atomistic, isolated, distinct "nuggets" of consciousness. Instead, every condensation of memory and seemingly independent memory-image is interwoven in a vast, practically limitless, virtual network of linguistic associations, webs of meaning, strata of feelings, layers of bodily tensions, and so forth (i.e., aforementioned "planes of consciousness").

As a way to suggest the complexity of memory, and how the various planes of memory interact, Bergson offers a second diagram that, as before, pictures the cone of memory intersecting with the plane of material existence. However, this time the cone is shown bisected into different cross-sections that represent the various "planes of consciousness" (*MM* 162).

The static geometric imagery of the cone and its various cross-sections is, however, potentially deceptive. Contrary to what the "cross-section" or "slice" imagery might suggest, these planes of consciousness, according to Bergson, "are not given as ready-made things superimposed the one on the other"; instead, "they exist virtually" (*MM* 242). As such, these various planes of consciousness are not meant to represent only certain restricted "slices" of our total memory. Instead, the planes of consciousness represent the variety of ways in which, at every moment of our existence, "our entire personality, with the totality of our recollections" either contracts or expands itself to just the level of generality or particularity that is needed in order to bring to the present moment the insight, or remembrance, or action that is most needed (*MM* 165).

The various planes of consciousness are therefore *not* more or less inclusive subsets of the totality of our memory. Rather, they represent varying "heights of *tension* or *tone* in [our] psychical life," varying ways in which we either loosen our attention on the present (in which case, specific, highly personal, concrete memory-images are more likely to arise) or sharply focus our attention on the immediacy of what is occurring in the present (in which case very generalized condensations of memory will be superimposed upon pure perceptions) (*ME* 147). In this way, Bergson argues, "the same psychical life . . . must be supposed to be repeated an endless number of times on the different stories of memory, and the same act of the mind may be performed at varying heights" (*MM* 105).

What Bergson is fighting against with this notion of planes of consciousness is the idea that was promoted by various associationists of his time that memories float around in consciousness as fragmented and isolated atoms. What Bergson is emphasizing, instead, is the notion that "psychic facts are bound up with each other, and are always given together to immediate consciousness as an undivided whole" (*MM* 166). In Bergson's understanding of memory, memory *as a whole* moves toward the present, contracting itself without dividing, offering those aspects of itself that can best facilitate effective action in the present moment.

Therefore, as Bergson notes, "between the plane of action . . . and the plane of pure memory, where our mind retains in all its details the picture of our past life . . . we can discover thousands of different planes of consciousness, a thousand integral and yet diverse repetitions of the whole of experience through which we have lived" (*MM* 241). (The fact that Bergson calls these planes of "consciousness" is fascinating, in that, for the most part, they are, at best, preconscious. We are rarely aware of the existence of these various planes of memory in-and-of-themselves, even while they are actively shaping every moment of our conscious experience.) Bergson goes on to suggest that at certain rare moments in our life, depending largely upon various bodily postures or attitudes (e.g., lying down with our eyes closed and breathing deeply and without effort, or practicing various yogic or meditative postures), we can contact the "wider" planes of consciousness that are closer to the base/top of the cone. When we are aligned with these "planes of consciousness," very specific memories of events that happened to us at certain times and places may flood our consciousness. Bergson argues, however, that because these highly personal recollections (which he links to dreams, idle speculations, and fantasy) are not "useful" to our ordinary functioning, it is much more common for us to be affected by levels of memory that are "lower" down the cone. These "narrower," "inner circles" of memory are where memory becomes increasingly impersonal and "distilled"; these are the planes of consciousness where memory "shrinks" or becomes "thinned and sharpened, so that it presents nothing thicker than the edge of a blade to actual experience, into which it will thus be able to penetrate" (*MM* 106).

COMPLETE PERCEPTION

Bergson argues that every moment of our lived experience is a preconscious, almost instantaneous constructive or creative process, in which perception and memory interact with each other in a variety of highly complex ways. For the sake of clarity, it is possible to analytically separate out several highly simplified "steps" of this interactive process. Beginning from the "side" of perception (that is, from the plane of the images of the material universe that intersects with the tip of the cone) we can say that:

1) Perceptual images are filtered and selected from the totality of the universal flux, creating our "pure perceptions" (a selection process that I claim is initiated by the activity of "*primal memory*").

2) This preselected subset of perceptual images stimulates an enormous cascade of neurochemical reactions in our sense organs. As Bergson puts it, the sense organs act, in effect, "like an immense keyboard" upon which the perceptual images play their "harmony of a thousand notes" (*MM* 128).

3) The neurochemical activities of our body, nervous system, and brain, having been stimulated by the various perceptual images, activate a range of possible motor responses (e.g., an image of a chair evokes a potential range of activities, such as sitting on it, moving it closer to the table, picking it up, and so forth).

4) The perceptual images (and the potential motor responses to them) provide a sketch that memory then attempts to fill in and flesh out so that we can act as effectively as possible in the world.

5) The various memory-images and/or condensations of memory (which are, in effect, different "combinations" of *habit memory* and *recollection memory*) attempt to "fill in" the perceptual gaps, in essence, by "playing" another "keyboard" (even if this keyboard is mental, not physical in nature), a process that in turn also sets in motion complex neurochemical patterns of reaction in the physiology of our body (*MM* 129).

6) The initial attempt by memory to overlay the perceptual images is typically not adequate. Therefore, according to Bergson, "an appeal is made to the deeper and more distant regions of memory" in order to fill in the perceptual "sketch" (*MM* 101). At this point, he notes, "any memory-image that is capable of interpreting our actual perception inserts itself so thoroughly into it that we are no longer able to discern what is perception and what is memory" (*MM* 103).

As Bergson further states, this back and forth between perceptual images and various strata/planes of memory (and the corresponding neurochemical changes that are catalyzed by the playing of these "keyboards") can and does "go on indefinitely—memory strengthening and enriching perception, which, in its turn becoming wider, draws into itself a growing number of complementary recollections" (*MM* 101). This back and forth process creates, in essence, a "kind of *circuit* in which the external object yields to us deeper and deeper parts of itself, as our memory adopts a correspondingly higher degree of tension in order to project recollections towards it" (*MM* 116; see figure 2, *MM* 132).

In order to illustrate the complex, almost instantaneous, preconscious interaction between memory and perception, Bergson offers the example of someone reading a book. As he points out, literate adults do not read letter by letter. Instead, "rapid reading is a real work of divination. Our mind notes here and there a few characteristic lines and fills all the intervals with memory-images which, projected on the paper, take the place of the real printed characters and may be mistaken for them. Thus we are constantly creating or reconstructing" (*MM* 103).

In this dynamic process, "perception-images" from the various letters on the page go toward our mind, only to be met by various memory-images that are, as it were, rushing out to greet these perception-images in order to superimpose themselves onto the shapes of the letters, enabling us to read the words and phrases that are, as a result of the work of memory, now infused with various depths of personal and cultural significance. As Bergson notes, the perceptual act of seeing words on the page (or hearing words that are spoken) only furnishes us "with guiding marks," it only draws "an outline which we fill with memories. . . . It is the memory which makes us see and hear" (*ME* 206–207). It is memory that completes perception, that "slips into it and supplies most of its content. . . . [It is] the meaning, before everything, which guides us in the reconstruction of forms and sounds. . . . Interpretation is therefore, in reality, a reconstruction" (*ME* 207). As Suzanne Guerlac insightfully points out, "it is as if the real, and the interpretation of the real, were almost the same thing."[1]

20

RUMINATIONS ON THE
HIDDEN POWER OF MEMORY

RUMINATION, PART ONE:
PSYCHIC CYSTS AND DISTORTED PERCEPTIONS

By now it should be clear that, according to Bergson's theory, our pure perceptions are created moment to moment by a process in which we unconsciously and yet almost instantaneously give our attention to only a tiny percentage of the pulsating, protoconscious material "images" of the universe, allowing the rest, in essence, to pass through completely unnoticed. Almost simultaneously, in a way that is equally unconscious and equally seamless, these pure perceptions are themselves "filled in" and given significance by various "strata" of memory. Therefore, according to Bergson, we are not passive witnesses of an utterly objective world. Rather, under the surface, utilizing memory in a way that escapes our notice, we are constantly, actively, creatively, shaping our experience of the world as well as our experience of ourselves.

What is crucial to remember about this "constructive" process is that most of it takes place utterly unconsciously, in-and-through the activity of different "planes" of memory, in-and-through the countless condensations of our past experiences as they are continually reworked and reshaped within us, becoming over time the hidden foundation of our beliefs, our attitudes, our hopes, our fears, and our prejudices.

These "planes of consciousness" (most of which paradoxically are hidden from our day-to-day awareness) are not an amorphous, homogeneous unity. Instead, in a way that is strikingly similar to how Bergson proposes (primarily in *Creative Evolution*) that our intellect "fragmentizes" the flux of the material universe into seemingly solid, clearly bounded, unchanging material objects, our subconscious appears to have a corresponding tendency toward fragmentation as well. Although memory is not spatial in nature, it appears that, even in this case, our "spatializing" tendencies have "frozen" or "hardened" the interpenetrating temporal flux of our subconscious into various "strata." (It is crucial to remember, however, that even at their most "frozen," these various strata of the subconscious are never completely separate from each other, but instead form differentiated "layers" of an interpenetrating, dynamic whole.)[1]

Within these strata, there seem to be widely differing "degrees" of "frozenness" or "hardness"—in other words, widely differing degrees to which these planes of consciousness either demonstrate "durée-like" qualities or do not.[2] Some of these "layers," for instance, seem to be extremely "durée-like"—that is, extremely porous, fluid, and interconnected. These are the planes of consciousness, I submit, that are at work within us when our thoughts, beliefs, and feelings are insightful, creative, and inspired. Coming from these levels, new ideas (and dreams, and desires, and intuitions) effortlessly percolate up within us, seemingly from out of nowhere. Aligned with these strata of consciousness, we just seem to *know* what to say or to do moment-to-moment without realizing why. In touch with these more "durée-like" qualities of our subconscious, the world around us seems to shine with an extra light; our mind is unusually clear; our feelings flow forth relatively unimpeded; and our body feels at ease, centered, and graceful.

There are also those crystallizations of thought/memory/feeling that are less overtly "durée-like"—that is, that are more "sluggish" or "stuck." These planes of consciousness are more resistant to change; they are more unwilling to synthesize in unexpected ways with other "layers" within. These planes of consciousness (or our attempts to move *between* these various planes) underlie those times when our thoughts are relatively mechanical, repetitive, and forced; or when new ideas or insights are difficult to attain; or when we are stubbornly attached to certain internal attitudes and perspectives. Influenced by these strata of consciousness, we can feel blocked, hesitant, and unsure of ourselves (or conversely, we can act in ways that are reactively defensive and self-righteous). Coming from these internal "layers" of memory, nothing in our lives seems to happen easily; our breathing is shallow; and our movements are painfully awkward. At these moments it can be difficult to access anything genuine within us; the world can seem dull and opaque; and life itself can feel like a continual struggle.

There also appear to be planes of consciousness within us in which certain repetitive patterns of memories and experiences have become knotted together and split off from conscious awareness, that have "congealed" within us into what might be called "psychic cysts" (the same "cysts" that were discussed toward the end of section 1). Bergson's discussion of these "independent growths" within the depths of the psyche is, admittedly, rather undeveloped (*TFW* 166).

Nonetheless, these highly habituated unconscious phenomena within us, which are seemingly endowed with a life of their own and can, in Bergson's words, "usurp the whole personality" (*TFW* 166), appear to correspond, almost perfectly, with aspects of our psyche that are frequently alluded to in certain neo-Freudian systems of thought (e.g., object relations theory and Self psychology).[3]

These various neo-Freudian psychological systems, for all of their numerous (and significant) differences, all assume that, hidden within the depths of our psyche, there exist numerous, difficult-to-access "layers" of "walled off" memories that we carry within us from our earliest experiences as a child. These early residues of traumatic, difficult-to-assimilate experiences (as well as our visceral reactions to these experiences) are rarely, if ever, fully integrated in our conscious awareness. (This difficulty in assimilation is perhaps not surprising, not only because these levels of the subconscious are so painful and defended, but also because they seem to occupy a "place" within the psyche that is extremely hard to grasp—a "place" that is no place, simultaneously "us" and "not us," created out of the fabric of relationality itself and yet sealed off and isolated in the hidden recesses of interiority.)

According to these psychotherapeutic perspectives, if we want to uncover the source of most of our psychological pain, if we want to begin to heal our neurosis, our depression, our anxiety attacks, our obsessive worrying, our compulsive addictive behavior, or our debilitating feelings of self-loathing, we need to turn our attention in the direction of what I am calling "psychic cysts"—that is, in the direction of the various parental imagoes within us (those more or less consolidated internalizations of the negative voices, and affective tone, of significant others), or in the direction of incompletely assimilated self-objects in our psyche (those terrifying and debilitating gaps in our feelings of inner solidity and self-worth).

Created long ago, in reaction to almost intolerable levels of stress and anxiety (arising either from repeated experiences of chaotic, cold, hateful, or unloving environments, or in reaction to seemingly overwhelming feelings of fear, hurt, anger, or despair), these cordoned-off, quasi-independent psychic cysts gradually took form as we attempted to defend ourselves from, or tried to cope with, extremely difficult-to-assimilate experiences by denying that they ever took place—that is, by the repeated process of cutting ourselves off from these painful, albeit naggingly insistent, memories.

While at some point in our personal history it might have been necessary to have forced these knots of memory from our conscious awareness in order to cope with whatever traumatic experience we found ourselves in, for most of us these twisted loops of self-hatred, fear, and despair have long since lost whatever useful function they might have initially served and are now (tragically) almost entirely maladaptive and destructive. Like thick ropes of memory that bind us, these psychic knots within are "us" at our most bound, our most contracted, our most wounded, our most habituated.

The power of these psychic knots over most of us is typically much greater than many realize. (It seems that it is almost a law of the psyche that the more something is forced out of consciousness, the more it secretly tends to run the show.) Their activity, therefore, can be difficult to detect. However, one clear indication of their influence is when we repeatedly make destructive choices in our lives (e.g., when we mysteriously seem always to choose intimate relationships with the wrong people) and when we have recurring negative life experiences (e.g., when we repeatedly fail to get and/or keep rewarding careers).

As soon as we accept the possibility that these "psychic cysts" might exist hidden within us, then it becomes much easier to explain these recurring negative choices and life experiences as the manifestation of various self-reinforcing vicious circles of belief, action, experience, and memory. If we can accept that these deeply embedded and distorted (yet taken-for-granted) outlooks on life will often prompt us to act or to express ourselves in destructive, harmful ways, then it becomes relatively easy to see how these actions would lead, not surprisingly, to hurtful negative life experiences that in turn would only serve to reinforce the congealed memory patterns themselves.

The activity of these psychic cysts within us can also be detected, I suggest, during those moments when we are caught off guard by an irrational, yet extremely charged, emotion (e.g., rage, despair, depression, terror) surging up seemingly out of nowhere. (Bergson himself speaks of "a violent anger roused by some accidental circumstance" as one example of those difficult-to-account-for episodes of knee-jerk, hyperexaggerated reactivity that we all tend to struggle with in our lives to a greater or lesser degree [*TFW* 166].) And finally, as Bergson himself notes, studies of hypnotic suggestion and multiple personalities also offer important evidence of the possibility that strata of our subconscious can be "populated" with a wide variety of semiautonomous "partial selves"[4] or stubbornly ingrained, seemingly self-activated "nodules" of memory (*TFW* 166).

There are numerous psychotherapeutic techniques that are designed to identify and name these various "complexes" within us. However, I am not convinced that it is always necessary (or even possible) to determine exactly which of these "personality fragments" is active within us during various negative emotional states or life situations. In fact, it seems quite likely to me that the very act of naming these complexes, while perhaps helpful in the short term, can also lead to an overly simplistic and formulaic approach to the subconscious and more subtly may also help to solidify and strengthen the complexes themselves.

It seems to me that Bergson's theoretical perspective can help us to understand that even when these psychic cysts are extremely entrenched, reactive, and resistant to change, they are, nonetheless, still only momentary patterns of tendencies taking place within the larger matrix of the totality of the subconscious, a totality that is extremely fluid, dynamic, interconnected—a totality that is also (I submit) moving toward increasing levels of complexity and integration. These memory patterns, congealed or not, are still manifestations of durée; they still have at least the potential to transform themselves into more fluid and more integrated expressions of our wholeness.

Nonetheless, when we are struggling to change a particular stubbornly engrained reactive tendency within ourselves, these walled off patterns of memory can feel extremely "stuck." This "stuckness" can in turn be felt, in an immediate and visceral way, in the kinesthetic sensations of our body (e.g., in the shortness of our breath or in the constriction of our chest). Bergson's notions of how memory can become embodied in our physical structure are, in this way, quite revealing. They correspond closely with the insights of many neo-Reichian body-mind therapeutic systems (e.g., bioenergetics, Rolfing, Feldenkrais work) that claim (in a variety of ways) that our deeply embedded, unconscious belief systems and affectively charged memories can and do impact our body in specific, almost predictable, ways. These mind-body systems of thought emphasize that, when we repeatedly undergo numerous early experiences of stressful external and/or internal environments, it is inevitable that our muscles, ligaments, tendons, and connective tissue, reacting to the pain and fear that we are feeling, will tense up in an inevitably doomed attempt to shield us from these intensely powerful negative feelings and sensations.

Unfortunately, if this psychophysical reactivity happens frequently enough, our once fluid, soft, and joyful bodies (e.g., observe the fluidity of an infant) become increasingly hardened, calcified, and segmented, until finally, to one extent or another, our bodies become as distorted (i.e., as armored, or held in, or blocked, or brittle) as our unconscious beliefs and attitudes themselves. Again, while at one point these psychophysical defense structures were perhaps needed (as a protection against negative internal feelings and/or hostile external environments), they now only weigh us down; they only cut us off from our innate connection to the pulsations of the universe, and consequently, numb us to the streaming of pleasure and deep feeling that, if we were less guarded, blocked, and walled off, would be continually flowing in and through us.

These psychophysical defense structures and our corresponding attempts to partition ourselves both psychologically and physiologically into a disjointed collection of isolated, numbed, and stunted parts only serve to further deaden us; they only make us more and more machine-like and robotic, more and more shut down and shut off from our depth, from others, and from the world around us. Blindly reacting to the encrusted and painful results of our previous reactivity, we then attempt to wall ourselves off even more, to deny the existence of any wounds within us, to push the hurtful remnants of our past even further down in order to keep them from surfacing into our awareness.

Eventually we convince ourselves that it is an extremely bad idea to ever attempt to uncover the source of our psychological pain. How much better, we think, to simply tighten up our perimeter; or to batten down the hatches; or to do whatever is necessary not to leave our known, comfortably familiar space of carefully defined cultural expectations and social interactions, our seemingly safe world of carefully defined roles and prepackaged behavior. Why risk turning our attention within if it only invites loss of control and inner turmoil?

In our reactive fear, we forget (or never learn) that there are other alternatives. For instance, how much better it would be for us if, when we felt sad, we could learn simply to let that feeling rise up within, trusting that it is good to experience that feeling fully and deeply, knowing that it will in its own time and in its own way organically shift to another complexly configured pattern of feeling. If we did not clamp that sadness down, if we did not force it from our awareness, then perhaps it would not have to fester unconsciously within until it finally turned into full-blown despair or depression.

This responsive, open, and accepting way of dealing with difficult emotional states is rarely an option for most individuals. Instead, I would argue (drawing upon various psychotherapeutic models and at least implicitly on Bergson) that for the vast majority of us, as we increasingly cut ourselves off from feeling, as we deny that anything is innately wrong, as we blame others for our own self-created suffering, we will inevitably and unconsciously project these deeply repressed and distorted memories (and the correspondingly distorted beliefs, expectations, and attitudes) onto the world around us; we will superimpose these forgotten, yet still active, remnants of our past unto our perception of the world, creating in turn numerous destructive and self-fulfilling prophecies.

Finally, the ever-shifting maze of distorting "funhouse" mirrors that we have projected onto the world—that we have erected almost completely under the radar—begins to show us a world that seemingly justifies all of our despair, doubt, suspicion, and fear (even as we might be utterly convinced that we are seeing the world with pristine clarity).

Thankfully, even in spite of these seemingly entrenched, congealed patterns, we are constantly changing and ceaselessly evolving in ways that we do not even realize. Thankfully, we have countless other dimensions of our being that are not so distorted and destructive. Thankfully, in-and-through-and-around all of these "denser," more stagnant, more walled-off dimensions of our psyche, there are also deeper, wider, wilder, freer, clearer, more alive, more vibrant, dimensions of our selfhood as well.

I would further suggest that these denser, more congealed aspects of our psyche do not emerge simply from our desperate attempts to shield ourselves from our early wounds. In addition, they are also (tragically and unnecessarily) recreated within us as a way to shore up our taken-for-granted sense of separation and egoic smallness; they are maintained as a way to pretend that the flux, both within us and around us, is not really happening; they are made and remade as a way to keep us from having to let down our guard, or to prevent us from giving ourselves fully to that immense aliveness that can be found, not only in the vast reaches of the cosmos that surrounds us, but also in the depths of our innermost being.

RUMINATION, PART TWO: FREEING OURSELVES, CREATING NEW WORLDS

It is not an easy task to recognize that we are literally stuck in a walled-off world of our own making. We all need help to realize that we are enmeshed in, and trapped by, our own self-created suffering. We all need help to see that the world that we experience does not come to us ready-made and prepackaged, but rather in ways that we rarely recognize is continually and dramatically molded and shaped by an overlay of memory (and hence, attitudes, beliefs, expectations, hopes, fears, and so on) that we superimpose upon it. We all need help to rid ourselves of the mistaken belief that we are isolated and powerless victims of a hostile and meaningless world. Other choices are possible. We can create a more alive, more fulfilling world for ourselves.

The hope for transformation and healing, not only for ourselves, but implicitly for the entire world, is that if we become aware of some of the distortions, ideologies, and masks that we have created, we can then slowly begin to let go of them. As we realize the extent to which our unconscious memories and beliefs affect the way in which we interact with the world; as we begin to acknowledge the repercussions that these unconscious memories have on our lives; as we begin to wake up and stop blindly accepting spoon-fed truths; as we take on these tasks, what we often discover is that it becomes increasingly possible for us, in our freedom, as embodiments of durée, as expressions of the élan vital, to become more porous and responsive to the promptings of our depths. It becomes increasingly possible to choose a different, more enlivening, empowering, and fulfilling set of beliefs, and consequently to co-create a different, more loving, more fluid, more open, more connected world in which to live and flourish.

Taking Bergson's understanding of memory perhaps further than he might have wished, I would suggest that we can be hopeful about initiating profound change within ourselves because (as will be discussed in much more depth further on) memory is not a passive, unchanging and unchangeable, imprint of past experiences. Instead, memory in its entirety, as it manifests in-and-as our subconscious, is highly creative and highly mutable; it is remarkably free and flowing; it is ceaselessly evolving into new and unpredictable forms—that is, it is durée at its best.

In fact, as I pointed out earlier, I would argue that even the denser, less permeable aspects of our subconscious are in reality nothing but a more "congealed," temporarily frozen form of durée itself. If we think about it, it is clear that even the most deeply sealed off, segmented, and reactive aspects of our subconscious are, even still, remarkably creative in that they are able, seemingly effortlessly, to create the worlds of experience we inhabit. And even when we, influenced by these aspects of our subconscious, behave in formulaic and predictable ways, even then we sometimes manage to surprise ourselves; even then something unexpected, and alive, can manage to express itself in-and-through all of our defenses. Furthermore, although these aspects of our subconscious may be heavily guarded, nonetheless, they *can* shift; they *can* respond over time to new and ideally healthier ways of viewing the world.

If we hope to transform ourselves, if we hope to heal these entrenched and tangled knots of consciousness, we might have more success if, instead of trying to root them out or attack them, we tried a different approach. These inner knots were originally created to defend ourselves against attack, so attempting to eradicate them using the same energy with which they were created is usually, at best, ineffective, and at worst, only serves to exacerbate the original wounds and to strengthen the defenses themselves. Our best hope for transformation is that over time, with patience, gentleness, and help from others, we can bring these buried knots of unconscious beliefs into awareness; or we can give these hidden and denied aspects of ourselves space to breathe, so that they can begin to heal within us. If we can start to have genuine compassion for these wounded and walled-off aspects of ourselves, it is possible that with the warmth of that compassion and self-acceptance we can slowly begin to thaw those frozen layers of consciousness so that they, and we, can become increasingly free, increasingly alive.

I agree with Bergson: we are not doomed to repeat the past. We have the very real potential to become increasingly conscious co-creators of our lives, shaping the ongoing flux of our experience. Because memory in-and-of itself is nothing but durée, because memory in a very real way is freedom itself, we can breathe new life into the seemingly static configurations of our past; we can consciously choose to let our memories arise, whether in the form of specific recollection images or in the form of body memory—that is, in-and-through visceral, affectively charged feelings. Then, in our freedom, we can understand and interpret these memories and feelings differently; we can switch the lens through which we view our past, ourselves, and the world around us.

Because we have this freedom, we also have a corresponding responsibility. Whether through therapy, or spiritual work, or through the profound transformation that can come through a high-quality education, we can choose to accept the responsibility, not only to unearth and reinterpret these buried dimensions of

our being, but also to open ourselves up to a set of radically different and potentially more valuable ideas and attitudes—a cluster of beliefs that will, in turn,
create a new set of experiences and memories, that will also, in turn, be superimposed upon our perceptions to create a better world for us to inhabit.

Of course, this sort of radical transformation does not happen overnight
and it does not happen easily. I suggest that we can be helped in this process by
consciously choosing to create a new environment, a new context, a new social
group, a new configuration of relationships that can mirror and model other
possibilities for us. These new experiences (e.g., of safety, hope, love, communion) can then act as a potent counterforce to the old destructive patterns.

In these liminal spaces and times (e.g., therapy sessions, yoga workshops,
drumming circles, charismatic church services, improvisational dance classes,
prayer meetings, healing retreats, meditation seminars, or even the lively give
and take of energized conversations with friends and colleagues) we can give ourselves the opportunity to try on new modes of being by cultivating an ever-deep-
ening connection to that fertile and open "space" of stillness and receptivity
within; we can create a support system that can assist us to die to old ways of
perceiving and acting, so that ultimately the potential is there to rejoin our
"normal" world of social interactions with more awareness, more freedom, and
more choice.

Of course, as Emile Durkheim pointed out more than a century ago, because
emotionally charged group settings can and do generate a potent matrix in which
various altered states of consciousness are likely to arise, we have to be aware that
the ideas that are communicated in-and-through these group contexts will have a
strong tendency to become quickly assimilated and affirmed within our psyche.[5]
If, for example, we have spent numerous hours singing and dancing and drumming (or meditating, or doing breath work, or chanting) together with others; and
if during those moments of "collective effervescence" our ego boundaries begin to
soften and we begin to feel an ecstatic sense of communion with wider, freer, more
joyous states of awareness; then the philosophical, theological, or political ideas
that are sanctioned by the authority figures of these groups—ideas that are
expressed either orally or through the study of texts that the group has affirmed—
will often begin to seem especially persuasive and attractive, having gained an association in our memory with these potent and pleasurable experiences.

The pronounced tendency of individuals to strongly affirm the ideas that
are associated in their memory with states of expanded awareness and with powerfully charged group contexts (e.g., tent revivals, mass rallies, possession rituals,
etc.) is arguably a major factor in the ability of different religious and political
movements throughout history to generate intensely loyal and committed fol-
lowers, to create people who believe fervently and passionately in a system of
ideas that have become internalized to the extent that their ongoing experience

of reality has been profoundly altered (and who are, therefore, likely to act in ways that confirm and intensify these tacit assumptive worlds).

In the past, some groups have condemned or discouraged any and all group contexts that generated nontypical or altered levels of awareness (e.g., the condemnation of "enthusiasts" in the late Middle Ages and the denouncing of Pentecostal practices from the pulpits of more "proper" evangelical churches, and so forth); however, we do not have to restrict ourselves to this rather one-dimensional approach. If we are aware that, by immersing ourselves in such a highly charged group context we will be more likely to adopt the ideas (and ideals) held by that group, and if we are aware that, by internalizing these ideas and ideals, we will then over time gradually change the "lens" through which we experience reality, then there will be a powerful incentive to choose to participate only in those groups that promote ideas and ideals that we are consciously hoping to cultivate within ourselves.

The primary point is that our memories are always going to shape, consciously or unconsciously, our experiences in the present. Therefore, it seems crucial that we, with as much clarity and energy as possible, decide which ideas (and ideals) we most wish to let go of and/or to transform, which new set of ideas and ideals we wish to internalize, and which set of practices and/or communal settings will best nurture this transformative process.

The hope is that we can begin, little by little, to reconfigure the world that we currently inhabit; the hope is that with some hard work and luck (and/or grace) we can gradually begin to change the underlying "note" of our being. Then, over time, depending upon which doorway (or doorways) of beliefs/practices/and support systems that we have stepped through, we might well begin to experience, for instance, a world that is more filled with God's presence than before; or a world in which we are more aligned and attuned moment by moment with our Buddha nature; or a world in which we have confronted our shadow material and are now connected with and integrating various archetypal energies; or a world in which we are more authentic, playful, sexual, and alive; or a world in which we feel the play of the Goddess in everyday life and in the pleasurable movements of our body; and so on.

It is hard to tell just how far all of this goes. Bergson himself was a critical realist. While he affirmed the innate fluidity of reality (both internally and externally), he did not believe that our descriptions of this reality were utterly arbitrary. While he does argue that each of us, inevitably, projects him- or herself out into the world and then interprets and understands that world via numerous conscious (and unconscious) "filters" that continually shape our experience of that reality, nonetheless, according to Bergson, there is a common world that we all share. There actually is, according to Bergson, a touchstone for truth; our truth claims are not utterly relative; they are not simply the artifacts of differing cultural practices, historical precedents, economic determinants, social locations, and linguistic patternings. We can, to a greater or lesser degree, have a direct, intuitive access to the depths of reality, even if at the same time that reality is always changing, is ever new.

Of course, if growth, newness, creativity, and freedom are indeed an inherent quality of the makeup of the universe itself, if there actually is a "built-in" evolutionary élan that is urging the universe forward in nonarbitrary, but open-ended directions (and Bergson clearly argues that all of this is true), then our desire to free ourselves from those aspects of ourselves that are deeply habituated and resistant to change (or to put it more positively, our longing to transform ourselves and the universe around us) is in-and-of-itself an expression of the essential evolutionary thrust of the universe itself; it is an indication of our alignment with levels of reality that are as true as they get, as trustworthy as they come.

Again, it is hard to tell how far we can go in our transformative, evolutionary development. If we learn to align ourselves with the élan vital in ever deeper ways; if we become more and more intuitive; if we cultivate within ourselves an openness to dimensions of reality that have previously been cut off from us; if we let go of the confining shell of our previous limiting and destructive beliefs, then it is difficult, if not impossible, to say exactly what we might discover (or in what unexpected ways we might transform). Admittedly, we have some hints, some indications of what might be possible, if we look at the lives of the saints and mystics. There we can vicariously perceive reverberations of love, wisdom, and compassion that, for the most part, and for most of us, are literally unimaginable. Nonetheless, if Bergson is correct, then even the feeblest desire to move in that direction, even the most fumbling initial willingness to long for more, is an indication that our hopes and dreams may some day, in a way that dramatically exceeds our expectations, become a vibrant, living reality.

21

THE PRESENCE OF THE PRESENT

THE PRESENCE OF THE PAST AND THE FUTURE OF PRESENCE

Bergson's theories on the nature of memory are, not surprisingly, intimately interwoven with his understanding of the relationship between memory and time, especially as time manifests itself as what we often for convenience's sake call the past, present, and future.

Of these three, the present is probably the most difficult to fully comprehend. To a large degree, this difficulty is directly related to the fact that time is constantly moving. And from within this ever-changing flux, it can be exceedingly difficult to pin down exactly "where" (or more accurately, "when") the present exists. Even our very attempts to pin down or to grasp the present seem to be inherently self-defeating. If the present actually could be pinned down or grasped, it would have stopped flowing, but as Bergson notes, "the real, concrete, live present—that of which I speak when I speak of my present perception—that present necessarily occupies a duration" (*MM* 137).

According to Bergson, time is not and cannot be composed of a series of static mathematical "instants" or "points" (i.e., a series of unchanging "nows") that when added together somehow turn into the river of time in which we actually live (*MM* 137). The present, therefore, rather oddly, is not something that *is* so much as it is something that is always being made, something that is always becoming. As Bergson points out, there actually is no present, if by the present we mean some idealized line that divides the past from the future. The present, understood in this commonsense sort of way, can never be "caught" in that, if we wait for it to happen, it will always remain out of our grasp in the future; but as soon as we think that it is, so to speak, present, it has already slipped into the past (*MM* 150).

However, the *concrete* present, the present as it is actually experienced in consciousness, is much more accessible. According to Bergson, the concrete, lived present can, in certain respects, be understood as the immediate past. As he points out, even in the tiniest moment of our perception (e.g., seeing a flash of light), billions of vibrations have taken place. Therefore, even in a microsecond of perception, we have gathered together *in our memory* a quantity of vibratory quanta that is literally unimaginable. (Bergson is speaking here of what I call "*primal memory*"—the type of memory that binds each seeming separate moment to the next, the type of memory that forms the duration of matter.) These "elementary vibrations," as Bergson puts it, are "translated" by our memory into our pure perceptions, a process that necessarily takes time (and takes place *in* time, *as* time). Therefore, as a consequence of the inescapably temporal nature of perception, as soon as we have perceived something it is already past. As Bergson notes, "in truth, every perception is already memory. *Practically, we perceive only the past*, the pure present being the invisible progress of the past gnawing into the future" (*MM* 150).

Our present in this way is always a difficult-to-grasp fusion of the past and the future. It is in the past because, as was just pointed out, the moment that we attempt to take hold of the present, it has already disappeared into the past; it is in the future because, as embodied beings with practical interests, we are tremendously concerned about the next moment. According to Bergson, our attention, our sensorimotor, bodily based awareness of the world around us is intensely focused moment-to-moment on the anticipated needs of the future. As Bergson notes, "my present is that which interests me, which lives for me, and in a word, that which summons me to action" (*MM* 137). Understood from this perspective, as Bergson indicates, "that which I call my present" is in certain respects "my attitude with regard to the immediate future; it is my impending action. My present is, then, sensori-motor" (*MM* 140).

Because our body is itself inherently sensorimotor (in that its primary task is to sense itself and the world around it and to perform actions), the present is also in a very important way intimately related to our consciousness of our body (and hence is intimately related to habit memory). Our body, in turn, is where "we directly feel the flux" of "that continuity of becoming which is reality itself"; it is our lifeline to actuality, to the materiality of existence, to that "present which is always beginning again" (*MM* 139). The present, therefore, is deeply intertwined with the flux of material existence, and our body is (from our perspective) situated at the very center of this material universe. Moment-to-moment our body is impacted by the universe and moment-to-moment it impacts the universe in turn. The body, for Bergson, therefore, "represents the actual state of my becoming, that part of my duration which is in process of growth" (*MM* 138). As such, the body and its ever-changing perception of the universe around it is "the pointed end" of our present, a present that is "ever moving, ever driven into the future by the weight of our past" (*MM* 243).

THE CHARACTER OF OUR PRESENT,
THE PRESENCE OF OUR CHARACTER

For Bergson, our present (as noted earlier) is not just focused on material existence; it is not just intertwined with our sensorimotor bodily awareness; it is not just actively oriented toward the future. It is also firmly rooted in the past, not just in-and-through the activity of our "primal memory," which binds one moment of perception to the next, but also via the ongoing process by which our pure perceptions are continually infused and filled in with memory (i.e., infused with the past) to become the experienced content of our concrete perceptions in the ever-moving stream of the present.

The past is also present within us in-and-through what we call our "character." According to Bergson, "the condensation of the history that we have lived from our birth—nay, even before our birth, since we bring with us prenatal dispositions," is immediately present within us (and can be felt as such) in our character (*CE* 5). In order to make any and all decisions, we draw upon, at least implicitly, this ever-present synthesis of our past that "conditions our present state, without being its necessary determinant" (*MM* 148). In fact, this "digest" of our past is, in many ways, more real to us than the external world in that our character is not something separate from us, but instead in certain respects *is* us. At every moment, in the margins of our awareness, we directly know, from within, our own character (i.e., the synthesis of our entire past) with an immediacy that is rivaled only by the sensory flux of those pure perceptions (i.e., that very small segment of the images of the universe that we admit into consciousness).

ATTENDING TO THE PRESENT

Our present is also in the past in yet another way in that our present can be understood, in a certain sense, as the period of duration that can be held together in our memory as an organic whole by the power of our attention.

Using an example that Bergson himself used while giving a lecture, let's say that I am pronouncing the word "conversation." In order for that word to have any meaning it has to be present in my consciousness as an integral whole. Therefore, my present includes at the very least the length of time that it takes to pronounce the word "conversation." Yet, at the same time, when I am pronouncing the syllable "tion" of the word "conversation," the first three syllables of the word are already in the past. The presence of the word "conversation," therefore, if it can be found anywhere, is in my memory; in other words, it is in my past.

Unfortunately, however, the relationship between attention and the present is even more complex than this. As Bergson points out, "when I pronounce the word 'conversation,' there is present in my mind not only the beginning, the middle, and the end of the word, but also the words which preceded it and all the beginning of the sentence; otherwise I would have lost the thread of my speech" (*ME* 69). Therefore, it appears that the present is not confined to the length of time it takes to pronounce a word like "conversation," but rather can be expanded to include the "amount" of duration (and the quality of attention, and the cohesiveness of memory) that is associated with pronouncing an entire sentence.

However, the complexity does not end here. As Bergson recognizes, sentences vary in their length. Therefore, in reality, the particular span of time that makes up the present varies according to the length of the sentence (and/or the power of a person's attention). As such, in order to extend the present further into the past, all that a person would have to do in essence is simply to change the punctuation in order to lengthen the sentence. The implication is clear:

> The distinction we make between our present and past is . . . if not arbitrary, at least relative to the extent of the field which our attention to life can embrace. The "present" occupies exactly as much space [so to speak] as this effort. As soon as this particular attention drops any part of what it held beneath its gaze, immediately that portion of the present thus dropped becomes *ipso facto* a part of the past. In a word, our present falls back into the past when we cease to attribute to it an immediate interest. (*CM* 179)

Pushing this argument to its limit, Bergson suggests that if he were not concerned with what was coming in the future but instead could remain fully immersed in speaking, giving that activity his full attention, then conceivably there would be no limit as to how long that sentence could become (the ultimate "run-on" sentence!), and consequently, there would be no limit as to how much of the past he could hold together in his consciousness.

Bergson argues that if we could somehow manage to give our full attention to the flow of life (an attention that would also have to be, as pointed out before, utterly uncontaminated with concerns about the future), if we could allow ourselves to become fully immersed in what we were doing and/or saying, then with this ability (an ability that, I suggest, is identical to the goal sought by those who practice mindfulness meditation) we could at least theoretically extend our present to include our "entire past history"—a present that would not be a frozen "instantaneity," made up of a "cluster of simultaneous parts," but rather an "undivided" and "continually moving" present (*CM* 180). An individual with this quality/level of attention (or mindfulness) would, according to Bergson, experience her or his present as an indivisible flowing melody, as "a perpetual present, although this perpetuity [would have] nothing in common with immutability . . . [but rather, would be] a present which endures" (*CM* 180).[1]

MINI-RUMINATION: LIVING IN THE NOW

This ability to live fully and completely in an expanded, fluid present is also a goal that is frequently described in the texts of many mystical traditions. Unfortunately, however, it often seems that when some naïve practitioners are, for instance, encouraged to "live in the now," they mistakenly interpret this to mean that they should limit their attention to the smallest possible "instant" of the present. However, a closer inspection of what mystics mean by "the now" shows (for the most part) that they do not advocate that we should reduce consciousness to the tiniest possible instant of the present; they do not propose that we should literally forget everything that happened in the past and have no sense of the future at all. Instead, what most mystical teachings emphasize is the need to free one's attention from an obsessive fretting over the past and an equally obsessive anxiety about the future in order to develop a quality of sustained, focused, centered attention that holds within itself (in a relaxed, "spacious" way) increasingly vast (and qualitatively rich) stretches of duration. The ideal is to be fully immersed in the flowing pulsations of the present to such an extent that the present, as it were, expands to include the totality of one's entire experience, so that the past and the future as abstract distinctions dissolve and are utterly absorbed into dynamic continuity of the "now." It is this present that is, as the name indicates, always present, not as a tiny atom of time, but rather as the ever-changing continuity of our consciousness.

THE INDIVISIBILITY OF MEMORY

For better or for worse, however, most of us are not mystics with a highly refined and cultivated ability to be continuously and attentively mindful of and absorbed into the present. For most of us, our power of attention is rather undeveloped. Therefore, our attention flits moment to moment to some new thought or new perception (often with little or no conscious instigation). However, even though our attention inevitably meanders in this way, these shifts in the quality of our awareness, according to Bergson, do not introduce a radical break into the flow of consciousness. Instead, consciousness flows on seamlessly, rooted in and floating on memory. In fact, as Bergson points out, if memory did not exist, there would be no consciousness in that "a consciousness unable to conserve its past, forgetting itself unceasingly, would be a consciousness perishing and having to be reborn at each moment. . . . All consciousness, then, is memory,—conservation and accumulation of the past in the present" (*ME* 8).

Bergson stresses that it is possible to feel directly within us the fact that our present is infused with a clear memory of what just occurred. We can feel, within our own being, an inner continuity of consciousness that is created because we have, in (and as) the flow of our present experience, memory of what just took place. Therefore, the past is, within our own experience, clearly preserved in the ongoing, indivisible flow of our consciousness.

We also can tell, within our own experience, that the "quantity" of the past that is preserved and interwoven with the present, in-and-as memory, varies widely depending upon the quality of our attention. When we forget what happened in the recent past, this forgetfulness happens, according to Bergson, not because the past (or our memory) has disappeared, but rather because our day-to-day consciousness is primarily interested in what is about to happen in the near future, that is, in the sensorimotor present. Because we are almost "solely preoccupied" with the task of "determining an undetermined future," our day-to-day "consciousness may shed a little of its light" on those memories from the past "which can be usefully combined with our present state"; however, the rest of our memories, the rest of our past, typically "remains in the dark" (*MM* 150). Bergson argues, therefore, that the past in a very real sense has not ceased to exist. Instead, it has simply ceased to be useful.[2]

Bergson argues that when we forget something (i.e., when we cannot summon specific memory-images into our conscious awareness) this does not happen because our memory at some mysterious point completely severs itself from the present and radically cuts itself off from the flow of consciousness. According to Bergson, memory is always present—it is just that our attention is elsewhere. (Remember: if memory is not present, then neither is consciousness.) Therefore, since memory never really "goes" anywhere, since it is always present (albeit "under our radar") in-and-through-and-as our ever-changing experiences, and since "that change is indivisible, and . . . in an indivisible change the past is one with the present," conceivably, *all* of the past experiences of every moment are preserved; *all* of our memories are implicitly or virtually or subconsciously present within consciousness (*CM* 183).

What this continuity of consciousness (and memory) means for Bergson is that "our whole past still exists," even if, significantly, it "exists subconsciously" (*ME* 70). And if all of our past exists "within us" (once again, spatial metaphors are problematic), if our past "preserves itself automatically," then we have no need to conceive of memory as some sort of "special faculty" that has the job of storing the past within us (*CM* 180). It is only when we ignore the "indivisibility of change"; it is only when we close ourselves to "the fact that our most distant past adheres to our present and constitutes with it a single and identical uninterrupted change"; it is only when we think that the past is for the most part destroyed and "that there is something extraordinary about the preservation of the past"—it is only in such cases that we need to imagine that there is some sort of "special faculty" (i.e., the brain) which manages somehow to record those parts of the past that are almost miraculously not destroyed (*CM* 180–181).

22

MEMORY AND THE BRAIN

WHERE, OH WHERE ARE OUR MEMORIES STORED?

Bergson's notion that memories do not need to be stored in the brain in order to survive unharmed appears at first glance to fly in the face of both common sense and decades (perhaps centuries) of scientific evidence.[1] Nonetheless, while Bergson's argument may seem quixotic, it is important to realize that he does not make such a claim lightly. To begin with, Bergson underscores that, if we look carefully at our memories, it is not self-evident that they need to be "stored" anywhere. As he points out, "we understand that physico-chemical phenomena take place *in* the brain, that the brain is *in* the body, the body *in* the air which surrounds it," and so on, but why do we have to assume that memories are contained *in* something? (*MM* 148). Bergson realizes that the almost inevitable and understandable temptation is to imagine that memories must somehow be contained within the brain. But as he hastens to point out, perhaps this taken-for-granted assumption is itself based on an overly materialistic (and spatial) understanding of mental phenomena.

What Bergson asks us to do is to take seriously the idea that perhaps memories are *not* physical (at least in the normal way that we understand "physical," i.e., they are not tangible, measurable, quantifiable objects in space). He insists that, if we look carefully at memory from the standpoint of the immediacy of our own experience, we will discover for ourselves that memory indeed does not seem to be "made" of the same "stuff" as the physical objects that surround us, at least insofar as memory cannot be touched, or seen, or smelled, or weighed, or measured. In *Matter and Memory*, Bergson works hard to convince his readers that memory (or spirit, or the mind—all essentially synonymous terms for Bergson) is, as he puts it, "absolutely independent of matter"[2] (*MM* 177). It is "spirit in its most tangible form" (*MM* 73).[3] What Bergson asks us to do, at least temporarily, is to trust the evidence of our own experience; he asks us to acknowledge that, if memory is indeed as it appears to be, "neither visible nor tangible," if we can accept the nonmateriality of memory, at least as a working hypothesis, then it becomes quite reasonable to ask why our memories should "need a container" and how they could, in fact, possibly even have one (*ME* 68).

According to Bergson, if our memories are anywhere, they are "in" the mind, they are "in" consciousness.[4] As Bergson repeatedly emphasizes, memories are not stored in the brain. Seen from a Bergsonian perspective, the brain is not best understood (as it often is) as some sort of highly sophisticated computer with an enormous storage capacity.

EXPERIMENTAL ATTEMPTS TO FIND MEMORIES IN THE BRAIN

We have to be careful to not overly quickly dismiss Bergson's assertion that memories are not located in the brain, even if this proposition might appear to fly in the face of decades of scientific data, and even if it seems to contradict the claims made by philosophers and scientists over the past few centuries. While it is true that the overwhelming majority of cognitive scientists and neurologists currently take for granted that memory can and should be fully explained in terms of neurochemical modifications within the brain (the so-called traces of past experience), what many people do not realize is that the evidence for these traces is neither powerful nor unambiguous.[5] In fact, as Rupert Sheldrake notes, "attempts to locate such traces within the brain and to analyze them have so far been unsuccessful."[6]

Sheldrake argues that scientists continue to believe that memories are stored in the brain because, at first glance, this claim appears to be supported by two highly convincing forms of evidence, that is, "that electrical stimulation of certain parts of the brain can evoke memories" and "that brain damage can lead to loss of memory."[7]

Perhaps the most well-known example of experimental evidence that appears to demonstrate that memories can be evoked when specific parts of the brain are stimulated with electricity is the research that was conducted by Wilder Penfield and his associates starting in the 1920s. During a series of operations on patients with various neurological disorders, Penfield and his colleagues stimulated different parts of their patients' brains with electrodes (although the patients' scalps were anesthetized, they remained fully conscious). When Penfield, for instance, used an electrode to give a mild electrical shock to specific parts of a patient's motor cortex, he discovered that the patient's arms or legs often made involuntary movements. Similarly, when an electrode was activated while touching the primary auditory or visual cortex of other patients, they often reported a range of auditory and visual hallucinations (e.g., flashes of light, buzzing sounds, and so forth). Remarkably, however, when regions of the temporal cortex of epileptic patients were stimulated with an electrode, some of these patients reported that they remembered specific scenes from their past (e.g., an evening at a concert or a telephone conversation) in vivid detail. Even more remarkably, when these same areas of the brain were touched with an electrode again (often without the patient's knowledge), the same "engram" (a term coined by Penfield to designate memory traces in specific parts of the brain) was elicited, with a similar degree of detail.[8]

Quite understandably, Penfield and countless other scientists influenced by his work concluded, based on these experiments, that memories were stored or "encoded" in highly specific portions of the brain. The only problem was that no one, including Penfield himself, was able to replicate these findings. In fact, at a certain point Penfield abandoned his original claim that engrams are, in fact, located in a specific area of the brain. As Penfield (perhaps ruefully) notes, "in 1951 I had proposed that certain parts of the temporal cortex should be called the 'memory cortex,' and suggested that the neuronal record was located there in the cortex near points at which the stimulating electrode may call forth an experiential response. This was a mistake. . . . The record is not in the cortex."[9]

What Penfield (and the vast majority of other scientists of his time) did not abandon, however, was the notion that there is a "record" of the past *somewhere* in the brain. Given the typically unexamined mechanistic metaphysical theory that undergirds most modern science, this notion is understandable: if everything that is real is made of dead matter blindly interacting according to natural laws, then memory must also be "made" of physical "stuff." And if memories are indeed physically present in the body, then it seems that the brain, with its enormous neuronal complexity, is a good place to look. Today, most scientists and theorists on the nature of consciousness operate under the assumption that, although the physical location of memory within the brain (and the mechanics of how it operates) is not currently known, this lack of knowledge is only a temporary setback: it is taken for granted that, given enough time, persistence, and experimental sophistication, it will become possible to map out the physical instantiation of memory within the brain in great detail.

The renowned American neuropsychologist Karl Lashley was one of the best-known proponents of the belief that, given sufficient experimental tenacity, the location of memory engrams within the brain can and will be unearthed. Lashley's own tenacity was more than amply demonstrated by his more than thirty years of experimentation. His basic experimental design was rather simple. Lashley would first train animals in a variety of tasks and then he would surgically cut out (or burn, often with his wife's curling iron) portions of the animals' brains (while the animals were kept alive). The assumption behind this gruesome experimentation was that, if the part of the animal's brain that contained the memories corresponding to the new skill that it had acquired had been destroyed, then the animal, after it recuperated, would no longer be able to demonstrate its newfound learning. (Lashley realized that another possible result of this procedure was that the animal's memory might be disrupted in another way, in that it might also have difficulty acquiring new skills.)[10]

Lashley assumed that his work would verify and amplify Penfield's assertion that there is a clear-cut location for engrams in the brain. However, all of his experimental results seemed to prove that Penfield's assertion was incorrect.[11] In one experiment, for instance, Lashley trained rats to jump through tiny doors, rewarding them for success with food. When he was convinced that the rats had mastered their task, he set out very systematically to find out where the memory was located by burning various parts of their brains. Unfortunately, this experiment did not lead to quite the result that Lashley had anticipated. While the rats' motor skills were often radically truncated due to the cauterization of large parts of their brains, they nonetheless persisted in their ability to demonstrate their new skill (albeit with much less grace than before). Lashley would burn more and more of the rats' brains, but although their motor functions would become increasingly impaired, they still attempted to jump through the doors to get to the food, even with the vast majority of their brain destroyed.[12]

Similarly, Lashley trained monkeys to open a variety of latch boxes. Once they had mastered this task, he surgically removed most of their motor cortexes. Although this operation paralyzed the monkeys, after eight to twelve weeks they would recover enough of their motor function that they were once again physically capable of opening the latches to the boxes. The question, however, was whether the monkeys would remember the skill that they had previously acquired before the operation? What Lashley repeatedly found was that, when the monkeys were shown the boxes, they promptly opened them without any initial fumbling or exploratory movements, conclusively demonstrating that they still retained their memory of this task, even with most of their motor cortex destroyed.[13]

In experiments with other animals, Lashley surgically removed large portions of other sections of their brains (e.g., the cerebral cortex and the cerebellum). Nonetheless, all of these surgically disabled animals were still able to demonstrate that they maintained their previous learned skills, even with massive levels of injury to highly significant parts of their brains. Eventually, in the light of all of this experimental evidence, Lashley concluded that learning in these animals was not best understood as a complex series of reflexes that created simple, straightforward "traces" in the nervous system and brain. Instead, he began to hypothesize that memory must be stored in multiple systems throughout the brain.[14]

Many other scientists, however, were not persuaded by this new way to understand memory and attempted to prove that Lashley's hypothesis of "distributed memory" was incorrect. Indiana University biologist Paul Pietsch, for instance, worked diligently to prove that memories are indeed located in specific parts of the brain. Pietsch's research focused on the brains of salamanders. Due to the remarkable physiological resilience that salamanders possess, when Pietsch surgically removed a brain from one of these amazing animals, it would not die but instead would simply become comatose. Furthermore, once the salamander's brain was reattached, the salamander would eventually recover and begin to function relatively normally.

Pietsch took advantage of this seemingly wondrous recuperative ability. What Pietsch did, in over seven hundred different experiments, was to cut out the brains of numerous salamanders and then, before putting the brains back, he would tamper with them in various ways—all in an attempt to show that memory was directly linked to specific sites in the brain. As Lynne McTaggart notes, "in successive experiments [Pietsch] reversed, cut out, sliced away, shuffled and even sausage-ground his test subjects' brains. But no matter how brutally mangled, or diminished in size, whenever whatever was left of the brains was returned to his subjects and the salamanders had recovered, they returned to normal behavior."[15] Based on the results of these experiments, even Pietsch finally converted to the view that memory is not stored in specific places in the brain, but rather is distributed in some unknown fashion throughout the brain.[16]

Although these experiments appear to demonstrate, rather graphically, that memory can survive the destruction of large portions of the brain, the mainstream response to findings such as these has been to echo (in various ways) Lashley and Pietsch's assertion that there must be multiple backup or redundant memory storage systems distributed throughout the brain. In this way, if memories are stored in one location and that site is destroyed, then the backup memory systems automatically kick in.[17] However, as Sheldrake astutely observes, while "this hypothesis, invented to account for the failure of attempts to find localized memory traces, follows naturally from the assumption that memories *must* be stored somewhere inside the brain . . . in the continuing absence of any direct evidence, it remains more a matter of faith than of fact."[18]

PHILOSOPHICAL PROBLEMS WITH THE MEMORY TRACE THEORY

The theory of memory traces in the brain has other problems besides a lack of experimental evidence. For instance, if we hypothesize that memories are stored somewhere in the brain (whether in specific locations or distributed throughout the brain's neural network), the question then becomes: how are these memories accessed and retrieved? For any sort of retrieval system to work, it must be able to identify the memories that it is searching for. However, in order to do this, the retrieval system itself must have some kind of memory, which implies that there would have to be another retrieval system to access these memory traces, and so on, ad infinitum.[19]

Bergson himself pointed out another problem with the memory trace theory. If we assume (as many did during Bergson's time) that auditory memories, for instance, are dormant in some sort of neurochemical form in the cells of the cortex, then how are these memories stored? As Bergson pointed out, even the same word, spoken by different people, or spoken by the same person in a different way, produces a different sound. Would there then need to be a separate memory for each of these different sounds? Or is the word itself, with each of its unique forms of pronunciation, given its own "memory-slot"? Or is each individual sentence separately recorded? Or does each word (or letter?) within the sentence have its own discrete "cubby-hole," with a separate (but related?) memory trace for clauses within the sentence and yet another one for the sentence itself? And how are these various sound, word, and sentence memories related to other auditory memories (since meaning never emerges in isolation, but rather, is integrally dependent upon the entire linguistic network)? (*ME* 64).

Furthermore, how should we understand the storage of visual memories? If each visual recollection of a perceived object were stored in the brain, there would have to be millions of memory traces for each object, because even a simple, stable object changes its form and color moment by moment depending upon changes in the observer's point of view. And if we add movement to the equation, how many trillions of memory traces would have to be created for each object as it shifts its appearance when it moves through time? (*ME* 64). Even the massive neuronal complexity of the brain might well be taxed by this "quantity" of memory storage.

For Bergson, the more fundamental philosophical issue is that listening to sounds, and remembering ideas, and understanding words, and seeing objects are all aspects of a continuous process that can only artificially be separated into discrete "things." What we analytically divide into discrete words or images is, in reality, an unbroken stream of fluid changes; words and visual images are only phases of an undivided continuum. Thought and perception are innately continuous, but psychologists and neurologists act as if it is possible to isolate out discrete memory-images from this continuum; they pretend that these thoughts and perceptions are "things," so that each can then have its own discrete location in the brain (*MM* 125).

Bergson also points out another philosophical problem with the notion that memories are stored in the brain. As he notes, if we want to believe that memories are located within the brain, "it is then necessary that the brain, in order to preserve the memory, should preserve itself" (*MM* 149). The problem, however, is that at every moment within the brain, there are countless complex and almost inconceivably rapid sequences of neurochemical activities. In-and-through all of this flux, how is it possible that there can be any stability to memory? How is it possible that our memories can stay safely tucked away somewhere, untouched by all of this flux?

Sheldrake agrees with Bergson that the neurochemical dynamism of the brain presents enormous difficulties for any understanding of how memories can persist over time. As he points out, "if memories are somehow stored in synapses, then the synapses themselves must remain stable over long periods of time: indeed, the nervous system as a whole must be stable if it is to act as a memory store."[20]

Until recently, this neuronal stability is exactly what most scientists took for granted. It was assumed that the nervous system and the brain were indeed extremely stable, at least in mature animals. The reigning "dogma" (challenged only by those who wanted to ruin their careers) was that by the age of three, the form and function of the human brain was relatively fixed. While it was recognized that new memories could be formed (and new skills could be learned), it was thought that the basic structure of the brain was as immutable as the color of our eyes.[21]

However, it is now becoming increasingly clear that the structure of the brain is much more dynamic than was once imagined. For instance, it was once thought that certain sections of the brain are "wired" for highly specific functions (a view that can be dated to 1861, when Paul Broca, a French surgeon, claimed that the ability to speak was located in the left frontal lobe of the brain). However, it is now known, for example, that if people lose their sight at a young age, that the visual cortex will not simply remain dormant, but instead will begin to become activated in response to touch, or sound, or language.[22] Similarly, it was once thought that no new neurons are created within the brain once maturity is reached. However, in 1998, Peter Eriksson of Sweden's Sahlgrenska University Hospital and his colleagues discovered that the brains of patients even in their sixties and seventies continued to create neurons.[23]

This degree of dynamism and adaptability within the structure and functioning of the brain and nervous system may well present a more nuanced understanding of the physiology of human beings than was possible with the previous assumptions about the immutability of the brain (which, in turn, offers us a much more hopeful sense of the possibilities for genuine personal and moral change). However, this new theoretical paradigm makes it much more difficult to claim that memory is "encoded" in some sort of physical memory traces.

The theory of memory traces within the brain, therefore, is far from conclusively proved. It is riddled with philosophical difficulties and is not supported by persuasive evidence. (As Sheldrake points out, one recent textbook, *Molecular Biology of the Cell*, asserts that "we still understand almost nothing about the cellular basis of memory in vertebrates—neither the detailed anatomy of the neural circuits responsible nor the molecular biology of the changes that experience produces in them.")[24]

BRAIN INJURY AND MEMORY: BERGSON'S PERSPECTIVE

As was pointed out earlier, one of the primary reasons why it is often assumed that memory is physically encoded in the brain is the indisputable fact that brain injury can destroy our ability to recollect past events. If Bergson is audacious enough to make the claim that memory is not stored in the brain, he has to address this issue forcefully, and he has to come up with convincing alternative explanations.

Bergson begins this task by arguing that there are two, equally viable, ways to understand the relationship between the brain and memory. The first way to understand this relationship is to claim that memories are contained in the brain. The second (which Bergson endorses) is to claim that, while memories are not in-and-of-themselves spatial or overtly physical in nature, in order for them to be of any use to us in our daily lives we have to somehow gain access to these memories and we have to physically express them in-and-through the body, that is, through words, gestures, sounds, postures, facial expressions, and so on. Bergson stresses that in order to accomplish either of these tasks, the body itself (especially the nervous system and the brain) must function properly. If it does not, then what looks like memory loss may perhaps be more accurately understood as difficulty in *accessing* or *expressing* memory.

The first (naturalistic) hypothesis argues that damage to a particular region of the brain, whether caused by injury or disease, destroys the memories that are stored in that area of the brain. The second (Bergsonian) hypothesis argues that injury to the brain does not in fact destroy the memories themselves, but rather either prevents a person from being able to tune into her or his memories or keeps the person from manifesting and using those memories through her or his ability to speak, write, move about effectively in the world, and so on (*MM* 99).

In order to better understand Bergson's arguments about the relationship between brain injury and memory, it is important to recall that Bergson emphasizes that there are two very different types of memory: habit memory and recollection memory. Both forms of memory are connected to the body (especially the brain), but this connection manifests itself in strikingly different ways.

To reiterate, habit memory is almost completely physical in its very nature; as Bergson puts it, habit memory is "acted rather than thought" (*MM* 237). In this form of memory, our body reacts more or less automatically with little or no conscious prior thought to various perceptions. This is the sort of memory that we primarily draw upon, for example, when we recite a poem from memory, or when we drive a car while holding a conversation, or when we play the piano in an "automatic" fashion.

Bergson is the first to admit that damage to the brain can severely cripple this form of memory. If someone, for example, due to a stroke or trauma from surgery can no longer remember how to recite a poem that she or he had previously memorized, Bergson would suggest that her or his difficulties are not the result of damage to stored memories in the traumatized sections of the brain. Instead, he would say that this type of problem with memory comes about at least in large part because of damage to those structures of the brain that had previously coordinated the complex physical capacities needed to recite this poem from memory.

According to Bergson, damage to the brain can also impact the second form of memory: "recollection memory." Bergson emphasizes that recollection memories in their "purest" form are "spiritual" in nature, that is, they are for all practical purposes nonphysical. These essentially nonphysical, nonspatial memories of the past are therefore not *directly* affected by injury to the brain. Nonetheless, in order for these nonphysical recollections to intersect effectively with our day-to-day existence, they cannot remain divorced from the physicality of our active and perceptual life. Therefore, what happens is that our free-floating fund of recollections of specific past events, impelled by the urgent needs of the present, become transformed into a form of memory that *can* become superimposed upon and seamlessly integrated with the world that we perceive.

As will be discussed in more detail further on, what Bergson argues is that under the surface of our awareness, with little or no conscious choice on our part, detailed recollections of specific incidents in the past change into an "in-between" form of memory, a form of memory that is lower down the "cone" of memory, a form of memory that mediates the worlds of spirit and physicality, a form of memory that can give significance to the world around us, a form of memory that enables a person to know, for example, that this particular form of color and shape is a Turkish rug or that series of rhythmic sounds is a Beatles' song.

Bergson argues that in the case of recollection memory, damage to the brain does not destroy the actual recollection memories themselves (as "spiritual" phenomena, they cannot be affected by physical events). Instead, as Bergson puts it, "the alleged destruction of memories by an injury to the brain is but a break in the continuous progress by which they [i.e., recollections] actualize themselves" (*MM* 126). According to Bergson, what injury to the brain does is to disrupt the ability of memory-images to be "inserted" effectively into our bodily, active, present moment existence; damage to the brain undercuts the ongoing, seemingly effortless ability of these tacit networks of meaning to transform the flux of perceptions into a three-dimensional world that is rich in significance. Recollections in-and-of themselves, therefore, are not destroyed. What are destroyed are the sensory or motor areas of the brain that enable these recollections either to be consciously accessed in the present (e.g., when we remember specific events from our past experience), or what are destroyed are the highly complex brain functions that enable these recollections (in the form of "memory-images") to effectively fuse, under the surface of our conscious awareness, with the ongoing flux of perceptions.

Perhaps Bergson's understanding of the relationship between memory and brain damage can be clarified by giving a few examples from *Matter and Memory*. Drawing upon the experimental evidence on brain pathology available to him at the time (especially the data relating to various kinds of aphasia, or disorders relating to language use), Bergson offers several examples of memory loss.[25] One patient, for example, as the result of a fall, had lost the ability to speak on his own. All that he could do was to parrot whatever was spoken in his vicinity. Another patient with brain damage was unable to understand anything that was said to him, but (similar to the first patient) repeated back word for word whatever he heard. As Bergson points out, for both of these patients, it was almost as if the auditory sensations were converting themselves automatically into bodily articulations.

From a Bergsonian perspective, neither of these examples of memory loss should be understood as resulting from damage to memory traces in the brain. Instead, they are better understood as the result of damage to those bodily mechanisms that, in the first case, had previously allowed the patient to express his thoughts and memories, and in the second case had previously facilitated the smooth integration of the meaning-giving "memory-images" unto the perceptual images (i.e., words) that the patient was hearing. All that was left, in both cases, was a rudimentary form of habit memory.

Bergson also notes that lesions in the brain are often correlated with a person's inability to remember specific incidents in her or his past. However, as Bergson points out, "if recollections were really deposited in the brain," then the destruction of brain tissue would permanently erase the memories that were stored there (*MM* 237). But even in Bergson's time, it was often acknowledged that patients with cerebral lesions would at times spontaneously regain their memories (which is hard to explain if the memories had been physically stored there). Therefore, Bergson argues, "things happen much more as if the brain served to recall the recollection, and not to store it" (*ME* 65). In light of this type of evidence, Bergson suggests that instead of clinging to the notion that the memories themselves are physically destroyed by damage to the brain, it is perhaps preferable to realize that what is lost is the ability of a person to bring his memories into a working relationship with the present; what is lost "is the whole faculty of remembering" itself (*MM* 237).

These examples attempt to illustrate how Bergson's way of understanding the relationship between memory and the brain allows us to make sense of different kinds of cerebral pathologies at least as well as the more conventional notion (i.e., that memories are contained in the brain). Bergson's perspective does not ignore or deny the crucial role that the brain plays in the process of remembering. He simply provides an alternate interpretation of the relationship between the brain and memory. In much the same way that a television repairman understands that damaging the wiring within a television disrupts the ability of the television to receive electromagnetic signals from the station (as well as the television's ability to change those signals into coherent patterns on the screen of the television), but would never claim that this damage to the television destroys the signals themselves, Bergson is very much aware that damage to the brain often does affect a person's ability to recall and to express her or his memories, but he is adamant that this physical damage does not destroy the actual memories that the brain is attempting to access and to articulate.

BRAIN INJURY AND MEMORY: CURRENT UNDERSTANDINGS

Mainstream psychology and neurology have studied memory loss (or amnesia) for well over a century. At this point in time, amnesia is currently divided into two primary categories: "retrograde" amnesia and "antegrade" amnesia. Retrograde amnesia occurs when a person cannot remember events that happened before (and immediately after) an injury, trauma, or sudden onset of disease to the brain or nervous system. (Interestingly, the types of memories that Bergson would call "habit memory" are usually not lost in retrograde amnesia—that is, the patient will usually retain sensorimotor skills, such as the ability to type or to drive a car.)

Retrograde amnesia is typically explained in two distinct ways. First, as was also the case in Bergson's time, it is often currently argued that amnesia occurs when the memory traces located in the part of the brain that was traumatized have been destroyed. This explanation, however, is difficult to defend since, as was noted earlier, patients frequently recover the ability to remember the memories that were supposedly destroyed.[26] Much more plausible (and closer to Bergson's understanding) is the contemporary theory that the trauma to the brain destroyed the ability of the person to *retrieve* memories from where they are stored, still unharmed, in the brain. (What this theory leaves unexplained, however, is the mysterious location of the memories themselves.)

The second form of amnesia, "antegrade" amnesia, occurs when a person can no longer create new long-term memories (again, as the result of a trauma, injury, or disease). In this condition, patients can commonly do tasks that involve "habit" or "bodily memory" (for instance, they can perform mathematical calculations, if done quickly, or they can dial a telephone number), but soon afterward they have difficulty remembering that they performed these actions.[27]

One contemporary mainstream explanation of antegrade amnesia claims that injury to the brain has destroyed the ability of the brain to form new memory traces. Bergson, of course, would interpret this defect somewhat differently. Although he would concur that trauma to the brain might well alter the quality of those recollections by damaging, for instance, the ability of the person to concentrate on a task, he would insist that recollection memories, in some form or another, *are* being created. The primary problem, he would argue, is that damage to the brain makes it difficult, if not impossible, for these recollections either to be accessed or to be communicated (through words, bodily gestures, and so forth). As Bergson stresses, "the brain's function is to choose from the past, to diminish it, to simplify it, to utilize it, but not to preserve it" (*CM* 182).

These two primary ways in which theorists currently classify amnesia are, not surprisingly, overly simplistic abstractions from the much more complex and messy reality of those who suffer from various neurological disorders. Some diseases, for instance, lead to highly specific effects on the patient's ability to recognize others or to recall events from the past. As Sheldrake points out, for instance, "the ability to recognize faces . . . may be lost as a result of a lesion in the secondary visual cortex in the right hemisphere. A sufferer may fail to recognize the faces of even his wife and children, although he still knows them by their voices and in other ways."[28] At other times, patients will be unable to recognize the significance of various objects, colors, sounds, and so forth (a syndrome called "agnosia"). Similarly, there are many different forms of aphasia (disorders of language use) and apraxia (the loss of abilities to manipulate objects in a coordinated way).

The standard explanations of these disorders vary widely. Some theorists posit, for instance, that agnosias result from defects in the higher levels of brain functioning which, when functioning normally, combine data from the sense organs into recognizable and nameable patterns. Others theorize that agnosias come about due to "disconnections between intact brain areas such as the language and visual regions of the cortex."[29] But interestingly, as Sheldrake emphasizes, *none* of the current mechanistic interpretations of agnosias attribute their onset "to the destruction of memory traces"; similarly, mainstream explanations of aphasias and apraxias as well "are generally attributed to disturbances of organized patterns of activity in the brain rather than to a loss of memory traces."[30]

When examining these current understandings of the genesis of various forms of memory disorder, it is crucial to understand that, while we may currently have a vastly more sophisticated and detailed understanding of the complex operations of the brain than was available when Bergson was alive, nonetheless, Bergson's way of understanding memory has *not* been superseded. All the facts about amnesia can plausibly be interpreted from *both* a materialistic/mechanistic perspective and from a Bergsonian/nonmechanistic perspective. It is simply not the case that the mechanistic perspective has all the evidence in its favor, while Bergson's perspective is a whimsical, antiquated, and outdated relic of the past. In fact, as Sheldrake notes, "the effects of brain damage on the loss of memory provide *no* persuasive evidence in favor of the materialist theory."[31]

Furthermore, I would like to suggest that Bergson's interpretation of the relationship between memory and the brain offers a perspective that is much more positive and hope filled than the standard mechanistic explanatory model. If we accept Bergson's vision of the interaction of memory and brain (or something like it), then if someone we love is suffering from a memory disorder (e.g., Alzheimer's), we are not compelled to believe that our loved one, with all of her or his memories, character traits, and personality quirks, has been reduced to nothing more than a steadily worsening set of stock mannerisms, robotic and repetitive phrases, and chaotic manifestations of negatively charged affect. Instead, we can rationally believe that this person whom we care about so deeply is indeed present somewhere, but that due to the brain damage caused by the disease, she or he (in the form of her or his intentions, memories, and ideas) is no longer capable of interacting effectively with our physical level of existence. (Drawing upon Bergson's perspective, we can also rationally believe that our loved one's consciousness itself survives, in some form, after the death of the physical body. But the subject of the postmortem survival of consciousness will have to wait until we have explored Bergson's understandings in a bit more detail later in this section.)

23

MIND AND MATTER AS
DIFFERENT RHYTHMS OF DURÉE

THE INTERWEAVING OF MIND AND MATTER

In *Matter and Memory*, Bergson repeatedly stresses the profound differences between matter and mind, a dualism that he had previously delineated and affirmed in *Time and Free Will*. Bergson takes on this task, at least in part, to convince us that the mind has an independence and efficacy of its own and can never be reduced to blind material forces. Time and time again in *Matter and Memory*, Bergson emphasizes the numerous, almost self-evident, contrasts between, on the one hand, the predictable, quantitative changes that take place in the material universe, and on the other hand, the unpredictable, qualitative shifts that occur within the flow of our consciousness.

However, a careful examination of *Matter and Memory* soon reveals that this explicit dualism between matter and the mind, while genuine and essential to Bergson's project, is also provisional. If Bergson were to affirm that matter and mind are two *utterly* different substances, then it would be difficult, if not impossible, for his metaphysical perspective to answer the Cartesian question of how these two utterly different substances can interact with each other at all (as they so clearly do in our everyday experience). Therefore, while *Matter and Memory* emphasizes the functional and practical differences between mind and matter, Bergson also insists that a close examination of both mind and matter reveals numerous ways in which, under the surface, these two phenomena may be much more similar than was previously suspected. According to Bergson, if we look carefully, we will discover that matter is much more "mind-like," and mind is much more "matter-like," than we might have imagined.

It has already been shown how Bergson nudges us away from thinking of the external universe as a mechanical interaction of "nugget-like" atoms, and instead has us picture the physical world as an interconnected, dynamic nexus of overlapping and interpenetrating "images," a world that, like our own consciousness, is a ceaselessly changing, intrinsically temporal, and cohesive matrix. Understood in this way, the universe is not separate from our own consciousness in that it is the very "stuff" out of which our own perceptions are created. Seen from this perspective, the material universe increasingly begins to look much less like a wind-up clock and much more like a materialized cosmic mind.

Simultaneously, even though Bergson works hard to convince us that memory is "in no degree an emanation of matter" (*MM* 182), he also emphasizes that memory is inseparable from the universe, at least the universe as it is grasped by our perceptions. As we saw earlier, although our pure perceptions are formed from the very "stuff" of the materiality of the cosmos itself, those pure perceptions could not be formed without the ceaseless underlying activity of memory. Memory (in the form of what I call "primal memory") is that which, under the surface of our conscious awareness, effortlessly selects from the ceaseless influx of cosmic information only that which applies to us, leaving the rest to pass through us unnoticed. In a very important sense, therefore, the very heart of materiality itself, if understood from a Bergsonian perspective, continually pulses with memory.

Memory is also present at the heart of materiality itself, if for no other reason than the undeniable fact that our pure perceptions *take time*. As Bergson points out, "'pure,' that is to say, instantaneous, perception is, in fact, only an ideal, an extreme. Every perception fills a certain depth of duration, prolongs the past into the present, and thereby partakes of memory" (*MM* 244). Understood in this way, memory is that which temporalizes and synthesizes what would otherwise be an unimaginable succession of timeless, static, and disconnected material instants. Memory, on this level, is what gives durational "depth" to materiality itself.

Therefore, while it is true that in *Matter and Memory* Bergson attempts to demonstrate the very real differences between pure perception (which is formed from the seemingly spatial, quantifiable, divisible "stuff" of the external universe) and memory (which is inherently temporal, qualitative, and interconnected), he also works hard to demonstrate how these *apparently* different substances are, in actual fact, always inextricably interwoven with each other. This interweaving occurs, not only on the level of our own concrete perceptions, when via the superimposition of our own *personal* memories, memory creates the ongoing, seamless, and meaning-full continuity of our conscious experience, but also at the most impersonal, overtly material, level of reality imaginable (*MM* 182).

QUANTITY AND QUALITY: THE DIFFERENCE OVERCOME

Bergson's brilliant revisioning of the nature of matter and mind allows us to cross an abyss that, for many scholars, has often seemed impassable: the philosophical gulf between quantity and quality.[1] The quantitative elements of existence (often misleadingly termed "primary qualities" in philosophical discussions during the past few centuries) are the measurable, predictable material units of existence, as opposed to the experienced "qualia" of our perceptions (often known in philosophy as "secondary qualities"). The *quantitative* level of reality can be seen, for example, in the spectrum of electromagnetic vibrations that underlie the *qualitative* experience of the color "red." The philosophical problem is that it is difficult to see how a collection of seemingly insentient, calculable, vibratory movements (that are in no way "red") can combine together to become our seamless, ever-evolving, conscious states of awareness (in this case, "red" *as we see it*).

Bergson does not attempt to overcome this problem by denying that a vibratory, quantitative reality exists underneath the qualia of our experienced sensations. He fully acknowledges that beyond our conscious awareness, there are countless vibrations that come together to create the material substratum of the world that science studies so well, the world of calculable, predictable, seemingly lawful interactions. Bergson accepts (and in fact, embraces) scientific evidence. However, he interprets that evidence in a way that is radically different from most conventional scientists and academics, in that according to him, these material vibrations are not inert, but instead have a degree of protoconsciousness inherent within them. As such, this quantitative reality is perhaps better understood as a different "quality" of quality itself. These vibrations are, from Bergson's perspective, simply a different rhythm of durée than our own, and as such, they possess a quality of durée that in-and-of-itself cannot be directly accessed by our conscious awareness.

What Bergson suggests is that, in order for us to experience the smallest moment of, for instance "red," billions of vibratory pulses of durée are condensed together in-and-through our memory to form our experience of that distinctive color. This understanding of quality and quantity is a radical shift from the more commonsense understanding that "subjective" experience is "inside," while "objective" reality is "outside." Seen from a Bergsonian perspective, "inside" and "outside," or "subjective" and "objective" are simply interactive poles of a single dynamic temporal continuum, in which "the subjective side of perception" contracts, or compresses, or condenses, via memory, the "objective" multitude of "successive vibrations into which this perception can be internally broken up" into the seamless flow of our ongoing conscious experience (*MM* 70–71). For Bergson, our "inside" perceptions are, in actuality, "out there." At every moment of perception we are touching, and touched by, the world that we are perceiving. Similarly, the "outside" world is never completely divorced from consciousness, from what is "inside," in that it too is simply a more "diffuse," more "habituated," more predictable rhythm of durée—the essential "stuff" of reality itself.

RHYTHMS OF DURÉE

What Bergson asks us to do here is very difficult. He asks us to stop thinking about reality in spatial (i.e., material, measurable, divisible) terms, and instead to start thinking of reality in terms of time.[2] Instead of conceiving of matter as the fundamental substance of reality, as is assumed by materialism, Bergson asks us to conceive of the possibility that everything, both mind and matter, consists of varying rhythms of durée; he asks us to imagine that both matter and mind are simply differing manifestations of a unified (albeit continually changing and intrinsically pluralistic) reality: durée.[3]

If Bergson is correct, if our thoughts, feelings, perceptions, and indeed matter itself are all different "tensions" or "vibrations" of durée, then matter and mind are not two utterly different substances. Instead, they are two ends of a single interactive spectrum of temporal becoming. If this is the case, then the mind-body problem simply evaporates and the host of day-to-day interactions between our mind and body that we all experience (e.g., I intend to raise my arm, and do so) are no longer philosophical conundrums—and this is no minor accomplishment.

However, it can be exceedingly difficult to imagine different levels of duration (which are, in fact, also different levels of consciousness) because of our deeply ingrained tendency to assume that there is only one "homogeneous and independent Time" (MM 207). But Bergson points out that it is quite possible to become consciously aware within ourselves of the qualitative uniqueness of different rhythms of duration. He notes, for instance, that most of us have experienced the dramatic contrast between dream time and waking time; we have felt how in the dream level of temporality, it can seem as if days or weeks have gone by, when in the waking level of reality perhaps only a few minutes have passed (MM 207). Similarly, we all have felt the qualitative difference between those moments when time seems to "stand still" and when it seems to catapult forward with breathtaking speed. (The difference in how time is experienced when high on drugs or drunk or in various trance states might also be good examples.) For Bergson, these felt differences in time (corresponding to or perhaps even identical to felt shifts in consciousness) have their own integrity and are completely real. But, for the most part we either ignore them because of the deeply embedded internalization of "clock time" or we dismiss (or devalue) these moments because of the taken-for-granted assumption that time always moves forward at the same rate, "the same for everything and for every one," independent of our consciousness (*MM* 207).

For Bergson, even the smallest, most minute micro-movements of physicality are nothing more than a "diluted" form of time, of durée, of consciousness "spread out over an infinitely larger number of moments . . . quivering . . . like a chrysalis within its envelope" (*MM* 247). Bergson posits, therefore, that there is not a difference in nature between the quantitative reality of matter and the qualitative reality of our consciousness. Instead, there is a gradated continuum of durée that ranges between temporal changes that are more predictable, more measurable, more divisible (i.e., matter) to temporal changes that are unpredictable, nonmeasurable, indivisible (i.e., our personal consciousness). As Bergson puts is, "between sensible qualities . . . and these same qualities treated as calculable changes [i.e., matter], there is therefore only a difference in rhythm of duration, a difference of internal tension" (*MM* 247).

According to Bergson, each moment of my perception "contracts into a single moment of my duration that which, taken in itself, spreads over an incalculable number of moments" (*MM* 208). Underneath our highly particularized quality of perception, "the material universe subsists exactly as it was"; the qualities that make up materiality "mark as many moments in their own existence as science distinguishes in it; and sensible qualities, without vanishing, are spread and diluted in an incomparably more divided duration" (*MM* 208). In this way, as Bergson goes on to note, "matter thus resolves itself into numberless [protoconscious] vibrations, all linked together in uninterrupted continuity, all bound up with each other, and traveling in every direction like shivers through an immense body" (*MM* 208).

For Bergson, physical reality itself is never atemporal. Every physical moment is a durational pulsation, even if the temporal length of that pulsation, especially on a quantum level, is incomparably more minute than the pulsations of our everyday consciousness. For Bergson, durée is a constant. What varies is the rhythm of that duration, that is, the "amount" of the past that has been compressed or condensed into a temporal moment.

Čapek points out, and I think correctly, that Bergson's theory that reality consists of different strata of durational tension or different rhythms of durée is "the most difficult, most elusive as well as the least known and least understood part of Bergson's thought."[4] In some ways, it might be helpful to begin by clarifying what Bergson is opposing. For instance, Bergson is clearly saying that time as it is understood in Newtonian physics is mistaken. As Keith Ansell Pearson points out, for Bergson, there is "no single, universal time spread out across the universe that is objectively valid for all systems"; there is no "homogeneous time that would be the same for everything and everyone."[5]

Instead, as Mullarkey points out, for Bergson, "time is serialized, tiered or stratified in a set of nested *durées*."[6] As Bergson sees it (at least by the end of

Matter and Memory), time is not unified; reality does not take place on a single plane. Instead, there are multiple dimensions of experience, multiple levels of reality (e.g., quantum, molecular, mineral, vegetal, animal, and human), each possessing a unique, albeit ever-changing, temporal rhythm.[7] Each of these levels of reality manifests a specific quality of temporality (and consciousness) and yet none of these levels are atomistically autonomous. Instead, each level or quality of experience emerges when countless other "lower" or "more diluted" rhythms of temporality are compressed together.[8]

According to Bergson, this compression of "lower" levels of duration takes place continually within us. As he points out, "when I open and close my eyes in rapid succession, I experience a succession of visual sensations each of which is the condensation of an extraordinarily long history unrolled in the external world" (*ME* 20). In other words, in the time that it takes for someone to open and shut his or her eyes as fast as possible, billions of vibrations, one following the next, are occurring on a subatomic level. These vibrations, which would take centuries if anyone were to attempt to count them individually, are condensed in our own level of durée into a single second of conscious experience. Understood in this way, "sensation condenses, into the duration which belongs to us and characterizes our consciousness, immense periods of what we can call by analogy the duration of things" (*ME* 21).

For Bergson, therefore, there are countless levels of experience (and time) other than our own; there are countless "planes" of durée, each of which fuses the past into the present to a different degree. According to Bergson, the universe as a whole consists of a wide spectrum of different levels of duration, ranging from the quasi-necessity of the duration of matter, through the largely instinctive duration of various rudimentary organisms, up to the highly conscious, flexible (if at times habitual) duration of human consciousness, and perhaps even beyond our normal levels of awareness to greater, more fluid, more creative, more intuitive modes of consciousness as well.[9]

Bergson even speculates that it is possible, and is indeed likely, that there exists a duration of consciousness with a "higher degree" of "tension" (or even better, "attention") than our own—one that is able to condense the entire history of humanity into a very short period of its own duration in the same way that we condense the "history" of the vibrations of matter into the ongoing flux of the perceptions of our conscious experience in any moment (*MM* 207). For Bergson, therefore, while we normally live our life convinced that there is only a single, homogenous Time, independent of our own state of awareness, in reality our everyday experience of time is merely one of a vast profusion of qualitatively different temporal possibilities, ranging from the unimaginably rapid durée of quantum phenomena to the equally unimaginable temporal experience of levels of consciousness that far exceed our own.

24

EMBODYING MEMORY

COPING WITH MEMORY

According to Bergson, if and when we realize that the brain's primary task is not to record memories; if and when we recognize "the continuity of the inner life and consequently of its indivisibility"; if and when we acknowledge that all of our past is subconsciously present within us, at that point what needs to be explained is not "the preservation of the past, but rather its apparent abolition"; what needs to be accounted for is not the remembering, but the forgetting (*CM* 181).

What accounts for this forgetting, in Bergson's scheme of things, is the crucially important work of that astonishingly complex organ: our brain. While it might not have been given the job of storing our memories, nonetheless, it has plenty to do in that, along with filtering out the vast majority of the images that make up the physical universe, it also has to "mask" the equally vast "quantity" of memories that are subconsciously present within us and "then to allow only what is practically useful to emerge through the mask" (*ME* 71). (The brain also, of course, does a lot more than these two tasks, but Bergson's focus is primarily on the brain's astonishing ability to respond with amazing sensitivity and speed to the cascade of "notes" that are "played" on its "keyboard" by both the influx of perceptual images pouring in through the senses and the ongoing torrent of memories, thoughts, and feelings that continually rise up from within us.)[1]

Bergson emphasizes that it is crucial that the brain keeps most of our memories from flooding into our awareness. If our brain was not able to screen out most of the memories that we carry with us under the surface then, according to Bergson, we would have tremendous difficulty concentrating on the task at hand and more generally functioning effectively in life. If our attention to the immediacy of life slackens, if we become lost in the past, if we are overly absorbed in (or overwhelmed by) a flood of fantasies or aberrant and irrelevant memories, thoughts, and feelings (i.e., various recollection memory-images), if our aware-ness is not sufficiently rooted in "the sensori-motor equilibrium of the body" (i.e., if our habit memory is not effectively integrated into our physiology), then as Bergson stresses, we will, almost inevitably, suffer from numerous mental problems (*MM* 174).

According to Bergson, mental disorders arise at least in part due to "an unloosing or a breaking of the tie which binds" our mind to our body; they emerge (again, at least in part) due to "a weakening or an impairing of our atten-tion to outward life" (*MM* 14–15). Bergson argues that the ongoing stream of perceptual information flowing into our senses, the affective sensations of the physicality of our body, as well as the tactile kinesthetic awareness of our body moving through space are that which, taken together, "fixes our mind, and gives it ballast and poise" (*MM* 173). If we are disconnected from the movements of our body, if our attention to the immediacy of the present is disrupted, then "the sense of the real grows weaker, or disappears" and mental problems will likely emerge (*MM* 175).[2] (Conversely, of course, the implication is that, if we want to become more integrated and mentally healthy, we might want to explore the therapeutic efficacy of spending more time in beautiful, peaceful environments, as well as the psychological and emotional value of processes such as yoga, dance, massage, sexuality, martial arts, and so on, that assist us in opening up to a full range of bodily sensations and that nurture the ability to be physically grounded and fluid in our movements in-and-through the world.)

RUMINATION: GETTING DREAMY AND GOING ON AUTOMATIC

Everyone moves through life moment to moment utilizing an ever-shifting com-bination of the various planes of memory. From a Bergsonian perspective, how-ever, problems arise if we are either too open to influxes from recollection memory or if we are overly influenced by the quasi-automatic reactivity of habit memory.[3] If recollection memory is overly dominant within us, we will tend to be abstracted, caught up in daydreams and fantasies and we will have difficulty not only engaging effectively (and pleasurably) with the physical world, but also in establishing meaningful and fulfilling relationships with others. Conversely, however, if we live primarily under the influence of habit memory, then we will frequently act on impulse, driven by ingrained, reactive patterns of behavior that are rarely, if ever, questioned, and we will often unconsciously mimic the behav-ior of others in our group. [4]

For myself, I can rather easily find the ways in which I struggle to deal with the difficulties that can arise when either one of these forms of memory is too influential within me. From the side of habit memory, for instance, I sometimes find myself (much more often than I like) saying or doing something in a completely rote, habitual, formulaic, and unconscious manner, acting as if I were a highly programmed robot rather than a human being with genuine freedom to choose my behavior. I am thinking here not only of those annoying relics of my cultural and familial upbringing (i.e., those idiosyncratic mannerisms and stock phrases that seem to be embedded in my personality), but also of more destructive, deeply reactive, patterns of behavior (e.g., my almost comically predictable tendency to get extremely agitated and angry, almost like a reflex, if someone says or does something that offends me).

On the side of recollection memory, I have for quite some time been aware of how I can at times become so immersed in what I am thinking, or studying, or writing, that I can become quite oblivious to my body or to the world around me. (My wife still teases me about the time that I hit my head so hard on the door of our car when I was getting in that she was concerned that I might have badly hurt myself, but when she shared her concerns with me after the fact, I had absolutely no idea what she was talking about. I could not remember even banging my head.) At times, I shudder at the numerous ways in which I embody the stereotype of the absent-minded professor (or, as William James, perhaps more compassionately and accurately put it, professors whose minds are elsewhere). I have frequently said only half in jest that I am not sure if I would have survived graduate school (or my life as a professor) if it were not for the ways in which my ongoing practice of yoga, tai chi, and aikido (to say nothing of the extremely beneficial effects of being in a committed relationship with a loving partner) have helped to ground me in my body and in my feelings.

Nonetheless, while I have clearly had to wrestle with the difficulties that come with overly powerful influxes of recollection memory and with overly engrained forms of habit memory, I am also often profoundly grateful that both of these forms of memory are as active as they are within me. For instance, without the porous permeability that allows the "doorway" into recollection memory to stay fairly open within me, I doubt that I could ever write a book such as this one and I doubt whether my dream life (or my spiritual life) would be anywhere near as rich and rewarding as it frequently is. The issue does not seem to be that I have a relatively open door to recollection memory. Instead, the real issue seems to be how well I am willing or able to integrate this influx into my daily life.

Similarly, on the side of habit memory, I also have countless, intensely habitual ways of behavior that I prize very highly. I am thinking here not only of the various physical skills that I have worked hard to attain (e.g., learning several tai chi forms or gaining a certain proficiency in speaking Portuguese), but also the numerous social skills and abilities that were, seemingly, deposited on my doorstep (e.g., learning to how to walk, how to dress myself, how to treat others with respect, how to speak English). In all of these cases, the habitual behavior that I learned is crucial to my effective functioning as a human being. The issue with habit memory seems to be less about "going on automatic" and more about the extent to which I *consciously* cultivated these habits within me or the extent to which these habits, even if they were unconsciously created, are now aligned with deeper, truer dimensions of myself.

In general, when dealing with memory, the primary task seems to be, as Bergson himself notes, how to become "well-balanced" or "nicely adapted to life" (*MM* 153); in other words, how to harmonize these two types of memories within ourselves. Of course, this task is not easy. It takes an enormous amount of effort and time before we are able to live consciously. Integrating the wisdom of past experience into the present in order to become increasingly reflective and self-aware (i.e., learning how to become open, in positive ways, to recollection memory) is arguably the task of a lifetime. Similarly, becoming more and more fluidly responsive to the changing needs of the present and increasingly able to draw freely upon the wisdom of the body (i.e., learning how to embody in positive ways the benefits of habit memory) is also an exceedingly difficult accomplishment. Weaving both of these two tasks together is, if possible, yet even more difficult. However, all of this difficulty (at least in my experience) is more than compensated by the inherent fulfillment and sense of accomplishment that arises within as we cultivate and nurture a life of balance, a life rooted in self-discovery and fluid responsiveness.

LEARNING PHYSICAL MOVEMENTS

The physicality of our bodily experience is very much at the center of Bergson's understandings of the seemingly most "spiritual" occurrences (e.g., as we will soon see, bodily sensations play a crucial role in his theory of dreams). For Bergson, memory, intellectual effort, and other cognitive activities are always rooted in the movements, sensations, and intelligence of the body.[5] Similarly, memory, thought, and efforts of attention (i.e., cognitive phenomena from "higher on the cone") are all complexly interwoven with any attempt to learn some sort of physical skill.

In order to more clearly understand Bergson's explanation of the process of how we learn a physical skill, let's envision that we have entered a dance studio for the first time. In order to learn the dance steps, we try to observe the movements of the instructor or advanced students. However, even if we pay close attention to the teacher's precise and graceful movements, because we lack a previous training in dance (and hence any memories of, or understandings about, dance), it is likely that we will be unable to remember much of what we are seeing and we will certainly not be able to replicate many, if any, of the steps. And yet, if we are to learn at all, we have to begin by watching the instructor as best we can. As Bergson perceptively notes, "in order to learn the dance, we must begin by seeing it danced, [yet] on the other hand we can only see it, in its details and even as a whole, when we have learnt to some extent to dance it" (*ME* 216).

After we have watched the instructor demonstrate the dance moves that we are attempting to learn, "we begin by imitating the movement as a whole . . . as we think we have seen it done" (*MM* 111). But while our visual perception of this movement (let's say, watching our instructor dance the samba) was a "*continuous* whole," our clumsy initial attempts to imitate that grace and fluidity rarely succeed. Especially in the beginning of our endeavor, it seems that the only way we can learn the dance is to break up the fluidity and continuity that we saw within the movements of the instructor into a "compound" made up of a rather disconnected and segmented series of smaller bodily movements (i.e., we might focus on how our feet should move, or our hands, or the posture of the torso, and so on, perhaps even having given names to these smaller, more basic units of movement as a way to capture them in our mind's eye).

With a great deal of effort, thought, and attention, we then attempt to repeat these various smaller movements, consciously focusing our attention on different aspects of the process, over and over again, consciously assessing how we did, thinking about how to improve, and so on. All of this mental effort (again, coming from "higher up the cone") interweaves with layer upon layer of bodily memory (coming from closer to the cone's tip) that is taking place as well, that is, the total, ever-changing kinesthetic gestalt of how the various attempts to move felt in our muscles, in the shifting of our weight, in the tension of our breath, and so on.

Ideally, over time, with the help of the teacher's instructions (e.g., "keep erect," "no, the other left foot"), this process of paying conscious attention to the small details of the movements that we have decomposed begins to bear fruit. Through numerous repetitions of these "broken up" movements, we are able, very gradually, in the habit memory of our own body *and* in the "mind's eye" of our recollection memory to recompose the original complex movement back to the fluid unity we saw embodied in the instructor in the beginning.

As Bergson points out, "the true effect of repetition is to decompose and then to recompose, and thus appeal to the intelligence of the body" (*MM* 111). This "intelligence of the body" fuses together memory, effort, and attention with the kinesthetic gestalt of our bodily experience. This type of visceral intelligence must with "each new attempt" work to "separate movements which were interpenetrating"; it must, each time, focus "the attention of the body to a new detail which had passed unperceived"; it must, each time, help us to physically "discriminate and classify," to teach "what is essential," to point out "one after another, within the total movement, the lines that mark off its internal structure. In this sense, a movement is learned when the body has been made to understand it" (*MM* 111–112). (Not surprisingly, this process of decomposing the teacher's original fluid, complexly interwoven, multifaceted physical movements into a more serialized, relatively unchanging set of discrete, smaller, and often named units of movement mirrors the process by which the intellect, according to Bergson, attempts to analyze and atomize the ever-changing, complexly textured, dynamic flux of consciousness—and matter—into a set of much more static and ideally nameable objects in order to deal with them more efficiently.)

Bergson also points out that in our attempts to learn, for instance, dance steps, we not only somehow have to manage to embody new movements (i.e., we have to create new habit memories), but we also often have to struggle unconsciously against a multitude of old kinesthetic memory-schemas that contradict the new ways of movement that we are attempting to master.

Let's say that we have perhaps earlier learned a variety of ballroom steps. Our internalizations of the habitual ways of moving and holding our body that are associated with this particular style of dance, while they might help to increase our bodily intelligence overall, might also subtly interfere with our ability to learn the unique and different ways of moving and holding our bodies that are associated with, for instance, breakdancing. More subtly, however, we might also have to struggle with more unconscious and pernicious bodily habit memories. For instance, perhaps as a child, our parents repeatedly and harshly told us to "sit still," or to "keep quiet," or to "behave" when we were running and jumping freely around the house. It is likely that after years of this type of conditioning, our body might almost reflexively clench and freeze when asked to perform certain types of more spontaneous movements in public.

According to Bergson, the difficulty that often accompanies our attempts to learn anything, either physically or intellectually, is not only created in large part by our need to try more or less fruitfully to fit old patterns of knowing or doing something onto a new situation, but also by our need to change (or let go of) these older memory schemas so that they can more easily fit the reality of what is at hand. As he puts it, "the interval between the difficult attempt and the easy execution, between the learning and the doing of the exercise" is itself often nothing more than our strained attempts to adapt our previous ways of acting and thinking to new situations (*ME* 219).

According to Bergson, many if not most of these old ways of knowing or acting are deeply unconscious. Unfortunately, therefore, when attempting to learn a physical activity, many people often have to struggle with a multitude of highly detrimental, unconscious memory patterns/attitudes (ranging "up" and "down" the cone of memory) that they unknowingly bring to the process. For example, while I might have consciously decided to learn a certain dance step, perhaps my subsequent efforts are undermined and sabotaged by unconscious fears of attempting something new in a public setting, or by my hidden (even to myself) belief that I am extremely clumsy and unable to move gracefully, or by my obscure, yet tenacious, resistance to working with authority figures. There-fore, the effort that is associated with learning a new physical activity does not just come from the strenuousness of the movements themselves, but also from a range of psychological factors as well.

MOVING INTUITIVELY

Bergson's account of how we learn a physical activity accurately mirrors my own often painfully difficult attempts to learn various physical skills (e.g., my ongo-ing attempts to become more proficient in aikido). However, there is one aspect of this learning process that Bergson, rather oddly, seems to ignore. He fails to emphasize how, after the initial step of decomposition, when someone has begun to embody the various movements with an increased level of skill, there comes a time when the initial process of putting forth a lot of conscious effort actually begins to undermine and block the subtler, deeper, levels of learning. During this intermediate level of learning, there is a stage in which the student has to actually *stop* trying so hard, has to *stop* thinking so much about what she or he is trying to do, and has to learn to simply let her or his body move. At this level of the process, what the student has to learn is not so much the mechanics of how to capably put together a set of specific detailed movements, but rather how to relax into the fluid continuity of the movement as a whole, how to open up and trust the wisdom of her or his bodily knowing, how to quiet and calm her or his thoughts, how to breathe and remain centered, and how to sense, and feel, and intuit, what is needed within the flux of the ever-changing situation. (This is especially important when what we are trying to learn is explicitly geared toward more open-ended, less formal, and more stressful situations, such as how to transfer what we have gained, for instance, "on the mat" in an aikido dojo to an effective response if we were attacked "on the street.")

Bergson does not explicitly mention this "middle way" of action—that is, this way of moving through life that is neither the haphazard, random, ungrace-ful style of movement demonstrated by someone with no background or training (and/or no desire for any physical self-cultivation), nor the intense, driven, effortful way of moving that is characteristic of someone who is consciously attempting to improve her or his physical ability. Nonetheless, Bergson's philo-sophical perspective at least implicitly has the potential to help us to understand and value this alternative, more intuitive, mode of calm, yet focused, poised, and attuned movement. However, because Bergson himself often seems to struggle against his own tendencies to overly stress the effort that is needed to think and behave intuitively (due to his understandable emphasis on how difficult it is to go against the typical, more fragmented and hyperintellectualized way of relating to life), I would suggest that we first examine how a creative and insightful philosopher from Japan, Yuasa Yasuo (1925–2005) attempted to articulate the various qualities of intuitive action.

Yuasa (his last name is listed first, in accordance with standard Japanese usage) wrestles with the mind-body relationship in ways that are strikingly similar to Bergson's (which is not surprising given that Yuasa was deeply interested in and influenced by Bergson's ideas). Yet, at the same time, perhaps due to Yuasa's ability to draw upon the work of various Eastern religious figures that were unknown to Bergson, he also took much of what is only implicit in Bergson's work and developed it in intriguing and valuable new directions.

Yuasa frequently argues that Western philosophical, psychological, and scientific ways of attempting to deal with the mind-body problem differ in significant respects from Japanese approaches to this same issue. For example, Western philosophers, according to Yuasa, tend to assume that the mind-body relationship is a basically stable, relatively universal phenomenon that varies little, if at all, from person to person. In Western investigations of the mind-body issue, therefore, a great deal of philosophical attention might be given, for example, to exploring the interconnections (or lack thereof) between, let's say, one's mental intention and the physical action of raising one's arm (a common example among thinkers in the philosophy of mind tradition).

Yuasa emphasizes that many, if not most, important Japanese thinker/practitioners (e.g., Dogen, Kukai, Nishida) typically begin with a quite different set of premises when they look into the mind-body relationship. These thinkers/practitioners assume as a fundamental given that the mind-body relationship is not something that is static. Instead, they stress that the mind-body relationship "changes through the training of the mind and body by means of cultivation (*shugyo*) or training (*keiko*)."[6] Therefore, from the Japanese point of view, instead of studying the intrinsic and quasi-universal mind-body connection that is presupposed by the Western example of "raising one's arm," another possibility presents itself: what if we were to study the acquired and exceptional mind-body unity illustrated by, for instance, Hank Aaron's baseball swing or Yo-Yo Ma's virtuoso cello performance? Looking at the mind-body issue from this perspective opens up the investigation in a very different way. Seen from this angle, we would focus less on examining what *is* (i.e., the intrinsic, seemingly ever-present, qualities of the mind-body relationship) and more on examining what *could be* (i.e., what hidden potential for skillful movement do we possess and how can these potentials become actualized?). That is, our concern would not be simply how to articulate the best theory to describe a universal phenomenon, but rather how to articulate and ideally cultivate a better understanding of the relationships among the "intellectual *theory*," the "somatic *practice*," and the "integrated *achievement*" of various physical skills in and through a careful examination of the performance of certain exceptional individuals.[7]

According to Yuasa, even the existential situation of the investigator of the mind-body relationship in the East is different in that "the mind-body issue is not simply a theoretical reflection," but rather "is originally a practical, lived experience (*taiken*), involving the mustering of one's whole mind and body."[8] The implication is that true knowledge about one's mind-body is not something that could, or even should, be simply a theoretical achievement. Instead, it can only be gained "through 'bodily recognition or realization' (*tainin* or *taitoku*), that is, through the utilization of one's total mind and body."[9] As Yuasa emphasizes, Dogen and Kukai were not academic philosophers in the Western sense. They did not speculate on the mind-body issue simply for the sake of intellectual clarity. Instead, they were realized Buddhist teachers who, after years of intense self-cultivation, wrote and taught on the mind-body issue as a way to prod their students toward the achievement of profound dimensions of felt, embodied, experiential realizations of the unity of the mind-body.

Later in this text I will show how Bergson himself, toward the end of his life, became increasingly interested in the life and teachings of mystics (especially certain Christian contemplatives) and how to a certain extent Yuasa's distinction between the mystical embodied East and the theoretical, disengaged West does not accurately reflect the nuances of even Bergson's own perspective. However, if we understand Yuasa's claims to be primarily a matter of emphasis and not some sort of cultural essentialism, then I would argue that there is much to be gained by his insights. Clearly, Western philosophy (with the possible exception of Aristotle, and those influenced by him, and even then primarily in the realm of ethics) has not devoted much attention to the cultivation of higher levels of mind-body capacities. Equally clearly (again, with the possible exception of certain Western mystically inclined philosophers, e.g., Plotinus and Meister Eckhart) the primary method of study preferred by Western philosophers has been intellectual, and not the explicitly embodied, experiential, and meditative methodology of Eastern practitioners—for example, Japanese thinkers such as Kukai and Dogen.

Nonetheless, in part perhaps due to Yuasa's own training in Western philosophical traditions, much of what he offers is itself somewhat Western (in his sense of the word) in that, while he primarily examines the issues that arise when we look carefully at the cultivation of the mind-body, his presentation is overtly intellectual and cross-cultural in nature.

One of Yuasa's most important and helpful contributions is to suggest that, as Thomas Kasulis points out in his introduction, "consciousness is double-layered."[10] Yuasa uses the term "bright consciousness" to describe our everyday conscious awareness (and our awareness of this awareness itself). Bright consciousness is Descartes' *cogito*; it is the realm of thought, of self-conscious awareness of one's mental processes. "Bright consciousness" is that form of awareness that has been most intensively studied by the Western philosophy of mind.

However, according to Yuasa, bright consciousness is itself rooted in something more fundamental, something that is not accessible to the shining, self-aware gaze of bright consciousness itself, that is, "dark consciousness." "Dark consciousness" is not "inferior" or "evil" consciousness. Rather, it is "hidden" consciousness; it is that level of our awareness that is typically not accessible to our everyday bright consciousness.

Kasulis argues that this dark consciousness "parallels, in part, the functions of the autonomic nervous system."[11] He also claims (I think misleadingly) that "psychoanalytically, [dark consciousness] resembles the unconscious in some ways."[12] (I would argue that a better comparison would be with the *subconscious* as articulated by William James and Fredrick Myers, in that repression, sexuality, and aggression are central to Freudian notions of the *unconscious*, but do not figure into either Myers' and James' notion of the subconscious or into Yuasa's descriptions of "dark consciousness.") Importantly, however, dark consciousness, as understood by Yuasa, also has numerous correlates with the "lived body examined by Merleau-Ponty and Bergson."[13]

Yuasa's notion of dark consciousness helps to clarify many of the same issues that are raised by Bergson's discussion of habit memory, but with some helpful shifts in orientation. In order to illustrate some of the ways in which bright and dark consciousness are operative within each of us, imagine, if you will, that you are driving a car.[14] Suddenly, out of nowhere, a dog steps into the road directly in the path of your car. You quickly swerve to avoid hitting the dog. If you think about what happened later (with your bright consciousness), you might say that you "simply reacted," but if you think about it more, it is rather amazing that in a split second your body somehow managed to orchestrate a highly complex series of maneuvers involving steering, braking, timing, and so on, all with no conscious thought or decisions on your part.

This type of bodily intelligence is what Yuasa refers to as dark consciousness. As an experienced driver, your dark consciousness was able, almost instantaneously, to cause the car to swerve to avoid hitting the dog only because you had previously undergone perhaps months of explicit instructions on how to drive a car as well as perhaps years of concrete practical experience behind the wheel. You did not just accidentally learn how to drive a car. Instead, this skill is something that you acquired with concerted and conscious effort. During this learning process you explicitly used your bright consciousness when you focused your attention, for instance, on how to use the brake effectively, or on how to let a car skid without losing control, and so on. Through these deliberate acts of will, thought, and attention, you were gradually able to internalize and embody the knowledge that could manifest spontaneously and effortlessly in and through your dark consciousness, during that single intense interaction with the dog. In that moment, your body just did what it did, without thinking of alternatives.

As Kasulis points out, in a very real sense "the *body*, not the mind, decided the action."[15]

Yuasa's distinction between bright and dark consciousness, while drawn primarily from his investigation into the cultivation or practice of yogic and Buddhist meditation techniques, as well as the training of those immersed in Japanese arts, such as poetry, the No drama, and the tea ceremony, also can and does apply to any attempt to train our dark consciousness to act effectively in our daily lives, whether that training involves explicit lessons (e.g., learning how to play the piano or ride a bicycle) or arises due to our immersion in an environment that is consciously oriented toward a goal of self improvement (e.g., taking part in psychotherapy sessions, participating in a structured monastic life, or attending graduate school).

In all of these cases, the beginning phase of learning is typically awkward and difficult. As our bright consciousness intentionally sets down new patterns of behavior, as we work hard to interweave new interpretive formulations onto outdated interpretive "maps," as we consciously attempt to overcome our resistance to the new ways of acting and responding, our body-mind in these difficult moments of "self consciousness" can feel rather sluggish, uncooperative, and dense. Gradually, however, the new ways of living, acting, thinking, and feeling become more and more "second nature." Increasingly, our actions begin, easily and effortlessly, without premeditation, to mirror the patterns set down originally by our bright consciousness. Ideally, of course, these "new and improved" ways of being in the world and interacting with others are not rote, conditioned, formulaic reactions, but rather are spontaneous, fluid, responses that are adaptive to ever-changing situations. What Yuasa is describing is not the attempt to force ourselves into some "one size fits all" mold, but rather is the end result of a long, intentional attempt to acquire a repertoire of physical skills, aesthetic and psychological sensibilities, and meditative abilities, that we can use to create a new and ideally better way to respond to life's ever-changing circumstances.

When we have reached that point when we "can act in the same way as an excellent musician plays a piece that has been mastered, or as an artist whose brush moves itself in accord with inspiration," at that point, according to Yuasa (drawing upon the work of another Japanese philosopher, Nishida Kitaro), "the body loses its objectivity as a thing and, as it were, is made subjective"; at this point in our personal development, "the functions of the mind and the body become unified . . . in the 'oneness of body and mind' (*shinjin ichinyo*)" and we can begin, increasingly, to live an intuitive life; we can embody Nishida's idea of "acting intuition" (*koiteki chokkan*), in which "the two moments of acting and intuition are always simultaneous and inseparable."[16]

In such moments, for example, when a gymnast is "performing his or her best techniques in a state of no-mind," or when a master pianist is "performing in total absorption," or when a gifted and experienced actor is "acting out his role on a stage, becoming the role itself," or when a professor is interacting with her students in the classroom in such a way that every moment shimmers, and the words flow eloquently and without effort, from her mouth—in such moments "there is only the smallest gap between the movements of the body and mind"; in such moments, according to Yuasa (referring, again, to Nishida's theoretical perspective), the body becomes, as it were, "subjectivized" while at the same time the mind "gives up being an ego-consciousness," and "enters the state of selfless samadhi or what may be called 'the self without being a self.'"[17]

This ability to "act as a self without being a self, to be guided by creative intuition" is, for both Yuasa and Nishida (and, at least implicitly, for Bergson as well) a way of acting that comes from an ongoing, ever-new alignment with the power that arises from "the region of the authentic self."[18] Here we experience a level of "knowing" in which we have tapped into "something" that is, from a certain perspective, the deepest level of selfhood, and yet from another perspective, is a level of consciousness that is much vaster, much freer, much more fluid, much more joyous, than the day-to-day personality/ego self with which we normally identify ourselves.

RUMINATION: BODILY INTUITIONS

Since I was a young man, I have been intrigued by how certain rhythmic, repetitive bodily movements often seemed to open up a smooth, steady flow of ideas, ideas that would seem simply to float up of their own accord from some unknown depths within me. For instance, when I was a teenager I had a part-time job mowing the lawns of several neighbors. I would spend hours during those hot, humid summer days in Florida, wearing nothing but a pair of cut-off shorts, my long hair tied back by a sweat band, completely absorbed in the process of pushing a heavy, partially self-propelled lawn mower back and forth, up and down those large lawns. There was something about the kinesthetic quality of feeling of my body moving with the strength and vigor of a young man, something about the pulsating vibrations of the engine coursing up my arms that quieted my mind, sparked numerous philosophical ruminations, and opened me up to a flood of unsought insights (some of which I shared in the beginning of section 1). During those times, it was as if something else, or someone else, would fill my mind with ideas and perceptions that shone with a luminosity and depth that made my typical teenage thoughts seem muddled and shallow, ideas that felt, as it were, good to think.

I also frequently noticed a similar phenomenon when, almost every morning, for nearly eight years in my twenties, typically in a large and open meditation hall with hundreds of others, I would spend an hour and a half chanting a long hymn in Sanskrit. Sitting poised, relaxed, and balanced on my meditation cushion, my mind focused and absorbed, my spine erect and elongated, my legs crossed easily in the half-lotus posture, my arms holding the chanting book in front of me, my breath coming in and out of my body in a rhythmic, repetitive way as I chanted the text, I would notice that some floodgate would open inside of myself and a stream of creative insights and solutions to problems would float unbidden into my awareness, never distracting me from my absorption in the chant, but simply arising pleasurably, easily, before my mind's eye, while I remained immersed in what I was doing.

Similarly, during the years that I have spent working on this book, there were many times in which, after hours of reading and thinking about Bergson's thought, I would take a break and go for a long walk along White Rock Lake in Dallas. What I would notice is that there was frequently something almost magical about the simple act of walking, with no agenda, with an easy, smooth, continuous pace, breathing deeply, my mind quiet, soaking in the expanse of the lake, the swooping and darting of the swallows, the honking of the geese, and the rustling of the wind as it blew through the lush high meadow grasses and the leaves of the cottonwood trees. During those moments, once again, it would be as if an inner doorway had opened and ideas and images and insights would bubble up effortlessly without any instigation on my part. My only task then (along with continuing to immerse myself in my walk and in the beauty around me) was to sit back in some peaceful, deeply still place within myself, and "take dictation" —that is, simply watch and remember the insights that would percolate up.

Something similar also often takes place when I lie down and let my body relax and let my breath slow down. In that fertile place between waking and sleep, a similar up-rush of unasked for insights and deeply gratifying inspirations will frequently fill my awareness. During those moments it is almost as if I am gripped by an "otherness," a type of power or presence, an electric sense of anticipation, a vague, inchoate knowledge that something vast, mysterious, and exciting is gestating under the surface of my conscious awareness. This "something," rather oddly, seems to be both me and not me. It is clearly not my ego; it has nothing to do with my will; it is not linked to any attempts to direct or focus my attention. At the same time, however, it does not feel foreign or alien to myself—rather, it seems to be rooted in, and rising up from, a source that is deep inside me, something that is real, true, "me."

In all of these examples, despite their variety, something similar seems to be taking place. My body, whether active or still, is very relaxed—even if, during the more active examples (e.g., mowing, chanting, or walking), it can also be fully engaged in what it is doing. During these moments, my attention is fully absorbed in the present, immersed in the unfolding of events either around me or within me (or both). My mind, which may have previously been intensely focused on a specific set of tasks, is then allowed to drift (even if it can also, amazingly, as in the chanting example, be fully focused on a very narrow, very familiar routine as well).

In all of these examples, I feel like I am "plugged in" to something greater. There is a felt sense of leaning back within myself, of floating on something that supports me, lifts me up, and energizes me. That something, as I mentioned, feels very much like "me," but with larger "boundaries" than my mind-body's normal sense of itself as an autonomous, clearly bounded psychophysical unit. During these moments, it is as if I am a scintillating bubble that is drifting on a warm ocean of rhythmical currents—but without any sense of myself as utterly passive or completely alone. (There is no clear-cut "membrane" that separates my "awareness-bubble" from the greater sea in which I am floating.) When I am connected in this way, I feel at ease and deeply peaceful. During these moments, life feels rich, full of promise and significance.

Conversely, there are also moments in my life when, seemingly out of nowhere, a type of inner wall arises between myself and this greater awareness. During these times, I feel isolated and edgy, as if I am cut off, not only from my own depths, but from my connection to others as well. When I get like this, it is as if I am a hamster, racing frantically on my wheel, going nowhere, feeling the pressure of time bearing down on me. When I feel this way, I find it hard to catch my breath and my body tenses against a vague, but visceral, upwelling of anxiety. My jaw clenches and I can sense a type of almost cellular tightness throughout my body. During these times, life can feel meaningless, sucked dry of its vitality, and it is almost as if I were two-dimensional, hollow, insubstantial, and outside of myself.

I have often wondered whether these two contrasting states of being are perhaps rather mild variations of two much more extreme, starkly different internal states: on the one hand, a state of severe mental fragmentation, crippling anxiety, and existential despair, and on the other hand, a state of ever-present joy, of divine wonder, of exalted mystical union. I would suggest that we all, to one extent or another, oscillate between these two poles of awareness in our daily lives.

For myself, the felt difference between these two contrasting states of experience does not offer any iron-clad evidence for the reality of deeper, richer, truer levels of awareness and life within. However, I believe that the contrast between these two modes of consciousness does suggest a way to begin to understand why Bergson's notion of cultivating an intuitive connection to the source of life within might be so appealing to some, in that it speaks to a state of being that I would argue we all know directly in our own experience, even if we rarely or explicitly acknowledge its existence.

Interestingly, Bergson does not speak as often as one might suspect about this visceral experience of bodily intuition, this moment-to-moment immersion into the flux of life, this attunement with something deep within. However, in "The Perception of Change" (an essay published originally in 1911, now found in *Creative Mind*), Bergson certainly moves forcefully (and eloquently) in that direction. In this essay he suggests that we are most completely ourselves when we recognize and joyously give ourselves to the ceaseless change that is going on both within us and around us. He claims that, if we can cultivate within ourselves (usually through philosophical study) an ongoing experience of the flux of universal becoming, then our rigid and frozen perception of life can be melted, and in doing so "everything comes to life around us, everything is revivified in us. A great impulse carries beings and things along. We feel ourselves uplifted, carried away, borne along by it" (*CM* 186). He points out that if we can let go of our fears that we will "drown in the torrent-like flow" of the movement of life; if we can release our anxiety that the world we have so carefully constructed will disintegrate; if we let go of these fears and habituations, then at that point we will discover, perhaps to our surprise, that we have gained a "feeling of greater joy and strength" than we might have imagined possible (*CM* 177, 124). Bergson claims that we will feel increased joy "because the reality invented before our eyes will give each one of us, unceasingly," the joy that seemingly only privileged artists possess—the joy of seeing, beneath the apparent "fixity and monotony" of our everyday lives the "ever-recurring novelty, the moving originality of things" (*CM* 124). We will feel greater strength because, by attuning ourselves to the ceaseless dance of creative energy that is life itself, "we shall feel we are participating, creators of ourselves, in the great work of creation which is the origin of all things and which goes on before our eyes," allowing us to become, therefore, conscious co-creators of our world (*CM* 124).

Although Bergson does not explicitly mention this, I would suggest, following Yuasa, that the "doorway" to the depths of our truest self and consequently the ability to connect more and more fully with the source of an intuitive, responsive openness to life does not just open as the result of philosophical study or emerge as a spontaneous gift arising from some mysterious place within. This doorway can also be opened consciously and intentionally via a variety of spiritual techniques that explicitly engage the physical body (e.g., yogic postures, chanting, breathing techniques, drumming, dancing, and so on).

For instance, I have frequently noticed that when I practice tai chi, if I stop consciously focusing on how to do the various movements correctly; if my mind begins to become calm and quiet; if I can immerse myself in the interconnected flow of one movement into the next; if I can relax into my breath and root myself into the earth and open myself to the sky, then what sometimes happens is that I begin to feel as if I am no longer moving my body, but instead that my body is being moved. In those rare, but precious moments, it feels as though my body is simply dancing in harmony with an unseen, but viscerally felt energy that pulses through me and the world; it is as if my body is no longer a cut off, utterly independent object, but rather is the physical (yet somehow "transparent") expression of the rhythmic currents of life energy moving in and through it.

When I think about these easy, effortless, rewarding moments, it is clear to me that my body was able to move in a way that explicitly mirrors Bergson's understanding of durée and the élan vital; that is, in those moments, it embodied a fluid, ever-changing, interconnected, continuous, and complex flux of temporal differences. What is not so clear to me, however, is whether my attempts to become more physically fluid, graceful, and "tuned in" have helped me in any way to become more fluid, graceful, and "tuned-in" during my daily life. I recognize that my mind almost inevitably becomes more still when I practice tai chi (which in-and-of-itself is quite a gift), but I am not sure whether my attempts to create in-and-through my practice of tai chi a type of physical template of a more flowing, open, attuned way to move through life (i.e., a more "durée-like" way to move) has catalyzed, in turn, any corresponding "durée-like" effects in my overall interactions with life as well.

What *is* clear to me is that there is no one-to-one, automatic correspondence between physical and psychological fluidity. I personally know many individuals who are amazingly flexible, graceful, and physically gifted, and yet who are also mentally rigid and emotionally shut down. Conversely, I also know some people who, even though they suffer from debilitating physical disabilities are very open, warm, and graceful in their interactions with others and with the world around them. It seems clear to me, therefore, that consciously learning to become more physically graceful does not automatically lead to a more spiritually graceful way of life.

At the same time, however, I am still convinced (along with Yuasa) that an intuitive, flowing, "tuned in" way of life *can* be consciously cultivated (at least to a certain extent). What makes this process so difficult to master, however, is that at some point in our development our tense, strained attempts to improve ourselves seem to become the very thing that blocks what we are trying so hard to attain. While in the beginning we might well have to work hard to overcome many deeply engrained habitual tendencies within us (e.g., the tendency to overanalyze everything or to try to control everything), at some point all of this hard work becomes self-defeating, because what needs to be dissolved is this often obsessive and anxiety-driven push toward perfection itself. At some point, we have to learn not to try so hard; we have to learn how to open up, to let go, to trust. We have to learn how to give ourselves fully to what is always effortlessly taking place at all times within us and around us—the flow of the totality of life itself.

Of course, this type of learning is itself the result of a type of effort, but it is a rather peculiar type of effort, an "effortless effort" if you will—a type of poised stillness, an alert, receptive responsiveness that does not force anything to happen, that does not try to figure everything out ahead of time, but rather without clenching, without attachment, subtly attunes to what is called for in the uniqueness of each particular configuration of events and then acts, spontaneously and appropriately.[19] The effort here, if there is one, is to learn how to get out of the way, how to be as transparent as possible, how to become aligned moment by moment with the often difficult-to-discern guidance and inspiration that arises from somewhere deep within, from a source that cannot be grasped and cannot be named. This process is almost by definition never perfect; it is never done; it is always renewed; and there are no guarantees. Still, it seems to me that here, if anywhere, is a life task worth taking on; here, if anywhere, is what it means to live intuitively.

25

BECOMING CONSCIOUS
OF THE SUBCONSCIOUS

CONSCIOUSNESS AND UNCONSCIOUSNESS

As we saw in the last chapter in Yuasa's discussion of "dark consciousness," everyone has had numerous experiences of doing something almost utterly automatically, giving it little or no attention, even if at least in retrospect it is clear that a striking amount of awareness and intentionality was taking place. We all have memories, for example, of "waking up" after driving for miles "on autopilot," amazed (and often somewhat shaken) by the fact that we have easily and effortlessly undergone amazingly complex procedures that needed conscious attention and choice and timing, and yet somehow managing to do all of this with our minds almost completely elsewhere (while, for instance, obsessing about a previous conversation or listening to a favorite CD). It is clear from our own experience that the boundaries between what is "in" our consciousness and what is "out" of our consciousness are by no means straightforward and easily determined.

Bergson's theoretical perspectives can help us to make sense of this fascinating interface between consciousness and unconsciousness. Unfortunately, however, Bergson's understandings of what is conscious and what is unconscious are themselves often difficult to unravel. As is hopefully becoming clear, Bergson often uses the terms "consciousness" and "unconsciousness" in a variety of often unspecified and deeply intertwined ways. However, I would argue that this terminological slippage and overlap did not happen unconsciously (as it were). As was pointed out in the beginning of section 1, although Bergson's first book was published in English as *Time and Free Will*, in the French it was entitled *Essai sur les données immédiates de la conscience* (*An Essay on the Immediate Data of*

Consciousness). As should be evident simply from the French title, in this text Bergson gives an enormous amount of careful attention to the issue of the nature of consciousness (as he also does in *Matter and Memory* and *Creative Evolution*).

In and through these (often quite different) explorations of the nature of consciousness, certain tropes appear time and again. One of the most familiar, albeit confusing, issues that frequently arises in these texts is the fact (verifiable within our own experience) that it is quite possible to be unconscious of consciousness itself.

For instance, as was pointed out in section 1, most of us are not typically aware of the fluidity, dynamism, creativity, and continuity of durée (i.e., consciousness) within us due to the "spatial grid" that we (unconsciously) superimpose over our day-to-day awareness. This spatialization of our consciousness prompts us to focus our attention outward and encourages us to think that our consciousness (if we give it any attention at all) is shaped similarly to the outer world. That is, we almost automatically suppose that our consciousness is as segmented and divided and "nameable" as the objects that seem to surround us, making it often quite difficult for us to become conscious of the true nature of consciousness itself.

Similarly, Bergson often argues that our memory is, for the most part, unconscious and yet in almost the same breath, he will add that the deeper levels of memory are "coextensive with consciousness" itself (*MM* 151). In other words, these levels of memory are said to be the most "durée-like" aspect of our being, and yet the vast majority of these profound levels of consciousness are veiled from our day-to-day conscious awareness.

And finally (if there actually ever is an end to these types of ruminations), in *Creative Evolution*, Bergson equates consciousness with the élan vital, making our own consciousness into simply one rather limited instantiation of a vaster, quasi-divine, cosmic evolutionary impetus. This expansion of consciousness's role (and concurrent qualities) was prefigured by the end of *Matter and Memory*, where Bergson claims that the entire flux of becoming, both matter and memory, is nothing but an ever-shifting spectrum of differing rhythms of durée (i.e., consciousness). Unfortunately (at least from the point of view of philosophical clarity), what is not readily apparent is how it is possible for this cosmic consciousness to operate within our own body and mind—as our very life itself, as the source and depth of our own personal consciousness—in a way that is for the vast majority of us almost completely unseen, unfelt, unexperienced. Once again, consciousness is hidden from consciousness—that is, consciousness is unconscious of consciousness.

To be fair, even though it might seem contradictory that we should so frequently be unconscious of our own consciousness, many contemporary researchers and theorists (working for instance, within the field of cognitive science) are also making similar claims, albeit coming from strikingly different sets of metaphysical assumptions.

For example, as a way to unpack his claim that "we know more than we know we know," David Myers, a contemporary research psychologist, argues that there are two distinct levels within us in which thinking, feeling, and memory operate: one level that is "conscious and deliberate" and another level that is "unconscious and automatic"; or put in another way (in the language of cognitive science): our brains accomplish their tasks via "dual processing."[1]

Myers underscores his claim that "we know more than we know we know" with the vivid example of "blindsight." He points out that there are certain individuals who have damaged the visual cortex in their brain as a result of a stroke or surgery and are, as a consequence, unable to see in certain parts of their visual field. In experiments with these individuals, if they are shown a sequence of sticks in sections of their visual field that are not functioning correctly, they will (understandably) report that they see nothing. However, if these same individuals are asked to guess whether the sticks are horizontal or vertical, they almost inevitably will give the correct response. The implication is that, on some level, they are conscious of the sticks, but on another level, they are not conscious of this consciousness. As Myers puts it, "there are, it seems, little minds—'parallel processing systems'—operating unseen" within these individuals.[2]

Myers' claim that there is something within us that can act (and know) independently of our conscious awareness is echoed by David Milner, who (very likely without knowing it!) follows in Bergson's footsteps (at least in certain respects) in his discussion of the brain's two visual systems. One of these systems (in a way somewhat similar to recollection memory) "gives us our conscious perceptions" while the other (in a way that is somewhat similar to habit memory) "guides our actions."[3] (Of course, Milner's claim that it is the brain that accomplishes these tasks is strikingly different from Bergson's own understanding, as is Milner's description of the second visual system as the "zombie within.")[4] To illustrate the distinction between these two parallel systems, Milner describes a brain-damaged woman who, when asked to estimate the size of an object with her thumb and forefinger could not do it; however, when she reached for the object, her thumb and forefinger were automatically able to move in the correct way. Once again we can see from this example, as Myers notes, that this woman "knows more than she is aware of."[5]

Myers gives several other examples of how, although we like to imagine that our conscious intentions and choices are in control of our actions, in reality something else under the surface is really in charge. For instance, Myers notes that when speaking, "strings of words effortlessly spill out of your mouth with near-perfect syntax. . . . It's as if there were servants downstairs, busily hammering together sentences that get piped up and fluidly shoved out of your mouth. You hardly have a clue how you do it."[6] Similarly, pianists make no conscious decisions about how to move their fingers, tennis players do not consciously think through each of their movements on the court, and our hands just seem to know what to do when signing our names.

As Myers puts it, "the new cognitive scientists agree" with the "older" theoretical perspectives (e.g., depth psychologists such as Freud, and by extension, philosophers such as Bergson and James) that "the mind is buzzing with influential happenings that are not reportably conscious."[7] The primary difference between the understandings of the cognitive scientists and the supposedly antiquated, superseded, and irrelevant perspective of thinkers like Bergson is that for the cognitive scientists, consciousness (including the hidden activity of consciousness we have been focusing on) is, at best, only a temporary, expedient way to talk about what is really going on—that is, complex neurochemical operations within the brain. As such, unconscious awareness is often pictured in a way that parallels many contemporary understandings of the neurochemical activity of the brain in that it is seen as the end result of the activity of a host of tiny, relatively unimportant and unintelligent "workers" within—that is, it is the product in the words of Myers of the "servants downstairs," or "the downstairs laborers watching the radar screens"; it is put together by the "little minds" that come together to make up "the zombie within."[8] These robotic minions take care of the grunt work, reserving "only the really important mental tasks" for "the executive desk, where your conscious mind . . . your mental CEO" works.[9]

RUMINATION: THE SUBCONSCIOUS AND SUPERCONSCIOUSNESS

The types of (strikingly capitalistic!) images that often emerge in the attempts by cognitive scientists to make sense of the unconscious activity of consciousness are in vivid contrast to the root metaphors and metaphysical assumptions that underlie Bergson's own work. While Bergson's descriptions of various types of unconscious activity can at times seem rather prosaic in that they often emphasize the utilitarian and evolutionary advantages of unconscious levels of awareness and action, Bergson never attempts to reduce these unconscious levels of dynamism to bits of matter robotically fulfilling predetermined tasks. Instead, what we find in Bergson's work (with certain exceptions) are deeply appreciative assessments of the powers and potentials of subconscious mental activity.

For Bergson, while our subconscious levels of awareness may be *filtered* in and through the brain (thus creating wide-ranging cerebral effects), these subconscious levels of awareness are not *produced* by the brain. Therefore, unlike the stupid underground workers portrayed by cognitive psychology that represent (very inadequately I might add) the multiplicity of our immensely complicated neural circuitry, our subconscious fields of awareness do not need a "boss" to unify them. Instead, in-and-through all of their plurality, these subconscious fields of memory and consciousness possess an inherent quality of continuity and cohesiveness that allows them to operate independently from our conscious awareness, with a degree of lucidity and appropriateness (and dare I say, wisdom) that is almost inevitably a dramatic improvement over the often rather lackluster abilities demonstrated by our conscious day-to-day awareness.

Using a Bergsonian lens to examine various forms of unconscious activity that take place within our own psyches (and bodies), what we see is not a mob of mechanistic drones toiling away under the surface, but rather an array of stunningly complex, intricately interwoven activities that seem to require an almost incomprehensible "amount" of consciousness in order to successfully occur, and yet which astonishingly take place with little or no conscious awareness on our part.

For instance, most of the autonomic activity that takes place within our own body (e.g., growing hair or digesting food or regulating our hormonal secretions) takes place completely unconsciously—and thankfully so, because our conscious levels of mental ability could never begin to accomplish even the most rudimentary (and still unimaginably complicated and interconnected) tasks that these unconscious levels of awareness effortlessly and ceaselessly perform.

Similarly, we are also unconscious of the numerous, dynamic, and highly creative planes of consciousness that form our memory—and yet every night, we witness the spontaneous and free-flowing manifestation of numerous richly configured dream worlds, worlds filled with levels of drama, pathos, and insights that, if we had consciously attempted to imagine, would be one-dimensional and prosaic in comparison. (As will be demonstrated further on, Bergson's own theory of dreaming is, oddly, rather "un-creative." Nonetheless, I suggest that this example of the subconscious creativity of our dream-life is faithful to the underlying thrust of Bergson's work as a whole.)

According to Bergson, we are also unconscious of the fact that fields of influence from the entire physical universe are continually flowing in and through us; even if at the same time in the depth of our being there is an underlying, deeply hidden awareness of our unity with the cosmos—a unitive awareness that, if countless mystical narratives are correct, can at times be unveiled within us with sudden, stunning, almost revelatory force, a unitive awareness that was not cobbled together with our own conscious efforts, but rather was always there, waiting to show itself.

If we look carefully at any of the examples we can find of unconscious activity (e.g., the neurochemical activity of the brain, the production of multilayered dream worlds), what we discover is that in every instance mind-bogglingly complex processes are taking place. Understood from a mechanistic, deterministic, and naturalistic framework, these processes are often thought to be not only unconscious, but also nonconscious; that is, it is assumed that consciousness is not needed in order for any of them to take place. Bergson, however, would strongly disagree.

According to Bergson (at least the Bergson of *Creative Evolution* and beyond), all of these processes offer quite dramatic indications, not only of consciousness, but also some sort of superconsciousness. In order for any of these unconscious processes to take place, unimaginably complicated and exquisitely timed levels of organization, intercommunication, aesthetic ability, creativity, and intentionality have to be simultaneously present. In other words, these processes, interpreted from a nonmechanistic, nondeterministic, nonreductionistic framework, give every indication of taking place within greater, wider, deeper (perhaps cosmic or divine) levels of mind. Interpreted in this way, all of these "unconscious" processes offer us quite evocative indications (not evidence) of the activity and presence of intensely powerful, highly developed levels of consciousness, even if almost all of this activity takes place below (or above) the threshold of our ordinary level of conscious awareness.

What is not so clear from this Bergsonian interpretive framework is exactly what (or who) is doing all of these various activities and exactly what is the nature of the relationship between these various levels of consciousness and our own particularized, mundane consciousness. It would be tempting to simply say that the whole show is run by the élan vital (i.e., by the cosmic mind) and simply leave it at that. And while, understood from a certain perspective, I think that this actually might indeed be the case, the élan vital is not some sort of homogeneous, static, unchanging Divine Substance that can or should offer us an easy resting place for our theories of the universe and our place within it. Instead, the élan vital, like our own consciousness, is an ever-new fusion of manyness and oneness; it is (and we are) an exuberant explosion of unexpected potentialities; it is (and we are) an unimaginably rich proliferation of levels of consciousness and temporality that always transcend any and all of our attempts to intellectually categorize.

As such, it seems to me that, instead of attempting to come to a neat and tidy metaphysical closure, it would be more in keeping with the multiplicity and richness of the élan vital that we open ourselves to a multitude of possible answers to our question: who (or what) is performing these awe-inspiringly complex tasks—within our bodies, within our minds, within the universe we inhabit—all with little or no conscious awareness on the part of our egoic minds?

We might for instance, along with Gustav Fechner, envision an interwoven, interpenetrating hierarchy of consciousnesses, each associated with differing magnitudes of physicality, that is, perhaps we should postulate that our individual consciousnesses are each rooted in or open up to (but are consciously unaware of) a more expansive level of consciousness, such as an "Earth soul," that is, in turn, nested in a "solar system soul," that is, in turn, part of a "galaxy soul," and so on.

We could also reexamine the ancient occult notions of "angelic" levels of consciousness that dwell within the depths of our being, even as they also are simultaneously each responsible for various "spheres" of personal, natural, planetary, and cosmic functioning.

We could also draw upon the highly detailed, mystically inspired inner maps of various Tantric sages (such as Sri Aurobindo) and their extremely complex understanding of overlapping vital and astral dimensions that are subconsciously (and superconsciously) present within the depths of our consciousness.

We could also begin to take seriously the possibility that the multitude of gods and goddesses, ancestors, buddhas and bodhisattvas, orishas and nature spirits, and the countless other divine beings that are affirmed within numerous religious traditions, along with the variety of subtle worlds that they are said to inhabit, actually do exist—in part as distinct, autonomous beings and worlds, but also as dynamic, overlapping, interpenetrating, ever-new manifestations of our own subconscious potentialities, as radiant configurations of consciousness that are present right now, here within us, around us, continually vibrant with activity, hidden under the surface of life as we know it.

As we think through the status of these various levels of subconscious realities, I would suggest that we also acknowledge, right up front, that the subconscious dimensions of our being are not all goodness and light, but also seem to be the source of much (if not most) of our mental and emotional (and often physical) suffering. It seems crucial that we at least attempt to make some sort of sense of the nature of the relationship between the various levels of "higher" consciousness which many claim are active in a hidden way within the depths of our being and the more pathological levels of awareness that also seem to be subconsciously present within us.

Personally, I think that it might be fruitful to examine the correspondence, not only between Bergson's work and the insights of object relations theory and Self psychology (a task that I touched upon, in a very rudimentary way, in an earlier rumination), but also the potential overlap between Bergson's ideas and those of Carl Jung, particularly his intriguing notion of a plurality of quasi-independent, powerfully charged, and highly ambivalent archetypal realities that are present in the depths of the psyche, archetypes that are both "us" and "not us," archetypes that are themselves grounded in a deeper, wider Self—a Self that is simultaneously individual and collective in nature.

Another potentially worthwhile avenue of exploration might be the relatively unknown, but highly sophisticated and empirically grounded work of Fredric Myers, especially his hypothesis of the Subliminal Self. For Myers, the Subliminal Self encompasses a vast spectrum of consciousness extending down into the depths where neurosis and multiple personalities dwell, and ascending to the heights where the inspirations of genius emerge and where we find states of ecstasy, clairvoyance, and prophetic dreams.[10]

There are numerous ways in which Bergson's work dovetails with all of these (quite diverse) perspectives. Due to the constraints of this book, I am not able to give here more than a quick appreciative nod in their direction. But perhaps in the future the fascinating overlap between Bergson and these (and other) metaphysical and psychological "maps" could be more carefully explored. My only hope, with this rumination, is to underscore the value of looking in a multitude of directions for ways to envision and understand our subconscious connection to the worlds within us and around us.

26

RECOLLECTION MEMORY, DREAMS, AND THE ÉLAN VITAL

Reading Bergson's work, it is often easy to assume that he wholeheartedly supports the value of opening up to the hidden depths of the psyche—and this assumption is not entirely incorrect. However, Bergson at times also appears subtly to downplay the value of certain transrational dimensions of the human mind. Bergson's less-than-ringing endorsement of the subconscious strata of the self is especially evident in his rather ambivalent depiction of recollection memory.

As we have seen, Bergson frequently argues that our recollection memory is for the most part ill suited to the practical needs of everyday life. He repeatedly stresses that, in order for us to function effectively, it is crucial that our specific recollections of the past remain cut off from our day-to-day awareness, except for those rather rare memories that can be "coordinated with the present perception" (*MM* 85). Bergson also points out, however, that there are certain moments in our lives in which these buried memory-images can and will cross the internal barriers that we have erected to prevent their emergence. During these moments, our minds can become flooded with "confused recollections, unrelated to the present circumstances," making it difficult for us to deal with the demands of everyday life (*MM* 85).

From Bergson's perspective, if we are fortunate, these incursions of recollection memory into our waking world will take place during those moments of restful relaxation when we can afford to daydream and let our mind wander without having to focus on any specific task. Bergson also emphasizes, however, that if these dream-like images should intrude upon our present awareness too often, with too much intensity, this "mingling [of] dream with reality" can "seriously disturb" our "intellectual equilibrium" (*MM* 84, 88).

It seems clear, therefore, that Bergson has a very mixed assessment of the value of recollection memory. On the one hand, he argues that our recollections of the past are relatively benign, something to be indulged in during idle, nonproductive moments of daydreaming and fantasy. On the other hand, this same grouping of memories seems to have a slightly more ominous aspect to itself as well in that it is something that needs to be kept safely at bay, something that can rather capriciously interfere with our practical lives, something that, at its worst, can even threaten our mental equilibrium.

Reading Bergson's ambivalence toward recollection memory in passages such as these, it can almost appear that the utilitarian claims of everyday life are more important to Bergson than the need to open oneself to the subconscious. Reading these types of passages, it can be easy to forget that the overall thrust of *Matter and Memory* is toward a highly positive reevaluation of the role of memory in our lives; it can be easy to forget that, according to Bergson, the closer we get to the depths of recollection within us, the closer we are to the dimensions of our being that are "coextensive with consciousness" (*MM* 151); it can be easy to forget that it is in the depths of recollection memory that we find "spirit in its most tangible form"; it can be easy to forget that the deeper we go within ourselves to the source of memory within us, the more that we find increasingly pure manifestations of durée (*MM* 73).

Given the fact that Bergson claims that the closer we come to *"pure memory"* (the virtual, open-ended, ever-renewed source of memory within us), the closer we are to pure durée; and given the fact that Bergson never revised or found fault with his analysis of durée in *Time and Free Will*, we would expect to find him making the assertion that recollection memory (which is relatively removed from the plane of materiality) possesses the qualities of durée that he worked so hard to articulate in his previous work, that is, fluidity, dynamism, creativity, freedom, newness, a fusion of difference and continuity, temporality, unpredictability, and so forth.

Oddly, however, when Bergson discusses recollection memory, he often speaks of it in exceedingly spatial ways. For instance, at one point, Bergson argues that this mode of memory "retains and ranges alongside of each other all our states in the order in which they occur, leaving to each fact its place and, consequently, marking its date, truly moving in the past and not, like [habit memory], in an ever renewed present" (*MM* 151). In this passage, it is almost as if recollection memory is seen as simply a type of mental storage facility or inner warehouse, where all of our memories of specific events that occurred in our personal history are kept. Or more anachronistically, in this passage we find Bergson describing recollection memory as if it were nothing more than a type of internal video camera, passively and neutrally recording (and even dating!) every event in our lives. (This passage is strikingly similar to how Bergson notes elsewhere that recollection memory retains "the image of the situations through which [we have] successively traveled . . . [laying] them side by side in the order in which they took place" [*MM* 84].)

These depictions of recollection memory are, in many ways, strikingly un-Bergsonian in that recollection memories are pictured, as it where, frozen in their place, separate, and lined up next to each other—a very spatial and seemingly static vision of what Bergson calls "true memory" (*MM* 151). However, it is clear that these isolated passages do not give an accurate impression of the overall thrust of Bergson's understanding of memory. As several interpreters of Bergson's work have pointed out, Bergson primarily emphasizes that memory should not be seen as some type of device for quasi-mechanically storing images from the past; instead, as a relatively pure manifestation of durée, memory (at least in its depths) is better understood to be fluid, unpredictable, and genuinely creative.

Pete Gunter, for instance, argues that, according to Bergson, "our personal past is neither a stamp collection of memory-images nor a set of causal factors more or less mechanically impelling us."[1] It is, instead, "a culmination of wider possibilities which funds our freedom."[2] Similarly, Keith Ansell Pearson emphasizes that, for Bergson, memory is not a "bare or brute material repetition of the past," but rather it has its own autonomy and acts within us as a "disruptive and creative power."[3] Understood in this way, memory for Bergson is not some sort of passive receptacle for the past. Instead, as Marie Cariou puts it, memory in its depths *"is creative imagination."*[4]

Jean Hyppolite also emphasizes the ways in which, for Bergson, memory has a meaning that is far different from the ways in which it is normally understood. As Hyppolite sees it, memory for Bergson "is not a particular faculty that is concerned with repeating or reproducing the past in the present; it is consciousness itself insofar as this consciousness is creative duration."[5] Hyppolite points out how, according to Bergson, memory is highly supple in that it spontaneously merges with the ever-changing flux of perceptions in order to help us meet "the demands of adapting to the world."[6] Nonetheless, as Hyppolite also emphasizes, we must be careful not to imagine that memory, when it acts in this way, is some sort of "mechanical combination of images, of ready-made memories [*souvenirs*], which, deposited somewhere in the brain or in the unconscious . . . come to complete the given situation."[7]

As Hyppolite notes, memory for Bergson is not some sort of highly complex machine; it is not a "set of images which are given ready-made in the unconscious."[8] Instead, "living memory" moves fluidly to meet and to interpret every situation, and in this way "its suppleness, its ability to dilate and contract, contrasts with the rigidity of every mechanism."⁹ As Hyppolite puts it, living memory is, therefore, not a collection of rigidly compartmentalized memories, but rather is "*one sole* personal past" that effortlessly modifies itself "according to the demands of a present situation"; it is that often hidden dimension of our being that effortlessly, and outside the range of our everyday awareness, enables us to live in a meaningful world and to respond to that world with varying degrees of freedom, fluidity, and creativity.¹⁰

RECOLLECTION MEMORY AND BERGSON'S THEORY OF DREAMS

While I am in complete agreement with this more "durée-like" way of understanding Bergson's view of memory, nonetheless, as was pointed out previously, Bergson's ambivalence toward recollection memory remains. His less-than-glowing attitude toward this level of memory is particularly evident in his almost utilitarian disparagement of some of the primary manifestations of recollection memory, especially dreams as well as the "play of fancy and the work of imagination" (*MM* 180).

Bergson's mixed assessment of the value of dreams is perhaps most evident in a lecture he gave at the Institut Psychologique in 1901, a lecture that was subsequently published as an essay in *Mind-Energy*. According to Bergson, the "stuff . . . dreams are made of" is primarily a mass of muted and obscurely noted sense impressions. This sense data can be internal, for example, the "color blotches" we perceive behind our eyelids (*ME* 105) or the internal sensations of the ear (its "buzzing, tinkling, whistling") (*ME* 108) or the various "disorders of digestion, breathing and circulation" (*ME* 112). This sense data can also be external, for example, the light from a candle penetrating the eyelids (which may invoke dreams that are "dominated by the idea of fire") (*ME* 107) or "contact of the body with the night-dress" (which may lead to dreams of being "lightly clad") (*ME* 109) or the bodily sensations of lying horizontally in bed (which Bergson theorizes can lead to dreams of flying, since lying in bed in this way can prompt you to feel that you are not "touching ground") (*ME* 109).

According to Bergson, this almost one-to-one relationship between what we physically feel in the margins of our awareness and the consequent form the dream takes within us is strikingly similar to how concrete perceptions are created in our waking life, in that Bergson theorizes that dreams are, in reality, little more than a combination of vaguely apprehended sensations fused with a shifting overlay of recollection memories.

Bergson argues that in both our waking and dream life our perceptions only give us a sketch of the external object, a sketch that then needs to be filled in with different types of memories. The primary difference is that in our dream life we no longer have the urgent need to accurately interpret the external world, a situation that gives our memory much more latitude to superimpose less "accurate" memories onto the vaguely apprehended sensations that are the underlying "stuff" of dreams. Bergson emphasizes, however, that in both cases (i.e., during dreams and in waking perceptions) the "finished product" of what we perceive is a complex fusion of perception and memory.

In his discussion on dreams, Bergson notes that we often mistakenly assume that perceiving something in our waking life (e.g., hearing a dog bark) is a very simple and straightforward process. It appears that all we have to do in order to hear something is passively to receive sonic information (e.g., the barking) from the outside world through our ears. However, as Bergson points out, hearing a dog bark is in actuality an enormously complex undertaking, one in which each of us makes "without suspecting it, a big effort" (*ME* 124). Just to hear a single bark, we have to compress all of our memory, all of our "accumulated experience" and overlay that sensation with the condensation of memory that "most resembles the sensation and can best interpret it," thereby fusing memory and sensation together seamlessly "as the tailor fits on and tightens a new garment" (*ME* 124–125).

Bergson argues that this preconscious process is ongoing and "ceaselessly renewed" every moment of our waking existence (*ME* 125). While in certain respects we can say that this interpretive process takes place quasi-automatically, with little or no conscious attention on our part, in other respects, according to Bergson, this state of "uninterrupted tension" takes tremendous effort and will (*ME* 125). As Bergson puts it (his emphasis), "*waking* and *willing* are one and the same" (*ME* 127). (Bergson does not clarify how it is possible that we can preconsciously will something to occur—another of the paradoxes of the nature of unconscious awareness that we have explored earlier. However, he does make the intriguing suggestion that this seemingly exhausting process of having to match memories with our pure perceptions leads to the very fatigue that sleep itself attempts to heal [*ME* 125].)

Bergson goes on in this essay to argue that during sleep we no longer have to give quite the same level of concerted attention to the sensations that press upon us; consequently our "tense" adaptation to the pressing needs of the present can relax. It is this disinterest in, and detachment from, the sensations of the waking world that opens the door to the mass of recollection memories buried deep within us. In our dream life, because memory no longer has to constantly adapt itself to reality, recollection memories are much more free, not only to arise within us, but also to superimpose themselves, one after the other, and often very rapidly, upon the relatively diffuse set of sensations we are obliquely perceiving (e.g., the "color blotches" behind our eyelids, the touch of sheets on our skin, and so forth). While we are dreaming, unlike in waking life, there is little or no concern with how well our memories "fit" the sensations themselves, since "very different memories will suit equally well the same dream sensation" (*ME* 128). For instance, we might indistinctly perceive some vague internal sensations, such as "black lines upon a white background," when we are lying in our bed with our eyes closed (*ME* 113). These sensations, in order to form dreams, are overlaid with numerous memories that are vaguely analogous to the sensations, producing in turn a wide range of associated dream images, for example, "a carpet, a chessboard, a printed page, or a host of other things" (*ME* 113).

Bergson's explanation of dreams is a seamless and natural extension of his theory of perception and it is, I would argue, somewhat convincing. I do not think that anyone would deny that there are some dreams in which our vague awareness of external or internal sensations is creatively reconfigured by our dream life (e.g., when sensations of a full bladder might result in, let's say, a dream of floating in an inner tube on a lake). However, in our post-Freudian (and post-Jungian) world, Bergson's dream theory can at times seem remarkably circumscribed and one-dimensional.[11] If Bergson's theory of the genesis of dreams could be modified so that it was less literalistic and heavy-handed, I think that it would be easier to appreciate what he *does* offer (especially his strikingly interactive emphasis on how our perceptions and bodily sensations can and do, at least to a certain extent, help to shape the form and feeling of our dreams).

THE CREATIVITY OF DREAMS

Nonetheless, the fact remains that Bergson often does give a painfully literalistic and unimaginative interpretation of what dreams signify. Even more puzzlingly, given his explicit connection between dreams, recollection memory, and ever-more-pure manifestations of durée, it can be startling to read that he also explicitly denies that dreams have the power to "create anything" (*ME* 113).

Bergson notes that we might wish to defend the creative capacity of dream life by giving examples of individuals who wake up having received a vivid creative insight (e.g., a musical composition, a scientific theory, or a literary composition) while dreaming. He argues, however, that these examples are not as straightforward as they might appear. Bergson relates, for instance, the story of Guiseppe Tartini, a musician from the eighteenth century, who "was toiling at a composition," but no inspirations would come (*ME* 113). Upon falling asleep, however, Tartini had a dream in which the devil appeared before him, "seized the violin and played the sonata" that Tartini had been attempting to compose (*ME* 113). Upon waking, therefore, all that Tartini had to do was to write down the sonata before he forgot what he had heard in the dream.

It might seem that this example clearly demonstrates the creative capacities of our dream life. Bergson, however, is not persuaded. He suggests, instead (in a way that is similar to Freud's notion of "secondary elaboration"), that perhaps Tartini's imagination retrospectively modified the dream, adding to it features that it really did not possess; in essence, he argues that Tartini's waking consciousness actually did most (if not all) of the work, even if Tartini himself was convinced that his dream deserved the credit for the composition.

Bergson goes on to offer another example of how it can mistakenly appear that our subconscious is the source of creativity, an example drawn from the writings of the Robert Louis Stevenson. As Bergson notes, Stevenson wrote an essay entitled "A Chapter on Dreams" in which he claims that many of his most original stories "were composed, or at least sketched, in dream" (*ME* 114). Bergson, once again, attempts to deflate this claim by pointing out that Stevenson admits that he periodically "lived in a psychical condition in which it was very hard to know whether he was asleep or awake" (*ME* 114). Bergson concludes from this observation that the real effort of composition actually occurred when Stevenson was awake, even if this effort was happening, as Bergson puts it, "in the subconscious" (*ME* 114). (Of course, what is rather puzzling about this observation is that even in Bergson's theorizing, dreams are formed in the subconscious. Therefore, if the source of Stevenson's creativity is also found "in the subconscious," it is not clear what significant difference it makes to claim that Stevenson was actually awake during these inspirational moments, since in both cases the actual source of the creativity was subconscious in nature.)

It seems, at least in this essay, that it is almost unimaginable to Bergson that our dream life could actually have the power to create something original. He is emphatic about this point: according to him, "when the mind is creating . . . it is not actually asleep" (*ME* 114). Dreams, according to Bergson, are basically "a resurrection of the past" in that they are constructed primarily from useless shards of recollection memories (*ME* 114). Like Freud's theory of the "day's residues" (but without Freud's much more sophisticated understanding of latent dream thoughts that are repressed and symbolically represented in a hidden form in the manifest dream content), Bergson postulates that the most basic "stuff" of dreams are inconsequential bits of recent memories that we have forgotten or are "fragments of broken memories, picked up here and there, presented to the consciousness of the dreamer in an incoherent form" (*ME* 114–115).[12]

Thankfully, Bergson's perspective on dreaming was not uniformly dismissive. Seven years later (in "Memory of the Present and False Recognition," an article published in December 1908, on the phenomenon of déjà vu) Bergson acknowledges that it is crucial to let go of the "preconceived idea" that dreams are nothing but "phantoms superadded to the solid perceptions and conceptions of our waking life" or "will-o-wisps which hover above it," and that it is important to recognize that dreams in actuality are "the substratum of our normal state" (*ME* 154–155). Here Bergson gives much more theoretical "weight" to our dreaming life, arguing that the levels of consciousness that are linked to dreaming do not just come into existence when we sleep, but rather are active beneath our conscious awareness at every moment. Here Bergson acknowledges that perhaps our dream life has in-and-of-itself crucial psychological and perhaps even ontological significance.

TIME AND DREAMS

Even with these theoretical modifications, I would argue that Bergson dramatically underestimates the creative activity of our dream life (as well as the creative capacity of our imaginative and visionary abilities). For Bergson to be so blind to the creativity of our inner life (at least in his understanding of dreaming) is, to put it mildly, rather odd. After all, as we have seen, it is Bergson who argues that the closer that we get to "pure" or "virtual" memory, the closer we are to the most unencumbered activity of durée within us. (Please forgive, again, the almost unavoidable spatial metaphors.) If this actually is the case, then it would seem that we should expect that those aspects of our being that are the most "durée-like," that is, our dreams, our imagination, and our intuition, would manifest in very durée-like ways, that is, we should expect that they would be *inherently* creative (along with numerous other qualities).

I would suggest that, as a matter of fact, our dream life does indeed demonstrate qualities that are more aligned with durée than our typical waking level of experience. For instance, while our normal waking experience of time is exceedingly spatial in nature (in that it often seems to be split up into discrete, countable, homogeneous units of time, almost as if we are always in the background of our awareness hearing the ticktock of an internalized clock measuring the seconds of our existence), the temporal quality of dreams is exceedingly fluid and dynamic. Speaking from my own experience, I have often woken up from a dream and casually noticed the time that I awoke, only to fall back asleep and then undergo a depth of dream experiences that seem from within the dream to take several hours or even days to occur. However, when I wake up, I discover that this seemingly quite prolonged temporal experience within my dream life took only a few minutes of measurable waking time.

To his credit, Bergson, in his essay on dreams, does comment that when we dream it is possible to compress into a few seconds of "clock time" a range of experiences that, to the dreamer, appear to go on for several days. To illustrate this point, he tells the wonderful story of a dream that is found in Alfred Maury's *Le Sommeil et les Rêves* (a dream that, by the way, is also found in Freud's *Interpretation of Dreams*). The dream goes like this:

I am in bed in my room, my mother at my pillow. I am dreaming of the Terror; I am present at scenes of massacre, I appear before the Revolution Tribunal; I see Robespierre, Marat, Fouquier-Tinville . . . ; I defend myself; I am convicted, condemned to death, driven in the tumbril to the Place de la Révolution; I ascend the scaffold; the executioner lays me on the fatal plank, tilts it forward, the knife falls; I feel my head separate from my body, I wake in a state of intense anguish, and I feel on my neck the curtain pole which has suddenly got detached and fallen on my cervical vertebrae, just like a guillotine knife. It had all taken place in an instant, as my mother bore witness. (*ME* 128–129)

As Maury emphasizes, the very last scene in the narrator's tremendously long and complex dream occurs when his head is cut off, a scene that corresponds notably with the physical reality of being hit on the neck by the curtain rod. If we believe that the physical occurrence of the curtain rod hitting the dreamer's neck was the event that was translated into the dream image of the guillotine knife cutting off his head (which would make sense given Bergson's theory), then a question should immediately arise within us: how do we account for all of the extremely intricate and temporally lengthy events that preceded the decapitation? While it might make logical sense to hypothesize that in the instant after the curtain rod hit his neck that his memories fused with the physical sensations to produce the dream image of being decapitated, it is much more difficult to account for all of the events that were experienced before the execution scene, a sequence of events that appeared to go on for a very long time, a sequence of events that seem to lead almost inevitably to the decapitation. What Bergson has to do, in essence, is to account for the fact that all of these events were compressed in waking life into the instant of time between feeling the curtain rod on his neck and waking up.

I want to be clear here. I do not have a problem with Bergson using this dream as an illustration of how dreams can dramatically compress temporal experience. In fact, these types of temporal shifts are exactly what we should expect to find when we are immersed in a level of consciousness that is more overtly "durée-like" than waking experience. What *is* problematic, however, with Bergson's explanation of this dream is that he seems oblivious to how a dream with such an intricate plotline and dramatic tension could manifest in little more than instant. This is not a dream created from "fragments of broken memories, picked up here and there, presented to the consciousness of the dreamer in an incoherent form" (*ME* 114–115). This is, instead, a dream that clearly illustrates the sheer creative exuberance of our dream life, a complex, dramatic synthesis that took form, absolutely effortlessly, with no intent or planning by the dreamer's ego in a stunningly brief period of time.[13]

DREAMS, "VIRTUAL" MEMORY, AND THE ÉLAN VITAL

An excerpt of a dream that I had on December 29, 2004:

> "Listen, listen," he said, as we lay drifting in the surging tidal swells of
> the ocean. "You can go much further if you align yourself with the
> waves than if you try to fight against them. You can even learn how to
> go the whole way underwater if you wish. Let me show you how." And
> with these words I awoke, abruptly, but not harshly, in my bed, lying
> flat on my back.

Dramatic shifts in temporal awareness are not the only ways in which
dreams (and imagination, intuition, and flashes of inspiration) demonstrate
"durée-like" qualities. It is clear to me that, when I look carefully at my own
dream life—for example, the aforementioned dream—my dreams manifest in a
very "durée-like" way. Every night, new worlds are effortlessly created within me,
worlds that are explicitly and undeniably made of consciousness, not matter.
These dream worlds are amazingly complex, detailed, nuanced, and multitex-
tured; they have intricate dramatic plots woven together with exquisite characterizations, humor, pathos, and suspense. In these worlds, every moment is new
and unanticipated, every moment is a ceaseless, uninterrupted, highly dynamic
flow of difference. In these worlds, especially when I examine them closely when
I wake up, I find a language of symbolism, a coded communication in which
heteronymous, often dramatically opposed, qualities are fused together and
interact seamlessly. In these worlds, I find metaphorical sleights of hand and
veiled hints of significance that when interpreted often reveal layer upon layer of
meaning and applicability to my daily life. These dream worlds also, crucially,
come into being without any planning or effort on the part of my will—it is as if
somewhere in my depths there exists, as Bergson would say (especially by the
time of *Creative Evolution*) an almost god-like level of creative ability, an ability
that manifests with utter freedom, seemingly for its own sake, regardless of
whether "I" want it to or not. In these worlds, I find (especially in "big dreams,"
those dreams that shine with lucidity and sing with significance) levels of insight
and guidance that feel as if they come, not only from somewhere deep within
me, but from a source of wisdom that feels, dare I say it, divine.[14]
    Bergson himself never suggested that the source of our dream life is any-
thing more than a psychological process. However, especially after *Creative Evolution*, it would not be far-fetched to imagine that Bergson himself might have
been willing to posit that dreams emerge, not simply from personal subconscious
sources, but also (simultaneously) from a more cosmic, transpersonal matrix as
well. Bergson relatively easily could have hypothesized that, in our depths, where

we find what Mullarkey calls "virtual" or "pure" memory—that imageless, open, dynamic matrix of memory within us—we *also* find our own private entryway into the depths of cosmic consciousness.

But Bergson never takes this step. While he does make a brief acknowledgment in *Matter and Memory* that "the activity of the mind goes far beyond the mass of accumulated memories, as this mass of memories itself is infinitely more than the sensations and movements of the present hour" (*MM* 173), as far as I can tell, he never went so far as to claim that our "virtual" memory might also be understood as an exceedingly pure manifestation of the élan vital within us, even though there appear to be numerous natural points of correspondence between the élan vital and "virtual" memory.

Nonetheless, even though Bergson never explicitly made the connection between the élan vital and "virtual" memory, he quite often pointed out the numerous and overt points of correspondence between the élan vital and durée. In *Creative Evolution*, Bergson suggests that, if we plunge into "the depths of our experience" and identify within ourselves those moments when we feel the most fully alive, the most creative, the most free, the most fluid, it is during these moments that it is possible to discover (and align ourselves with) the élan vital, the superconscious evolutionary energy that he claims is ceaselessly active within us, *as us* (*CE* 199). According to Bergson, the most "durée-like" quality of our experience is itself the élan vital—that vital principle "in which we participate and whose eternity is not to be an eternity of immutability, but an eternity of life" (*CM* 186). For Bergson, the same vital impetus that expresses itself in the blossoms of spring, in the flight of a bird over a pond, and in the brilliant light of the sun, also courses within us, in the pumping of our blood, in the flexing of our muscles, and (perhaps most importantly) in the ever-changing dynamic flux of our consciousness.

For Bergson our own consciousness (i.e., durée) is one of the clearest mirrors of the élan vital.[15] He points out that our consciousness and the élan vital are both continually growing, both are ceaselessly changing forms, both are constantly taking on shapes that are ever new (*CM* 21). This continual evolution of both the élan vital and our personal consciousness, this shared ability to effortlessly reshape the past into forms which could not have been predicted, this mutual temporal dynamism, indicates to Bergson that life and consciousness are not two separate substances. Instead, as he puts it, "life is connected either with consciousness or with something that resembles it" (*CE* 179).

The consciousness that Bergson claims is connected to the energy of life is not simply human consciousness (although that is the only consciousness of which we can be directly and immediately aware). Nor is it just the consciousness that seems to be present in different degrees within all organisms (although that is one of its primary manifestations). Instead, Bergson suggests that the level of consciousness that is connected to the élan vital is an "enormous field" of creative awareness that is expressed in and through all organisms as well as in all of the countless forms assumed by matter.[16]

The élan vital, for Bergson, is the ceaselessly creative cosmic consciousness, both singular and plural at the same time, which propels the universe forward in a free, yet nonarbitrary way, toward an open-ended future. Bergson claims that this "consciousness, or rather supra-consciousness" is the creative cosmic vitality that continuously creates new worlds from a dynamic center of being "like rockets in a fire-works display" (*CE* 261, 248). This divine center of cosmic creativity (which Bergson, in a rare use of theological language, explicitly labels as "God"), is not a separate object, nor is it a being that is "already made" (*CE* 248). Instead, "God," seen in this light, is a "continuity of shooting out"; "God" is "unceasing life, action, freedom," and as such, is the dynamic source of ceaseless creative activity—the same creative activity that takes the form of the ongoing flux of our consciousness, the same creative activity which can be experienced "in ourselves when we act freely" (*CE* 248).

What I would like to suggest is that it is congruent with the overall thrust of Bergson's thought to make an explicit connection between "pure" or "virtual" memory and the élan vital. "Pure" or "virtual" memory is not a collection of recollection memory-images. Rather, it is the open, dynamic, *virtual* matrix of memory; it is that aspect of ourselves that is, as we saw, "spirit in its most tangible form" (*MM* 73); it is that dimension of our being that, according to Bergson, is the most "durée-like" in nature. Since, as was shown previously, the élan vital is also understood to be sheer durée, to be durée in its very essence; and since Bergson himself claims that we come to know the élan vital within ourselves in-and-as our own personal consciousness; it does not seem to be much of a theoretical leap also to claim that we can find an extremely pure manifestation of the élan vital present within the depths of our *subconscious* as well.

Certainly by the time of *Creative Evolution*, if not well before, Bergson would seem to have little if any reluctance to posit the active, creative presence of a cosmic consciousness within each of us. It is very clear, for him, that our personal consciousness is a direct manifestation of the élan vital. It is equally clear that the élan vital, for Bergson, is that which seemingly effortlessly coordinates and directs and impels the countless, astonishingly intricate physiological activities that come together to make up all living organisms, including our own physical bodies. Why not then also say that it is the élan vital itself that performs the equally astonishing task moment-by-moment of seamlessly fusing together memory and perception to create our concrete, ongoing conscious experience of life? Why not claim that it is the élan vital that chooses out of the vast torrent of images flowing through us, which images we will note and which ones we will filter out? Why not simply state that it is the élan vital that is the source of what I term "primal memory"—that is, that it is the élan vital which in-and-through memory provides the temporal connection of one moment to the next on all levels, from the quantum realms up to our own consciousness and possibly beyond? And finally, why not simply assert that the élan vital itself is the source of that wondrous capacity to create dreams: those exceedingly complex, dynamic, multifaceted worlds of consciousness that effortlessly blossom within our own being every night?

It is clearly not possible for our egoic level of awareness to do any of these tasks. Therefore, if Bergson is willing to discuss a quasi-divine cosmic consciousness that undergirds and activates all of the physical processes in the external universe, then why not also posit that this same superconsciousness manifests within us in the most intimate workings of our subconscious being? Why not assert that the élan vital expresses itself in-and-as the creative fountainhead of our "virtual" or "pure" memory?

To acknowledge that a superconscious awareness/power is operative within our depths does not necessarily negate each person's lived experience of particularity and uniqueness, nor does it diminish the value of our conscious experience of individual freedom and choice. It is not as if we have to philosophically choose between either some sort of all-consuming monistic Oneness which obliterates any and all differences, or a universe composed of a collection of isolated, atomistic parts, cut off from any deeper connection to something greater. A Bergsonian worldview is essentially both/and—it stresses that both oneness and manyness continually coexist, that ceaseless change is present in and through underlying continuity.

From this perspective, therefore, it is quite possible, and indeed likely, that we are simultaneously human and (in a way that is hidden to most of us) divine. And as we will see later, in the all-too-brief discussion of Bergson's final text, *The Two Sources of Morality and Religion*, Bergson himself posits that the evolutionary thrust of the universe is moving humanity in the direction of waking up to this subconscious connection to divinity. For him, the various mystics and saints of different traditions are, in fact, harbingers of a new species of human beings, those individuals who have become most fully themselves by intuitively and consciously aligning themselves, moment to moment, with the élan vital.

27

BERGSON AND
NON-ORDINARY EXPERIENCES

RUMINATION: A NEO-BERGSONIAN
UNDERSTANDING OF NON-ORDINARY EXPERIENCES

According to Bergson, our day-to-day experience of the world is continually shaped, under the surface of our conscious awareness, by our ongoing choice to focus on and respond to only a very limited "amount" of the universal flux that surrounds and interpenetrates us. We therefore perceive and interpret only those aspects of the universe that are necessary in order to act in any given situation. But if this is the case, if our predominant mode of attunement with the world and each other is pragmatic, then it becomes *possible that numerous other worlds of experience exist.*[1] Bergson addresses this possibility in these remarkable lines:

> Nothing would prevent other worlds corresponding to another choice, from existing with it in the same place and the same time: in this way twenty different broadcasting stations throw out simultaneously twenty different concerts which coexist without any one of them mingling its sounds with the music of another, each one being heard, complete and alone, in the apparatus which has chosen for its reception the wavelength of that particular station. (*CM* 69–70)

In these lines, we have what I call Bergson's "radio reception theory of consciousness." From this perspective, our everyday mundane level of consciousness is simply one "channel" out of theoretically unlimited alternate possibilities, a "channel" of consciousness whose function is simply to play the "music" that is appropriate to our day-to-day practical functioning in the physical world. According to Bergson, there are countless "planes" or, if you will, "channels" of durée. This fascinating theory that countless different worlds might well concurrently coexist with our own, each of which can be accessed by a corresponding quality of inner receptivity, offers a fertile theoretical framework from which to understand the genesis of various paranormal and religious phenomena, that is, phenomena that ordinarily pass above or below our pragmatic experience but which are neither unreal, nor, with the right "tuning," inaccessible to experience.

From a Bergsonian perspective, we can postulate that the experiences that fill the pages of religious texts and ethnographies (e.g., telepathy, clairvoyance, mediumship, visionary encounters, and so on) are moments when, for a variety of reasons, individuals "change channels" and tune into dimensions of reality with which they are already connected subconsciously.[2] Perhaps, as Bergson speculates, these types of experiences arise if and when the "mechanisms" which are "expressly designed to screen" the enormous flood of information we receive from the universe stopped functioning effectively. If this were to happen, then the "door which they kept shut" would be partially opened, thereby letting in levels of information that would normally be excluded from our more mundane awareness (TS 315).

When attempting to grasp Bergson's etiology of paranormal phenomena, it is crucial to recognize that, according to Bergson, our brains are not designed to simply screen out the vast majority of the perceptions that together make up our physical universe. They also screen out a concurrent, perhaps even more extensive, torrent of coexisting, interpenetrating memories, thoughts, and feelings. To a certain extent these subconscious memories, thoughts, and feelings correlate with our personal biography. However, Bergson also postulates that some of what we remember, think, and feel may in fact originate from minds other than our own. Bergson emphasizes that our minds, in a way that is far more pronounced than matter, overlap and interpenetrate each other—and in fact transcend spatial boundaries altogether.[3] (As we have seen, Bergson argues, quite explicitly, that because consciousness is not spatial in nature, it is incorrect to think that our memories and thoughts are confined within the physical structure of our brain). This freedom from spatial limitations means that it is not at all clear where, for instance, my mind ends and yours begins. (Even the need to measure and determine such boundaries itself betrays a deeply rooted spatial orientation.) Bergson suggests, therefore, that it is quite possible that our minds are continually blending and overlapping with other minds (perhaps even nonhuman minds) in a reciprocal flow of mental information below the surface of our awareness.

Bergson notes that "if such intercommunication exists, nature will have taken precautions to render it harmless, and most likely certain mechanisms are specially charged with the duty of throwing back, into the unconscious, images so introduced" (*ME* 97). As Gunter points out, it would be "literally unthinkable" to have to function in a world where we had to deal, not only with our own mind, but also with the thoughts and feelings and memories of others. Therefore, it is crucial that our "brains and sense organs . . . function with respect to any supposed 'psi' phenomena . . . in the same way that they function with regard to our physical surroundings: they must exclude, and simplify, making concentration on ordinary problems possible."[4]

Nonetheless, according to Bergson, it is quite likely that telepathic communication between minds still does take place "under the radar" almost continuously, not just for especially gifted psychics, but for everyone (in much the same way that radio or television waves are ubiquitous). However, for most of us, most of the time, this telepathic awareness does not rise to the surface of consciousness, primarily because our brains (and I would add a variety of psychological defense structures) prevent us from being overwhelmed with this mostly extraneous information. Even so, Bergson goes on to suggest that it is quite possible that certain thoughts, memories, images, or feelings from other minds might occasionally manage, for various reasons, to slip past these physical and psychological mechanisms.

Extending and applying this Bergsonian insight, I would argue that our own tacit assumption of "how much" of the information (both physical and nonphysical) that passes under the surface of conscious awareness is "permitted" to slip past the filter of our brains is itself profoundly shaped by a complex set of cultural and historical factors. Clearly, non-Western cultures (and even certain segments of Western culture) both now and in other periods of history have had profoundly different assumptions as to what is "allowed" to enter into conscious awareness. In fact, I would argue that spiritual techniques, such as meditative practices, chanting, contemplative prayer, fasting, dancing, prolonged periods of silence, ingestion of psychoactive substances, and so on, are actually various ways in which individuals in numerous cultures have attempted consciously to nurture the capacity to open themselves up to "quantities" (and perhaps more importantly *qualities*) of information present below the surface of awareness that many of us in the West might reject, a priori, as either irrelevant or delusive.

This neo-Bergsonian "filter" or "radio reception" model of consciousness can help us understand a variety of phenomena that have been frequently examined by psychologists, anthropologists, and scholars of religious studies. If we start from this neo-Bergsonian perspective, it becomes possible to take seriously the numerous claims made by a variety of mystics, visionaries, and shamans throughout history and in numerous cultures, for example, the claim that spiritual beings have come to them in their dreams and visions or conversely the claim that these dreamers/visionaries have traveled to nonphysical worlds and have had powerful interactions with spiritual beings. Seen from a neo-Bergson-ian point of view, these types of transformative spiritual experiences no longer have to be understood, as numerous theorists have claimed in the past, as evidence of psychological instability (at least in many, if not most cases). They also do not automatically have to be regarded as the meaningless result of the mechanical neurological activity within the brain, nor do they have to be seen as nothing more than the sum total of the psychological, economic, and cultural factors at work within an individual.

Rather, what this neo-Bergsonian point of view allows us to do is to note that, while we need to give careful attention to physiological, psychological, economic, and cultural factors in understanding the genesis of these types of experiences, we can *also* posit that there could be transpersonal, transcultural, transhistorical factors at work as well. To the extent that these experiences always appear in-and-through the various strata of a person's memory, we need to acknowledge the numerous ways in which these experiences are inevitably shaped by numerous psychological, historical, and cultural influences. However, coming from this neo-Bergsonian standpoint, we can also argue that there might well be levels of consciousness that, while interpenetrating our own, also transcend our normal sense of self. It is possible that our own subconscious may well overlap with countless "higher" and more inclusive "superconscious strata" of awareness and volition; strata that are simultaneously "self" and "other," strata of consciousness that we typically ignore or filter out of our daily conscious awareness, but that nonetheless might well occasionally manifest themselves powerfully within the psyches of mystics, shamans, and visionaries; levels of consciousness that while interpenetrating our own, might well also possess their own ontological distinctiveness and agency.

Giving theoretical weight to these levels of consciousness allows scholars of religious studies (and cultural anthropologists as well as anyone else who is interested in better understanding the origin and dynamics of powerful mystical and religious experiences) to integrate and harmonize two important, albeit often opposing, tasks: to honor the "outsider" social-scientific explanatory theories of religious life, while also respecting the claims made from the "insider" point of view, which invariably takes for granted that these types of experiences emerge from real encounters with real spiritual beings—spiritual beings who live in alternate dimensions of reality, but who can and do interact with our own more mundane level of existence.

This alternative "gnostic" way of approaching religious and mystical experiences (a term I borrow from Jeffrey Kripal's work) is difficult to do well, in that it attempts to knit together highly reductive explanatory systems with modes of understanding that dramatically challenge many of the most fundamental assumptions upon which our post-Enlightenment worldview is based.[5] In the past, when paranormal and religious phenomena have been examined from the context of an Enlightenment mindset, it was often the case that these types of "non-ordinary" events were frequently ignored, or were dismissed as superstitious relics of backward, irrational cultures, or were reduced to nothing more than a conflux of various psychological, sociological, cultural, economic, or physiological forces. Given the fact that many (if not most) of the Enlightenment (and post-Enlightenment) theorists of religion assumed a classical Newtonian physics and tended to have internalized a highly positivistic and/or rationalistic set of presuppositions, and also typically understood the universe from either a Cartesian or materialistic point of view, these reductive explanations of paranormal and religious phenomena made quite a bit of sense. In many ways, it is understandable that someone who takes for granted a Cartesian separation of mind and matter as well as a Newtonian fracturing of the universe into a multitude of solid objects "lawfully" interacting in space, would consider most, if not all, narratives of paranormal experiences to be evidence of irrationality, delusion, and/or pathology. However, given a different set of foundational assumptions about the nature of external reality and the nature of the psyche, we can easily begin to understand these types of "atypical" phenomena in much more nonreductive (albeit equally complex and sophisticated) ways.

A neo-Bergsonian understanding of non-ordinary experiences allows us to claim that many (if not most) paranormal phenomena are decidedly not delusions or superstitious nonsense; in fact, we can argue that they might well be manifestations of a *more* profound, *more* inclusive quality of perception (or at the very least a level of perception that is an equally valid and valuable alternative to our more prosaic modes of experience). If Bergson is correct, if we are indeed, beneath the surface of our ordinary awareness, continually connected with the entire universe; if the apparent clear-cut separation between objects is not ontologically real, but instead is created by the filtering mechanisms of the brain as well as by unconscious, deeply engrained patterns of memory and belief, then perhaps different spiritual disciplines (e.g., chanting, fasting, meditation, dancing, ritualized ingestion of sacred plants, and so on) simply serve to open up the inner floodgates in a ritually controlled and culturally sanctioned fashion, allowing practitioners to more easily and effectively absorb and integrate the powerful information that is pouring into them from different currents of the ocean of the ever-changing images that make up the universe as we know it.[6] Perhaps, therefore, many religious/mystical/visionary experiences are indications that it is possible to see (and to know) *more*, and are perhaps even indications that we can see and know *better*, than is typically possible from within the context of our everyday level of consciousness.

If Bergson's vision is correct, then it should be the case that if we were able, through sheer hard work or innate ability, to concentrate the previously scattered and diffuse levels of our thought, will, desire, and attention to a single, steady, intensely focused "direction," and/or if we were able to discipline our mind so that we could open up to physical and mental levels of connection to the universe that had been previously filtered from our consciousness, then we should be able (to a greater or lesser degree) to receive information that is unavailable to our senses about what is happening either far away or in the minds of other beings (i.e., clairvoyance and telepathy should be possible).[7] Given this same set of assumptions (assumptions that I would suggest underlie many if not most spiritual/mystical traditions) then we should also be able to create purposeful changes in our physical world (i.e., a range of "magical" phenomena and healing abilities should be possible).

Scholars of religious studies are well aware that these types of "magical" or "supernormal" experiences or events have frequently been described (and often consciously cultivated) by a variety of mystics, shamans, saints, and healers throughout our history on this planet.[8] However, all too often, these claims have been dismissed or condemned by many of these same academics (a reaction that I would argue is engendered at least in part due to the influence of the internalization of our culture's powerfully affirmed and often taken-for-granted naturalistic or mechanistic belief systems). A neo-Bergsonian perspective offers us another alternative.

A neo-Bergsonian perspective, for instance, allows us to reconsider the validity of the claims made by mesmerists in the late nineteenth century that individuals who have opened themselves via a profound trance state to a deeply felt connection to the healing power and presence of the Infinite can heal a multitude of previously incurable diseases in others. This perspective also, for instance, opens us to the possibility that the disciplined practice of Taoist visualization techniques might actually cultivate the numerous paranormal abilities that their scriptures describe (e.g., the ability to see inside the body of another; the ability to travel nonphysically to faraway places and/or to other dimensions of reality; and so forth). If this neo-Bergsonian vision is correct, then these claims as well as a host of others would all need to be reevaluated.

I think that it is also important to emphasize that it is not only the more "spectacular" forms of paranormal and/or religious experience that can be reevaluated from a neo-Bergsonian framework. This perspective can also account for a variety of seemingly more prosaic levels of intuitive awareness as well, modes of experience that frequently occur within many of us, but which we often choose to ignore or deny.

I know for myself that this theoretical framework helps me to understand, for example, the numerous times in which, while working on this book, I would suddenly wake up in the middle of the night, only to watch amazed and bemused (although also a bit dismayed due to my lack of sleep) as some unknown source within my own depths, after apparently having noted insights and connections that my conscious self had overlooked, would release an ongoing stream of insistent, almost electric ideas into my conscious awareness. During those nights of inspiration, it seemed to me that this "otherness" within (which was also, importantly, a "me-ness" as well) had the most important task; that is, "it" had the responsibility of doing the actual creative work. As for my semiconscious, only half-awake egoic self, "its" job was primarily to pay attention to this flood of realizations that had somewhere been germinating deep within me and to periodically jot them down before they were forgotten.[9]

From the point of view of Bergson's "radio reception" theory, we can say that our intuitive insights, while not inevitably accurate, are also not simply psychological in nature, but rather have a deeper ontological dimension as well. If Bergson is correct, if our selfhood/identity really is an ongoing project rather than a pre-given, static nugget of soul within us; if we really are, under the surface of our conscious awareness, much more open to the currents of thoughts, feelings, and memories of those that surround us than we typically imagine, then we will inevitably be affected, for good or ill, by the prejudices, hatreds, fears, loves, joys, enthusiasm, and wisdom of those around us. If we can stop thinking that our brain produces our thoughts and feelings and can realize, instead, that it is a highly sophisticated receiver (and transmitter) of various mental phenomena, then we can understand that it is not abnormal but, in fact, should be expected that to a greater or lesser degree we can "pick up" or "tune into" or "resonate with" the thoughts, feelings, desires, inspirations, intuitions, and even sensations of other beings.[10]

This neo-Bergsonian point of view allows us to legitimately claim that our sense that someone is sexually attracted to us (or conversely, the sense of danger or wrongness that we pick up from someone) is not irrational, nor is it simply based on subtle bodily cues, but instead may well be rooted in an accurate perception of what is actually occurring under the surface of our normal sensory perceptions. This neo-Bergsonian perspective also gives us a framework from which to suggest that perhaps something more than simply quirks of our psychology underlie those trance-like moments when we are composing a song, or are painting a picture, or are playing the piano, or are writing a story and it seems as if something or someone else is working in and through us: perhaps we are in truth inspired by some deeper strata of the universe (and/or deeper levels of our selfhood). Similarly: perhaps the subtle awareness of a dearly loved, but deceased relative watching over and protecting and guiding us is not simply a wish fulfillment rooted in unresolved grief; perhaps our empathetic feelings about our pets or even wild animals are not subjective anthropomorphic projections unto other species, but actually reflect a genuine, albeit muted, awareness of a deeper underlying ontological connection with these beings; perhaps all of these phenomena, in actuality, are varieties of ways in which we are tuning into and acknowledging the flow of subliminal information that we constantly

receive from the mysterious universe that surrounds and interpenetrates us, but
which we (for a variety of evolutionary, cultural, and psychological reasons) typically ignore or choose not to see.

If we can begin to let go of the idea that we are bounded, atomistic, billiard
balls of dead matter that bump against each other in mechanistically predictable
ways; if we can begin, instead, to view ourselves as something closer to a relatively stable whirlpool in a surging sea of consciousness; if we can begin to see
ourselves as a dynamic yet cohesive, utterly unique, patterning of consciousness
that is open to influxes from other configurations of consciousness (of perhaps
different "densities"), then it also becomes increasingly possible to make sense of
numerous sociological phenomena that might previously have been exceedingly
puzzling, for example, the underlying dynamics of crowd contagion, mob hyste-
ria, and ritual effervescence (as well as a host of more overtly "psychological"
phenomena, such as empathy, transference, and countertransference).

This neo-Bergsonian perspective would also suggest that the Buddhists (and
the Hindus, and the Christians, and so on) are correct when they insist that the
quality of the company that we keep is crucial to our spiritual (and psychological) well-being (especially if we expand the notion of "keeping good company"
to include the books we read, the movies we watch, the events that we participate in, and so on). Perhaps we really are viscerally affected by others; perhaps
we really are uplifted (and even healed) by the prayers and good wishes and
hopes of those that surround us. Conversely, perhaps we actually are influenced
under the surface and to various degrees by the fears and anger and despair of
the people with whom we interact.

I would also suggest that it is quite likely that an unconscious fear of being
"overwhelmed" by what is streaming into us moment by moment may be at
least one factor in the complex codes of pollution and purity that have been set
up by many religious traditions. Perhaps the various taboos and castes and clans
come about (again at least in part) due to the unconscious desire to create more
secure boundaries between "us" and "them"; perhaps these social structures are
erected to a certain extent due to the desire to "protect" ourselves from the
seemingly invasive "otherness" of what we are tacitly sensing both around and
within ourselves.

Nonetheless, even if these religious structures do, in fact, emerge (at least
partially) as defensive reactions against seemingly invasive currents of otherness,
I would suggest that a neo-Bergsonian awareness of our porous boundaries need
not (and in fact, should not) lead us to the fear-based desire to shore up our
defenses even more; it should not encourage us to work harder to shield ourselves even more effectively from others. We do not have to choose between
either a blasted-open, fragmented, overwhelmed, and chaotic self or a sealed up,
thick-walled, isolated, closed-hearted, and deeply lonely self. We do not have to
think that we are either powerless pawns of a multitude of influences pouring

into us from all sides or that we are utterly autonomous, clearly defined, egoic agents making crisp logical decisions. Instead, over time we can begin to viscerally experience that there is a depth within us; we can slowly begin to open ourselves up to the felt sense that we are at all times resting in, and inextricably connected to and moving in, vaster, deeper, and freer dimensions of consciousness; we can begin little by little to realize that underneath our typical day-to-day awareness there are dimensions of vastness, love, presence, and power that we might have hardly dared to hope exist.

However, as Bergson himself would doubtless be the first to admit, it also cannot be denied that, at least in certain instances, the opening of the inner floodgates might well produce less than positive consequences. Although Bergson himself does not explicitly address this issue, I would postulate that many forms of mental illness (as well as various types of negative possession states) could well be the result, at least partially, of an inability to cope with the torrent of incoming information from various strata (both "physical" and "mental") of the cosmic flux that interacts, in destructive ways, with a person's immature or distorted psychological structures. Perhaps certain forms of mental illness occur when, due to a complex series of physical, social, and emotional reasons, a person's brain and psychological defense mechanisms are no longer able to screen out a sufficient amount of the incoming torrent of information that continually pours into us all, leading to a variety of maladaptive attempts to cope with this "too-much-ness."

Maybe some of the individuals suffering from psychosis really are hearing voices, really are seeing visions, really are feeling powerful "divine" surges of mysterious energy, but these voices, these visions, these pulses of energy are not only interpreted via the lens of their personal, painful history, but more radically are *shaped* by that history into the individual's felt experience of persecutory voices, frightening visions, and overwhelming currents of energy. Maybe these individuals really are plugged into something that is extremely powerful; maybe they actually (at least potentially and under the surface) are "tuning into" nonphysical beings; maybe they actually can pick up on the feelings and thoughts of others. Unfortunately, however, due to a complex conjunction of physiological problems, environmental stressors, and psychological history, the fragile defense structures of these individuals, unlike other arguably more spiritually developed individuals, such as mystics, saints, and shamans, are simply not prepared to handle the levels of consciousness and energy that come into their systems—and/or the prism of their psychological matrix (sadly) refracts these currents of awareness in highly distorted and problematic ways.[11]

Furthermore, on an even more speculative note, I would argue that there is no a priori reason to restrict the etiology of mental illness and/or negative possessions to an inability to screen out sufficient amounts of this subconscious influx. It is also possible (as many if not most non-Western cultures and premodern

Western cultures have insisted) that ontologically distinct transphysical beings might well hypothetically exist in the "realms" of consciousness outside the scope of our everyday awareness, and it is equally possible that not all of these beings are uniformly benevolent. The unseen levels of reality (both within and around us) may also include beings with different degrees of malevolent or negative intentions (e.g., various types of demonic beings, suffering and confused disincarnate human spirits, and so forth). If a person's psyche is subject to hostile and unwanted incursions from these beings (and/or from human individuals who are consciously or unconsciously sending hostile intentions to this individual) and if the psychic "energies" from these beings attack a person who is physically weakened and/or psychologically damaged or traumatized, then these types of invasive psychic incursions might well be another source of the obsessive, persecutory, fearful, and/or hostile thoughts and perceptions that characterize various forms of mental illness and/or negative possession states.

It is important to remember, however, that these sorts of highly speculative (and purposefully provocative) hypotheses need not completely negate more conventional, social-scientific understandings of the dynamics of mental illness, sorcery, and negative possession states. Adopting a neo-Bergsonian perspective does not mean returning, unreflectively, to a premodern worldview, but rather, would encourage a creative synthesis of various explanatory systems into a more inclusive, more integrated, whole. It is true, nonetheless, that a neo-Bergsonian understanding of the genesis of these types of phenomena would strongly challenge any sort of monolithic and coercive reductionism, and would open the door to a respectful reexamination and reinterpretation of how these phenomena have been understood by other cultures in the not-so-distant past.

I would argue that this neo-Bergsonian way of understanding the relationship between mysticism and mental illness is at least potentially more helpful and illuminating than other more reductive accounts. While a neo-Bergsonian standpoint might well determine that certain types of non-ordinary experiences are indeed potentially destructive or debilitating, this perspective would not automatically assume that any and all paranormal experiences are inherently delusional (as unfortunately often happens when theorists approach these experiences with the tacit and often unexamined metaphysical belief that other dimensions of reality simply do not exist). Instead, if and when this negative assessment was to be made, it could and should emerge only after applying a complex cluster of pragmatic criteria.[12]

Not that long ago, scholars often claimed that the shamans, mystics, or mediums they were studying were deluded and deranged simply because they saw visions, heard voices, and acted in unusual ways. However, if we accept a neo-Bergsonian perspective, we would have the much more difficult task of assessing whether a particular shaman, mystic, or medium is mentally ill (or conversely whether the shaman/mystic/medium is psychologically mature, socially effective, and spiritually powerful) by noting a variety of pragmatic factors, factors that at least tacitly help to influence how shamans/mystics/mediums are assessed by those from within their own culture: Is she or he actually successful, at least for the most part, in the curing sessions that take place? Does this individual, via her or his trance states, typically manage to relay accurate and helpful information?[13] Is she or he in-and-through her or his alternate state of consciousness able to find game for their tribe or able to discover where a lost/stolen item is located, or able to serve as an agent for reconciliation within the strained social matrix of their community? Are the songs, poems, and stories that are "received" by these individuals aesthetically beautiful and/or philosophically profound and/or relevant? If these sorts of putatively positive events regularly occur (and there is bountiful anecdotal evidence that indicates that they do indeed often take place), then unless we have an a priori conviction that shamans/mystics/mediums are deluded or that spiritual levels of reality are by definition illegitimate, then it appears we have every right to argue that these individuals are not only *not* delusional, but that they are in fact frequently exemplars of highly positive personal and social qualities, qualities that we might do well to cultivate (at least to a certain extent) within ourselves.

Admittedly, if the lives of shamans/mystics/mediums are examined carefully, we frequently see indications, especially in the early phases of their careers, that they have difficulty in navigating the complexities of day-to-day existence. From a neo-Bergsonian perspective, however, this initial disorientation is quite understandable, in that the neophyte shaman/mystic/medium would be seen as having to adjust, often quite suddenly, to an influx of vast, previously hidden dimensions of consciousness into their mundane awareness. However, I would suggest that there is also ample evidence that, given enough time in a supportive context (e.g., apprenticeships with more advanced shamans or training in a monastic environment with spiritually mature elders) that many (if not most) of these individuals can and do successfully integrate these deeper/vaster dimensions of consciousness into their own personal level of awareness. In fact, this ability to attune themselves harmoniously to other levels of consciousness is, at least arguably, one reason why many mystics (and shamans and other visionaries) eventually manage to become highly effective, highly creative, highly charismatic healers, teachers, counselors, leaders, and catalysts of cultural change.

Extending Bergson's argument somewhat, I would suggest that it is quite possible that the contagious, persuasive, transformative power (i.e., the charisma) of the saints, mystics, and shamans may not simply be reducible to effective public-speaking skills or to a highly honed ability to manipulate others and/or their public image, or to the capacity to play on the gullibility and naïveté of their followers/clients. Instead, if we begin to open up to the possibility that each of us is not in actuality a clearly bounded (albeit enormously complex) quasi-mechanical physical mass, but instead is an even more complex, highly dynamic, interactive vortex of varying rhythms of consciousness (some of which make up our living bodies), then we can begin to understand that there might well be an ontological basis for charisma in all of its various forms (e.g., healing, prophecy, reconciliation, leadership, teaching, etc.). Some people might simply be more open, more tapped into "higher" or "more evolved" dimensions of reality. Some people may in fact be more attuned with the evolutionary conscious energy of the cosmos, may in fact be more "transparent" in that they allow more of this élan vital to flow through them with less distortion, less obstructions, than others can presently allow.

Bergson claims (correctly I would argue) in the *Two Sources* that certain select individuals (i.e., the saints and mystics, and I would add, the shamans and mediums of various traditions) have managed to "open up the valve" within them that normally keeps most of us cut off from our innate connection to this cosmic consciousness—this universal life force, this divine evolutionary impetus. Bergson suggests that, in their own lives, they demonstrate that it is not only possible, but highly worthwhile to be plugged into a matrix of god-like potentiality, creativity, and love. (In the *Two Sources*, based on his examination of mysticism, Bergson claims—unlike in *Creative Evolution*—that love is an essential aspect of the élan vital.)

Opening up to these subliminal levels of our being, aligning ourselves more and more with the cosmic élan that is the source of our creativity, our joy, our love, our deepest and truest insights, need not be seen as a submission to an alien other, nor as a way to dissolve our uniqueness into an ocean of universal sameness. Instead, nurturing our attunement with this evolutionary cosmic power can be understood as how we can begin to discover, within our own experience, that the taproot of our self plunges into the beating, ever-new heart of all that is; it can be a way for us to begin to transform ourselves each in our own way into modern-day mystics and visionaries.

In *The Two Sources*, Bergson speaks at length about the consciousness of the mystics.[14] (While Bergson primarily focuses on Christian mystics, I would argue that genuine mysticism is not limited to any one religious tradition.)[15] In Bergson's eyes, the mystics are those individuals who have succeeded in establishing "a contact," a "partial coincidence, with the creative effort [of life]," an effort that is "of God, if it is not God himself" (*TS* 220). The mystics are those individuals who have developed their intuitive connection to the cosmic currents of life to the highest degree imaginable. Bergson writes that as the mystics give themselves more and more freely to the "irresistible impulse," to the "boundless impetus" that they discover in their depths, their awareness plunges into "a superabundance of life" and they are able, in spite of their apparent outer weakness, to accomplish amazing feats (*TS* 232). He suggests that, increasingly guided from within by "an innate knowledge" that comes from their intuitive attunement with the divine, the mystics are prompted moment-to-moment as to "the step to be taken, the decisive act" (*TS* 232). Then, having dissolved within themselves the distinction between acting and being acted upon, these mystics are able to put forth "a vast expenditure of energy"; however, they rarely seem to tire because "this energy is supplied as it is required" and all they have to do is to open themselves to that "superabundance of vitality" that "flows from a spring which is the very source of life" (*TS* 232).

According to Bergson, these mystics, even while remaining individuals, have transcended the "limitations imposed on the species by its material nature" and in this way, in-and-through their own lives, they continue and extend the creative divine activity (*TS* 220). Bergson suggests that if all of us could somehow soar as high as these mystics, then "nature would not have stopped at the human species," for individuals who have transformed themselves in this way are in actuality more than human (*TS* 213). Bergson argues that, through their example, these mystics have "blazed a trail" that we may all someday walk; by taking this journey into the fountainhead of their own consciousness, they have shown all of us the potentials that lie dormant within (*TS* 258). Bergson claims that, through their love and their profound insights, these mystics have done what others could not do—that is, they have helped to catalyze "a radical transformation of humanity" (*TS* 239). In-and-through their own spiritual development, they have assisted in the evolutionary process of the cosmos, an evolutionary development in which the divine seeks "to create creators" (*TS* 255). According to Bergson, each of these mystics, each in his or her own way, has helped to create "a divine humanity" (*TS* 239). By doing so, as the final sentence of *The Two Sources* notes, they have helped to fulfill "the essential function of the universe" which is nothing less than "the making of gods" (*TS* 317)—not gods as omniscient, omnipotent divine beings, but rather gods as human beings who have opened themselves fully to their divine source and are therefore able to manifest, with little or no impediment, the creativity, vitality, freedom, and love that is their true nature and birthright.[16]

BERGSON'S PARTICIPATION IN "PSYCHICAL RESEARCH"

My attempts to apply Bergson's "filter" theory to a variety of non-ordinary phenomena might seem surprising to those scholars who are primarily familiar with Bergson in-and-through the current philosophical fascination with the thought of Gilles Deleuze. (Deleuze strongly deemphasizes the "spiritual" aspects of Bergson's work, as do many other recent scholars of Bergson's thought.)[17] However, it is by no means difficult to connect Bergson's work in *Matter and Memory* to his interest in paranormal phenomena. As Gunter points out:

It may seem a long way from the theories of *Matter and Memory* to the problems of parapsychology, but the two are in fact closely related. Bergson's concept of mind-body relations, with its "filter" theory of perception and its supposition that nature everywhere "interpenetrates," give rise quite naturally to a theory both of how "psi phenomena" are possible and why we are ordinarily unaware of them.[18]

Similarly, R. C. Grogin, in his brilliant analysis of the creative interplay between Bergson and the interest in occultism and psychical research in pre–World War I France, argues that "*Matter and Memory* was not merely a negative attack on the mechanistic orthodoxies of the nineteenth century"; instead, "the real theme of *Matter and Memory*" is the reality of paranormal phenomena, such as telepathy and the survival of consciousness after death.[19] (I think that Grogin is mistaken in this claim, given that, as we will see further on, Bergson's interest in such phenomena began after the publication of *Matter and Memory*. However, it is clear that the metaphysics of *Matter and Memory* offers a fertile framework for understanding non-ordinary phenomena.)

In the latter decades of his life, Bergson became increasingly interested in understanding the genesis of these non-ordinary modes of consciousness. This theoretical interest was neither peripheral nor passing. Bergson worked closely for many years with several well-known scholars and scientists who studied psi phenomena in the late nineteenth century and the early twentieth century: his colleague Pierre Janet at the Collège de France; Théodule Ribot and Charles Richet at the Sorbonne; and William James in America. He also worked more obliquely with thinkers such as Frederic Myers, Hans Driesch, Sigmund Freud, and Carl Jung. According to Grogin, these "psychical researchers" (in addition to Bergson's academic colleagues in philosophy) were the people "who understood him best. . . . They worked along parallel lines with Bergson, rubbed shoulders with him at conferences, discussion groups and laboratories, and were preoccupied with the same problems that he grappled with. They always recognized that Bergson was one of theirs—that he was one of the truly original theoreticians of psychical research."[20] (Grogin also points out that members of Bergson's own family were very interested in the occult. For instance, Bergson's sister Mina was married to Samuel MacGregor Mathers, who in the 1890s was the leader of the Order of the Golden Dawn, arguably the most famous occult organization of the period. Mina herself apparently "was instrumental in initiating" W. B. Yeats, the most well-known member of the order, and "caused something of a sensation in Paris," when she and other members of the order "staged a theatrical performance at La Bodinière Theatre, called the Rite of Isis.")[21]

Other scholars who are familiar with Bergson's work and life have commented on the overlap between Bergson's philosophy and psi research, and on the degree to which Bergson himself was interested in the paranormal. Bertrand

Méheust, for instance, in his magisterial two-volume study of mesmerism in France, points out that Bergson's interest in paranormal phenomena was an open secret in the society of his time.[22] Not only was he elected the president of the British Society for Psychical Research in 1913, but his presidential address for the society, entitled " 'Phantasms of the Living' and Psychical Research," given in that same year was only one of several (admittedly brief) articles or notes that he published in his lifetime on the subject of psi phenomena.

Bergson's first article on non-ordinary phenomena was, as Leonard Eslick points out, "a skeptical critique of telepathy experiments carried out with hypnotic subjects," that was published in 1886.[23] Bergson's initial skepticism, however, gradually shifted, and by 1900, Bergson decided to join the Institut Psychologique Internationale (or, as it was eventually renamed, the Institut Général Psychologique), a newly formed society dedicated to a careful study of non-ordinary phenomena.[24]

By 1903, in a four-page, rather informal paper published in the *Bulletin de l'Institut général psychologique*, Bergson is clearly curious about how others have examined and tested the fact that some people during séances perceive columns of light and that these columns of light appear to correlate with measurements of high-frequency radiation. In this short piece, as Méheust points out, Bergson is wary of the possibility of deception, yet he also insists that it is crucial to take such phenomena seriously.[25] This attitude of cautious interest in psi phenomena is also evident in another short piece published in 1904 in which Bergson asks questions about the study of changes in the respiration of hypnotic subjects during various stages of hypnosis. This interest continues in Bergson's two-page review of Boirac's *La Psychologie inconnue*, written in 1908, in which he approvingly notes the author's attempts to classify various psi phenomena (including hypnosis).[26]

Perhaps most intriguing, however, is the fact that Bergson participated (in 1905 and 1906) in at least four séances (Grogin claims that it was six) designed to test the alleged telekinesis of Eusapia Palladino, a controversial yet allegedly quite powerful medium of that time. Grogin points out that during these séances, Bergson "witnessed the full gamut of the 'phenomena' that made the medium famous: levitations, table-rapping, furniture-moving, flying objects and flashing lights."[27]

Grogin's assessment draws largely on two pages of extremely terse and cryptic notes published in 1906 that all-too-briefly describe what took place during these séances. While the notes are exceedingly elliptical, it is clear that Bergson was an active participant and that he did indeed witness several mysterious and striking phenomena. For example, during one séance Palladino reported that she felt herself becoming physically lighter and asked that her claim be checked using the scale that, fortunately, was present at the séance. (Her claim was subsequently verified.) During another séance various witnesses (including Bergson and Madame Curie) asserted that they clearly saw a dark arm appear beside a curtain and forcibly touch a man several times on the shoulder. Finally, during yet another séance, in which all of the participants sat around a table with their hands clearly visible on the table top, Palladino asked Bergson, as an outside observer, to closely watch her knees under the séance table—a request that she seemingly made so that it would be clear that she did nothing physically to cause the subsequent phenomena. Bergson, in the interest of science, agreed. Immediately after this request, the séance table rose suddenly into the air, even though another witness asserted that he never let go of Palladino's hand during the entire time that the table was levitating. (Holding the hands of mediums and watching their knees under the table were common, and commonsense, procedures of the time designed to prevent trickery [*M* 673–674]).

From these notes, it is clear that, while Bergson attended relatively few séances with Palladino, he was able to observe, nonetheless, a relatively wide and dramatic range of telekinetic phenomena. Even so, as Méheust emphasizes, Bergson remained deeply divided about these séances. On the one hand, he was convinced in certain respects that Palladino was trying to trick the researchers. On the other hand, he was equally convinced that some of the phenomena that he witnessed were so extraordinary that they resisted any rational explanation.[28] Méheust also points out that, in an interview with George Menuier in 1910 (and Bergson rarely granted interviews), Bergson reiterated his perplexity with the phenomena that he had witnessed during the séances with Palladino, while nonetheless asserting that after examining the various documents published for over twenty-five years on the topic of telepathy he was convinced that there was stronger evidence in favor of telepathy than against it. In fact, as Bergson put it, if he had to bet for or against the reality of telepathy, he would bet in its favor without any hesitation.[29]

"'PHANTASMS OF THE LIVING' AND PSYCHICAL RESEARCH"

Bergson's stature among the wide-ranging group of philosophers, psychologists, and scientists who were interested in researching non-ordinary phenomena in Europe in the early twentieth century is perhaps most clearly indicated by the fact that he was elected the president of the British Society for Psychical Research in 1913. Bergson's attitudes toward non-ordinary phenomena (especially telepathy and clairvoyance), as well as the ways in which he believes that his own philosophical understanding of the mind-body relationship offers at least one potentially helpful way to make sense of their genesis, is clearly enunciated in the presidential address that Bergson gave to the society in London on May 28, 1913: "'Phantasms of the Living' and Psychical Research."

Bergson begins by saying that he is puzzled by the honor that the society has bestowed on him because he "has done nothing to deserve it," in that, as he claims, "it is only by reading" that he knows "anything of the phenomena with which the Society deals" (*ME* 75). This claim, which is itself rather interesting given his experiences with Palladino, becomes even more puzzling when he goes on to assert in this public forum that "I have seen nothing myself, I have examined nothing myself" (*ME* 75). Whether reluctant to reveal his own admittedly rather scanty background in this area or simply demurring modestly to the "ingenuity, the penetration, the patience, the tenacity" that has been shown by those present in the hall while studying psi phenomena, it is clear that Bergson admires those who have persevered in their research, especially in the face of "the prejudices of a great part of the scientific world" (*ME* 75, 76). Bergson clearly opposes these prejudices, pointing out how behind the mockery of those who even refuse to examine critically the evidence for psychical phenomena "there is, present and invisible, a certain metaphysic unconscious of itself,—unconscious and therefore inconsistent, unconscious and therefore incapable of continually remodeling itself on observation and experience as every philosophy worthy of the name must do" (*ME* 77).

Bergson will, later in the talk, offer his own philosophy as a more conscious and therefore more supple and ideally valuable alternative to the taken-for-granted mechanistic materialism that was so prevalent during his day. But before proceeding in this direction, Bergson examines several important methodological issues.

Bergson first asserts (without bothering to give any reasons to support his assertion) that psi phenomena are facts, facts similar to those studied by natural science. For him, these facts are subject to laws and can therefore be repeated again and again, unlike the specificity and particularity of historical facts (e.g., the Battle of Austerlitz) that happen only once and can never repeat themselves. He postulates that, similar to electricity and magnetism, telepathy "is operating at every moment and everywhere, but with too little intensity to be noticed or else in such a way that a cerebral mechanism stops the effect, for our benefit, at the very moment at which it is about to clear the threshold of consciousness" (*ME* 79–80). He also claims that, if and when we finally understand the underlying dynamics of the operation of telepathy, then in much the same way as it is now no longer necessary to wait for a thunderstorm in order to see the effect of electricity, it will no longer be necessary to wait for spontaneous telepathic events, such as the appearance of a "phantasm of the living"—that is, apparitions of individuals, often sick or dying, who appear unexpectedly to friends or loved ones, often miles away, apparitions that were studied in the monumental two-volume work *Phantasms of the Living*, published in 1886, and spearheaded by Edmund Gurney, a founding figure of the Society for Psychical Research.[30]

What Bergson notes, however, is that even though telepathy, to his mind at least, is a lawful and entirely natural phenomenon, nonetheless, it appears that the only way to study it is with "an entirely different method, one which stands midway between that of the historian and that of the magistrate"—that is, a method in which researchers study documents, examine witnesses, assess their reliability, and so forth (*ME* 80). Bergson comments that, after becoming aware of the sheer number of reliable cases and after seeing the care and thoroughness in which these cases were examined, he is "led to believe in telepathy, just as [he] believe[s] in the defeat of the Invincible Armada" (*ME* 81). He admits that this belief has neither "the mathematical certainty" given by a demonstration of the Pythagorean theorem nor the empirical certainty seen in the verification of one of Galileo's laws; however, "it has at least all the certainty which we can obtain in historical or judicial matters" (*ME* 81). Nonetheless, as Bergson notes, this level of evidence is simply not compelling to most scientists. Therefore, as he notes, because "psychical research" is unable to be produced under strict laboratory conditions, it is considered as not only unscientific, but even unreal. (Bergson was actually incorrect in his assertion that paranormal phenomena are unable to be studied experimentally. Even by the time of this talk there had been a number of fascinating experiments, and by the beginning of the twenty-first century, there have been thousands.)

Bergson goes on to give an example of a frequent strategy used by those who are skeptical of the conclusions of psychical research. He describes a dinner party that he attended during which the conversation focused on psi phenomena. An eminent physician at the party offered a story given to him by a woman who he considered to be intelligent and trustworthy. This woman's husband, an officer, was killed in battle. According to the doctor, "at the very moment when the husband fell, the wife had the vision of the scene, a clear vision, in all points conformable to the reality" (*ME* 82). The doctor went on to say that this story may *seem* to be evidence for the existence of telepathy or clairvoyance, but as he went on to note it is important to remember that this was quite likely not the only time that the woman had dreamed that her husband had died—and clearly those other dreams turned out to be false. The physician went on to say, "We notice cases in which the vision turns out to be true, but take no count of the others" (*ME* 83). He concluded that, if we actually took full account of *all* the evidence, then psychical phenomena would be simply understood as the work of coincidence or chance.

Not surprisingly, Bergson disagrees. He comments that after this conversation a young girl said to him that "'It seems to me that the doctor argued wrongly just now'" (*ME* 83). Agreeing with the young girl, Bergson notes that there was indeed a fallacy in the doctor's argument (*ME* 83). According to Bergson, the doctor's fallacy was that he overlooked the specificity of the vision. As Bergson points out, if a painter had, in his imagination, attempted to paint a picture with a level of specificity equal to that of the wife's vision, a picture that showed in minute detail exactly how the real soldiers moved and how they looked, there is absolutely no chance that the painter could succeed in that the scene is "decomposable into an infinity of details all independent of one another" so that "an infinite number of coincidences is needed in order that chance should make a fancied scene the reproduction of a real scene" (ME 84).

Bergson further argues that it is mathematically impossible for a painter to produce an utterly accurate picture of the scene even if, as Bergson points out, "we leave out the coincidence *in time*, that is, the fact that two scenes whose content is identical have chosen for their apparition the same moment" (ME 85). Given this double infinity (so to speak), and given the fact that "the lady who had the vision of a part of a battle was in the situation of that painter" in that "her imagination executed a picture," Bergson is willing to conclude that "if the picture was the reproduction of a real scene, it must, by every necessity, be because she perceived that scene or was in communication with a consciousness that perceived it" (ME 85).

Bergson goes on to claim that, while he has no way to ascertain whether the story that the doctor told was true or false, nonetheless, "if this were proved to me, if I could be sure that even the countenance of one soldier unknown by her, present at the scene, had appeared to her such as it was in reality,—then, even if it should be proved to me that there had been thousands of false visions, and even though there had never been a veridical hallucination except this one," then that would be sufficient to prove the possibility of perceiving objects and events at a distance in a way that our senses cannot normally accomplish (ME 85).[31]

Bergson, drawing upon his "filter theory of consciousness," suggests that it is possible that "we perceive virtually many more things than we perceive actually, and that here, once more, the part that our body plays is that of shutting out from consciousness all that is of no practical interest to us, all that does not lend itself to our action" (ME 95–96). Given this he asks if it is not also possible that "around our normal perception" there is an unconscious "fringe of perceptions" associated with psi phenomena that occasionally enters into our consciousness "in exceptional cases or in predisposed subjects?" (ME 96).

Bergson emphasizes that the experimental method is based on the ability to measure physical phenomena, but as he goes on to note, "it is of the essence of mental things that they do not lend themselves to measurement" (ME 87). For Bergson, consciousness by its very nature is not spatial; hence it cannot be measured. Reiterating much of what he explored earlier in *Matter and Memory*, Bergson argues that "consciousness is not a function of the brain"; therefore, it can and does transcend physical boundaries (ME 93). This freedom from spatial limitations means that it is quite possible that our minds are continually blending and overlapping with other minds in a reciprocal flow of mental information below the surface of our awareness. As Bergson notes: "between different minds there may be continually taking place changes analogous to the phenomena of endosmosis. If such intercommunication exists, nature will have taken precautions to render it harmless, and most likely certain mechanisms are specially charged with the duty of throwing back, into the unconscious, images so introduced" (*ME* 97). However, if this mental "intercommunication" is indeed continually taking place under the surface of our everyday awareness, then he suggests that it is quite possible, even likely, that certain images might occasionally slip past this mechanism, leading to moments of telepathic and clairvoyant knowledge.

It appears, therefore, that Bergson postulates two seemingly distinct ways in which non-ordinary states of consciousness may arise: *either* 1) they surface when the brain is less "successful" than normal at filtering out the countless images of the *physical world* that are ceaselessly flowing through us, *or* 2) they occur when the brain fails to keep our personal consciousness screened off from the underlying flux of overlapping *minds* that is present under the surface of our awareness at every moment. However, it is crucial to recall (as was emphasized earlier) that this seemingly Cartesian division of labor is simply a manifestation of the complexity of Bergson's metaphysical perspective. While Bergson (at least after *Matter and Memory*) acknowledges a *functional* distinction between mind and matter, he also stresses that both mind and matter are simply differing manifestations of a unified (albeit continually changing and intrinsically pluralistic) reality: durée.

Bergson's interest in non-ordinary phenomena did not disappear after 1913. Several decades later, with the publication of *The Two Sources*, Bergson comments that he believes that "telepathic phenomena" have been verified by the "mutual corroboration of thousands of statements which have been collected on the subject" (*TS* 316). He emphasizes that while it is important to be discriminating about what evidence to accept, nonetheless, if only a portion of this evidence were to be accepted as valid, it would have a transforming effect on humanity's willingness to begin to accept the reality of that which it cannot touch or see directly. Bergson admits that the information that we gain from psychical research may well only deal with "the inferior portion" of our consciousness; it may well only focus on "the lowest degree of spirituality" (*TS* 316). Nevertheless, he argues that the acceptance of psi phenomena would help humanity to open up to the possibility of the existence of other levels of spiritual reality as well.

28

BERGSON AND THE AFTERLIFE

BERGSON ON THE SURVIVAL OF CONSCIOUSNESS
AFTER THE DEATH OF THE PHYSICAL BODY

It is clear that Bergson's theories about psi phenomena were integrally linked in his mind with a wide range of related "spiritual" issues. One of the most important of these issues is the possible survival of our consciousness after the death of the physical body. Bergson did not give a lot of concerted theoretical attention to this issue, even though he was for a time the president of an organization (the Society for Psychical Research) that dedicated an enormous amount of time and energy to attempting to do just this. Nonetheless, in "The Soul and the Body," a lecture that he gave in Paris on April 28, 1912, as well as in "'Phantasms of the Living' and Psychical Research," Bergson reveals at least a little of his own understanding about the possibility of the survival of consciousness after the death of the physical body.

For example, in "The Soul and the Body" Bergson notes that, if we agree with his conclusion that the mind is for the most part independent of the brain, then it becomes reasonable to speculate that the "preservation and even intensification of personality are not only possible, but even probable after the disintegration of the body" (*ME* 35). Bergson then expands upon this observation in his presidential address to the SPR later the next year:

> The more we become accustomed to this idea of a consciousness overflowing the organism, the more natural we find it to suppose that the soul survives the body. Were, indeed, the mental molded exactly on the

257

cerebral, were there nothing more in a human mind than what is inscribed in a human brain, we might have to admit that consciousness must share the fate of the body and die with it. But if the facts . . . lead us, on the contrary, to regard the mental life as much more vast than the cerebral life, survival becomes so probable that the burden of proof come to lie on him who denies it rather than on him who affirms it; for the one and only reason we can have for believing in an extinction of consciousness after death is that we see the body become disorganized; and this reason has no longer any value, if the independence of almost the totality of consciousness in regard to the body is also a fact of experience. (*ME* 97–98)

Like his close friend William James, Bergson considers himself an empiricist, but an empiricist of a special kind: a "radical" empiricist. Bergson (like James) argues that it is crucial for us to take seriously, not only the facts revealed to us under controlled laboratory conditions, but also the facts of experience that reveal themselves to us via careful introspection as well as the facts that we can adduce in-and-through an equally careful investigation of the narratives of "nonordinary" experiences, such as intuitions, creative insights, mystical experiences, and the phenomena studied by the psychical researchers of his time (e.g., clairvoyance, telepathy, mediumistic events, and so on). Bergson is adamant that he does not want to take the route taken by those philosophers who, following Plato, simply define the soul as that which is immortal. Instead, in keeping with his colleagues in the Society for Psychical Research, he wants the issue of the survival of consciousness after the death of the physical body to be approached empirically, via experience, so that it can be "progressively, and [yet] always partially, solved" (*TS* 263).

Bergson has his own "best guesses" about the deeper significance of death and what happens to our consciousness after going through this passage. He posits that our consciousness, during the time it spends interwoven with the material world, "is tempering itself like steel and preparing itself for a more efficient action, for an intenser life . . . a life of striving, a need of invention, a creative evolution"—all activities that, to his way of thinking, take place, at least potentially, in the afterlife (*ME* 35). He also imagines that after death we might well rise to the level of the moral plane that we have attained already in this life, in much the same way "as the balloon set free takes the position in the air which its density assigns it" (*ME* 35). Nonetheless, he is quite clear that these musings are only one of many possible scenarios. As an empiricist, he emphasizes that our understanding of the nature of the afterlife should be based only upon "a prolongation and a profound investigation" of the experiences of everyday life, as well as other more non-ordinary experiences (i.e., mystical and psi experiences), and that therefore, "the problem must remain open" (*TS* 264). Bergson is, nonetheless, hopeful in that he believes that in this investigation there is "the possibility of endless progress" (*TS* 264).

RUMINATION: NEO-BERGSONIAN GLIMPSES OF THE AFTERLIFE

In my own musings on what might happen to our consciousness after the death of the physical body, I have been (not surprisingly) deeply impacted by my work on Bergson (as well as William James, and increasingly, Frederic Myers, one of the founders of the Society for Psychical Research). However, before I begin any creative speculations on this issue, I would like to affirm as clearly as possible my strong belief that it is crucial to adhere to theoretical humility when we are discussing the nature of the afterlife. It is problematic enough to claim that we have anything close to a clear and trustworthy understanding of our present earthly existence. Our epistemological modesty, however, has to become even *more* pronounced, I would suggest, whenever we discuss survival after death. We will likely never know for certain what happens after death until it happens to us—even then, I would argue that we will only know what *our* level of postmortem experience reveals. There is no reason to assume that we become omniscient or illusion-free beings after death. Our own postmortem experience might still be only a small part of the picture; it might well be distorted; there might well be countless dimensions of knowledge about post/trans-physical reality available that are out of the reach of our postmortem perceptual abilities—levels of awareness that would only become available to us if we possessed the requisite level of spiritual development/evolution.

I am all in favor of articulating our own vision of what might happen after the death of the physical body—and (like Bergson) I think that it is critical that we attempt to support that vision with evidence from a variety of sources. However, I think that it is crucial always to be aware that much, if not most, of our understanding of what happens after death may well remain shrouded in mystery.

Nonetheless, a keen awareness of the inevitable limitations of our theorizing (as well as the potential for distortion and wishful thinking) does not mean that it is useless to argue vigorously against the reigning materialistic nihilism that is so prevalent and powerful in many subsets of our contemporary culture, or more positively to defend the notion that survival after death is not only possible, but I would claim even likely. In many ways, the following rumination attempts to take on exactly this task.

To begin with, I would like to suggest, along with Bergson, that a close examination of our present quality of consciousness can give us some important clues about the nature of consciousness after the death of the physical body. I think that it is especially useful to acknowledge Bergson's analysis of our ordinary consciousness as a simultaneous co-arising of perpetual difference/change *and* ongoing, seamless continuity. It is crucial to keep both aspects of this para-doxical pairing together.

However, for the moment I would like to focus on the continuity side of the dyad. I would argue, again along with Bergson, that a careful introspective analysis of our moment-to-moment experience demonstrates that there are no gaps, no "holes" in our experience. Rather, in-and-through the continual flux of sheer difference in our consciousness we always discover ceaseless continuity. There is constant change in the *contents* of consciousness, but there are no empty "spaces," no moments, however small, of sheer unconsciousness; in other words, I would argue that consciousness is *not* particulate in nature. (Whitehead and at least some Buddhists, I suggest, are wrong about this.) Instead, I would argue that our own experience reveals that consciousness is a continually present whole, even if it is also always shifting, always flowing.

For instance, I (for one) never experience myself "blipping" in and out of existence. Instead, the transition moments in my awareness—for example, waking up or going to sleep—are more a matter of shifting from one state of awareness to another than moments in which I truly go unconscious. We might think that deep sleep, for example, is a case of sheer unconsciousness, but I would disagree. I worked for several years in a sleep lab. Every time that we would wake someone up when their EEG readings correlated with the stage of deep sleep, the research subjects never reported that their consciousness was simply not there. They never reported any sense of emerging out of an utter blank—a sheer nothingness. Instead, they would typically say that they experi-enced themselves as "drifting," or "floating." In deep sleep, they were typically not aware of their body or of their surroundings. Nonetheless, consciousness was still present. (In fact, for many of them, their consciousness was so vivid that they often had difficulty believing that they had actually been asleep at the moment we woke them up.) I suggest, therefore, that consciousness, as such, is *always* present, even in those moments when it seems to disappear—for example, when we faint, or pass out, or undergo anesthesia. I hypothesize that what we call "unconsciousness" is really an unconsciousness of the external physical world combined with a temporary forgetfulness of the stream of one's own personal memory.

What this ongoing continuity of consciousness suggests (especially when combined with Bergson's highly sophisticated analysis of the continuity of memory on subconscious levels of our being) is that there is no a priori reason to suppose that this continuity, this ceaseless and seamless flowing of our selfhood, will somehow dissolve with the death of the physical body.

This is especially the case if we postulate, along with Bergson, that our mind/memory/consciousness is functionally separate from the body/matter/physicality (even if, as was pointed out earlier, this functional duality is ontologically resolved by Bergson into a dynamic, temporal oneness) *and* if we agree with Bergson (as well as James and Myers) that the brain does not produce consciousness, but rather acts as a type of dynamic filter/receiver/tuner for preexisting wider/deeper states of consciousness. If this is true (and I am convinced that there is good evidence that it is) and if consciousness actually is not dependent upon the brain for its existence, but instead has its own independent, flowing, continuous existence, then it seems to me that after the death of our physical body we should perhaps expect a radical change in the *form* of our consciousness, but not its utter disappearance.

I am also convinced by Bergson's suggestion (echoed, once again, by James and Myers) that reality consists of a multitude of overlapping, interpenetrating, ever-changing "fields" of awareness and that our assumption that reality consists of unchanging, static "things" or "objects" that are separated in space (and are therefore countable and measurable) is simply not correct. I think that the pan-experientialists, the panentheists, the panpsychics are basically correct: the universe is not dead matter, but rather it consists of different degrees of consciousness/life/experience. I consider the universe to be a complex, multidimensional network of ever-changing, overlapping, interpenetrating rhythms of consciousness/experience. In such a universe, I think that it is clear (based, for one, on the mountain of evidence collected by psi researchers) that our boundaries are nowhere near as fixed and clear-cut as we might have thought. While I think that individuality and uniqueness and personality is a crucial aspect of this living universe, I also believe that the seeming solidity of our physical body has convinced us, wrongly, that our self is also similarly bounded, spatial, and contained. I think, instead, that our selfhood is much more porous, much more multidimensional, much more complex and layered, than we might have imagined—and that this multidimensionality is an integral aspect of our selfhood even now, even while we are so strongly identified with our physicality. So I can only imagine how fluid, how overlapping, how freely and creatively intertwined with other fields of existence we will find ourselves after the death of our physical body.

I am also convinced by Bergson's (and again James' and Myers') analysis and defense of the continual creativity and deeply rooted freedom of our consciousness, a creativity and freedom that interacts in fascinating ways with the perhaps more difficult-to-discern freedom and creativity that is inherent in the multitude of levels of reality that we are currently navigating. I suggest that we live in a highly participatory universe, one in which consciousness, while functionally distinct from physical reality, is ontologically always helping to construct and shape the most fundamental levels of experience. If this dynamic, interactive interplay between our own consciousness and the wider/deeper levels of reality is taking place now, while we have a physical body, if our experience is even now powerfully shaped by the interaction between, on the one hand, our thoughts, expectations, memories, and desires, and on the other hand, the streaming flux of the otherness of the reality around us, then why should not the same be true to an even greater extent in the after-death realms of experience? I see no reason to assume that this interactive, universal, creative dynamism disappears simply because of the death and decay of the physical body.

Therefore, it seems quite likely to me that how we envision postmortem existence, the variety of religious beliefs (both conscious and preconscious) that we have about what will happen after death (e.g., reincarnation, sensual heavens, ghostly shadow worlds, merger with God, and so forth), as well as our own conscious and subconscious beliefs about what we deserve and how compassionate or not we believe the "unseen world" to be, will strongly shape the quality and form of our postmortem experience. I do not think that there is just some utterly objective after-death realm of experience "out there" or "up there" waiting for us. Instead, I am convinced that our level of imagination (or lack of it), the audacity of our hopes or the tenacity of our fears, the complex layering of our beliefs (especially our subconscious beliefs and assumptions) will help to create a unique after-death quality of experience for each of us.

I want to be clear, however. I do not think that our postmortem experience will be utterly plastic, that it will be simply subjective. Instead, similar to our current level of experience, I think that our postmortem existence will be a subjective *and* objective *co-created* reality, or more accurately, that it will be a reality in which the subject/object dichotomy itself will be transcended even more completely and obviously than is currently possible on this level of reality. I imagine that after death we will "arrive" in a dimension of reality that has a degree of "otherness," that "pushes back" in a way that is similar to our current level of physical existence; however, this dimension of experience will be powerfully shaped and formed by the ongoing creative continuity of our memories, hopes, fears, beliefs—on both conscious and subconscious levels. What this co-created, participatory notion of after-death experience implies is that our after-death experience will most likely be extremely variable—a variability that the plurality of different cultural beliefs about the afterlife both reflects, and more subtly, helps to shape.

If we do indeed draw to us (or help to shape) the world of our experience after the death of our physical body and if this process is based on the quality of consciousness/heart that we have attained during this lifetime, then it seems that a realization of this fact would underscore the crucial need for us to attempt to shift our own "note" of consciousness, our own "vibratory rate" before death. It seems to me that the more that we take responsibility, right now, before death, for opening our hearts, for aligning ourselves with light, for awakening to our connection with the deepest levels of the cosmos, for creating for ourselves a body of spirit, light, freedom, creativity, compassion, and love, then the more that we will not only be prepared to enter, fully, freely, and consciously into that critical transition between life and death, but that we will also be able to draw to us and help to co-create the most spiritually evolved post-mortem world imaginable.

Obviously, this understanding is highly congruent with the Tibetan Buddhist teachings of the importance of spiritual work in this lifetime in order to prepare to make the most of our entrance into the bardo realms as well as a variety of other alchemical and tantric/mystical perspectives on the relationship between our current spiritual practices and our experience of life after death—teachings that stress that our disciplined attempts to transmute our current experience of this world leads to increased possibilities of freedom, joy, and awareness in the next world (as well as helps to bring transformative energies into this level of existence).[1]

From this perspective, freeing ourselves now, working to change the "note" of our physical/mental/emotional existence at this moment (both for ourselves and for the sake of others) sets a momentum going, creates an overall trajectory that might well help to create a template that will carry on into our postmortem existence. Therefore, if this is true, then we can and should take responsibility for what will happen to us in the other life while we are still in this life—we can and should consciously work to alter ourselves for the better, to work to open our hearts up more fully, to allow ourselves to envision more richly, and to hope more daringly.

In addition, I think that it is critically important as part of our spiritual work that we also learn how to become more and more familiar with the "territory" of out-of-body levels of experience now, before death. Whether we immerse ourselves in shamanic/yogic experiences of "voyaging" in nonphysical, visionary worlds; or practice dream yoga; or explore various visionary realities via the medium of entheogens; or become increasingly attuned to various subtle energies through intensive training in various esoteric programs or spiritual healing schools, I would suggest that consciously opening up to and creating experiences that help us to disentangle ourselves from a literally hide-bound sense of ourselves will almost certainly serve us well in our after-death levels of experience.

I would also add that I am convinced that we are never alone in any of this: that we can and do receive crucial help in this process, whether through initiatory transmissions or influxes of grace, from other more spiritually advanced beings—beings with a higher vibratory rate than our own, beings who are simultaneously (from one perspective) deeper dimensions of our selfhood and (understood from another perspective) have a high degree of ontological "otherness."

I am convinced that these beings, as well as the other worlds that I suggest we access after death (worlds which are simultaneously present right now in other dimensions of reality), are wonderfully, outrageously, wild and weird—and that we are better off admitting this fact upfront, in order that we can just relax into the strange, untamed beauty of it.

However, this openness to being surprised and delighted by the unexpected, this insistence on the creative unpredictability of the afterlife, does not mean that I do not think that we cannot articulate better and more nuanced understandings of what we might well run into after death and how to make the most out of that experience. It seems to me that it is clearly possible to get information as to the nature and quality of non-ordinary states of consciousness; that is, those states of awareness when we are not quite as identified with our physical self as we are in our ordinary life. We can, and I think should, gather data from trance/possession experiences, from narratives of people under anesthesia, from accounts drawn from the spiritualist movement, from research into near-death experiences, from disciplined investigations of memories of past lives, from ethnographic explorations of shamanic journeys or out-of-body experiences, from introspective analyses of experiences with various entheogens, and so on. However, given the inherent, inescapable creativity of the consciousness that I think manifests itself in-and-through this multifaceted universe, we should simply expect that there would be a wide range of what appear to be mutually contradictory indications ("evidence" seems too strong a term) of what might take place after the death of our physical form. All of this data may simply allow us to access different vantage points on the shimmering variability and mutability of the afterlife. Therefore, I suggest that we should applaud this proliferating pluralism of perspectives rather than become discouraged at its tangled, twisted profusion.

I would also like to suggest that, if we want to learn more about the possible textures and "mechanics" of the after-death experience, we might want to look more carefully into dreaming. It seems to me that dreams are a shamefully neglected source of hypotheses about life after the death of the physical body. I think that the manner in which our culture understands dreams, either as a purely random and meaningless blowing off of steam from overheated neurons or as a purely psychological realm of symbolic experience, is highly truncated and restrictive. At the very least, we have to acknowledge that many other cultures (and even our own at earlier stages in its history) have certainly understood dreams differently, have claimed that powerful, vivid dreams can and often do give us trustworthy, albeit not complete, information about alternate, nonphysical worlds (as well as often highly specific, useful, and veridical information about this world).[2]

As I pointed out in an earlier chapter, it is striking to me that each of us has an experience, every night, of consciousness creating effortlessly and ceaselessly, with no conscious intention on our part, extremely elaborate, intricate, detailed, and (relatively) cohesive worlds. In these "inner" worlds (because who knows "where" these worlds actually are), we are certainly not subject to the same spatial/temporal limitations as in our normal daily physical experience. In our dreams, we have created a world that, perhaps like postmortem existence, is rather fluid—a world that seems to be more overtly responsive to our desires and fears and expectations than our current physical level of existence. In our dream worlds, the subject/object boundaries are also not as clear-cut as they appear to be in our waking existence. Dream landscapes, although they certainly seem "physical" when we are in the dream itself, are in truth made of our own consciousness. We (at least subconsciously) are the ones who have created this dream world—and in order to make our way in and through it, we at times have also created for ourselves a clearly formed "dream-body" (even if at other times, we seem bodiless, more like a formless observer, an invisible "point of view" witnessing the unfolding of events). Yet, in neither situation are we completely restricted to the point of view of an observer (whether embodied or not), since the world that we are observing and interacting with is simultaneously "us"—in that it is made of our own consciousness. Given this rather odd state of affairs, it does not seem a stretch to hypothesize that perhaps one task that our dream experience takes on is to train ourselves to become accustomed to postmortem levels of existence—modes of existence that, as I mentioned previously, may also be nonphysical, may also possess a fluid subject/object interplay, may also be the result of the god-like creativity of consciousness itself.

I want to emphasize, however, that I do not think that dreams *only* serve to prepare us for death—far from it. Many times dreams seem to be ways for us to work through, in a less restricted way than is possible in our waking experience, a whole panoply of obscure desires, unacknowledged fears, hidden regrets, and so on. Dreams, it seems to me, give us the permission (and ability) to try on and to go through a multitude of situations, as well as offer us (at least on some level of our being) the opportunity to learn and to grow from these experiences—not all of them pleasant or comfortable, by any means.

In the past, I would typically cringe when I privately speculated on the possible affinity between dream experience and postmortem experience. I did not like considering that scenario. To be trapped in a perpetual dream experience seemed to me to be at best a mode of existence that was clearly second-rate and nowhere near as satisfactory and fulfilling as waking experience and at worst almost a quasi-hellish purgatory, with (at times) its randomness and seeming chaos, its discomfort and overall sense of incompleteness.

However, I have begun to wonder whether my physicality itself, as a type of "anchor" in this world of matter, may well be at least partially responsible for why much of my dream experience is often so fragmentary, conflicted, and unsatisfactory. Perhaps Bergson is at least partially correct about the role that physical sensations play in forming dream experiences. Perhaps, let's say, the tension in my chest, or the pressure in my stomach from undigested food or gas, or the soreness and aches of my muscles and joints are all registering somewhere; perhaps all of this lingering, peripheral awareness of my physical existence is grist for the "dream creativity source" to mold into those types of dreams that seem so restless and rootless, so plagued with dissatisfaction and anxiety. If this is the case, then perhaps, after the death of my physical body, my dream creativity will be less "pulled down" into the "heaviness" of physical existence and will be free to manifest, more purely and freely, modes of experience that are more aligned with the "note" of "higher" dimensions of reality.

I would also like to reiterate that it is quite likely that the various "dream" worlds of postmortem existence would not be identical to our world. In these worlds it is quite likely that the subject/object distinction, for instance, would not be quite so clear-cut and the presumptions of natural law would not always apply. Nonetheless, these levels of postmortem existence would still be "worlds"—worlds of distinct forms; worlds with color, shape, and relative consistency; worlds that have characters; worlds that have drama; worlds in which individuals could make choices, could be sad and happy, could grow and learn and love—worlds of memories and hopes and fears. They would also be worlds that are more clearly and distinctly shaped by each "individual's" own perceptual "lens" or "filters." As such, depending upon the level and quality of our prior spiritual work, these worlds may well be much more vivid, more alive than our current world; they may be worlds that are more clearly and obviously made of light, love, and energy; they may be worlds in which consciousness is more freely and fully itself: that is, worlds that are joyous, alive, and creative.

I also do not think that it is unreasonable to hypothesize that death may well be experienced as a type of "waking up" into another preexisting dimension of reality.

When I was much younger, I had several very powerful dreams in which I died in the dream (usually from a car crash). In these dreams, I have sufficient time to be aware that I may well die very soon, and therefore I make the most of this opportunity to prepare for my death. In these dreams, I gather myself into the center of my being; I align my heart with a powerful longing for spiritual freedom; I open up my consciousness to the presence of light and love; and I ask for assistance from whoever/whatever is there to guide me through this moment. Then, at the moment of death itself (which is never painful), I feel myself rising up, drawn in part at least by my very desire to make the most of this transition time. At a certain point, what inevitably happens, however, is that I break through a type of bubble-like "membrane" and "wake up" into a life that was already in process. At this point I realize that what I had thought was my real life was, instead (ironically), a dream-like fragment of my true existence, which was actually taking place on this higher, "richer" level of reality. (Unfortunately, I do not have equally clear recollections as to the specific nature of the quality and texture of my experience at this level of existence.)

Here is another suggestion about the relationship between dreams and the afterlife: I think that we can gather information about postmortem levels of experience from those occasional spectacular dreams that we are gifted with—

those lucid, highly charged, emotionally rewarding, revelatory dreams. What I am talking about here are those Big Dreams, dreams that feel more real than our waking experience, dreams that are more luscious, more uplifting, more consoling than our current waking experience, dreams that you mourn having to leave, dreams that kindle a deep sense of longing and nostalgia for what you have lost.

I had such a dream a few years ago. It happened on the night of April 6, 2007, around 3:00 in the morning. I woke up and yet I was still fully aware of the dream reality that I had been in before. I was fully conscious of myself in the bed. Yet, during this whole period of time, the "valves" between my waking experience and my dream experience were open "both ways," so that my dream world and my waking world were distinct, yet simultaneously flowing into each other. During the next thirty minutes to an hour it was as if the "vertical" dimension of my being had become integrated with, and available to, my waking awareness. During this time I was simply a conduit of pulsations, surges of cosmic energy/life/blessings that were flowing in and through "me." (Here, I am not talking about the typical, waking consciousness of my usual self-identity, but rather a highly transparent, expanded "me.") Even the strong coughs that would often explode from my chest were not simply the physiological symptoms of the pneumonia that I was suffering from at that time, but were also in a more profound way energetic shock waves of blessings/life/energy that were coursing down from the deeper/wider dimension of my being (the "vertical" dimension) and out through the infinitely complex and interconnected and always changing web of pathways of light or dancing movement that I sensed was undergirding or creating my waking reality.

During this entire time period, I felt as though I was this transparent, pulsating, hugely expanded presence that was actively choosing, shaping, creating, and making reality. My wider/deeper self seemed to possess its own unique "note"—a clear-cut, distinctive sense of individuality, selfhood, and internal cohesion. Nonetheless, at the same time, my consciousness was also continually and integrally connected to and aligned with, even joyously dancing and singing with—co-creating with—*others*. Together, we were consciously choosing to be interwoven constituents of a wider/deeper group consciousness, joining together in a harmonious, pulsating, powerful, "pumping" of light/energy/blessings in and through "us" and "down" into "my" present waking reality.

As I began to emerge out of that open, expanded state, some images arose in my mind that partially helped me (especially when I mulled over these images afterward) to give a type of concreteness to certain aspects of that experience. The first one was a modification of Bergson's inverted cone: the cone of memory, with its tip intersecting with the plane of perception. During my time in that altered state of consciousness, I possessed a similar sense of opening up like a cone, but my experience of that opening up was more organic, less bounded, and more diaphanous. I was more like a transparent, crystalline spider made of movement/music/light and joy that was dancing and creating a "web" of ever-changing, pulsating, utterly diverse, interwoven, energy/light pathways stream-ing out into the universe—an ever-shifting, overlapping grid of highly differentiated, constantly throbbing colors of light/energy conduits.

An alternative variation of this image was that of a jellyfish, a simultane-ously collective yet cohesive being made of light, floating and traveling in light, pumping and throbbing light in-and-through itself, light that was coursing down through its beautiful crystalline tendrils into our world.

And finally, the solitariness of each of these images was compensated by yet another image: a collective dance of multiple male and female Natarajas (the iconic Hindu image of God dancing) erotically, ecstatically, intertwining—a col-lective, free, creative dance of many beings (who were, at the same time, para-doxically, one being), all rhythmically attuning to the song of existence, dancing light and life into our world with abandon and a sense of utter fulfillment.

To me, this dream or vision brought some really good news: it seems likely to me that even now, in our present state of waking awareness, as James puts it, "over our heads," we actually *are* part and parcel of a deeper/wider/freer self, a self that is connected to our physical world and our physical body, but is not dependent upon it. (It is quite the reverse in fact.) Aligned with Bergson (and, of course, James and Myers), I tend to think that we are multidimensional and that the self that we typically identify with is a precipitate—a congealing of a deeper, more extensive and expansive selfhood (a selfhood that might well be, simultane-ously, a collective reality).

Bergson, James, and Myers were not, of course, the only ones to think this way. For instance, it appears that numerous Australian aboriginal peoples have had a very similar understanding, a worldview that claims that there are multi-ple levels of reality and that, right now, we inhabit all of these various levels in the form of what they call "ancestors"—ancestors who are continually "dream-ing" the "lower" worlds into existence, sending pulsations of light, life, and energy into those lower worlds so that these worlds can flourish. According to these aboriginal people, one job of our spiritual work in this world is to recali-brate the energetic and vibratory quality of our experience so that it is more fully and completely aligned with/attuned to these deeper, concurrently existing dimensions of our selfhood (a job that, for them, is accomplished by a complex series of initiatory events). Seen from this perspective, perhaps (at least at times), what we often call out-of-body journeying is, more accurately, a process by which we journey in-and-through alternate dimensions of our own con-sciousness, a consciousness that is not so neatly divided into "us" over here and "the world" over there, a consciousness that is continually creating worlds within worlds within worlds, worlds that are themselves inextricably interwoven with our own subjectivity and which continually manifest themselves in a wide variety of unpredictable ways.

I think that it is almost certain that there will be much more to life after death than we can even begin to imagine or comprehend—for example, a multitude of different levels of trans-subjective "heavenly" worlds or states of ecstatic merger or divine radiance. I envision worlds of deep connection, freedom, and creativity; worlds of increased depth and quality of feeling; worlds of full, rich, open sensual experience; worlds filled with bodies of beauty, bodies of light and love, bodies that are not frozen with fear, bodies that are not crippled with limitations and cellular tension, bodies that do not cage us, but rather bodies that help us to center and ground, bodies that allow us to relate to others in a loving, sensual no-holds-barred way, bodies that give a focus to our desire to love and to receive love fully and without restrictions.

Again, I have had several powerful dream experiences of these "heavenly" worlds, worlds in which I was a fully embodied being, sharing an almost unimaginably joyous and free experience of mutual love and sensual connection with other beautiful, open, embodied men and women—a world of deep, freely flowing feelings, given and received, a world of intimate connection beyond anything possible in this life, a world of continual, joyous creativity, a world of utterly vivid and stunningly beautiful colors and patterns that live and breathe, a world in which those dreams that we have buried and not dared even to admit that we have had are fulfilled beyond our wildest hopes, a world that I "woke up" from with my heart pounding with a deep longing, a world that still fuels an aching nostalgia within me.

There have even been moments in my life in which it seems that something of the glow and freedom of those worlds transfuses my experience of this world, moments of sensing or perceiving a shimmering perfection shining in and through the ordinary events of my life, moments in which I can bask in a world that is right here, right now, translucent and inherently fulfilling, a world of continual growth and divine presence, a world broadcasting luminous reminders of the hidden yet deeply present worlds of my dreams.

SOME FINAL WORDS

In my initial, ludicrously ambitious, vision of the structure and contents of this book, I had hoped to examine Bergson's entire corpus (an intention that paid off, at least to a certain extent, in that I was prompted to give substantial time to a rather detailed investigation of all of Bergson's published works). However, I eventually had to face the fact that I was not going to be able to give anywhere near the same quality of attention to Bergson's later works as I have given to *Time and Free Will* and *Matter and Memory*. This collision between my desire for completeness and the limitations of time and space was perhaps inevitable, but I still wish that it could have been otherwise, in that each of Bergson's later texts, in their own unique way, is richly rewarding, and each deserves much more sustained and careful attention than I was able to give.

For instance, in *Creative Evolution*, Bergson articulates a fascinating understanding of evolution, one that offers an intriguing "third way" between intelligent design theorists and neo-Darwinians. In this same work, as well as in his important essay *Introduction to Metaphysics*, Bergson also crafts an illuminating examination of the epistemological interaction between rationality and intuition in which he affirms the crucial role that the intellect (and science) plays in understanding the world around us, while also highlighting the inevitable difficulties that the intellect faces when attempting to adequately address the dynamism and complexity of life. In both *Creative Evolution* and *Introduction to Metaphysics*, Bergson's affirmation of the vital role played by intuition is not (contra Russell) a form of antirationalism, but instead, is a nuanced, sophisticated examination of the value and validity (and potential limitations) of various modes of transrational knowledge.

And finally, in *The Two Sources of Morality and Religion*, Bergson advances an intriguing theoretical investigation into the biological roots of social cohesion, mythological belief, magical praxis, morality, and religion, as well as a ringing affirmation of the crucial significance of mystics in the ethical and spiritual evolution of human beings.[3] In this dense, multilayered (and at times, it must be said, somewhat problematic) text, Bergson straddles two worlds: 1) an analytically rigorous, quasi-Durkheimian sociological evaluation of the ways in which "closed" ("us versus them") social structures create correspondingly rigid and static moral codes and/or religious institutions, and 2) a quasi-poetic paean of the virtues of mysticism in promoting not only a dynamic intuitive awareness of one's connection to the universe, but also an open-ended, vibrant, nonexclusive ethical life.

Because I was so acutely aware of the way in which each of Bergson's texts seamlessly emerges from, and builds upon, the ideas explored in his previous works (while also managing to offer something that is genuinely, and often strikingly, new) I felt that it was crucial for *Living Consciousness* to explore, in some depth, the foundational assumptions that are encoded in *Time and Free Will* and in *Matter and Memory*, not only to demonstrate the profundity of his thought, but also to give at least some sense of how Bergson's early work offers a perspective on the nature of consciousness and reality that remains dramatically relevant today.

I can only hope that *Living Consciousness* has succeeded, at least to a certain extent, in depicting Bergson's powerful affirmation of freedom, creativity, and temporal dynamism, and that this work has also offered at least a glimpse of Bergson's complex and sophisticated ontology. Bergson's interactive nondualism offers, I suggest, a much-needed corrective to the worldview that is so often assumed today by many influential philosophers, social theorists, and scientists, a worldview that tells us that we are nothing more than atomistic cogs in a mindless, uncaring, mechanistic universe. For myself at least, Bergson's participatory, enactive vision of our relationship with the universe, a vision that affirms that we ceaselessly, under the surface, help to create and shape our experience of ourselves and others, is not only theoretically compelling, but also aesthetically evocative (as well as, at least potentially, pragmatically effective). Personally, I believe that our contemporary world is crying out for such a vision, one in which each one of us is seen as integrally connected to wider, deeper dimensions of a dynamic, multileveled, and open-ended reality, a reality in which we matter, a reality that is enriched, and creatively shaped, moment by moment, by the choices that we make.

Living Consciousness by no means pretends to be the final word on Bergson. However, I would like to think that, at the very least, readers will leave this volume with their curiosity whetted. My hope was not to create some sort of homogeneous consensus among readers that Bergson's thought offers all of the answers to today's philosophical dilemmas. Rather, I wrote this book with the desire that readers will come away from it enriched by a vibrant and evocative understanding of the nature of consciousness and reality; awakened to the possibility that this universe is perhaps much more alive, much more interconnected, than was previously imagined; and energized to fashion their own, deeply personal, and ideally transformative, intuitive vision of the world in which they wish to live.

NOTES

A BRIEF BIO-HISTORICAL PREAMBLE

1. Emmanuel Levinas, *Ethics and Infinity*, trans. Richard A. Cohen (Pittsburgh: Duquesne University Press, 1985), 37.
2. Arguably the best biography of Bergson is Philippe Soulez, complétée par Frédéric Worms, *Bergson: Biographie* (Paris: Flammarion, 1997). However, detailed biographical investigation into Bergson's personal life was curtailed by Bergson's decision, in his last will, dated February 9, 1937, to expressly forbid the publication of his manuscripts, letters, or notes after his death.
3. Jacques Chevalier, *Henri Bergson*, trans. Lilian A. Clare (Freeport, New York: Books for Libraries Press, 1970), 53–55.
4. Enid Starkie, "Bergson and Literature," in Thomas Hanna, ed., *The Bergsonian Heritage* (New York: Columbia University Press, 1962), 92.
5. Marcel Bataillon, untitled contribution in *The Bergsonian Heritage*, 109–110.
6. Gabriel Marcel, untitled contribution in *The Bergsonian Heritage*, 126–127.
7. Chevalier, *Henri Bergson*, 60.
8. Ibid., 61.
9. Sanford Schwartz, "Bergson and the Politics of Vitalism," in Frederick Burwick and Paul Douglas, eds., *The Crisis in Modernism* (New York: Cambridge University Press, 1992), 298.
10. William James' letter to Bergson, June 13, 1907, in Ralph Barton Perry, *The Thought and Character of William James*, 2 vols. (Boston: Little, Brown, and Co., 1935), 345.
11. Cited in Joseph Chiari, *Twentieth-Century French Thought* (New York: Gordian Press, 1975), 32.
12. Tom Quirk, *Bergson and American Culture* (Chapel Hill, North Carolina: University of North Carolina Press, 1990), 69.

273

13. Ibid., 53.
14. *Living Age* (March 16, 1912), cited in *Bergson and American Culture*, 68.
15. Henry F. May, *The End of American Innocence* (New York: Oxford University Press, 1979), 228.
16. Frederick Burwick and Paul Douglas, "Introduction," *The Crisis in Modernism*, 3.
17. Quoted in Chevalier, *Henri Bergson*, 65.
18. Ibid.
19. Louise Collier Willcox, "Impressions of M. Bergson," *Harper's Weekly* (March 8, 1913), 6. Cited in *Bergson and American Culture*, 67–68.
20. Schwartz, in *The Crisis in Modernism*, 297.
21. R. C. Grogin, *The Bergsonian Controversy in France, 1900–1914* (Calgary: University of Calgary Press, 1988), 190.
22. Schwartz, in *The Crisis in Modernism*, 299.
23. Starkie, in *The Bergsonian Heritage*, 81.
24. Jacques Maritain, *La philosophie bergsonienne* (1913, 3rd ed., 1948), xiv. Cited in Leszek Kolakowski, *Bergson* (New York: Oxford University Press, 1985), 97.
25. Kolakowski, *Bergson*, 98.
26. Ibid.
27. Ibid., 98–99.
28. *Pascendi dominici gregis*, 71–97, in *The Papal Encyclicals: 1903–1939*, trans. Claudia Carlen (Wilmington, North Carolina: McGrath Publishing Co., 1981), 89. Cited in *Bergson and American Culture*, 60.
29. Ibid.
30. P. A. Y. Gunter, "Bergson," in *A Companion to Continental Philosophy* (Hoboken, New Jersey: Wiley-Blackwell, 1999), 179.
31. Soulez, *Bergson: Biographie*, 164–165.
32. Kolakowski, *Bergson*, 72.
33. Cited in Ian W. Alexander, *Bergson: Philosopher of Reflection* (New York: Hillary House, 1957), 69. Alexander also points out that M. Romeyer "related a conversation held with Bergson as early as 1933 when the latter declared his adherence to the principle of the divinity of the Catholic Church as linked with that of Christ." B. Romeyer, "Caractéristiques religieuses du spiritualisme de Bergson," in "*Bergson et Bergsonisme,*" *Archives de philosophie* 17, cahier 1, (Paris: 1947), 32.
34. *Bergson: Philosopher of Reflection*, 70. Alexander points out that "M. Wahl made this revelation in the course of a *soutenance de thèse* at the Sorbonne. See the report in *Le Monde*, 19th May, 1954."
35. Suzanne Guerlac, *Thinking in Time* (Ithaca, New York: Cornell University Press, 2006), 3. Interestingly, there does not seem to be any evidence of Hegel's influence on Bergson. As Milič Čapek notes, at the International

Philosophical Congress in Bologna in 1911, Bergson met Benedetto Croce, "a critical disciple of Hegel's thought," for the first time, and it "was then that Croce called Bergson's attention to certain points common to Bergson and Hegel. Bergson was apparently completely unaware of it . . . and when Croce suggested that he read *Phenomenologie des Geistes* so he could see the process-like character of Hegel's philosophy, Bergson with a disarming sincerity and to Croce's great amazement admitted that he never had read Hegel! He promised to read him, but Croce, recalling this conversation thirty-eight years later in 1949, doubted that he ever kept this promise." Milič Čapek, *Bergson and Modern Physics* (Dordrecht, Holland: D. Reidel Publishing Co., 1971), 172, quoting Jules Chaix-Ruy, "Vitalité et élan vital: Bergson et Croce," *Études bergsoniennes*, 5 (Albin Michel, 1960), 145.

36. Elizabeth Grosz, *The Nick of Time* (Durham, North Carolina: Duke University Press, 2004), 156. Čapek points out that Bertrand Russell was among the most virulent of Bergson's philosophical opponents, noting that "Russell's attitude to Bergson was not only that of philosophical disagreement, but of positive, almost personal dislike." Čapek, *Bergson and Modern Physics*, 335. Russell's descriptions of Bergson's work not only frequently misrepresent Bergson's thought, but also often verge on caricature and at times are tinged with a clearly discernible desire to ridicule Bergson. For instance, Russell's "analysis" of Bergson's doctrine of intuition claims that intuition is strongest "in ants, bees, and Bergson." Bertrand Russell, *The Philosophy of Bergson* (London: Macmillan, 1914), 3. Čapek suggests that Russell's animosity toward Bergson may have had a very personal origin: his "suspicion that Bergson 'lured' Whitehead away from him." *Bergson and Modern Physics*, 335. Tom Quirk also claims that "Bergsonism had something to do with the dissolution of two of the most famous intellectual friendships of the twentieth century: that of Alfred North Whitehead and Bertrand Russell and of Carl Jung and Sigmund Freud." *Bergson and American Culture*, 59. Quirk references Bertrand Russell, *The Autobiography of Bertrand Russell* (New York: Bantam Books, 1967), 166 and Nathan G. Hale, *Freud and the Americans* (New York: Oxford University Press, 1971), 197.

37. As Richard Lehan points out: "Bergson's influence, direct or indirect, on modern literature cannot be denied or de-emphasized." *The Crisis in Modernism*, 323. Quirk, in his careful study on Bergson's impact on the Progressive Era, provides an excellent list of bibliographical references on literature dealing with "the influence of Bergson on modern writers." *Bergson and American Culture*, 506. As Quirk points out, some excellent general studies include George Poulet, *Studies in Human Nature* (Baltimore: Johns Hopkins University Press, 1956); Margaret Church, *Time and Reality* (Chapel Hill: University of North Carolina Press, 1949); and Shiv Kumar, *Bergson and the*

Stream of Consciousness Novel (New York: New York University Press, 1963). Quirk also lists numerous other studies that focus on Bergson's influence on specific literary figures. Bergson's influence on Nikos Kazantzakis is particularly evident. Several well-regarded studies have been written: Peter A. Bien, "Nikos Kazantzakis," *Columbia Essays on Modern Writers* 62 (New York: Columbia University Press, 1972), 26–38; James F. Lea, *Kazantzakis: The Politics of Salvation* (Tuscaloosa, Alabama: University of Alabama Press, 1979), 20–25; Morton P. Levitt, *The Cretan Glance* (Columbus, Ohio: Ohio State University Press, 1980), 88–109.

38. *Bergson and Modern Physics*, 306.

39. *The Crisis in Modernism*, 230–244. Gunter has also written an excellent analysis of the correspondence between Bergson's thought and that of C.G. Jung (a correspondence that was due, at least in part, to several lines of historical influence). See P. A. Y. Gunter, "Bergson and Jung," *Journal of the History of Ideas* 43, no. 4 (October–December 1982): 635–652. William Barrett also argues that "Henri Bergson cannot really be omitted from any historical sketch of modern existential philosophy. Without Bergson the whole atmosphere in which Existentialists have philosophized would not have been what it was." William Barrett, *Irrational Man* (Garden City, New York: Doubleday, 1958), 13. Similarly, Annie Cohen-Solal, a biographer of Sartre, points out that during the years of Sartre's "intellectual gestation," Bergson played "a crucial, intense, revelatory role." Annie Cohen-Solal, *Sartre: A Life*, trans. A. Cancogni (New York: Pantheon, 1987), 11.

40. *The Crisis in Modernism*, 325–327; 330–367.

41. Richard A. Cohen, "Philo, Spinoza, Bergson: The Rise of an Ecological Age," in John Mullarkey, ed., *The New Bergson* (New York: Manchester University Press, 1999), 27. As Yuasa Yasuo and Minoru Yamaguchi both point out, the work of Nishida Kitaro, arguably the most important of modern Japanese philosophers, was also influenced by Bergson's thought. Yasuo Yuasa, *The Body*, T. P. Kasulis, ed., trans. Nagatomo Shigenori and T. P. Kasulis (Albany, New York: State University of New York Press, 1987), 64, and Minoru Yamaguchi, *The Intuition of Zen and Bergson* (Japan: Herder Agency, 1969), 20.

42. Hugh Tomlinson and Barbara Habberjam, the translators of *Bergsonism*, note in their introduction that "the affinities between Deleuze and Bergson led Gillian Rose to speak of his work as "the new Bergsonism." Gillian Rose, *Dialectic of Nihilism* (Oxford: Basil Blackwell, 1984), chapter 6. Cited in *Bergsonism*, 9. However, as the translators correctly note, Deleuze took up "and transformed . . . Bergsonian notions in his own errant campaigns for constructive pluralism." *Bergsonism*, 8. Deleuze himself was quite open about the ways in which he shifted basic Bergsonian ideas to serve his own ends, calling it "a kind of buggery . . . or immaculate conception" in which

he imagined himself "getting onto the back of an author, and giving him a child, which would be his and which would at the same time be a monster. . . . My book on Bergson seems to me a classic case of this." Cited in "Lettre à Michel Cressole," in Michel Cressole, *Deleuze* (Paris: Editions Universitaires, 1973), 111. One of the best examinations of the ways in which Deleuze uses (and I would claim at times abuses) Bergson's thought is Guerlac, *Thinking in Time*, 173–196. As Guerlac correctly points out, "if there is a 'return' to Bergson today . . . it is largely due to Gilles Deleuze whose own work has etched the contours of the New Bergson. This is not only because Deleuze wrote about Bergson; it is also because Deleuze's own thought is deeply engaged with that of his predecessor, even when Bergson is not explicitly mentioned." *Thinking in Time*, 175.

43. As Keith Ansell Pearson notes, "the significance of Bergson's attempt to think duration in a new way . . . was recognized and perhaps best appreciated by Levinas who wished to underline the importance of Bergsonism 'for the entire problematic of contemporary philosophy.'" Keith Ansell Pearson, *Philosophy and the Adventure of the Virtual* (New York: Routledge, 2002), 10, quoting Emmanuel Levinas, *Time and the Other*, trans. R. A. Cohen (Pittsburgh: Duquesne University Press, 1987), 132. John Mullarkey claims that "what Levinas has done is to take Bergson's philosophy of novelty and moralize it: 'the absolutely new' becomes the Other." John Mullarkey, *Bergson and Philosophy* (Notre Dame, Indiana: University of Notre Dame Press, 2000), 109. See also Pierre Trotignon, "Auttre Voie, Meme Voix: Lévinas et Bergson," in Catherine Chalier and Miguel Abensour, eds., *Emmanuel Lévinas* (Paris: Editions de l'Herne, 1991), 288.

44. As Elizabeth Grosz insightfully points out, even though "Bergson's works have languished largely in obscurity for well over half a century," nonetheless, regardless of their limitations, they "remain of dynamic relevance to understanding the ontology and politics of temporality. . . . his work is not without very significant implications for how we might reconsider the preeminent but unrecognized discourses of temporality—history, sociology, psychology, politics, and so on—as disciplines and methods of analysis bound up with duration." *The Nick of Time*, 241.

45. Recent texts on Bergson's work that, to a greater or lesser extent, are influenced by, or responding to, the poststructuralist perspective of Gilles Deleuze are (listed chronologically): John Mullarkey, *Bergson and Philosophy* (Notre Dame, Indiana: University of Notre Dame Press, 2000); Keith Ansell Pearson, *Philosophy and the Adventure of the Virtual* (New York: Routledge, 2002); Leonard Lawlor, *The Challenge of Bergsonism* (New York: Continuum, 2003); Elizabeth Grosz, *The Nick of Time* (Durham, North Carolina: Duke University Press, 2004); Suzanne Guerlac, *Thinking in Time* (Ithaca, New York: Cornell University Press, 2006).

INTRODUCTION

1. I am not alone in pointing out the normative overtones of Bergson's work. John Mullarkey, for instance, points out that while Bergson's earlier works are "boldly empirical," nonetheless, the "import" of that empiricism is "ultimately ethical." *Bergson and Philosophy* (Notre Dame, Indiana: University of Notre Dame Press, 2000), 3.
2. My claim that any philosophical examination of Bergson's work should, in itself, manifest at least some of the creativity and change that is at the heart of Bergson's thought, is echoed by Mullarkey, who notes that "one might justifiably ask how a work that extols continual creative transformation can be systematically examined without having at once its content artificially petrified and its spirit betrayed?" *Bergson and Philosophy*, 7.
3. As Bergson emphasizes in a discussion with members of the Société de Philosophie in 1901, "we need to be on the lookout for automatism" (*M* 495).
4. While I deeply appreciate (and agree with) the vast majority of Elizabeth Grosz's insights on Bergson, I am puzzled by her claim that "in his earlier works, *Time and Free Will* and *Matter and Memory*, Bergson understands matter as thoroughly inert, imbued only with spatial but not with durational properties." *The Nick of Time* (Durham, North Carolina: Duke University Press, 2004), 198. I would argue, in contrast (and I believe that most scholars of Bergson would agree with my assessment) that the change in Bergson's understanding of the nature of matter is evident by the time of *Matter and Memory*.
5. Research into psi phenomena is vast, therefore what follows (listed alphabetically by author's last name) is, at best, a small sampling, and one that focuses somewhat on research into the purported survival of consciousness after the death of the physical body. Robert Almeder, *Death and Personal Survival* (Lanham, Maryland: Littlefield Adams, 1992); Carl B. Becker, *Paranormal Experience and Survival of Death* (Albany, New York: State University of New York Press, 1993); William Braud, *Distant Mental Influence* (Charlottesville, Virginia: Hampton Roads, 2003); Stephen E. Braude, *Immortal Remains* (Lanham, Maryland: Rowman & Littlefield, 2003); Richard S. Broughton, *Parapsychology* (New York: Ballantine Books, 1991); David Ray Griffin, *Parapsychology, Philosophy, and Spirituality* (Albany, New York: State University of New York Press, 1997); Jeffrey Iverson, *In Search of the Dead* (New York: HarperSanFrancisco, 1992); Edward F. Kelly and Rafael G. Locke, *Altered States of Consciousness and Psi* (New York: Parapsychology Foundation, 2009); Edward F. Kelly et al., *Irreducible Mind* (Lanham, Maryland: Rowman & Littlefield, 2007); Dean Radin, *Entangled Minds* (New York: Paraview Pocket Books, 2006); Dean Radin, *The Conscious Universe* (New

York: HarperEdge, 1997); Russell Targ and Harold E. Puthoff, *Mind Reach* (Charlottesville, Virginia: Hampton Roads, 1977); Charles Tart, *The End of Materialism* (Oakland, California: New Harbinger Publications, 2009); Jim B. Tucker, *Life Before Life* (New York: St. Martin's Press, 2005).

CHAPTER 1. THE NATURE OF CONSCIOUSNESS

1. Susan Blackmore, *Consciousness: An Introduction* (New York: Oxford University Press, 2004), 23.
2. I have written about this "awakening" experience previously in my book *Exploring Unseen Worlds: William James and the Philosophy of Mysticism* (Albany, New York: State University of New York Press, 1997). In that text, I discussed this experience in order to illustrate how mystical experiences do not seem to be simply the products of our cultural background, but, instead, can themselves create significant changes in our prior assumptions of the nature of selfhood and reality. I also pointed out how, at least in this case, there is a type of stubborn "given-ness" to these sorts of experiences that can resist and negate certain types of arbitrary or inaccurate interpretations. The function of this chapter's exploration of this experience is quite different, in that here I am primarily interested in demonstrating the origins of my own interest in the nature of consciousness. My willingness to give accounts of specific moments from my own introspective work is one way in which I have attempted to give some real-life "heft" and specificity to the often unavoidable (yet admittedly helpful) generalizations that often characterize philosophical work.
3. Bergson rarely comments on the bifurcation of consciousness into the knower and known. The following is one of the few times in which he does: "How would it [durée] appear to a consciousness which desired only to see it without measuring it, which would then grasp it without stopping it, which in short, would take itself as object, and which, spectator and actor alike, at once spontaneous and reflective, would bring ever closer together— to the point where they would coincide,—the attention which is fixed, and time which passes?" (*CM* 12). I can only speculate why the bifurcation of consciousness is so rarely, and incompletely, addressed by Bergson, while so many thinkers within the Sankhya and Advaita Vedanta traditions (as well as numerous Western philosophers) have given so much attention to this issue with their emphasis on the seeming immutability of the inner "witness." For Bergson, durée is sheer change itself. Therefore, if durée, in its purity, is an inseparable fusion of subject and object, knower and known, then one has to assume that, for Bergson, the knower is also understood to be changing as well.

4. Harald Höffding, *La philosophie de Bergson* (Paris: Alcan, 1916), 160.
5. As we will see in section 2, in Bergson's second book, *Matter and Memory*, his depiction of durée expands and alters dramatically—the stress on immediacy recedes to the background as he probes deeply and brilliantly, if at times somewhat speculatively, into the nature of matter, perception, the unconscious, and memory. It is easy, as an interpreter of Bergson, to be so swept up by the power and sweeping scope of *Matter and Memory*—and its daring, if dauntingly abstract, formulations of the multiple levels of durée, the structure of matter, and the unseen depths of the unconscious—to assume that Bergson left behind the (relatively) straightforward portrayal of consciousness found in *Time and Free Will*. But a closer examination of Bergson's corpus reveals a different story: time and time again in the writings after *Matter and Memory* he returns to the portrayal of durée that he worked out so carefully in *Time and Free Will*. It is this understanding of durée which appears often side by side with the alternate perspective on durée that is articulated in *Matter and Memory*. (Bergson, unlike some of his more recent commentators, does not seem to see any tension between the durée of *Time and Free Will* and the durée of *Matter and Memory*.)
6. Maurice Merleau-Ponty, untitled contribution in Thomas Hanna, ed., *The Bergsonian Heritage* (New York: Columbia University Press, 1962), 136.
7. Ibid.
8. Čapek comes right to the point when he writes: "Without exaggeration, there is hardly anything less immediate, less given, than Bergson's 'immediate data.' The word 'immediate' was ill chosen by Bergson because what he meant by it was certainly not 'immediate de facto' but rather 'immediate de jure.' In other words, the introspective datum is immediate when it is freed from irrelevant and extraneous elements which, so to speak, 'mediatize' it." Milič Čapek, *Bergson and Modern Physics* (Dordrecht, Holland: D. Reidel Publishing Co., 1971), 86.
9. Guerlac notes that "Bergson turns the Kantian perspective inside out. He asks whether we do not unconsciously tend to construct our understanding of the inner world according to forms borrowed from the way we view the external world." Suzanne Guerlac, *Thinking in Time* (Ithaca, New York: Cornell University Press, 2006), 94.
10. Interestingly, in a note in the introduction of *Creative Mind*, Bergson points out that this analogy (i.e., how the illusion of movement is created on a movie screen by lining up a series of snapshots very close together) is dependent upon an underlying movement in order to create this illusion: "What the cinematograph [movie projector] shows us in movement on the screen is the series of immobile views of the film; it is, of course, understood that what is projected on this screen, over and above these immobile views themselves, is the movement within the projector" (*CM* 301, note 1).

11. *Bergson and Modern Physics*, 120.
12. Ibid.
13. Ibid., 152.
14. Ibid., 90.
15. Bergson's understanding of the simultaneous oneness and manyness of consciousness is beginning to be mirrored in the findings of current research into consciousness. As Blackmore notes, G. M. Edelman and G. Tononi argue that there are "two key features of consciousness, 'that each conscious state is an indivisible whole and, at the same time, that each person can chose among an immense number of different conscious states.' . . . That is, they want to explain both the integration or unity of consciousness, and its differentiation or complexity." G. M. Edelman and G. Tononi, "Reentry and the Dynamic Core: Neural Correlates of Conscious Experience," in T. Metzinger, ed., *Neural Correlates of Consciousness* (Cambridge, Massachusetts: MIT Press, 2000), 139. Cited in *Consciousness: An Introduction*, 251.
16. Ian W. Alexander, *Bergson: Philosopher of Reflection* (New York: Hillary House, 1957), 22. Guerlac, however, implicitly disputes Alexander's suggestion (on page 22) that durée manifests the "heterogeneity of organic growth." According to her, "time is discontinuous. . . . Although Bergson uses vitalist images . . . this does not mean he is thinking time on the model of a smooth progression or something like organic growth." *Thinking in Time*, 92, note 48. Guerlac (on the same page) argues that duration is "not a continuous temporality but a discontinuous time." This is one of the few times in which I have difficulty agreeing with Guerlac's interpretation of Bergson's work.
17. *Bergson: Philosopher of Reflection*, 22.

CHAPTER 2. AUTHENTICITY

1. John Mullarkey, *Bergson and Philosophy* (Notre Dame, Indiana: University of Notre Dame Press, 2000), 19–20.
2. Suzanne Guerlac, *Thinking in Time* (Ithaca, New York: Cornell University Press, 2006), 76.
3. A. A. Luce, *Bergson's Doctrine of Intuition* (New York: Macmillan, 1922), 60; Frederick Burwick and Paul Douglas, eds., *The Crisis in Modernism* (New York: Cambridge University Press, 1992), 5.
4. Garrett Barden, "Method in Philosophy," in John Mullarkey, ed., *The New Bergson* (New York: Manchester University Press, 1999), 35.
5. *Bergson and Philosophy*, 20. Mullarkey cites (*TFW* 169).
6. In a similar vein, Guerlac notes that "the collective obsession with space that characterizes Western culture may even involve a kind of defense, in the

psychoanalytic sense, on the part of the superficial self, against the fluidity of psychic operations in what Bergson calls their natural, or nonalienated state." *Thinking in Time*, 76.

7. It can be touching to see Bergson's attempts to lessen the existential shock of his message of universal change. For instance, he tries to reassure his readers that "change, if they consent to look directly at it without an interposed veil, will very quickly appear to them to be the most substantial and durable thing possible" (*CM* 177).

8. I would go so far as to claim that, if we were to fully accomplish the task of perceiving each and every moment *sub specie durationis*, this achievement would be phenomenologically equivalent to what certain Mahayana Buddhists describe in their accounts of enlightenment. Such a radical alteration of perception would be not only an awakening to who we already are under the surface, but also a way of experiencing all of life as ever-new, flowing, and interconnected.

CHAPTER 3. TIME

1. Leonard Lawlor so strongly emphasizes the temporal nature of durée that he asserts: "We can define duration with two simple claims. The first is perhaps at the heart of Bergson's philosophy: the past survives. The second follows from the first: the moment coming from the future is absolutely new." Leonard Lawlor, *The Challenge of Bergsonism* (New York: Continuum, 2003), 80.

2. A. R. Lacey, *Bergson* (New York: Routledge, 1989), 17.

3. A. A. Luce, *Bergson's Doctrine of Intuition* (New York: Macmillan, 1922),40.

4. Interestingly, however, even clock time can be shown to depend upon the lived, experienced time of durée. As Solomon points out, "the clock [is able to] serve as a measure of duration simply because each of its units of movement—each oscillation of the pendulum—is *felt* by us to be equal in duration." Joseph Solomon, *Bergson* (Port Washington, New York: Kennikat Press, 1970), 22.

5. Solomon, *Bergson*, 23.

6. For Bergson, durée is inherently irreversible. Chevalier stresses this aspect of durée by saying that: "The most fundamental trait of duration . . . is *irreversibility*," an irreversibility that is intrinsically connected to unforeseeability and real contingency." Jacques Chevalier, *Henri Bergson*, trans. Lilian A. Clare (Freeport, New York: Books for Libraries Press, 1970), 153.

7. P. A. Y. Gunter, "Bergson," in David Ray Griffin et al., eds., *Founders of Constructive Postmodern Philosophy* (Albany, New York: State University of New York Press, 1993), 135.

8. Charles R. Schmidtke, "Bergson and Gerontology," in Andrew C. Papanico-laou and P. A. Y. Gunter, eds., *Bergson and Modern Science* (New York: Harwood Academic Publishers, 1987), 232.

9. Milič Čapek, *Bergson and Modern Physics* (Dordrecht, Holland: D. Reidel Publishing Co., 1971), 91.

10. Thomas Hanna, ed., *The Bergsonian Heritage* (New York: Columbia University Press, 1962), 136.

CHAPTER 4. DO OUR FEELINGS MEASURE UP?

1. As Guerlac emphasizes, "*Quantity* tells us how much there is of something. *Quality* tells us how things feel to us—bright, dark, hot, cold, happy, lonesome, or beautiful." *Thinking in Time* (Ithaca, New York: Cornell University Press, 2006), 45.

2. John Mullarkey, *Bergson and Philosophy* (Notre Dame, Indiana: University of Notre Dame Press, 2000), 23.

3. Amazingly, Deleuze claims that "for Bergson, duration was not . . . the non-measurable. Rather, it was that which divided only by changing in kind, that which was susceptible to measurement only by varying its metrical principle at each stage of the division." Gilles Deleuze, *Bergsonism*, trans. Hugh Tomlinson and Barbara Habberjam (New York: Zone Books, 1991), 40. While I am supportive of creative appropriations and reinterpretations of previous philosophical work, I also think that it is crucial to begin by accurately representing as much as possible the particulars of that philosopher's perspective. In this case, Deleuze offers a flagrant distortion of Bergson's perspective. Bergson never says in *Time and Free Will* (which is the text that Deleuze is discussing in this passage) that durée is measurable. Instead, he goes to great lengths to emphasize exactly the opposite point.

4. A. R. Lacey, *Bergson* (New York: Routledge, 1989), 1–2.

5. F. C. T. Moore, *Bergson: Thinking Backwards* (New York: Cambridge University Press, 1996), 45.

CHAPTER 5. PHYSICAL DETERMINISM

1. Suzanne Guerlac, *Thinking in Time* (Ithaca, New York: Cornell University Press, 2006),78.

2. Idella J. Gallagher, *Morality in Evolution* (The Hague, Netherlands: Martinus Nijhoff, 1970), 43.

3. As Guerlac points out, while Bergson was not opposed to scientific investigations of the material world, nonetheless, if "we extend scientific modes of

thinking to ourselves, Bergson insisted, we would become like things. If we try to measure and count our feelings, to explain and predict our motives and actions, we will be transformed into automatons—without freedom, without beauty, without passion, and without dreams." *Thinking in Time*, 42.

4. Frederick Burwick and Paul Douglas, eds., *The Crisis in Modernism* (New York: Cambridge University Press, 1992), 280.

5. Ibid.

6. Pierre-Simon Laplace, "Introduction à théorie analytique des probablités," *Oeuvres completes*, vol. vii. (Paris, 1886), vi. Cited in (*CE* 38).

7. G. W. Leibniz, "Vom Verhängnisse," cited in Ernst Cassirer, *Determinism and Indeterminism in Modern Physics* (New Haven: Yale University Press, 1956), 12.

8. J. G. Fichte, *Die Bestimmung des Menschen, Sämmtliche Werke* II (Berlin, 1845), 182–183. Cited in Milič Čapek, *Bergson and Modern Physics* (Dordrecht, Holland: D. Reidel Publishing Co., 1971), 102.

9. *Bergson and Modern Physics*, 103.

10. Rupert Sheldrake, *The Presence of the Past* (Rochester, Vermont: Park Street Press, 1988), 3.

11. Ibid., 4.

12. Ibid.

13. Ibid.

14. Ibid., 7.

15. Cited in E. A. Burtt, *The Metaphysical Foundations of Modern Physical Science* (London: Kegan, Paul, Trench and Trubner, 1932), 9. See also *The Presence of the Past*, 6–7.

16. Immanuel Kant, *Critique of Practical Reason and Other Works on the Theory of Ethics*, trans. T. K. Abbot (London: Longmans, Green, 1909), 193. Cited in *Bergson and Modern Physics*, 102.

CHAPTER 6. ALTERNATIVE UNDERSTANDINGS OF THE SELF

1. Garrett Barden, "Method in Philosophy," in John Mullarkey, ed., *The New Bergson* (New York: Manchester University Press, 1999), 35.

2. Čapek notes that "simultaneously and independently of Bergson, the very same negation of psychological atomism was energetically put forth by William James." Milič Čapek, *Bergson and Modern Physics* (Dordrecht, Holland: D. Reidel Publishing Co., 1971), 95.

3. Leszek Kolakowski, *Bergson* (New York: Oxford University Press, 1985), 20.

4. *Bulletin*, Feb., 1903, 102. Cited in Jacques Chevalier, *Henri Bergson*, trans. Lilian A. Clare (Freeport, New York: Books for Libraries Press, 1970), 138.

CHAPTER 7. FREEDOM

1. Guerlac points out that "Bergson stands Kant on his head. For whereas Kant places freedom in the moral realm, beyond time and space, Bergson places it within time understood as heterogeneous duration. Instead of erecting a barrier between time and freedom, Bergson situates freedom within time (reconceived as duration) and in closest proximity to us—at the heart of our immediate experience." Suzanne Guerlac, *Thinking in Time* (Ithaca, New York: Cornell University Press, 2006), 102–103.

2. Milič Čapek, *Bergson and Modern Physics* (Dordrecht, Holland: D. Reidel Publishing Co., 1971), 90.

3. Joseph Solomon, *Bergson* (Port Washington, New York: Kennikat Press, 1970),38.

4. Cited in Idella J. Gallagher, *Morality in Evolution* (The Hague, Netherlands: Martinus Nijhoff, 1970), 32.

5. A. A. Luce, *Bergson's Doctrine of Intuition* (New York: Macmillan, 1922), 57. For the sake of clarity, I substituted the word "motivates" for the word "motives" that is found in the original text.

6. In later works such as *Creative Evolution*, Bergson does not just limit mind/spirit/consciousness to human beings. Instead, he postulates a vast, universal spectrum of opposing tendencies—life versus matter, freedom versus determinism, and so on. As Luce comments, Bergson's vision seems to postulate that there is "in Nature a scale of freedom, just as there is a scale of life. . . . It may well be that freedom is an upgrade tendency, realized in the universe in varying degrees, counteracting the downgrade tendency towards the automatic and the mechanical." *Bergson's Doctrine of Intuition*, 58.

7. Barden comments that when we come to realize the creativity of the self, we discover that what lies in the future is not "what is already implied in present knowledge but the invention of the radically new." Garrett Barden, "Method in Philosophy," in John Mullarkey, ed., *The New Bergson* (New York: Manchester University Press, 1999), 36. He goes on to note that "the understanding that our future is more than our present . . . allows one to break out of the confining circle variously described by Collingwood, Foucault and Rorty, among others" in that "radical relativism involves a static conception or image of mind in which the mind is conceived as a closed system, the future states of which are contained in its present and consequently calculable in principle"; for Bergson, however, as Barden goes on to add, "the mind is not a closed system." *The New Bergson*, 36.

8. *Bergson's Doctrine of Intuition*, 53.

9. David Ray Griffin, *Unsnarling the World-Knot* (Berkeley: University of California Press, 1998), 15.

10. Technically, "soft-core common sense" beliefs: 1) are not universal, and 2) can be denied without any inconsistency. The fact that they are not universal is clearly recognized in retrospect after they have been overturned. The fact that they can be denied without any inconsistency means that these beliefs are such that they can be challenged (and even replaced if a new idea comes along that is seen to be superior) without having to overcome any intrinsic hurdles.

11. John R. Searle, *The Rediscovery of the Mind* (Cambridge, Massachusetts: MIT Press, 1992), 3; cited in *Unsnarling the World-Knot*, 19. See also *Unsnarling the World-Knot*, 37.

12. As Guerlac points out, "illusions of common sense are one thing. Claims to scientific truth are quite another, and much more dangerous. These must be vigorously contested philosophically, Bergson implies, or we will find ourselves living in a culture of automatons." *Thinking in Time*, 58.

13. John R. Searle, *Minds, Brains and Science* (London: British Broadcasting Corporation, 1984), 97.

14. Thomas Nagel, *The View from Nowhere* (New York: Oxford University Press, 1986), 123. Cited in *Unsnarling the World-Knot*, 38.

15. Chiari notes that "Bergson sees creation as continuous freedom and man himself as making or continuously creating himself through his freedom. This is, in some ways, very Sartrian." I think that, at least in this instance, it might be more appropriate to say that Sartre is very Bergsonian. Joseph Chiari, *Twentieth-Century French Thought* (New York: Gordian Press, 1975), 39.

16. Bergson suggests that "free acts are exceptional [i.e., very rare] even on the part of those who are most given to controlling and reasoning out what they do" (*TFW* 167). I would argue that he perhaps should have said that free acts are exceedingly rare, *especially* for those who seek to control and reason out what they do!

17. Gallagher, however, argues that "Bergson's view of the nature and function of intellect prevented him from allowing it an essential role in the free act. The essence of the free act is spontaneity and unforeseeability and not rationality." Idella J. Gallagher, *Morality in Evolution* The Hague, Netherlands: Martinus Nijhoff, 1970), 65.

18. For Bergson, there is no such thing as "the moment," if it is envisioned as an isolated and single mathematical point in time. Instead, "the moment" or the present is rooted in our entire past and is dynamically pushing toward the future. As Luce notes, for Bergson, "my present is my past on tip-toe." *Bergson's Doctrine of Intuition*, 103.

19. As Vladimir Jankélévitch mentions, "there are no recipes for creating, for beginning, and for giving, but only for imitating, continuing, and conserving." Thomas Hanna, ed., *The Bergsonian Heritage* (New York: Columbia University Press, 1962), 164.

20. The distinction between impulsiveness and spontaneity is my own, not Bergson's.

21. As I argue in more detail in section 2, there are multiple reasons why these "psychic cysts" are created, why certain ideas and beliefs hidden within us seem to take on a life of their own and at times will appear to take control of our body and mind in ways that are strikingly similar to the possession states described in the literature of cultural anthropology. Mullarkey points out that even Bergson is willing to use this type of terminology. He notes that "in a course given on the concept of personality between 1910 and 1911, [Bergson] goes so far as to liken [the nature of the self] to the pathology of multiple personality and to a series of 'possessions.' (M, 858). Jacques Maritain noted with disfavor that 'it is . . . impossible, in the Bergsonian thesis, to say or to think I'." John Mullarkey, *Bergson and Philosophy* (Notre Dame, Indiana: University of Notre Dame Press, 2000), 20; citing Jacques Maritain, *Bergsonian Philosophy and Thomism*, trans. Mabelle L. Andison and J. Gordon Andison (New York: Greenwood Press, 1948), 231.

22. As Gunter insightfully comments, "We are reluctant to be free, [Bergson] points out, in a way that had undoubted impact on later French existentialism. We are ordinarily freer than we want to be." P. A. Y. Gunter, "Bergson," in *A Companion to Continental Philosophy* (Hoboken, New Jersey: Wiley-Blackwell, 1999), 174–175.

23. I agree with Jankélévitch's observation that "*Time and Free Will* says that the free man is he who totalizes himself, but it does not tell us what must be done; it does not tell us what our duty is." *The Bergsonian Heritage*, 159. However, Jankélévitch then goes on to claim that, for Bergson, the person "who is thoroughly himself cannot be evil; is not *Time and Free Will* a little optimistic in that?" *The Bergsonian Heritage*, 159. I am not sure where in *Time and Free Will* Jankélévitch finds Bergson making this claim. As far as I can tell, Bergson in *Time and Free Will* never explicitly argues that, if we act in accordance with our deep-seated self, all of our actions will be morally good (although by *The Two Sources of Morality and Religion*, he does argue that the saints and mystics are those who act in alignment with their depths, with the élan vital). Bergson's claim in *Time and Free Will* is only that when we are aligned with our depths our actions will be free. Freedom is precisely that which allows us to make genuine choices—and the choice between morally good and morally reprehensible actions is one of those choices.

CHAPTER 8. THE WORLD "OUT THERE"

1. Milič Čapek, *Bergson and Modern Physics* (Dordrecht, Holland: D. Reidel Publishing Co., 1971), 91. John Mullarkey points out, correctly, that it is

overly simplistic to portray Bergson's understanding of time and space in *Time and Free Will* as utterly dualistic. John Mullarkey, *Bergson and Philosophy* (Notre Dame, Indiana: University of Notre Dame Press, 2000), 10. However, as Mullarkey also emphasizes, there is a dramatic shift in Bergson's discussion of durée after *Time and Free Will*, a shift that, oddly, Bergson never overtly acknowledges. I would suggest that the vision of durée that Bergson articulates in *Time and Free Will* is the seed out of which the later versions of durée blossom—but this seed remains fully alive and active and is not a discarded empty husk.

2. Gilles Deleuze, *Bergsonism*, trans. Hugh Tomlinson and Barbara Habberjam (New York: Zone Books, 1991), 34.

3. Čapek argues, convincingly, that "the most concise and also most accurate term by which Bergson's concept of matter is described is 'extensive becoming.'" *Bergson and Modern Physics*, 212.

CHAPTER 9. MOVEMENT

1. As Elizabeth Grosz helpfully points out, "Bergson seeks change in itself, change that does not simply ripple over unchanging things, change that is not carried along by things but that problematizes the very stability of what counts as an immobility, a thing, that which is cut out from its environment." Elizabeth Grosz, *The Nick of Time* (Durham, North Carolina: Duke University Press, 2004), 194.

2. As Jacques Chevalier archly notes, science "measures movement by bringing it to a standstill, [in the same way that it] analyzes life by killing it." Jacques Chevalier, *Henri Bergson*, trans. Lilian A. Clare (Freeport, New York: Books for Libraries Press, 1970), 83.

3. Marie Cariou, "The Keyboards of Forgetting," in John Mullarkey, ed., *The New Bergson* (New York: Manchester University Press, 1999), 110.

4. Gregory Vlastos, "Zeno of Elea," *The Encyclopedia of Philosophy*, Vol. 8. (New York: Macmillan Publishing, 1972), 372–375.

5. Andrew C. Papanicolaou, "Bergson's Psycho-physical Theory," in Andrew C. Papanicolaou and P. A. Y. Gunter, eds., *Bergson and Modern Thought* (New York: Harwood Academic Publishers, 1987), 70.

6. Keith Ansell Pearson, *Philosophy and the Adventure of the Virtual* (New York: Routledge, 2002), 22.

7. Cariou claims that Bergson misses Zeno's use of irony. She argues that "Zeno was probably more Bergsonian than Bergson thought." *The New Bergson*, 111.

8. Vladimir Jankélévitch, "With the Whole Soul," in Thomas Hanna, ed., *The Bergsonian Heritage* (New York: Columbia University Press, 1962), 162.

CHAPTER 10. AN ATOMISTIC UNDERSTANDING OF REALITY

1. Rupert Sheldrake, *The Presence of the Past* (Rochester, Vermont: Park Street Press, 1988), 27.
2. Ibid.
3. Fritjof Capra, *The Tao of Physics* (New York: Bantam Books, 1977), 43.
4. Milič Čapek, *Bergson and Modern Physics* (Dordrecht, Holland: D. Reidel Publishing Co., 1971), 270.
5. Ibid., 260. Čapek cites Jean Piaget, "A propos de la psychologie de l'atomisme," *Thales* 5 (1949): 3–7.
6. This question of when food becomes "me" was of crucial importance in the Middle Ages, with the belief in the real presence of Christ in the Eucharist. For instance, how does one treat the "body of Christ," if the recipient has coughed part of it out or thrown it up? For a detailed discussion of these (and other related) issues, see Caroline Walker Bynum, *Holy Feast and Holy Fast* (Berkeley: University of California Press, 1987).
7. Mary Douglas, *Purity and Danger* (New York: Routledge, 1966). For a valuable psychoanalytic perspective on toilet training, and the charged significance of bodily boundaries, see Erik H. Erikson, *Childhood and Society* (New York: W. W. Norton, 1950), 48–108.
8. *The Presence of the Past*, 97.

CHAPTER 11. GOING BEYOND CLASSICAL PHYSICS

1. Bertrand Russell, "A Free Man's Worship," *Mysticism and Logic and Other Essays* (London: Pelican Books, 1953), 51. Cited in Milič Čapek, *Bergson and Modern Physics* (Dordrecht, Holland: D. Reidel Publishing Co., 1971), 10.
2. Cited in *Bergson and Modern Physics*, 11.
3. I am deeply grateful to both Henry Stapp, theoretical physicist par excellence, and Fred Olness, chair of Southern Methodist University's physics department, for their close and careful reading of my original (much longer and more detailed) discussion of the relationships between the findings of quantum mechanics and Bergson's thought. (Unfortunately, editorial constraints meant that I had to make the difficult choice to not include in this text most of what they read.) I particularly remember one lunch with Fred in which I expressed my concern that, because of my reliance on secondary texts, I might unknowingly be presenting a perspective that some physicists would scorn. Fred promptly reassured me that not only was my presentation resolutely mainstream, but that it actually was not weird enough!
4. Fritjof Capra, *The Tao of Physics* (New York: Bantam Books, 1977), 211.

5. Andrew C. Papanicolaou, "Bergson's Psycho-physical Theory," in Andrew C. Papanicolaou and P. A. Y. Gunter, eds., *Bergson and Modern Thought* (New York: Harwood Academic Publishers, 1987), 85–86.

6. *The Tao of Physics*, 282. Of course, a worldview that argues that there are no "things," but only an interwoven, ceaseless creation of new patterns in the flux, is not only Bergsonian, but also a perspective that is strikingly similar to the teachings of both Taoism and Mahayana Buddhism.

7. David Bohm and B. Hiley, "On the Intuitive Understanding of Nonlocality as Implied by Quantum Theory," *Foundations of Physics* 5 (1975): 96, 102. Cited in *The Tao of Physics*, 124.

8. *Bergson and Modern Physics*, 274. Čapek's emphasis.

9. Rupert Sheldrake, *The Presence of the Past* (Rochester, Vermont: Park Street Press, 1988),4.

10. As Čapek and others have pointed out, the relationship of Bergson's thought to that of Einstein is complex. While Bergson criticized certain aspects of relativity theory in the comments on Einstein's work that he made in *Durée et simultanéité* (published in 1923), he was not, in actuality, objecting to most of the specifics of the theory. However, it was easy for many people to focus exclusively on some of the specifics of Bergson's critique and to forget the "implicit agreement between his philosophy and the relativistic physics" as well as "those agreements which he explicitly pointed out." *Bergson and Modern Physics*, 235–236. As Pete A. Y. Gunter makes clear, even though Bergson in *Durée et simultanéité* argues against certain of Einstein's ideas, in many ways his thought mirrors some of the central assertions of relativity theory. For instance, Bergson proposed, several years before Einstein (in 1896, with the publication of *Matter and Memory*) that perhaps it was best to conceive of energy and mass as "aspects of one fundamental reality"; he articulated a theory "in which distinct objects are construed as aspects of a fundamental physical interconnectedness"; he proposed that time is not uniform, but rather that "there are different rhythms of duration"; and he argued that "motion is less the translation of a distinct body through an empty space than the transformation of an entire situation." P. A. Y. Gunter, "Henri Bergson," in David Ray Griffin et al., eds., *Founders of Constructive Postmodern Philosophy* (Albany, New York: State University of New York Press, 1993), 138. However, to complicate matters, it appears that Bergson himself also at times did not see some of these implicit agreements, due perhaps to "his justified criticism of certain interpretations of the relativity theory"; at times he entered, therefore (at least in the view of Čapek), into an "indefensible criticism" of the very aspects of the special theory of relativity that were explicitly aligned with his own philosophy. *Bergson and Modern Physics*, 236.

11. *Bergson and Modern Physics*, x.

12. Ibid., ix.
13. Louis de Broglie, "The Concepts of Contemporary Physics and Bergson's Ideas on Time and Motion," in P. A. Y. Gunter (ed. and trans.), *Bergson and the Evolution of Physics* (Knoxville: University of Tennessee Press, 1969), 47.
14. Ibid.
15. P. A. Y. Gunter, "Bergson," in *A Companion to Continental Philosophy* (Hoboken, New Jersey: Wiley-Blackwell, 1999), 175.

CHAPTER 12. MELODIES OF THE SELF AND WORLD

1. Bergson was delighted that his views of matter had been echoed, in many respects, by the work of Alfred North Whitehead, who as Bergson points out, eventually began to think of a piece of iron as "a melodic continuity" (*CM* 85). Čapek notes that Bergson was most likely paraphrasing a passage from Whitehead, in 1919, where he, "after insisting that durationless instants do not exist anywhere in concrete experience . . . concluded: 'it is equally true of a molecule of iron or of a musical phrase.'" Alfred North Whitehead, *An Enquiry Concerning the Principles of Natural Knowledge* (Cambridge: Cambridge University Press, 1919), 196. Cited in Milič Čapek, *Bergson and Modern Physics* (Dordrecht, Holland: D. Reidel Publishing Co., 1971), 318.
2. A. R. Lacey, *Bergson* (New York: Routledge, 1989), 96.
3. Ibid.
4. Čapek correctly notes that William James makes much the same observation when James points out that "even a single and 'isolated' tone is not isolated, since it is perceived in the context of antecedent silence." *Bergson and Modern Physics*, 32.
5. Ibid., 325.
6. For an alternative, and illuminating, use of jazz improvisation to illustrate metaphysical themes (this time from a Ch'an perspective), see Peter D. Hershock, *Liberating Intimacy* (Albany: State University of New York Press, 1996), 75–80.
7. As A. A. Luce notes in his poetic fashion, "when one tries to intuit the essence of personal being, one feels as if one were attempting to stay a stream; the ego seems an arrest of a current of being, the hanging wave of a flowing tide." A. A. Luce, *Bergson's Doctrine of Intuition* (New York: Macmillan, 1922), 102.
8. Eric Matthews, "Bergson's Concept of a Person," in John Mullarkey, ed., *The New Bergson* (New York: Manchester University Press, 1999), 133. Pearson notes that interpreters of Bergson have debated whether or not Bergson depicts a self that is a manifestation of sheer difference or possesses

an inherent unity. He lists two contrasting perspectives on this issue: J. Crary, *Suspensions of Perception, Attention, Spectacle and Modern Culture* (Cambridge, Massachusetts: MIT Press, 1999) and A. Game, *Undoing the Social* (Milton Keynes, United Kingdom: Open University Press, 1991). As Pearson points out, "where Crary sees Bergson as relying on a notion of a unified ego and a consciousness grounded in praxis (326) Game astutely shows that for Bergson 'there is no unitary, singular self' (1991: 102)." *Philosophy and the Adventure of the Virtual*, 226, note 23.

9. A. R. Lacey, *Bergson*, 95. Lacey is citing a passage from *Durée et simultanéité*.

10. As Elizabeth Grosz points out, "Bergson is concerned with finding the appropriate limits of scientific analysis, and with what it is that scientific methodologies must leave out. . . . Instead of making philosophy a form of passive acceptance of the givenness of the discourses and practices of the sciences, he makes it a productive concern that both functions *alongside* the sciences, operating with different aims and methods but able to make collateral use of the sciences as much as the arts, and also functioning as it were *underneath* the sciences, making explicit their unacknowledged commitment to philosophical and ultimately ontological concepts." Elizabeth Grosz, *The Nick of Time* (Durham, North Carolina: Duke University Press, 2004), 156–157.

11. Grosz echoes my emphasis on the ways in which Bergson's work offers an alternative to both foundationalist and antifoundationalist thinkers. As she notes, "both his earliest critics, who affirm the more or less limitless value of science and logic in explaining and ordering the real (Russell, Huxley), and his postmodern opponents, who affirm that the real is only ever accessible through synthesis (Derrida and deconstructionism, common characterizations of postmodernism), share a belief in the coincidence of epistemology/representation/discourse with the real, the collapse of ontology into epistemology. If there is a real that cannot be measured, represented, or known, then it remains, so it is believed, below philosophy's threshold of relevance. What these otherwise antagonistic positions—positivism, postmodernism—share, it seems, is that representations, whether mathematical (Russell) or discursive (for Derrida), are our only means of access to the real, the way we signify or construct the real." *The Nick of Time*, 192.

CHAPTER 13. CONTEMPORARY UNDERSTANDINGS OF CONSCIOUSNESS

1. As David Ray Griffin points out, "the mind-body problem, which Arthur Schopenhauer called the 'world-knot,' has arguably been the central problem in modern philosophy since its inception in the seventeenth century." David Ray Griffin, *Unsnarling the World-Knot* (Berkeley: University of California Press, 1998), 1.

2. In this section, where I offer an overview of current philosophical and psychological discussions on the mind-body problem, I am indebted to two texts: *Unsnarling the World-Knot*, by David Ray Griffin, and *Consciousness: An Introduction*, by Susan Blackmore (see note 3 for bibliographical information on Blackmore's text). Griffin's detailed and thorough analysis finally hammered home what I had known for quite some time: that *Matter and Memory* is perhaps even more relevant to today's philosophical climate than it was when it was written. Blackmore's clearly written and wide-ranging work, in its turn, helped me to pull all the pieces together, and gave me the broad overview of consciousness studies that I had been searching for during my research. While I disagree with certain aspects of both authors' work, on the whole I have tremendous respect for the clarity and scope of both texts. Finally, in this section I frequently quote from the works of several philosophers of mind (e.g., Thomas Nagel, John Searle). Because I was at times alerted to their work in either Griffin or Blackmore's texts, in my own references, whenever possible, I first give the bibliographical information of the original quote, and then give the page number in which it is found in Griffin or Blackmore.

3. Philosophers of mind are keenly aware of the issues that arise when exploring the nature of subjective experience. As Blackmore notes: "What is it like to be a bat? This is one of the most famous questions ever asked in the history of consciousness studies. First posed in 1950 it was made famous in a 1974 paper of that name by American philosopher Thomas Nagel." Susan Blackmore, *Consciousness: An Introduction* (New York: Oxford University Press, 2004), 22.

4. To underscore the difficulties associated with attempts to link consciousness with spatial locations, try asking yourself: "Is my consciousness in the room that I am in, or is the room in my consciousness?"

5. David Chalmers, "The Puzzle of Conscious Experience," *Scientific American* (December 1995): 63.

6. *Consciousness: An Introduction*, 19.

7. Edward F. Kelly et al., *Irreducible Mind* (Lanham, Maryland: Rowman & Littlefield, 2007), 25.

8. A. A. Luce, *Bergson's Doctrine of Intuition* (New York: Macmillan, 1922), 63.

9. Milič Čapek, "Bergson's Theory of the Mind-Brain Relation," in Andrew C. Papanicolaou and P. A. Y. Gunter, eds., *Bergson and Modern Thought* (New York: Harwood Academic Publishers, 1987), 133.

10. Ibid., 134.

11. Ted Honderich, "Mind, Brain, and Self-Conscious Mind," in Colin Blakemore and Susan Greenfield, eds., *Mindwaves* (Oxford: Basil Blackwell, 1987), 445-58; cited in *Unsnarling the World-Knot*, 37.

12. M. Minsky, *Society of Mind* (New York: Simon & Schuster, 1986), 287; cited in *Consciousness: An Introduction*, 13.

13. S. Greenfield, *Brain Story* (London: BBC, 2000), 14; cited in *Consciousness: An Introduction*, 13. There is, however, far from unanimity among various materialist theorists on the specific place within our brain where consciousness is generated. See *Consciousness: An Introduction*, 232 for a discussion of some of the options that are currently offered by various materialists.

14. Francis Crick, *The Astonishing Hypothesis* (New York: Scribner, 1994), 3; cited in *Consciousness: An Introduction*, 73.

15. *Consciousness: An Introduction*, 25.

16. Daniel Dennett, "Quining Qualia," in A. J. Marcel and E. Bisiach, eds., *Consciousness in Contemporary Society* (Oxford: Oxford University Press, 1988), 42; cited in *Consciousness: An Introduction*, 25.

17. Paul M. Churchland, *Scientific Realism and the Plasticity of Mind* (Cambridge: Cambridge University Press, 1979), 119.

18. Milič Čapek, "Bergson's Theory of the Mind-Brain Relation," in Andrew C. Papanicolaou and P. A.Y. Gunter, eds., *Bergson and Modern Thought* (New York: Harwood Academic Publishers, 1987), 130.

19. Galen Strawson, *Mental Reality* (Cambridge, Massachusetts: MIT Press, 1994), 51; cited in *Unsnarling the World-Knot*, 35.

20. *Mental Reality*, 53; cited in *Unsnarling the World-Knot*, 35.

21. *Consciousness: An Introduction*, 242.

22. John R. Searle, *The Rediscovery of the Mind* (Cambridge, Massachusetts: MIT Press, 1992), 130; cited in *Unsnarling the World-Knot*, 52.

23. John C. Eccles, *How the Self Controls Its Brain* (Berlin: Springer-Verlag, 1994), 22; cited in *Unsnarling the World-Knot*, 52.

24. Daniel Dennett, *Brainstorms* (Sussex: Harvester Press, 1978), 81; cited in John Mullarkey, *Bergson and Philosophy* (Notre Dame, Indiana: University of Notre Dame Press, 2000), 60.

25. *Bergson and Philosophy*, 60. M. R. Bennet and P. M. S. Hacker refer to strategies such as Dennett's homunculus theory as the "mereological fallacy." See M. R. Bennet and P. M. S. Hacker, *Philosophical Foundations of Neuroscience* (Oxford: Blackwell, 2003). I am grateful to Ed Kelly for pointing out this reference.

26. As Griffin helpfully points out, panpsychism is not vitalism: "Vitalism is the doctrine that nature, prior to the emergence of life, operated solely in terms of mechanistic principles, but that with life an entirely new causal force emerged. This kind of dualism is an example of exactly what panexperientialists want to overcome." *Unsnarling the World-Knot*, 93.

27. *Consciousness: An Introduction*, 148.

28. *Unsnarling the World-Knot*, 60.

29. Ibid., 61.

30. *The Rediscovery of the Mind*, 74, 81; cited in *Unsnarling the World-Knot*, 61.

31. Owen Flanagan, *Consciousness Reconsidered* (Cambridge, Massachusetts:

MIT Press, 1992), 35; cited in *Unsnarling the World-Knot*, 61.

32. Julius Adler and Wing-Wai Tse, "Decision-making in Bacteria," *Science* 184 (June 21, 1974): 1292–1294.

33. J. J. C. Smart, "Materialism," in C. V. Borst, ed., *The Mind-Brain Identity Theory* (London: Macmillan, 1979), 168f; cited in *Unsnarling the World-Knot*, 63.

34. *Unsnarling the World-Knot*, 63.

35. Thomas Nagel, *Mortal Questions* (London: Cambridge University Press, 1979), 189; cited in *Unsnarling the World-Knot*, 64.

36. Nicholas Humphrey, *A History of the Mind* (London: Chatto and Windus, 1992), 180f; cited in *Unsnarling the World-Knot*, 70.

37. *Unsnarling the World-Knot*, 70.

38. Ibid., 70–71.

39. *Consciousness: An Introduction*, 154.

40. John C. Eccles, *Facing Reality* (Heidelberg: Springer-Verlag, 1970), 173; cited in *Unsnarling the World-Knot*, 65.

41. *Unsnarling the World-Knot*, 65.

42. Ibid., 64.

43. Colin McGinn, *The Problem of Consciousness* (Oxford: Basil Blackwell, 1991), 45; cited in *Unsnarling the World-Knot*, 67.

44. *The Problem of Consciousness*, 18; cited in *Unsnarling the World-Knot*, 72.

45. *Unsnarling the World-Knot*, 72.

46. Ibid., 73.

47. *Consciousness: An Introduction*, 34. Some theorists however, claim that the notion of "easy problems" in consciousness studies is itself mistaken. See for instance E. J. Lowe, "There Are No Easy Problems of Consciousness," in Jonathan Shear, ed., *Explaining Consciousness* (Cambridge, Massachusetts: MIT Press, 1997), 117–123 and David Hodgson, "The Easy Problems Ain't So Easy," in Jonathan Shear, ed., *Explaining Consciousness* (Cambridge, Massachusetts: MIT Press, 1997), 125–131.

48. Karl R. Popper and John C. Eccles, *The Self and Its Brain* (Heidelberg: Springer-Verlag, 1977), 105; cited in *Unsnarling the World-Knot*, 3.

49. *Consciousness: An Introduction*, 32.

50. *The Problem of Consciousness*, 1–2, 7; cited in *Unsnarling the World-Knot*, 4.

51. William Seager, *Metaphysics of Consciousness* (New York: Routledge, 1991), 195.

52. *Mental Reality*, 50.

53. Thomas Nagel, *The View from Nowhere* (New York: Oxford University Press, 1986), 10; cited in *Unsnarling the World-Knot*, 5.

54. *Mental Reality*, 75, 108; cited in *Unsnarling the World-Knot*, 6. See also Galen Strawson et al., "Nature: Why Physicalism Entails Panpsychism," in Anthony Freeman, ed., *Consciousness and Its Place in Nature* (Exeter, United Kingdom: Imprint Academic, 2006).

55. *Consciousness: An Introduction*, 11.
56. *Unsnarling the World-Knot*, 78.
57. Ibid., 93. Panpsychism as a viable philosophical option is beginning to show new signs of life. In addition to the work of Galen Strawson (cited in note 54), see for instance David Skrbina, *Panpsychism in the West* (Cambridge: Massachusetts: MIT Press, 2005) and Henry P. Stapp, *The Mindful Universe* (Berlin: Springer, 2007).
58. *Unsnarling the World-Knot*, 91.
59. Ibid., 175.
60. Ibid., 79. As Blackmore points out, if we accept panpsychism, then numerous, and legitimate, theoretical questions have to be addressed, such as "is a stone aware? Is every scrap of sand, or each molecule or atom within it? What would it mean for something as simple as an electron to have mental attributes? And why should there simultaneously be physical and mental properties to everything?" *Consciousness: An Introduction*, 11. These sorts of philosophical questions deserve a detailed and careful response; however, for the moment, it is perhaps worth noting, as Griffin indicates, that "most forms of panpsychism do *not* attribute *consciousness* (as distinct from experience, feeling, sentience, or protoconsciousness)" to rudimentary forms of matter. *Unsnarling the World-Knot*, 80.
61. *Unsnarling the World-Knot*, 80.
62. *A History of the Mind*, 193; cited in *Unsnarling the World-Knot*, 80.
63. *Unsnarling the World-Knot*, 80.
64. *The Problem of Consciousness*, note 2; cited in *Unsnarling the World-Knot*, 82.
65. Ibid.; cited in *Unsnarling the World-Knot*, 82.
66. *Unsnarling the World-Knot*, 82.
67. *The Rediscovery of the Mind*, 3; cited in *Unsnarling the World-Knot*, 12.
68. *Unsnarling the World-Knot*, 11.

CHAPTER 14. IMAGES OF THE UNIVERSE

1. *Matter and Memory* is a masterpiece—it is a subtle, detailed, brilliantly unorthodox work. But unfortunately, in order to penetrate into the heart of this masterpiece, one must first pass through dense, seemingly impenetrable walls of highly technical philosophical prose. It is my hope that what follows successfully "translates" *Matter and Memory* in a way that allows it to be more easily grasped, while not losing the gift of its finely calibrated insights. For a recent, extremely detailed, commentary and analysis of *Matter and Memory*, see Frédéric Worms, *Introduction à Matière et mémoire de Bergson* (Paris: Presses Universitaires de France, 1997).
2. The French word for Bergson's technical term "image" is also "image" and

has the same visual connotations as the English word. However, as Elizabeth Grosz helpfully points out, although matter for Bergson is "imagistic," nonetheless, this does not imply "that it is reduced to the imagistic perception of a subject (i.e., idealism) or that the image is necessarily or in any privileged manner visual." Elizabeth Grosz, *The Nick of Time* (Durham, North Carolina: Duke University Press, 2004), 163.

3. The "object" that seems to exist "over there" is, in Gunter's vivid phrasing, "never simply located at any one place, but is connected by fields of energy to all parts of nature. In a sense, it is everywhere." P. A. Y. Gunter, "Henri Bergson," in David Ray Griffin et al., eds., *Founders of Constructive Postmodern Philosophy* (Albany, New York: State University of New York Press, 1993), 140.

4. David Skrbina, however, lists numerous scientist-philosophers who, as part of the early development of scientific thought, *were* open to some version of panpsychism (e.g., William Gilbert, Johannes Kepler, Gottfried Leibniz, Julien LaMettrie, Johann Herder, Gustav Fechner, Ernst Haeckel, Ernst Mach). Skrbina also discusses several notable scientists in the early to mid-twentieth century who endorsed panpsychism (e.g., Sir Arthur Eddington, J. B. S. Haldane, Sir Charles Scott Sherrington, W. E. Agar, Sir Julian Huxley, Sewall Wright, Bernhard Rensch, Gregory Bateson, A. Cochran, Charles Birch, Freeman Dyson, Danah Zohar, Rupert Sheldrake, Stuart Hameroff, and David Bohm. See David Skrbina, *Panpsychism in the West* (Cambridge: Massachusetts: MIT Press, 2005), 185–206. For another recent endorsement of a form of panpsychism by a notable quantum physicist, see Henry P. Stapp, *The Mindful Universe* (Berlin: Springer, 2007).

5. Frédéric Worms, "La Théorie bergsonienne des plans de conscience: genèse, structure et signification de *Matière et mémoire*," in Philippe Gallois and Gérard Forzy, eds., *Bergson et les neurosciences* (Le Plessis-Robinson: Insitut Synthélabo, 1997), 103.

6. Maurice Merleau-Ponty, untitled contribution in Thomas Hanna, ed., *The Bergsonian Heritage* (New York: Columbia University Press, 1962), 138.

7. F. C. T. Moore, *Bergson: Thinking Backwards* (New York: Cambridge University Press, 1996), 27.

8. We often forget how differently the world that we experience through our senses is from the world that is experienced by different species of organisms, whose sense organs screen out or emphasize quite different "portions" of the universal flux. Milič Čapek helpfully underscores the fact that the process of selection by which each of the various "animal milieu" is carved out of the total surrounding universe by various species of organisms is not so much a conscious selection by each organism, but rather, is the end product of vast eons of evolutionary selectivity within each species. Milič Čapek, *Bergson and Modern Physics* (Dordrecht, Holland: D. Reidel Publishing Co.,

1971), 36. For some fascinating accounts of the different sense capacities of various organisms (e.g., the ability of bees to perceive ultraviolet rays; the perception of ultrasonic vibrations in bats, porpoises, and moths; and how insects can sense sexual odors several miles away, see the following texts: Karl von Frisch, *Bees, Their Vision, Chemical Senses and Language* (Ithaca, New York: Cornell University Press, 1950), 6–11; Vitus Dröscher, *The Mysterious Sense of Animals* (New York: Dutton, 1965), 23–26; Lorus and Margery Milne, *The Senses of Animals and Men* (New York: Athenaeum, 1962), 131.

9. Unfortunately, in *Living Consciousness*, I am not able to give Bergson's multiple understandings of intuition the detailed attention that they so clearly deserve. However, in this chapter, I refer to those understandings of intuition that focus primarily on intuition as that which allows one to become increasingly attuned to the élan vital, that is, to the more cosmic levels of durée. This understanding of intuition is in contrast to Bergson's earlier, less cosmic, understandings of intuition. As many Bergson scholars have correctly noted, Bergson originally focused on intuition as that learned (and extremely arduous) capacity to come to know, from the inside, one's own personal durée—an immediacy of knowing that can then be extended to other qualities of durée as well. Many scholars of Bergson, perhaps influenced by Deleuze, and keen to emphasize the ways in which intuition is a valid, respectable mode of knowledge, often tend to stress the ways in which Bergson understands intuition as a rigorous "method" of comprehending durée and life. These scholars will often claim, as Grosz does, that intuition is "not to be confused with feelings, sympathy or empathy, or being in tune with." *The Nick of Time*, 235. While I sympathize (so to speak) with the desire of Bergson scholars to minimize the popular "head in the clouds" stereotype of intuition, nonetheless, I also think that doing so risks losing some of the richness of Bergson's attempts to approach the (literally!) inexpressible qualities of intuition from multiple vantage points—some of which are explicitly about "tuning into" the élan vital and are hence rather more "spiritual" or "cosmic" than many scholars appear to be comfortable acknowledging.

CHAPTER 15. NONLOCALITY AND BERGSON'S UNIVERSE OF IMAGES

1. Gary Zukav, *The Dancing Wu Li Masters* (New York: William Morrow, 1980), 282. Henry Stapp, a noted quantum physicist, wrote in 1975 that "Bell's theorem is the most profound discovery of science." Henry Stapp, "Bell's Theorem and World Process," *Il Nuovo Cimento* 29B (1975): 271; cited in *The Dancing Wu Li Masters*, 299.

2. *The Dancing Wu Li Masters*, 283.
3. Ibid., 286.
4. Albert Einstein, "Autobiographical Notes," in Paul Schilpp, ed., *Albert Einstein, Philosopher-Scientist* (New York: Harper and Row, 1949), 87; cited in *The Dancing Wu Li Masters*, 289.
5. Michael Talbot, *The Holographic Universe* (New York: HarperCollins, 1991), 52.
6. Ibid.
7. *The Dancing Wu Li Masters*, 47.
8. Ibid.
9. Ibid.
10. Milič Čapek, *Bergson and Modern Physics* (Dordrecht, Holland: D. Reidel Publishing Co., 1971), 278.
11. Lynne McTaggart, *The Field* (New York: HarperCollins, 2002), 2.
12. Paul Davis, *Superforce* (New York: Simon and Schuster, 1984), 48; cited in *The Holographic Universe*, 53.
13. For terse, yet insightful, descriptions of superdeterminism and the Many Worlds theory (as they relate to Bell's theorem), see *The Dancing Wu Li Masters*, 302–307.
14. *The Holographic Universe*, 47.
15. Ibid.
16. Ibid., 48.
17. David Bohm, "A New Theory of the Relationship of Mind and Matter," *Journal of the American Society of Psychical Research* 80, no. 2 (1986): 129; cited in David Skrbina, *Panpsychism in the West* (Cambridge: Massachusetts: MIT Press, 2005)204.
18. *Panpsychism in the West*, 131.
19. Ibid.
20. Ibid., 206.
21. David Bohm, "Hidden Variables and the Implicate Order," in Basil J. Hiley and F. David Peat eds., *Quantum Implications* (London: Routledge and Kegan Paul, 1987), 38; cited in *The Holographic Universe*, 41.
22. David Bohm, "A New Theory of the Relationship of Mind and Matter," 114, cited in *Panpsychism in the West*, 205.

CHAPTER 16. PERCEPTIONS AND THE BRAIN

1. P. A. Y. Gunter, "Bergson," in *A Companion to Continental Philosophy* (Hoboken, New Jersey: Wiley-Blackwell, 1999), 177.
2. Bergson rarely abandoned or altered his previous understandings, and terse summations of early works frequently appear in the body of later works.

3. Susan Blackmore, *Consciousness: An Introduction* (New York: Oxford University Press, 2004), 227.

4. Ibid.

5. Ibid., 227, 228.

6. Ed Kelly, in a private communication, notes that "there are only a few such cases [i.e., high-functioning individuals with the hydrocephalus], and they are all slow-onset, with the cortex essentially all there, but compressed." Nonetheless, the fact that someone can have an IQ of over 100 with a paper-thin layer of brain tissue should raise numerous questions as to the form of correlation that exists between the brain and consciousness.

7. Roger Lewin, "Is Your Brain Really Necessary?" *Science* 210 (December 12, 1980): 1232–1234.

8. I would argue that the evidence from the extensive research on NDEs—near-death experiences—is also an extremely compelling reason to reexamine materialist assumptions of the relationship between the brain and the mind. For a nuanced discussion of the philosophical implications of this evidence, see Carl B. Becker, *Paranormal Experience and Survival of Death* (Albany, New York: State University of New York Press, 1993), 77–119; David Ray Griffin, *Parapsychology, Philosophy, and Spirituality* (Albany, New York: State University of New York Press, 1997), 229–268; Emily Williams Kelly et al., "Unusual Experiences Near Death and Related Phenomena," in Edward F. Kelly et al., *Irreducible Mind* (Lanham, Maryland: Rowman & Littlefield), 367–421. For an excellent reader on the subject, see Lee W. Bailey and Jenny Yates, eds., *The Near-Death Experience* (New York: Routledge, 1996).

9. Leonard Lawlor, *The Challenge of Bergsonism* (New York: Continuum, 2003), 16. Bergson's notion of the brain as a conduit between incoming sensory nerves and outgoing motor nerves is clearly a vast oversimplification. It is obvious that the brain is not just an organ designed to make our responses operate less like reflex actions. For example, the brain does not simply deal with external information (i.e., perceptual data). It also has the complex, and crucial, task of monitoring and regulating the internal environment of the body. Bergson's discussion of this aspect of the brain is, admittedly, undeveloped (as is his related discussion of "affections").

10. George Wald, "Consciousness and Cosmology," in Andrew C. Papanicolaou and P. A. Y. Gunter, eds., *Bergson and Modern Thought* (New York: Harwood Academic Publishers, 1987), 349–350.

11. Ibid., 350. Wald's television metaphor echoes a way of understanding the relationship between the brain and states of consciousness that was extensively discussed and developed in Europe and America in the late nineteenth century, by thinkers such as William James, F. C. S. Schiller, and F. W. H. Myers. Edward and Emily Kelly call this perspective the "filter" or "transmission" theory. For a thorough and insightful discussion of the value

and potential difficulties of this perspective, see *Irreducible Mind*, 28–29 and 606–638. I discuss William James' elaboration of this theoretical outlook in G. William Barnard, *Exploring Unseen Worlds* (Albany, New York: State University of New York Press, 1997), 163–170.

CHAPTER 17. THE INTERACTION OF PERCEPTION AND MEMORY

1. Suzanne Guerlac appears to agree with my discussion of "primal memory," noting that the "kind of impersonal memory alluded to . . . in connection with Pure Perception" acts as a type of "memory thread onto which external instantaneous visions would be strung like beads." Suzanne Guerlac, *Thinking in Time* (Ithaca, New York: Cornell University Press, 2006), 118.
2. Once again, Bergson's understanding is similar to that of William James, who describes each moment of experience as a fusion of two types of knowledge: "knowledge by acquaintance"—the raw data of our sense experience—and "knowledge-about"—the culturally mediated, linguistic, preconscious, internalized information about that sense experience. For a fuller discussion, see chapter 2 of *Exploring Unseen Worlds*.
3. Deleuze underscores the potential negative consequences of the selectivity of our perceptions, a selectivity generated by our memories, of which our beliefs form an important subset: "As Bergson says, we do not perceive the thing or the image in its entirety, we always perceive less of it, we perceive only what we are interested in perceiving, or rather what is in our interest to perceive, by virtue of our economic interests, ideological beliefs and psychological demands. We therefore normally perceive only clichés." Gilles Deleuze, *Cinema* 2, H. Tomlinson and R. Galeta, trans. (London: Athlone Press, 1989/1985), 20.
4. Ian W. Alexander, *Bergson: Philosopher of Reflection* (New York: Hillary House, 1957), 42–43.

CHAPTER 18. MOVING FROM PERCEPTION TO MEMORY

1. These terms (habit memory and recollection memory) are my attempt to offer consistent names for these two different forms of memory. Bergson himself uses many different designations. Lawler argues, insightfully, that there is a close connection between Bergson's understanding of habit memory and Bergson's description, in *The Two Sources*, of the ways in which we tacitly embody a culture's set of moral and social imperatives, a process that Bergson terms "the totality of obligation." Leonard Lawler, *The Challenge of Bergsonism* (New York: Continuum, 2003), 33, referring to (*TS* 27).

CHAPTER 19. THE INTERWEAVING OF RECOLLECTION
MEMORY AND HABIT MEMORY

1. Suzanne Guerlac, *Thinking in Time* (Ithaca, New York: Cornell University Press, 2006), 136.

CHAPTER 20. RUMINATIONS ON THE HIDDEN POWER OF MEMORY

1. Keith Ansell Pearson points out that Deleuze emphasizes the stratification of memory as well. Deleuze however draws upon the image of a crystal, in which the past is complexified "into regions, sheets and strata of time." Keith Ansell Pearson, *Philosophy and the Adventure of the Virtual* (New York: Routledge, 2002), 183. I am in agreement with Deleuze's stress on the stratification of memory, especially because of its overlap with certain aspects of object relations thought. My only caution is that the metaphor of the crystal can lead us to think that memory is somehow "hard" and "unmoving" like a crystal, rather than supple and alive. Deleuze, however, appears to consciously oppose more organic metaphors (as Pearson notes, "Deleuze transforms the image of time from an organic one to a crystal one.") *Philosophy and the Adventure of the Virtual*, 182. Bergson himself was critically aware of the need to approach these nonspatial "realms" of experience with a variety of often conflicting metaphors; bearing this necessity in mind therefore, I would suggest that perhaps Jung's more organic image of the subconscious as a rhizome (found in the beginning of *Memories, Dreams, Reflections*) is equally powerful and suggestive, in that the visible mushroom (i.e., our everyday consciousness) is only the outer manifestation of a deeply hidden, complexly interwoven, subterranean reality. See C. G. Jung, *Memories, Dreams, Reflections* (New York: Vintage Books, 1989), 4.

2. Mullarkey appears to concur with my discussion of the different layers of mentality within us. As he notes, "there are stereotypical thoughts when, as living automata, we exist at a superficial level; but there are also complex, creative thoughts and emotions wherein our whole personality is involved and which can never be repeated. In other words, there are tones or levels to mentality." John Mullarkey, *Bergson and Philosophy* (Notre Dame, Indiana: University of Notre Dame Press, 2000), 37.

3. While Marie Cariou explores the connections between the ideas of Bergson and Freud, I would argue that Bergson's notion of the unconscious is much closer to the interactive, relational model of neo-Freudian schools (e.g., object relations theorists and Self psychology) than to Freud's own model of the unconscious. The unconscious for Bergson (as opposed to Freud) is *not* inherently charged with sexual and aggressive energy, it is not a hidden battlefield between timeless desires that want satisfaction at any cost and puni-

tive internal censorship that seeks to squash and deny anything less than moral perfection. See Marie Cariou, *Lectures bergsoniennes* (Paris: Presses Universitaires de France, 1990), 33–79. For a helpful overview of object relations theory in psychoanalysis, see Jay R. Greenberg and Stephen A. Mitchell, *Object Relations in Psychoanalytic Theory* (Cambridge: Harvard University Press, 1983).

4. For a fascinating discussion of these semiautonomous "partial selves," see Adam Crabtree, "Automatism and Secondary Centers of Consciousness," in Edward Kelly et al., *Irreducible Mind* (Lanham, Maryland: Rowman & Littlefield, 2007), 301–365. See also Adam Crabtree, *From Mesmer to Freud* (New Haven: Yale University Press, 1993) and F. W. H. Myers, *Human Personality and Its Survival of Bodily Death* (Charlottesville, Virginia: Hampton Roads Publishing, 1961).

5. Emile Durkheim, *The Elementary Forms of Religious Life*, Karen E. Fields, trans. (New York: The Free Press, 1995).

CHAPTER 21. THE PRESENCE OF THE PAST

1. This entire discussion of how the present is inevitably interwoven with the past dramatically undermines Deleuze's claim that there is a difference in kind between the past and the present. See especially chapter 3, "Memory as Virtual Coexistence," in Gilles Deleuze, Hugh Tomlinson, and Barbara Habberjam, trans., *Bergsonism* (New York: Zone Books, 1988).

2. Marie Cariou, "Bergson: The Keyboards of Forgetting," Melissa McMahon, trans., in John Mullarkey, ed., *The New Bergson* (New York: Manchester University Press, 1999), 104. Marie Cariou offers an important objection to Bergson's theory of forgetting. Bergson repeatedly emphasizes that we remember only what is useful in the present, however, as Cariou notes, it is often the case that we are often not able, in the present, to remember memories that would be, in fact, quite useful. (Conversely, we also at times obsessively remember events that are not useful!) Cariou suggests that forgetting is not as simple as Bergson claims. Rather, it is "a phenomenon of intense psychical complexity in which a whole work of elaboration, condensation, [and] figuration is accomplished," a process which also occurs in the production of dreams, a process which is related to, and translates, "a war of desires" within our unconscious. Ibid.

CHAPTER 22. MEMORY AND THE BRAIN

1. Rupert Sheldrake is one of the few contemporary scientists who agrees with Bergson's claim that memories are not stored in the brain. Sheldrake's theory

of "morphic resonance" is highly controversial, but he is open about his debt to Bergson. Sheldrake notes that "the conventional idea that memory must be explicable in terms of physical traces within the nervous system is . . . an assumption rather than an empirical fact. . . . The most stimulating critique [of this assumption] still remains Henri Bergson's *Matter and Memory*." Rupert Sheldrake, *The Presence of the Past* (Rochester, Vermont: Park Street Press, 1988), 215. For an insightful critique of Sheldrake's theory of morphic resonance, see Stephen E. Braude, "Radical Provincialism in the Life Sciences: A Review of Rupert Sheldrake's *A New Science of Life*," *The Journal of the American Society for Psychical Research* 77 (January 1983): 63–78.

2. The French word *esprit* means both "mind" and "spirit."

3. Andrew C. Papanicolaou, "Bergson's Psycho-physical Theory," in Andrew C. Papanicolaou and P.A. Y. Gunter, eds., *Bergson and Modern Thought* (New York: Harwood Academic Publishers, 1987), 97. As Papanicolaou points out, "The terms pure memory, spirit, duration and impersonal consciousness are synonymous and are interchangeably used throughout the text of *Matter and Memory*." Ibid.

4. Of course, to say that something is "in" consciousness is extremely problematic from a Bergsonian perspective!

5. *The Presence of the Past*, 160.

6. Ibid.

7. Ibid., 216.

8. W. Penfield and L. Roberts, *Speech and Brain Mechanisms* (Princeton: Princeton University Press, 1959). For a clear and thoughtful summation of Penfield's research, see *The Presence of the Past*, 219–220, and Lynne McTaggart, *The Field* (New York: HarperCollins, 2002), 77.

9. Penfield is quoted here in F. A. Wolf, *Star Wave* (New York: Macmillan, 1984), 175.

10. *The Presence of the Past*, 163.

11. *The Field*, 77.

12. Ibid., 78. See also Michael Talbot, *The Holographic Universe* (New York: HarperCollins, 1991), 11–13.

13. *The Presence of the Past*, 163.

14. Ibid., 164: Lashley's conclusion that memory is not stored in specific locations, but rather is distributed throughout the brain in highly complex ways, was further developed by a former student of Lashley's: Karl Pribram. Pribram became famous for his theory that memories are stored in the brain in a way that is analogous to how information is stored in the interference patterns in a hologram. See K. H. Pribram, *Languages of the Brain* (Englewood Cliffs, New Jersey: Prentice Hall, 1971).

15. *The Field*, 86.

16. *The Holographic Universe*, 26.
17. For a discussion of multiple "backup" memory systems, see Keith Ansell Pearson, *Philosophy and the Adventure of the Virtual* (New York: Routledge, 2002), 223, note 7: "Contemporary approaches in neuroscience work with the idea of there being multiple systems of memory with different brain organizations and that depend on different brain systems." Pearson references L. R. Squire, "Memory and Brain Systems," in S. Rose, ed., *From Brains to Consciousness?* (London: Allen Lane, 1998), 53–72 and D. L. Schacter, *Searching for Memory: The Brain, the Mind, and the Past* (New York: Basic Books, 1996), 169ff.
18. *The Presence of the Past*, 164.
19. Ibid., 216, Sheldrake references H. A. Bursen, *Dismantling the Memory Machine* (Dordrecht, Holland: Reidel, 1978).
20. *The Presence of the Past*, 166.
21. For a detailed and fascinating account of the neuroplasticity of the brain, see Norman Doidge, *The Brain That Changes Itself* (New York: Viking, 2008).
22. See: Sharon Begley, *Train Your Mind, Change Your Brain* (New York: Ballantine Books, 2007). Sheldrake gives further evidence of the plasticity of the nervous systems of mature animals in *The Presence of the Past*, 166.
23. Sharon Begley, *Newsweek*, July 2, 2007, 63.
24. *The Presence of the Past*, 168, no citation given. Sheldrake cites several works that critique the trace theory of memory (in addition to the previously cited *Dismantling the Memory Machine*): N. Malcolm, *Memory and Mind* (Ithaca, New York: Cornell University Press, 1977) and J. Russell, *Explaining Mental Life* (London: Macmillan, 1984).
25. For a lucid and concise depiction of the history of aphasia, and Bergson's role in how this cluster of disorders came to be understood, see Arthur L. Benton, "Bergson and Freud on Aphasia," in Andrew C. Papanicolaou and P. A. Y. Gunter, eds., *Bergson and Modern Thought* (New York: Harwood Academic Publishers, 1987), 176–186.
26. *The Presence of the Past*, 217.
27. Susan Blackmore, *Consciousness: An Introduction* (New York: Oxford University Press, 2004), 258.
28. *The Presence of the Past*, 218. See also Oliver Sacks, *The Man Who Mistook His Wife for a Hat* (London: Duckworth, 1985).
29. *The Presence of the Past*, 218.
30. Ibid. Sheldrake cites H. Gardner, *The Shattered Mind* (New York: Vintage Books, 1974); A. R. Luria, "The Functional Organization of the Brain," *Scientific American* 222, no. 3 (1970): 66–78; and A. R. Luria, *The Working Brain* (Harmondsworth: Penguin, 1973).
31. *The Presence of the Past*, 217—my emphasis.

CHAPTER 23. MIND AND MATTER AS DIFFERENT RHYTHMS OF DURÉE

1. Grosz underscores the ways in which these two types of difference (i.e., between quantity and quality) are linked to two contrasting political strategies. Quantitative difference emphasizes the differences of degree between one category of subjects (e.g., women, homosexuals, ethnic or political minorities) and another category (e.g., men, heterosexuals, ethnic or political majorities). Qualitative difference, on the other hand, is a type of "noncalculable difference," it is a difference that cannot be specified in advance, a difference that is "not a measureable difference between two given, discernible, different things—men and women, for example—but an incalculable and continuous process, not something produced by something in the process of production." Elizabeth Grosz, *The Nick of Time* (Durham, North Carolina: Duke University Press, 2004), 160.

2. As Pete Gunter notes, Bergson's originality is "to reconceive mind and body not as radically different kinds of substances, but as different modes of duration." P. A. Y. Gunter, "Bergson and the War Against Nature," in John Mullarkey, ed., *The New Bergson* (New York: Manchester University Press, 1999), 172. Mullarkey echoes and amplifies this comment when he points out that "while both matter and mind endure" they nonetheless "differ in their orientations." John Mullarkey, *Bergson and Philosophy* (Notre Dame, Indiana: Notre Dame University Press, 2000) 55. For Mullarkey, what we call "matter" is "materialization," while "mind" also is a process, a process of "an ever-increasing condensation of different rhythms into its *durée*." Ibid.

3. According to Pearson, Bergson does not fully decide that duration is "immanent to the universe" until *Creative Evolution*, where duration becomes the "key notion of thinking the idea of a creative (nonmechanical and nonfinalist) evolution." Keith Ansell Pearson, *Philosophy and the Adventure of the Virtual* (New York: Routledge, 2002), 36. Guerlac appears to disagree with Pearson, noting how in *Matter and Memory*, Bergson "speaks of the continuous becoming of duration, now understood as 'universal becoming.'" Suzanne Guerlac, *Thinking in Time* (Ithaca, New York: Cornell University Press, 2006), 150. Guerlac references *MM* 151. In a note, Guerlac comments that "we see here that, contrary to what many critics have suggested, Bergson does not wait until *Creative Evolution* to evoke duration as an ontological fact." Ibid. I agree with Guerlac on this issue.

4. Milič Čapek, *Bergson and Modern Physics* (Dordrecht, Holland: D. Reidel Publishing Co., 1971), 214–215.

5. *Philosophy and the Adventure of the Virtual*, 57, 164.

6. *Bergson and Philosophy*, 145.

7. Timothy Murphy points out that Bergson's notion of duration as a "virtual multiplicity capable of generating many different actual time-flows" is

aligned with many current theoretical perspectives. For instance, the idea of a virtual temporal multiplicity is now being reassessed by Deleuze, Bohm, and Ilya Prigogine, and "the rapidly expanding field of complex dynamics and fractal geometry, is another, more direct heir of Bergson's studies in duration." Timothy S. Murphy, "Beneath Relativity: Bergson and Bohm on Absolute Time," in John Mullarkey, ed., *The New Bergson* (New York: Manchester University Press, 1999), 77. In a different vein, scholars of religious studies, such as Mircea Eliade and Lawrence Sullivan comment on the non-homogeneity of time, noting how the internalization of different cultural assumptions about time, as well as the concrete participation in various ceremonies, can create a different quality of temporal experience. See for instance Mircea Eliade, *The Myth of the Eternal Return* (Princeton: Princeton University Press, 2005) and Lawrence E. Sullivan, *Icanchu's Drum* (New York: Macmillan, 1988).

8. Bergson's notion of a multileveled, "nested" temporal reality is quite congruent with Arthur Koestler's notion of "holons" (a term he coined in 1967).

9. Eslick claims that this movement up the temporal hierarchy mirrors the "ascent towards *spirit*" that is "described in *Creative Evolution* in terms of the effort of the *élan vital* to overcome the downward pull of matter by the creative emergence of diverging life forms, but which is consummated at the summit by human *intuition*, a sympathetic identification with universal Life, including, in the mystics, the Divine Life itself." Leonard Eslick, "Bergson, Whitehead, and Psychical Research," in Andrew C. Papanicolaou and P. A. Y. Gunter, eds., *Bergson and Modern Thought* (New York: Harwood Academic Publishers, 1987), 362.

CHAPTER 24. EMBODYING MEMORY

1. In this instance I am consciously using Bergson's metaphor of the "keyboard" in a different way than he does in *Matter and Memory* (see, for instance, *MM* 129). In this case, the brain itself is the keyboard, one that is simultaneously "played" from both "directions," that is, from the direction of the plane of the physical universe, and from the direction of the memories flowing in from the cone of memory.

2. If Bergson is correct, and there is indeed a clear-cut connection between a lack of bodily awareness and mental illness (and a close examination of individuals suffering from various extreme forms of mental illness and their problems with embodiment seems to strongly support this perspective), then perhaps we might question the overall effectiveness, at least in certain cases, of "talk therapy" and reassess the potential therapeutic value of working in a more physically engaged manner with clients/patients. Perhaps the

willingness to skillfully use various forms of dance, movement, noninvasive touch, or work with bodily posture (e.g., Alexander technique, Feldenkrais training, yoga, tai chi, deep tissue work, Reichian techniques, and so forth) needs to be reevaluated as a highly effective way to help those who suffer from mental problems to "inhabit" their bodies more fully, and consequently, to become increasingly capable of healthy interactions with others and the world around them. However, I would also argue that mental illness (or dreaming) is not necessarily the only end result of lack of bodily awareness. As demonstrated by the yogic tradition, there are also a host of potentially positive qualities that can emerge from a disciplined, intentional disengagement from sense experience, when the body is intentionally stilled through the practice of yogic postures, and the mind is turned within. This type of disidentification with the physical body can lead to profound states of meditative absorption, as well as numerous other spiritually powerful and transformative experiences.

3. Perhaps the clearest articulation of Bergson's understanding of the problems that can occur when we live with an overemphasis on habit memory takes place in his small book *Laughter*, originally published in 1900: *Laughter: An Essay on the Meaning of the Comic*, trans. Cloudesley Brereton and Fred Rothwell (London: Macmillan, 1911). [*Laughter* was published originally as two articles entitled "Le rire," *Revue de Paris* 7, nos. 23, 24 (1900): 512–544, 759–798; *Revue de Paris* 8, no. 1 (1900): 146–179.] In *Laughter*, Bergson discusses the crucial need to preserve our humanity in the midst of overly mechanical societies, pointing out the danger of allowing ourselves to be manipulated by the culture around us, lulled into "the easy automatism of acquired habits" and the thoughtless acceptance of ready-made ideas (*Laughter* 19). He notes that on the one hand, we live in "the quiet humdrum life that reason and society have fashioned for us,"—a static life of habitual routine (*Laughter* 158). On the other hand, just below the surface, we have a self that is dynamic, spontaneous, and alive. According to Bergson, an overly mechanistic rigidity of "body, mind and character" not only threatens our own delicate balance between "tension and elasticity," but also menaces society as a whole (*Laughter* 21). This mechanical rigidity within ourselves, and within others, is itself the "real cause of laughter" (*Laughter* 34). As he points out, "this rigidity is the comic . . . and laughter is its corrective" (*Laughter* 21). For Bergson, laughter does not arise as the result of conscious reflection, but rather, is the spontaneous expression of deeper dimensions of our humanity. And what do we laugh at? The mechanical rigidity of people who give "us the impression of being a thing" (*Laughter* 58). Or, put in another way, "the attitudes, gestures and movements of the human body are laughable in exact proportion as that body reminds us of a mere machine" (*Laughter* 29).

4. Bergson, as far as I am aware, does not explicitly connect the sort of behavior that would be expected in individuals with a preponderance of habit memory with his discussion of the "superficial self" in *Time and Free Will*, but there seems to be a clear connection between the two.

5. Mullarkey points out, correctly, that Bergson's emphasis on the body was radically innovative, especially his conceptualization of the "intelligence of the body" and "bodily memory." John Mullarkey, *Bergson and Philosophy* (Notre Dame, Indiana: Notre Dame University Press, 2000), 49.

6. Yasuo Yuasa, *The Body*, T. P. Kasulis, ed., and trans. Nagatomo Shigenori and T. P. Kasulis (Albany, New York: State University of New York Press, 1987), 18.

7. Ibid., 4.

8. Ibid., 18.

9. Ibid., 25.

10. Ibid., 4.

11. Ibid., 5.

12. Ibid., 4.

13. Ibid., 5.

14. The case of swerving the car to avoid hitting the dog in the road comes directly from Kasulis. *The Body*, 5.

15. Ibid.

16. Ibid., 70, 50.

17. Ibid., 200, 72.

18. Ibid., 224.

19. For an illuminating discussion of this sort of intuitive movement, from the perspective of various Chinese philosophical systems, see Edward Slingerland, *Effortless Action* (New York: Oxford University Press, 2003).

CHAPTER 25. BECOMING CONSCIOUS OF THE SUBCONSCIOUS

1. David G. Myers, *Intuition: Its Powers and Perils* (New Haven, Connecticut: Yale University Press, 2002), 4.

2. Ibid.

3. David Milner, "Sight Unseen," Presentation to the Royal Society of Edinburgh, Human Nature conference, August 2000; cited in *Intuition: Its Powers and Perils*, 4.

4. Ibid.

5. *Intuition: Its Powers and Perils*, 5.

6. Ibid., 15–16.

7. Ibid., 23.

8. Ibid., 25.

9. Ibid., 15.
10. For F. W. H. Myers' notion of the Subliminal Self, see his *Human Personality and Its Survival of Bodily Death* (Charlottesville, Virginia: Hampton Roads Publishing, 1961) as well as Emily Williams Kelly, "F. W. H. Myers and the Empirical Study of the Mind-Body Problem," in Edward F. Kelly et al., *Irreducible Mind* (Lanham, Maryland: Rowman & Littlefield, 2007).

CHAPTER 26. RECOLLECTION MEMORY, DREAMS, AND THE ÉLAN VITAL

1. P. A. Y. Gunter, "Bergson," in *A Companion to Continental Philosophy* (Hoboken, New Jersey: Wiley-Blackwell, 1999), 177.
2. Ibid.
3. Keith Ansell Pearson, *Philosophy and the Adventure of the Virtual* (New York: Routledge, 2002), 182.
4. In John Mullarkey, ed., *The New Bergson* (New York: Manchester University Press, 1999), 103.
5. Leonard Lawlor, *The Challenge of Bergsonism* (New York: Continuum, 2003), 112. Appendix II: English Translation of Jean Hyppolite's "Aspects divers de la mémoire chez Bergson" ("Various Aspects of Memory in Bergson"), Athena V. Colman, trans. (1949).
6. Ibid., 117.
7. Ibid., 117–118.
8. Ibid., 118.
9. Ibid.
10. Ibid., 119.
11. Interestingly, Bergson does mention in a footnote that "at the time when this lecture [on dreams] was given, Freud's *Traumdeutung* [*The Interpretation of Dreams*] had appeared, but 'psychoanalysis' had not reached anything like its present development" (*ME* 131). It is not clear how long after 1901 this footnote was written, but given Bergson's apparent awareness of Freud's work, it is striking that Bergson seemingly did not revise his lecture when it was published in *Mind-Energy* (a collection of his lectures and essays) to include a more nuanced portrayal of Freud's theory. Bergson does briefly note "those repressed tendencies to which the Freudian school have devoted a great amount of research," but this reference is primarily directed to the fact that "if, at night, we dream of the events of the day, it is insignificant incidents, not important facts, which will have the best chance of reappearing"—not exactly a nuanced or well-rounded portrayal of the Freudian notion of repression (*ME* 131).
12. Marie Cariou makes the insightful observation that "Bergson is less attentive than Freud to the way in which [memory] reappears disguised, meta-

morphosed, transferred and even sometimes transfigured." *The New Bergson*, 109.

13. To be fair, Bergson actually does attempt to explain the temporal compression that is experienced in certain dreams. For him, these types of dreams are the result of the capacity of memory to foreshorten experience. According to Bergson, when memory is freed from the need to adopt itself to the pressures of external reality, it can "rush along with a dizzy rapidity, like a cinematograph film when the speed of the unwinding is not held in check" (*ME* 130). Personally, however, this is a very unsatisfying explanation in that it (oddly!) offers a most un-Bergsonian way of viewing memory/consciousness as a static, prearranged, series of linear images that are stored away somewhere, images that, with the press of a button (or the crash of a curtain rod) are mechanically unrolled before us.

14. For an insightful discussion of the religious meaning of dreams in various cultures, see Kelly Bulkeley, *The Wilderness of Dreams* (Albany, New York: State University of New York Press, 1994).

15. As Leszek Kolakowski comments, "The central idea of Bergson's cosmology is this: the Whole is of the same nature as myself. The time-generating life of the consciousness is the model for the universe." Leszek Kolakowski, *Bergson* (New York: Oxford University Press, 1985), 70.

16. It is difficult at times to decide the exact relationship between the élan vital and matter. At times they appear to be antagonistic opponents, as two primordial and opposite cosmic principles. However, I would argue that more fundamentally, the élan vital is simply another way to think through durée, and as such, is the dynamic force/consciousness that is present in both organic and non-organic forms.

CHAPTER 27. BERGSON AND NON-ORDINARY EXPERIENCES

1. It is perhaps worth reemphasizing that only rarely do we *consciously* choose which images to focus on (and hence which "world of experience" we will inhabit). These choices (if we can stretch the word somewhat), take place with little or no conscious effort of will on our part, and occur quasi-instantaneously prompted by subconscious planes of memory, which in turn are dramatically influenced by our biological needs. I also wish to thank Alex Lefebvre for the editorial suggestions that he made, several of which I have incorporated into this section of the chapter.

2. There is one form of psi phenomena that Bergson's theoretical perspective would have difficulty explaining, or even acknowledging: precognition. Bergson's repeated emphasis on the open-ended, genuinely creative nature of durée makes it extremely difficult, if not impossible, to conceive of a ready-made future that exists just waiting to be accessed during moments of

precognition. The inherent conflict between this theoretical closure to pre-cognition and the (often quite striking) evidence of its existence that has been gathered by parapsychologists over the past few centuries, is explored, quite thoughtfully (albeit from a Whiteheadian perspective) in David Ray Griffin, *Parapsychology, Philosophy, and Spirituality* (Albany, New York: State University of New York Press, 1997), 90–95.

3. Robert Jahn and Brenda Dunne, two prominent parapsychologists, agree with Bergson that one of the primary difficulties that stands in the way of any scientific acceptance of psi phenomena is that "the commonly prevail-ing conceptualization of consciousness is basically particulate in nature. That is, an individual consciousness is normally presumed to be rather well localized in physical space and time, interacting only with a few specific aspects of its environment and with a few others similarly localized con-sciousnesses at any given time." They stress that it is only when we can let go of thinking that our consciousness is confined within the boundaries of our physical bodies, and reenvision our consciousness as wave-like in nature (similar to the wave-like nature of quantum realities), that telepathy, clair-voyance, and psychokinesis begin to have the possibility of being under-stood and accepted as real possibilities. Robert G. Jahn and Brenda J. Dunne, "Consciousness, Quantum Mechanics, and Random Physical Processes," in Andrew C. Papanicolaou and P. A. Y. Gunter, eds., *Bergson and Modern Thought* (New York: Harwood Academic Publishers, 1987), 299.

4. P. A. Y. Gunter, "Henri Bergson," in David Ray Griffin et al., eds., *Founders of Postmodern Constructive Philosophy* (Albany: State University of New York Press, 1993), 141.

5. Jeffrey J. Kripal, *The Serpent's Gift* (Chicago: University of Chicago Press, 2007). For a similar methodological perspective, see Jorge N. Ferrer and Jacob H. Sherman, eds., *The Participatory Turn* (Albany, New York: State University of New York Press, 2008).

6. My argument that various spiritual disciplines can serve to open up the filter of the brain, and can allow us to perceive levels of the universe that are typically screened from our sight, consciously echoes the work of Aldous Huxley. Huxley drew upon Bergson's understanding of the genesis of per-ception to formulate his theories of the "Mind at Large," a theory which he used to help explain the experiences he had taking mescaline in 1953. See Aldous Huxley, *The Doors of Perception and Heaven and Hell* (New York: HarperCollins, 2004).

7. For a fascinating discussion of the role of supernormal abilities in the lives of mystics, see Jess Byron Hollenback, *Mysticism: Experience, Response, and Empowerment* (University Park, Pennsylvania: Pennsylvania State University Press, 1996).

8. I would argue that paranormal mental and physical abilities have been repeatedly confirmed by an enormous body of evidence collected in very disciplined and careful ways, for example, by numerous psi researchers from the mid-1800s on. See the bibliographical information in note 5 in the introduction to this text for a small sampling of the material written on this topic.

9. I have found Frederic Myers' work to be particularly helpful in understanding this psychological dynamic. See F. W. H. Myers, *Human Personality and Its Survival of Bodily Death* (Charlottesville, Virginia: Hampton Roads Publishing, 1961).

10. It is important to emphasize that, seen from this neo-Bergsonian perspective, not all of these beings would necessarily have to be human, nor would all of them have to currently possess a physical body. Admittedly, from a neo-Bergsonian perspective it is difficult, if not impossible, to make a clear-cut distinction between influxes from previously hidden subconscious (or superconscious) planes of consciousness and the activity of seemingly independent spiritual beings, a difficulty that is also seen in the work of William James, Frederic Myers, and Carl Jung.

11. Interestingly, William James discussed the possibility that at times malevolent nonphysical beings might well be part of the cause of mental illness, in addition to various psychological factors. See Lecture Five ("Demonical Possession) in Eugene Taylor, *William James on Exceptional Mental States* (Amherst, Massachusetts: University of Massachusetts Press, 1984).

12. I explore, in much greater detail, some of the issues that arise in any attempt to make a pragmatic assessment of non-ordinary states of consciousness in chapter 5 of G. William Barnard, *Exploring Unseen Worlds: William James and the Philosophy of Mysticism* (Albany, New York: State University of New York Press, 1997), 273–357.

13. Several autobiographical accounts written/narrated by Native American shamans describe the nonsensory reception of highly specific information, such as which plants to pick to heal particular diseases, where to go to hunt, and so forth, as well as seemingly "miraculous" healing events. See for instance, Thomas E. Mails, *Fools Crow: Wisdom and Power* (Tulsa, Oklahoma: Council Oak Books, 1991); John G. Neihardt, *Black Elk Speaks* (Lincoln, Nebraska: University of Nebraska Press, 1961); Martin Prechtel, *Secrets of the Talking Jaguar* (New York: Jeremy P. Tarcher/Putnam, 1998).

14. R. C. Grogin notes that some interpreters of Bergson's work "have tried to link Bergson to the Jewish mystical tradition and specifically to the Kabbala. . . . Bergson once acknowledged that he had taken instruction in Hebrew, but was quite clear in maintaining that he had ignored the Kabbala." R. C. Grogin, *The Bergsonian Controversy in France 1900–1914* (Calgary: University of Calgary Press, 1988), 61, note 31.

15. At this point in time I can only present a small sampling of Bergson's thoughts about mysticism, primarily as a way to demonstrate the congruence between Bergson's earlier and later work.

16. Bergson actually says that the universe is a "machine for the making of gods," a puzzling metaphor given his stress on the unmechanistic nature of life.

17. Recent texts on Bergson's work that, to a greater or lesser extent, are influenced by, or responding to, the poststructuralist perspective of Gilles Deleuze are: John Mullarkey, *Bergson and Philosophy* (Notre Dame, Indiana: University of Notre Dame Press, 2000); Keith Ansell Pearson, *Philosophy and the Adventure of the Virtual* (New York: Routledge, 2002); Leonard Lawlor, *The Challenge of Bergsonism* (New York: Continuum, 2003); Elizabeth Grosz, *The Nick of Time* (Durham, North Carolina: Duke University Press, 2004); Suzanne Guerlac, *Thinking in Time* (Ithaca, New York: Cornell University Press, 2006).

18. *Founders of Constructive Postmodern Philosophy*, 141.

19. *The Bergsonian Controversy in France 1900–1914*, 56.

20. Ibid., 58.

21. Ibid., 40. Grogin also points out that Bergson's stress on empirical research meant that he was not personally involved in occult activities. "According to his brother-in-law, MacGregor Mathers, Bergson was not the least bit interested in magic: 'I have shown him everything that magic can do and it has had no effect on him.'" *The Bergsonian Controversy in France 1900–1914*, 43. Grogin references Ellic Howe, *Magicians of the Golden Dawn: A Documentary History of a Magical Order, 1887–1923* (London: Routledge and Kegan Paul, 1972), 113. Grogin goes on to note, however, that "interestingly, Bergson's sister claimed that some of their 'tiresome relatives' were into magic, and years later Bergson's daughter turned to the occult herself." *The Bergsonian Controversy in France 1900–1914*, 40.

22. See Bertrand Méheust, *Somnambulisme et médiumnité: Tome 1, Le défi du magnétisme.* (Le Plessis Robinson, France: Institut Synthélabo pour le Progres de la Connaissance, 1999) and Bertrand Méheust, *Somnambulisme et médiumnité: Tome 2, Le choc des sciences psychiques,* (Le Plessis Robinson, France: Institut Synthélabo pour le Progres de la Connaissance, 1999).

23. *Bergson and Modern Thought*, 354; (*M* 333–341).

24. M. Brady Brower gives a careful and detailed account of the tumultuous formation and development of this society. Originally named the Institut Psychique International, its name was almost immediately changed to Institut Général Psychologique due, in large part, to concerns by several participants that the organization would be perceived as too closely linked to the Society for Psychical Research that was active at the time in England and America. M. Brady Brower, *Unruly Spirits: The Science of Psychic Phenomena in Modern France* (Chicago: University of Illinois Press, 2010), 51–52.

25. (*M* 606–609); *Somnambulisme et médiumnité: Tome 2, Le choc des sciences psychiques*, 242.
26. (*M* 639–642; 760–762); Leonard Eslick, "Bergson, Whitehead, and Psychical Research," in Andrew C. Papanicolaou and P. A. Y. Gunter, eds., *Bergson and Modern Thought* (New York: Harwood Academic Publishers, 1987), 354. Bergson's interest in psi phenomena was also evident in 1919. A secondhand account of Bergson's talk at a Strasbourg Conference on the Soul, published in 1919, noted Bergson's discussion of psychical research within the larger context of the mind-body problem, as well as the importance of a spiritual point of view (which Bergson associates with France, England, and America) in order to overcome materialism and mechanism (which he, not surprisingly, associates with Germany) (*M* 1316–1319).
27. *The Bergsonian Controversy in France 1900–1914*, 52. Grogin cites Julies Courtier, "Rapport sur les séances d'Eusapia Palladino à l'Institut général psychologique, 1905–1908," *Bulletin de l'Institut général psychologique* 8, no. 5–6 (1908): 415–546.
28. *Somnambulisme et médiumnité: Tome 2, Le choc des sciences psychiques*, 242. Stephen Braude, in a wonderfully thoughtful examination of the controversies surrounding Palladino, echoes Bergson's assessment. Braude notes that while Palladino was several times caught cheating, nonetheless, her attempts to cheat were very crude and easily detected, and in several rigorously controlled séances that took place in Naples in 1908, three highly skeptical and experienced investigators were eventually convinced that many of the phenomena produced by Palladino were genuine. Stephen E. Braude, *The Gold Leaf Lady and Other Parapsychological Investigations* (Chicago: University of Chicago Press, 2007), 46–52.
29. Georges Meunier, *Ce qu'ils pensent du merveilleux* (Paris: Albin Michel, 1910), 85; *Somnambulisme et médiumnité: Tome 2, Le choc des sciences psychiques*, 243.
30. Edmund Gurney, Frederic W. H. Myers, and Frank Podmore, *Phantasms of the Living*, 2 vols. (London: Rooms of the Society for Psychical Research, 1886). This massive (and impressive) tome has been out of print for decades. However, the Esalen Center for Theory and Research has performed an amazing academic service: they have a virtual (and searchable) version of this text on their website www.esalenctr.org (in the heading "scholarly resources") as well as the complete two volume work of Frederic Myers' *Human Personality and Its Survival of Bodily Death*. This version of *Human Personality* is also included, as a cd, in the hardcover version of Edward F. Kelly et al., *Irreducible Mind* (Lanham, Maryland: Rowman & Littlefield, 2007). For an insightful, and fascinating, discussion of the Society for Psychical Research, see Deborah Blum, *Ghost Hunters* (New York: Penguin Books, 2006).

31. William James had a similar attitude toward veridical non-ordinary experiences. For the definitive text on James' exploration of psychic phenomena, see William James, *Essays in Psychical Research* (Cambridge, Massachusetts: Harvard University Press, 1986).

CHAPTER 28. BERGSON AND THE AFTERLIFE

1. The scholarship on Tibetan Buddhist attitudes toward the afterlife is extensive. Two classic texts are Francesca Fremantle and Chogyam Trungpa, trans., *The Tibetan Book of the Dead* (Boulder, Colorado: Shambhala Publications, 1975) and Sogyal Rinpoche, *The Tibetan Book of Living and Dying* (New York: HarperSanFrancisco, 1993). For a strikingly similar perspective, but from a neo-Platonic/esoteric/Christian perspective, see Kyriacos C. Markides, *The Magus of Strovolos* (New York: Penguin Books, 1985).

2. For a lucid and engaging discussion of the vivid contrast between our contemporary, Western attitude toward dreams and the varied ways in which different religious traditions have understood the significance of dreaming, see Kelly Bulkeley, *Visions of the Night* (Albany, New York: State University of New York Press, 1999). For a fascinating examination of the interface between dreaming and visionary life among the Native American peoples of the Great Plains, see Lee Irwin, *The Dream Seekers* (Norman, Oklahoma: University of Oklahoma Press, 1994). For an intriguing investigation of the metaphysical implications of dreaming in Hindu culture, see Wendy Doniger O'Flaherty, *Dreams, Illusion and Other Realities* (Chicago: University of Chicago Press, 1984).

3. In *Humanité*, Clinton Timothy Curle provides an extremely thoughtful, and fascinating, description of how Bergson's perspective in *The Two Sources* was extremely important in the creation of the United Nations' Universal Declaration of Human Rights in 1948. See Clinton Timothy Curle, *Humanité* (Toronto: University of Toronto Press, 2007).

BIBLIOGRAPHY

Adler, Julius, and Wing-Wai Tse. "Decision-making in Bacteria." *Science* 184 (June 21, 1974): 1292–1294.

Alexander, Ian W. *Bergson: Philosopher of Reflection*. New York: Hillary House, 1957.

Almeder, Robert. *Death and Personal Survival*. Lanham, Maryland: Littlefield Adams, 1992.

Bailey, Lee W., and Jenny Yates, eds. *The Near-Death Experience*. New York: Routledge, 1996.

Barlow, Michel. *Henri Bergson*. Paris: Editions Universitaires, 1966.

Barnard, G. William. *Exploring Unseen Worlds: William James and the Philosophy of Mysticism*. Albany, New York: State University of New York Press, 1997.

Barrett, William. *Irrational Man*. Garden City, New York: Doubleday, 1958.

Becker, Carl B. *Paranormal Experience and Survival of Death*. Albany, New York: State University of New York Press, 1993.

Begley, Sharon. *Train Your Mind, Change Your Brain*. New York: Ballantine Books, 2007.

Bien, Peter A. "Nikos Kazantzakis." *Columbia Essays on Modern Writers* 62. New York: Columbia University Press, 1972. 26–38.

Bennett, M. R., and P. M. S. Hacker. *Philosophical Foundations of Neuroscience*. Oxford: Blackwell, 2003.

Blackmore, Susan. *Consciousness: An Introduction*. New York: Oxford University Press, 2004.

Blakemore, Colin, and Susan Greenfield, eds. *Mindwaves*. Oxford: Basil Blackwell, 1987.

Blum, Deborah. *Ghost Hunters*. New York: Penguin Books, 2006.

Bohm, David, and Basil Hiley. "On the Intuitive Understanding of Nonlocality as Implied by Quantum Theory." *Foundations of Physics* 5 (1975): 93–109.

Bohm, David. "A New Theory of the Relationship of Mind and Matter." *Journal of the American Society of Psychical Research* 80, no. 2 (1986): 113–135.

———. "Hidden Variables and the Implicate Order." In *Quantum Implications*, eds. Basil J. Hiley and F. David Peat. London: Routledge and Kegan Paul, 1987. 33–45.

Borst, Clive Vernon, ed. *The Mind-Brain Identity Theory*. London: Macmillan, 1979.

Braud, William. *Distant Mental Influence*. Charlottesville, Virginia: Hampton Roads, 2003.

Braude, Stephen E. "Radical Provincialism in the Life Sciences: A Review of Rupert Sheldrake's *A New Science of Life*." *The Journal of the American Society for Psychical Research* 77 (January, 1983): 63–78.

———. *Immortal Remains*. Lanham, Maryland: Rowman & Littlefield, 2003.

———. *The Gold Leaf Lady and Other Parapsychological Investigations*. Chicago: University of Chicago Press, 2007.

Broughton, Richard S. *Parapsychology*. New York: Ballantine Books, 1991.

Brower, M. Brady. *Unruly Spirits*. Chicago: University of Illinois Press, 2010.

Bulkeley, Kelly. *The Wilderness of Dreams*. Albany, New York: State University of New York Press, 1994.

———. *Visions of the Night*. Albany, New York: State University of New York Press, 1999.

Bursen, H. A. *Dismantling the Memory Machine*. Dordrecht, Holland: Reidel, 1978.

Burtt, Edwin Arthur. *The Metaphysical Foundations of Modern Physical Science*. London: Kegan, Paul, Trench and Trubner, 1932.

Burwick, Frederick, and Paul Douglas, eds. *The Crisis in Modernism*. New York: Cambridge University Press, 1992.

Bynum, Caroline Walker. *Holy Feast and Holy Fast*. Berkeley: University of California Press, 1987.

Čapek, Milič. *Bergson and Modern Physics*. Dordrecht, Holland: D. Reidel Publishing Co., 1971.

Capra, Fritjof. *The Tao of Physics*. New York: Bantam Books, 1977.

Cariou, Marie. *Bergson et le fait mystique*. Paris: Éditions Aubier Montaigne, 1976.

———. *Lectures bergsoniennes*. Paris: Presses Universitaires de France, 1990.

Carr, H. Wildon. *Henri Bergson: The Philosophy of Change*. Port Washington, New York: Kennikat Press, 1970.

Cassirer, Ernst. *Determinism and Indeterminism in Modern Physics*. New Haven: Yale University Press, 1956.

Chaix-Ruy, Jules. "Vitalité et élan vital: Bergson et Croce." *Études bergsoniennes* 5 (Albin Michel, 1960).

Chalmers, David. "The Puzzle of Conscious Experience." *Scientific American* (December 1995): 62–68.

Chevalier, Jacques. *Henri Bergson*, trans. Lilian A. Clare. Freeport, New York: Books for Libraries Press, 1970.

Chiari, Joseph. *Twentieth-Century French Thought*. New York: Gordian Press, 1975.

Church, Margaret. *Time and Reality*. Chapel Hill: University of North Carolina Press, 1949.

Churchland, Paul M. *Scientific Realism and the Plasticity of Mind*. Cambridge: Cambridge University Press, 1979.

Cohen-Solal, Annie. *Sartre: A Life*, trans. A. Cancogni. New York: Pantheon, 1987.

Courtier, Julies. "Rapport sur les séances d'Eusapia Palladino à lInstitut général psychologique, 1905–1908." *Bulletin de l'Institut général psychologique* 8, no. 5-6 (1908): 415–546.

Crabtree, Adam. *From Mesmer to Freud*. New Haven: Yale University Press, 1993.

Crary, J. *Suspensions of Perception, Attention, Spectacle and Modern Culture*. Cambridge, Massachusetts: MIT Press, 1999.

Cressole, Michel. *Deleuze*. Paris: Editions Universitaires, 1973.

Cresson, André. *Bergson: Sa vie, son oeuvre*. Paris: Presses Universitaires de France, 1946.

Crick, Francis. *The Astonishing Hypothesis*. New York: Scribner, 1994.

Curle, Clinton Timothy. *Humanité*. Toronto: University of Toronto Press, 2007.

Davis, Paul. *Superforce*. New York: Simon and Schuster, 1984.

Deleuze, Gilles. *Cinema 2*. H. Tomlinson and R. Galeta, trans. London: Athlone Press, 1989/1985.

———. *Bergsonism*. Hugh Tomlinson and Barbara Habberjam, trans. New York: Zone Books, 1991.

Dennett, Daniel. *Brainstorms*. Sussex: Harvester Press, 1978.

Doidge, Norman. *The Brain That Changes Itself*. New York: Viking, 2008.

Dröscher, Vitus. *The Mysterious Sense of Animals*. New York: Dutton, 1965.

Douglas, Mary. *Purity and Danger*. New York: Routledge, 1966.

Durkheim, Emile. *The Elementary Forms of Religious Life*. Karen E. Fields, trans. New York: The Free Press, 1995.

Eccles, John C. *Facing Reality*. Heidelberg: Springer-Verlag, 1970.

———. *How the Self Controls Its Brain*. Heidelberg: Springer-Verlag, 1994.

Edelman, Gerald M., and Guilio Tononi. "Reentry and the Dynamic Core: Neural Correlates of Conscious Experience." In *Neural Correlates of Consciousness*, ed. Thomas Metzinger. Cambridge, Massachusetts: MIT Press, 2000. 139–152.

Eliade, Mircea. *The Myth of the Eternal Return*. Princeton: Princeton University Press, 2005.

Erikson, Erik H. *Childhood and Society*. New York: W. W. Norton, 1950.

Flanagan, Owen. *Consciousness Reconsidered*. Cambridge, Massachusetts: MIT Press, 1992.

Fremantle, Francesca, and Chogyam Trungpa, trans. *The Tibetan Book of the Dead*. Boulder, Colorado: Shambhala Publications, 1975.

Frisch, Karl von. *Bees, Their Vision, Chemical Senses and Language*. Ithaca, New York: Cornell University Press, 1950.

Gallagher, Idella J. *Morality in Evolution*. The Hague, Netherlands: Martinus Nijhoff, 1970.

Gallois, Philippe, and Gérard Forzy, eds. *Bergson et les neurosciences*. Le Plessis-Robinson: Insitut Synthélabo, 1997.

Game, Ann. *Undoing the Social*. Milton Keynes, United Kingdom: Open University Press, 1991.

Gardner, Howard. *The Shattered Mind*. New York: Vintage Books, 1974.

Greenberg, Jay R., and Stephen A. Mitchell. *Object Relations in Psychoanalytic Theory*. Cambridge: Harvard University Press, 1983.

Greenfield, Susan. *Brain Story*. London: BBC, 2000.

Griffin, David Ray, et al., eds. *Founders of Constructive Postmodern Philosophy*. Albany, New York: State University of New York Press, 1993.

Griffin, David Ray. *Parapsychology, Philosophy, and Spirituality*. Albany, New York: State University of New York Press, 1997.

———. *Unsnarling the World-Knot*. Berkeley: University of California Press, 1998.

Grogin, R. C. *The Bergsonian Controversy in France 1900–1914*. Calgary: University of Calgary Press, 1988.

Grosz, Elizabeth. *The Nick of Time*. Durham, North Carolina: Duke University Press, 2004.

Guerlac, Suzanne. *Thinking in Time*. Ithaca, New York: Cornell University Press, 2006.

Guitton, Jean. *La vocation de Bergson*. Paris: Librairie Gallimard, 1960.

Gunter, Peter A. Y., ed. *Bergson and the Evolution of Physics*. Knoxville: University of Tennessee Press, 1969.

———. "Bergson and Jung." *Journal of the History of Ideas* 43, no. 4 (October–December 1982): 635–652.

———. "Bergson." In *A Companion to Continental Philosophy*. Hoboken, New Jersey: Wiley-Blackwell, 1999. 173–182.

Gurney, Edmund, Frederic W. H. Myers, and Frank Podmore. *Phantasms of the Living*, 2 vols. London: Rooms of the Society for Psychical Research, 1886.

Hale, Nathan G. *Freud and the Americans*. New York: Oxford University Press, 1971.

Hanna, Thomas, ed. *The Bergsonian Heritage.* New York: Columbia University Press, 1962.

Hershock, Peter D. *Liberating Intimacy.* Albany, New York: State University of New York Press, 1996.

Höffding, Harald. *La philosophie de Bergson.* Paris: Alcan, 1916.

Hollenback, Jess Byron. *Mysticism: Experience, Response, and Empowerment.* University Park, Pennsylvania: Pennsylvania State University Press, 1996.

Howe, Ellic. *Magicians of the Golden Dawn: A Documentary History of a Magical Order, 1887–1923.* London: Routledge and Kegan Paul, 1972.

Hude, Henri. *Bergson.* Vols. I and II. Paris: Editions Universitaires, 1989, 1990.

Humphrey, Nicholas. *A History of the Mind.* London: Chatto and Windus, 1992.

Huxley, Aldous. *The Doors of Perception and Heaven and Hell.* New York: HarperCollins, 2004.

Irwin, Lee. *The Dream Seekers.* Norman, Oklahoma: University of Oklahoma Press, 1994.

Iverson, Jeffrey. *In Search of the Dead.* New York: HarperSanFrancisco, 1992.

James, William. *Essays in Psychical Research.* Cambridge, Massachusetts: Harvard University Press, 1986.

Jankélévitch, Vladimir. *Henri Bergson.* Paris: Presses Universitaires de France, 1959.

Jung, Carl G. *Memories, Dreams, Reflections.* New York: Vintage Books, 1989.

Kallen, Horace. *William James and Henri Bergson.* Chicago: University of Chicago Press, 1914.

Kant, Immanuel. *Critique of Practical Reason and Other Works on the Theory of Ethics.* T. K. Abbot, trans. London: Longmans, Green, 1909.

Kelly, Edward F., and Rafael G. Locke. *Altered States of Consciousness and Psi.* New York: Parapsychology Foundation, Inc., 2009.

Kelly, Edward F., et al. *Irreducible Mind.* Lanham, Maryland: Rowman & Littlefield, 2007.

Kelley, John Joseph. *Bergson's Mysticism.* Fribourg, Switzerland: St. Paul's Press, 1954.

Kolakowski, Leszek. *Bergson.* New York: Oxford University Press, 1985.

Kumar, Shiv. *Bergson and the Stream of Consciousness Novel.* New York: New York University Press, 1963.

Lacey, A. R. *Bergson.* New York: Routledge, 1989.

Lawlor, Leonard. *The Challenge of Bergsonism.* New York: Continuum, 2003.

Lea, James F. *Kazantzakis: The Politics of Salvation.* Tuscaloosa, Alabama: University of Alabama Press, 1979.

Le Roy, Edouard. *The New Philosophy of Henri Bergson.* New York: Henry Holt and Co., 1914.

Levinas, Emmanuel. *Ethics and Infinity.* Richard A. Cohen, trans. Pittsburgh: Duquesne University Press, 1985.

————. *Time and the Other.* Richard A. Cohen, trans. Pittsburgh: Duquesne University Press, 1987.

Levitt, Morton P. *The Cretan Glance.* Columbus, Ohio: Ohio State University Press, 1980.

Lewin, Roger. "Is Your Brain Really Necessary?" *Science* 210 (December 12, 1980): 1232–1234.

Loisy, Alfred. *Y a-ti-il Deux Sources de la Religion et de la Morale.* Paris: Émile Nourry, 1933.

Luce, A. A. *Bergson's Doctrine of Intuition.* New York: Macmillan, 1922.

Luria, A. R. "The Functional Organization of the Brain." *Scientific American* 222, no. 3 (1970): 66–78.

————. *The Working Brain.* Harmondsworth: Penguin, 1973.

Mails, Thomas E. *Fools Crow: Wisdom and Power.* Tulsa, Oklahoma: Council Oak Books, 1991.

Malcolm, N. *Memory and Mind.* Ithaca, New York: Cornell University Press, 1977.

Marcel, Anthony J., and Edoardo Bisiach, eds. *Consciousness in Contemporary Society.* Oxford: Oxford University Press, 1988.

Maritain, Jacques. *La Philosophie bergsonienne.* Paris: Librairie Marcel Rivière, 1930.

————. *Bergsonian Philosophy and Thomism.* Mabelle L. Andison and J. Gordon Andison, trans. New York: Greenwood Press, 1948.

Markides, Kyriacos C. *The Magus of Strovolos.* New York: Penguin Books, 1985.

May, Henry F. *The End of American Innocence.* New York: Oxford University Press, 1979.

McGinn, Colin. *The Problem of Consciousness.* Oxford: Basil Blackwell, 1991.

McTaggart, Lynne. *The Field.* New York: HarperCollins, 2002.

Méheust, Bertrand. *Somnambulisme et médiumnité: Tome 1, Le défi du magnétisme.* Le Plessis Robinson, France: Institut Synthélabo pour le Progres de la Connaissance, 1999.

————. *Somnambulisme et médiumnité: Tome 2, Le choc des sciences psychiques.* Le Plessis Robinson, France: Institut Synthélabo pour le Progres de la Connaissance, 1999.

Meunier, Georges. *Ce qu'ils pensent du merveilleux.* Paris: Albin Michel, 1910.

Milne, Lorus, and Margery Milne. *The Senses of Animals and Men.* New York: Athenaeum, 1962.

Miller, Lucius. *Bergson and Religion.* New York: Henry Holt and Co., 1916.

Minsky, Marvin. *Society of Mind.* New York: Simon and Schuster, 1986.

Moore, F. C. T. *Bergson: Thinking Backwards.* New York: Cambridge University Press, 1996.

Mullarkey, John, ed. *The New Bergson.* New York: Manchester University Press, 1999.

———. *Bergson and Philosophy.* Notre Dame, Indiana: University of Notre Dame Press, 2000.

Myers, David G. *Intuition: Its Powers and Perils.* New Haven, Connecticut: Yale University Press, 2002.

Myers, Frederic W. H. *Human Personality and Its Survival of Bodily Death.* Charlottesville, Virginia: Hampton Roads Publishing, 1961.

Nagel, Thomas. *Mortal Questions.* London: Cambridge University Press, 1979.

———. *The View from Nowhere.* New York: Oxford University Press, 1986.

Neihardt, John G. *Black Elk Speaks.* Lincoln, Nebraska: University of Nebraska Press, 1961.

O'Flaherty, Wendy Doniger. *Dreams, Illusion and Other Realities.* Chicago: University of Chicago Press, 1984.

Papanicolaou, Andrew C., and Pete A. Y. Gunter, eds. *Bergson and Modern Thought.* New York: Harwood Academic Publishers, 1987.

Pearson, Keith Ansell. *Philosophy and the Adventure of the Virtual.* New York: Routledge, 2002.

Perry, Ralph Barton. *The Thought and Character of William James*, 2 vols. Boston: Little, Brown, and Co., 1935.

Philonenko, Alexis. *Bergson, ou, De la philosophie comme science rigoureuse.* Paris: Les Éditions du Cerf, 1994.

Pilkington, A. E. *Bergson and His Influence.* Cambridge: Cambridge University Press, 1976.

Poulet, George. *Studies in Human Nature.* Baltimore: Johns Hopkins University Press, 1956.

Popper, Karl R., and John C. Eccles. *The Self and Its Brain.* Heidelberg: Springer-Verlag, 1977.

Prechtel, Martin. *Secrets of the Talking Jaguar.* New York: Jeremy P. Tarcher/Putnam, 1998.

Pribram, Karl H. *Languages of the Brain.* Englewood Cliffs, New Jersey: Prentice Hall, 1971.

Quirk, Tom. *Bergson and American Culture.* Chapel Hill, North Carolina: The University of North Carolina Press, 1990.

Radin, Dean. *The Conscious Universe.* New York: HarperEdge, 1997.

———. *Entangled Minds.* New York: Paraview Pocket Books, 2006.

Romeyer, B. "Caractéristiques religieuses du spiritualisme de Bergson." In "*Bergson et Bergsonisme.*" *Archives de philosophie* 17, cahier 1 (Paris 1947). No page numbers listed.

Rose, Gillian. *Dialectic of Nihilism.* Oxford: Basil Blackwell, 1984.

Russell, Bertrand. *The Philosophy of Bergson.* London: Macmillan, 1914.

———. *Mysticism and Logic and Other Essays.* London: Pelican Books, 1953.

———. *The Autobiography of Bertrand Russell.* New York: Bantam Books, 1967.

Russell, James. *Explaining Mental Life.* London: Macmillan, 1984.

Sacks, Oliver. *The Man Who Mistook His Wife for a Hat*. London: Duckworth, 1985.

Schacter, Daniel L. *Searching for Memory: The Brain, the Mind, and the Past*. New York: Basic Books, 1996.

Scharfstein, Ben-Ami. *Roots of Bergson's Philosophy*. New York: Columbia University Press, 1943.

Schilpp, Paul, ed. *Albert Einstein, Philosopher-Scientist*. New York: Harper and Row, 1949.

Seager, William. *Metaphysics of Consciousness*. New York: Routledge, 1991.

Searle, John R. *Minds, Brains and Science*. London: British Broadcasting Corporation, 1984.

———. *The Rediscovery of the Mind*. Cambridge, Massachusetts: MIT Press, 1992.

Shear, Jonathan, ed. *Explaining Consciousness*. Cambridge, Massachusetts: MIT Press, 1997.

Sheldrake, Rupert. *The Presence of the Past*. Rochester, Vermont: Park Street Press, 1988.

Skrbina, David. *Panpsychism in the West*. Cambridge: Massachusetts: MIT Press, 2005.

Slingerland, Edward. *Effortless Action*. New York: Oxford University Press, 2003.

Sogyal Rinpoche. *The Tibetan Book of Living and Dying*. New York: HarperSanFrancisco, 1993.

Solomon, Joseph. *Bergson*. Port Washington, New York: Kennikat Press, 1970.

Soulez, Philippe, complétée par Frédéric Worms. *Bergson: Biographie*. Paris: Flammarion, 1997.

Squire, Larry R. "Memory and Brain Systems." In *From Brains to Consciousness?* S. Rose, ed. London: Allen Lane, 1998. 53–72.

Stapp, Henry P. *The Mindful Universe*. Berlin: Springer, 2007.

Strawson, Galen. *Mental Reality*. Cambridge, Massachusetts: MIT Press, 1994.

Strawson, Galen et al. "Nature: Why Physicalism Entails Panpsychism." In *Consciousness and Its Place in Nature*. Anthony Freeman, ed. Exeter, United Kingdom: Imprint Academic, 2006. 117–128.

Sullivan, Lawrence E. *Icanchu's Drum*. New York: Macmillan, 1988.

Talbot, Michael. *The Holographic Universe*. New York: HarperCollins, 1991.

Targ, Russell, and Harold E. Puthoff. *Mind Reach*. Charlottesville, Virginia: Hampton Roads, 1977.

Tart, Charles. *The End of Materialism*. Oakland, California: New Harbinger Publications, 2009.

Taylor, Eugene. *William James on Exceptional Mental States*. Amherst, Massachusetts: University of Massachusetts Press, 1984.

Trotignon, Pierre. "Auttre voie, meme voix: Lévinas et Bergson." In *Emmanuel Lévinas*. Catherine Chalier and Miguel Abensour, eds. Paris: Editions de l'Herne, 1991. 287–293.

———. *L'Idée de vie chez Bergson*. Paris: Presses Universitaires de France, 1968.

Tucker, Jim B. *Life Before Life*. New York: St. Martin's Press, 2005.

Vlastos, Gregory. "Zeno of Elea." In *The Encyclopedia of Philosophy*, Vol. 8. New York: Macmillan Publishing, 1972.

Whitehead, Alfred North. *An Enquiry Concerning the Principles of Natural Knowledge*. Cambridge: Cambridge University Press, 1919.

Wilder, Penfield, and Lamar Roberts. *Speech and Brain Mechanisms*. Princeton: Princeton University Press, 1959.

Wolf, Fred A. *Star Wave*. New York: Macmillan, 1984.

Worms, Frédéric. *Introduction à matière et mémoire de Bergson*. Paris: Presses Universitaires de France, 1997.

Yamaguchi, Minoru. *The Intuition of Zen and Bergson*. Japan: Herder Agency, 1969.

Yuasa, Yasuo. *The Body*. T. P. Kasulis, ed., and Nagatomo Shigenori and T. P. Kasulis trans. Albany, New York: State University of New York Press, 1987.

Zukav, Gary. *The Dancing Wu Li Masters*. New York: William Morrow, 1980.

INDEX

Académie Française: Bergson's election to, xix

Action Française, xix

Advaita Vedanta, 279n3

Agar, W. E., 297n4

agnosia, 191

Alexander, Ian, xxi, 15, 150, 281n16

Alexander technique, 308n2

aikido, 201, 205

amnesia: forms of, 190; mainstream understandings of, 190. *See also under* brain, injury to, related to memory loss

aphasia: Bergson's explanations of, 189; forms of, 189, 191; history of, 305n25. *See also under* brain, injury to, related to memory loss

apraxia, 191

Aristotle, 207

Aspect, Alain, 132, 133

associationism, 46–50. *See also* determinism, psychological

atomism: biological genesis of, 79; Greek version of, 78; psychological versions of, 46–47, 284n2, 312n3; quantum physics disproves, 84; theoretical usefulness of, 79. *See also* associationism

attention: link to continuity of memory, 175–77

Aurobindo, Sri, 222

authenticity: bodily indications of, 26–27; difficulty of, 22–23, 25; freedom to create, 22; link to fluid responsiveness (technical term), 23; qualities of , 22. *See also* fluid responsiveness (technical term); selfhood

Barden, Garrett, 20, 48, 285n7

Barnard, Sandra, 148–49

Barrett, William, 276n39

Bataillon, Marcel, xvii

Bateson, Gregory, 297n4

beliefs: effects on experience, 170–71, 301nn2–3; organic nature of, 18; unassimilated, 18–19

Bell, J. S., 130

Bell's theorem, 130, 132, 133, 134, 135, 298n1, 299n13. *See also* non-locality (technical term); quantum mechanics (physics)

Bennet, M. R., 294n25

Benton, Arthur L., 305n25

Bergson, Henri: academic discourse, relevance to modern, xxiv–xxv, 277nn42–45; Bohm, David, comparison to, 135–36; Catholic Modernism, influence on, xix–xx; celebrity, xviii; conservatives, support by, xviii, xix; English skills of, xv; feminism, support

327